ALL QUIET IN PEKING

UNDER TURBULENT SKIES

Liu Heping

Translated by
Teng Jimeng

SINOIST

ACA Publishing Ltd
University House
11-13 Lower Grosvenor Place,
London SW1W 0EX, UK
Tel: +44 20 3289 3885
E-mail: info@alaincharlesasia.com
www.alaincharlesasia.com
www.sinoistbooks.com

Beijing Office
Tel: +86(0)10 8472 1250

Author: Liu Heping
Translator: Teng Jimeng

Published by Sinoist Books (an imprint of ACA Publishing Ltd) in arrangement with Guangdong Flower City Publishing House Co., Ltd.

Original Chinese Text © 北平无战事 *(Bei Ping Wu Zhan Shi)* 2019, Guangdong Flower City Publishing House Co., Ltd, Guangdong, China

English Translation text © 2022 ACA Publishing Ltd, London, UK

ALL RIGHTS RESERVED. NO PART OF THIS PUBLICATION MAY BE REPRODUCED IN MATERIAL FORM, BY ANY MEANS, WHETHER GRAPHIC, ELECTRONIC, MECHANICAL OR OTHER, INCLUDING PHOTOCOPYING OR INFORMATION STORAGE, IN WHOLE OR IN PART, AND MAY NOT BE USED TO PREPARE OTHER PUBLICATIONS WITHOUT WRITTEN PERMISSION FROM THE PUBLISHER.

This novel is entirely a work of fiction. The names, characters and incidents portrayed in it are the work of the author's imagination. Any resemblance to actual persons, living or dead, events or localities is entirely coincidental.

Paperback ISBN: 978-1-910760-85-7
eBook ISBN: 978-1-910760-86-4

A catalogue record for *All Quiet in Peking (Book One): Under Turbulent Skies* is available from the National Bibliographic Service of the British Library.

UNDER TURBULENT SKIES

BOOK I OF THE ALL QUIET IN PEKING SERIES

LIU HEPING

Translated by
TENG JIMENG

SINOIST BOOKS

LIST OF CHARACTERS

Fang Buting - governor of the Central Bank's Peking branch
Xie Peidong - brother-in-law of, and assistant to, Fang Buting. CPC underground agent
Fang Meng'ao - colonel in the National Revolutionary Army Air Force, instructor at Jianqiao Aviation Academy and captain of the Peking Economic Inspection Brigade. Son of Fang Buting and brother of Fang Mengwei
Cui Zhongshi - deputy treasury director at the Central Bank's Peking branch, CPC underground agent
Fang Mengwei - Fang Buting's youngest son, deputy commissioner of the Peking Police Bureau and deputy director of the Investigation Department of the Peking Garrison headquarters
He Qicang - vice-chancellor of Yenching University and economic adviser to the Kuomintang government
He Xiaoyu - Yenching University student and Vice-Chancellor He Qicang's daughter
Xie Mulan - Yenching University student, daughter of Xie Peidong and cousin of Fang Mengwei and Fang Meng'ao
Chiang Ching-kuo - eldest son of Chiang Kai-shek, also known as Comrade Jianfeng
Zeng Keda - inspector-general of the Ministry of Defence's Cadre Reserve Bureau

Hou Juntang - deputy director of the Air Force Operations Department
Lin Dawei - former staff member of the Air Force Operations Department, CPC Underground agent
Fu Zuoyi - commander-in-chief of the North China Headquarters for the Suppression of Communist Insurgency
Xu Tieying - director of the Liaison Office of the Communications Bureau of the Kuomintang Central Membership Committee, chief superintendent of Peking Municipal Police Bureau
Du Wancheng - general auditor of the Ministry of Finance, head of the Five-Member Working Group
Ma Linshen - deputy director of the Kuomintang's Central Commission on Citizens' Food Distribution
Wang Benquan - secretary of the Central Bank
Ma Hanshan - deputy director of the Peking Citizens' Food-Distribution Committee, and director of the Civil Affairs Bureau of Peking Municipality
Gu Weijun - Chinese ambassador to the US
Yan Chunming - professor, and head of the Communist Party's Student Committee at Yenching University
Cheng Xiaoyun - second wife of Fang Buting
Wang Yunwu - minister of the Ministry of Finance
Liang Jinglun - Yenching University professor, assistant to He Qicang and leading member of the Iron and Blood Congress of Nation-Saving
Shao Yuangang - member of the Youth Aviation Brigade

A huge establishment disappeared almost instantaneously, leaving behind a high wall, with history on one side and the people on the other.

The tide ebbs and flows as the moon rises and falls.

Wang Chong
Critical Essays

CHAPTER 1

It was the height of summer in 1948, the time of the new moon. In the black markets of Peking, rice was selling for as much as 360,000 *fabi* a half kilo. On the morning of 5 July, the Kuomintang-controlled Senate announced that refugee students from Northeast China, all fifteen thousand of them, would no longer receive rations. United in a loud and bitter protest, the students surrounded the residence of the Senate leader, Xu Huidong. Shots were fired, casualties mounted and by nightfall eighteen had died, 109 were injured and thirty-seven were in prison. On a day that would later go down in history as the "Fifth of July Incident", martial law arrived in Peking.

That night, a telegram was sent from the headquarters of the Central Bank of the Republic of China to Fang Buting, the bank's Peking branch governor, and delivered to his first floor office.

Fang Buting glanced down at the telegram, closed his eyes, took a deep breath, opened his eyes again and said: "Read it."

Xie Peidong was his brother-in-law as well as his assistant. Having transcribed the coded message, Xie put down his pen and stood to deliver it. Taking his voice down a notch to disguise a distinct tremble, he tried to read calmly, in a vain attempt to lessen the telegram's impact.

A message from the Central Bank of the Kuomintang government to the governor of the Peking branch. At 9.30pm, the government received a diplomatic note from US Ambassador John Leighton Stuart to the effect that their government has received information regarding the following incident:

"At every official level, the Peking Citizens' Food-Distribution Committee has been smuggling and reselling daily necessities meant for citizens. The infractions are listed in full and are clearly attributable to the Peking branch of the Central Bank."

The ambassador's note concluded that if the Kuomintang government failed to provide an adequate response, America intended to suspend all aid forthwith.

How did the US obtain this mysterious piece of intelligence at such speed, and how could they give such a rapid response? How damaging is this leak? Should the Central Bank take a stance, and if so, how should the government in turn respond to the American diplomatic note? We eagerly await the advice of the governor of the Peking branch, Fang Buting.

MIDDAY, TELEGRAM OFFICE OF THE CENTRAL BANK, SHANGHAI

Silence. Fang Buting had made a habit of not rushing decisions. But on this occasion, he spat out a word that sent shivers down his brother-in-law's spine: "Communists!"

"Governor!" said a shocked Xie Peidong who, as a stickler for propriety, still managed to address him by his proper title. "How should we reply to head office?"

"'Sorrows as high as mountains, as deep as the ocean, the peaks and depths of which I cannot see,'" said Fang Buting, muttering a line from a poem by Du Fu while looking out into the night sky beyond his balcony. He continued: "American intelligence on which this report is based has been leaked by someone here..."

Xie Peidong was speechless.

"I need to see Cui Zhongshi," Fang Buting concluded, facing his assistant. "Summon him immediately."

Xie Peidong hardly dared remind Fang that Cui had left for

Nanking that very same afternoon. He took a moment before plucking up the courage.

Fang Buting looked up abruptly. "What on earth is he doing there?"

"Meng'ao is due to be tried in Nanking tomorrow."

That was Fang Buting's wake-up call. All his past misgivings and doubts came together with a jolt, and in an urgent voice, he gave Xie the order: "Call Cui Zhongshi. Tell him to stop what he's doing and return to Peking this instant."

"But what about rescuing Meng'ao?"

"Should we really be letting one Communist save another?"

"You mean Cui is as much a Communist as Meng'ao?"

Fang Buting looked again at the telegram in Xie's hand. "Such detailed information on the contraband? How could the Americans know this much? Records like this are only kept here at the Peking branch. Apart from us two, only Cui Zhongshi knows the full extent of it."

Xie Peidong's face fell, but he still didn't want to believe it. "Governor, don't forget that our Mr Soong and Mr Kung both keep full accounts."

Xie's words reminded Fang of something: the power of instinct to turn a vague suspicion into a solid truth. When he was at Harvard studying for his PhD in Finance and Economics, his Anthropology professor had taught him that "intuition comes to you suddenly in a tricky situation". How many times had his instinct proven him right?

More determinedly this time, he told Xie Peidong: "I don't care whose backs those Commies are hiding behind, no one hides behind mine! Call Nanking. Go to Shanghai. Bring me Cui Zhongshi this minute."

There was a direct line to Nanking's Ministry of Finance and another to the Central Bank headquarters in Shanghai. Xie Peidong dialled Nanking first.

The Ministry of Finance confirmed that Cui Zhongshi had arrived that morning, but left early. He was apparently on his way to the Central Bank in Shanghai. Xie spoke to the Central Bank duty officer in Shanghai; Cui Zhongshi had not yet arrived.

"Did Cui Zhongshi say where he was planning to go?" Xie asked Fang.

"Details regarding the rescue of Meng'ao were part of the discussion. Meng'ao will know what they talked about."

As Xie Peidong was still holding the Nanking special line receiver, Fang Buting picked up the other phone. "Peking Police Bureau?"

"Who's calling?" was the stiff response.

"Can I speak to Fang Mengwei?"

"Who's calling, please?"

"His father."

"I'm sorry. Deputy Commissioner Fang is on duty. We're taking action against Communist insurgents tonight."

"What do you mean? Who's coordinating it?" yelled Fang Buting down the line. Pestering this police officer seemed of no use. "Call the deputy commissioner right away. Tell him he's needed at home."

"Yes sir. But what reason should we give to the garrison headquarters?"

"No reason at all. Tell him to come home, and if he wants to keep arresting students, he should arrest me before them. And if he does decide to kill any students, he will have to kill me first."

Fang Buting slammed down the phone before the officer could reply. It wasn't long before the phone rang again. Deliberately, Fang waited before answering. "Is that Mengwei?"

"Yes, this is your son," thundered the caller. But it wasn't. The voice was older and trembled with anger and agitation. Fang Buting was stunned by the deafening roar and held the phone a little distance from his ear.

"I'm at the hospital with the police and army to arrest injured students. How many will suffer this evening?"

The voice was so loud that even Xie Peidong, standing a few steps away, could hear every word. He watched Fang Buting quietly.

Fang Buting kept his cool. "Brother Qicang, my friend, where are you now? Which hospital? I'll be with you as soon as I can."

Less agitated now and with some vitality in his voice, He Qicang replied: "As vice-chancellor of Yenching University, where else do you think I'd be? The University Hospital. Get in your car and be here in twenty minutes!"

Xie Peidong tried to pass Fang Buting his hat. "Governor, you should take some of the soldiers who are guarding the vault. It's not safe out there."

Fang ignored him. At the door, he turned and said: "Send the Central Bank my answer: 'We at the Peking branch have no record of smuggling or reselling daily necessities. We have leaked no secrets either. Investigate us any time you wish.' As for Cui Zhongshi, you must reach him one way or another and get him to return to Peking at once." With those words, he walked out.

The environment outside was less oppressive than in the stifling and tense first-floor office. A ground-floor hallway decorated with wooden wall panels and with rooms on all sides led directly to a central building. A straight staircase connected Fang's office in the east and a curved one to the bedrooms in the west. Down the hallway to the east was a capacious reception room, while in the western part there was a large dining hall. In Peking, only a few such Western-style buildings remained in the legation quarter of Dongjiao Minxiang. Fang's building had been purchased directly by the Central Bank to be his home and office following the restoration of Kuomintang rule at the end of the War of Resistance Against Japanese Aggression. He felt it demonstrated the importance of Peking's banking operations.

Governor Fang Buting was walking down the eastern staircase when the living room clock chimed. He paused. The clock struck two, three, four.

The night was particularly dark. The resonance of the bell sounded to Fang Buting like a human voice. Although he heard no lyrics, he imagined them:

The floating, scattered clouds,
The bright moon shines on the people as they arrive.
Today is the happiest reunion.

Xie Peidong seemed to hear it too from behind the office door as he gazed after Fang Buting. Such auditory hallucinations always arrive unexpectedly and end for no reason at all.

As Fang Buting moved through the building with heavy footsteps, Xie felt a matching rise in the heaviness of his own heart. Xie watched him go downstairs and disappear into the living room.

It was a moonless night in a city governed by martial law, and the blackout was smothering. But light came, as it always does, with the glimmer of dawn.

Yenching University Hospital was powered by diesel generators donated by the United States.

It was now apparent that three squadrons were arranged neatly in the compound more than a dozen metres from the building: a squadron of soldiers from the Fourth Corps of the Kuomintang Central Army, a squadron of gendarmerie from the Peking Garrison headquarters and a squadron of policemen from the Peking Police Bureau. Soldiers from both the Central Army and the Peking Garrison were equipped with American weapons, including helmets and modern guns, whereas the police squadron were dressed in black uniforms, replete with shields and batons.

Dozens of Yenching faculty members were sitting on the stone steps facing the troops. A single young police officer stood between the two sides. His name was Fang Mengwei. He was Governor Fang's younger son and not only deputy commissioner of the Peking Police Bureau, but also deputy director of the Investigation Department of the Peking Garrison headquarters.

The soldiers and police behind him represented the state, while the academic staff in front of him were the face of the country. Fang Mengwei was unsure what he himself represented. All he knew was that as soon as he raised his hand, he would be letting the state crush the face of the country.

All eyes of the squadrons faced his back, yet he did not dare meet the gaze of the professors on the stone steps. Professor He Qicang, vice-chancellor of Yenching University and economic adviser to the Kuomintang government, was right in the middle.

Behind the academics on the other side of a row of glass doors thronged a crowd of refugee students from the Northeast.

What worried Fang Mengwei most of all was the presence of

three particular people staring in his direction. To his left was a young woman dressed in Yenching University uniform replete with school badge. She was Vice-Chancellor He Qicang's daughter, He Xiaoyu. To his right was a young woman dressed identically. She was Xie Mulan, his own cousin. In the middle stood He Qicang's assistant, Professor Liang Jinglun. His long robe and handsome face made him instantly recognisable.

Known as the youngest scholar in Yenching University, Liang was suspected of being a major player in the Communist Party-controlled Urban Works Department's Student Committee, and was on the "most wanted" lists of both the Peking Garrison and the Municipal Police. But every time they came to arrest him, his name would be removed from the list. He was the vice-chancellor's right-hand man and as such, could roam among the students, picking favours with his good looks and thoughtful countenance. Whenever Fang Mengwei heard the three characters that made up his name, Liang Jinglun, he felt distinctly nauseous.

The task at hand brought him back to his senses. He looked at the sky, noticed the tender light of dawn and raised his right hand. The troops responded immediately by standing to attention, clipping their heels in unison. But this time he raised his hand just high enough to reveal his wrist and check the time. It was already ten past four in the morning.

"Ready!" commanded the captain of the special service company standing before the Fourth Corps, even though he did not have the authority. Pressed against the chests of the Fourth Corps men, a barrage of carbine muzzles tilted forward.

"Forward! March!" continued the captain. The soldiers goose-stepped towards the professors in front of the building, intent on flattening them underfoot. He Qicang's eyes were trained on the wall of soldiers, and he straightened up. Nervously, the other professors followed his example. There was a commotion from behind the glass doors, as the students stood up to see what was going on. Xie Mulan waved and shouted to Fang Mengwei, but while Fang could see her, he couldn't hear what she was saying. He closed his eyes, and when the soldiers were less than five metres from the stone steps, he roared: "Halt!"

Fang Mengwei strode over to the captain of the special service company and asked: "Did anyone tell you who you should take orders from?"

The captain of the special service company protested: "I have orders that arrests must be made before daybreak, and it is already dawn. Mr Fang, your police force may not have to carry out military orders, but we are the state army. We must carry out our orders."

Fang Mengwei pulled out his Peking Garrison headquarters ID card from his coat pocket. "Then I'll address you with military orders! Platoon One!" A squad of the gendarmerie from the Police Command rushed over to the captain. "Keep an eye on him. If he doesn't follow my orders, arrest him." With this, the captain of the special service company originally deployed to bring in the students was held at gunpoint by a squadron of gendarmes.

Fang addressed the special service company, frozen by the turn of events: "I order you, in my capacity as commander of the Peking Garrison, to act in concerted effort. Now listen up, and turn back!"

This order appeared to be more effective than the one given by the special service company captain. The squadron turned back as one.

"Return to your original positions. Now!" The squadron returned, using their steps to measure the distance with utmost precision. As they turned, their carbines again rested on their chests.

"Deputy Commissioner Fang!" the captain called out. "Permission to call the Army Corps' commander-in-chief, Li Wen, as deputy commander-in-chief of the Peking Garrison."

Fang Mengwei walked over to the captain and whispered: "You want to make the call? The vice-chancellor sitting in the middle could call Ambassador Leighton Stuart at any time. Could Commander-in-Chief Li say the same?"

The captain went quiet. Ignoring him, Fang Mengwei turned and walked over to He Qicang, who was sitting on the stone steps. He saluted him, military style, heels clipping the ground. "Vice-Chancellor He, we are simply carrying out military orders. Please forgive us."

He Qicang glanced at his face and then looked over Fang's shoulder at the army and police squadrons behind him. "Son, look at you. Look at those youngsters inside. It's pathetic to see children hunting down other children. And for what? I insist you ask the gentlemen who sent you here, Fu Zuoyi and Chen Jicheng, to seek me out. I'll be waiting." With these words, he looked back up at the sky.

Somewhat embarrassed, Fang Mengwei squatted down and whispered: "Uncle He, did you call Ambassador Leighton Stuart?"

"Things are not yet that desperate." He Qicang turned sharply towards Fang Mengwei and continued: "How could you make such a mess of things and then ask the Americans for help? This is no kind of national government! Shame on all of you. If the government can't save its own face, then we, the people, shall!"

Fang Mengwei lowered his head. "But what am I supposed to do now?"

"Just wait another ten minutes and you'll see."

"What are you talking about?"

"I told you to wait ten minutes!" said He Qicang in a raised voice.

"What on earth for? I don't get it."

"What don't you understand? You've just got to wait another ten minutes."

Fang Mengwei's eyes brightened. "Is Vice-President Li coming?" He sighed in expectation. Standing up, he shouted to the squadron: "Ten minutes. Wait for new orders."

The soldiers and policemen had no need to wait since at that instant, the road to the hospital gate was illuminated by headlights. Blurred by shadows, a car appeared. The only person supposed to ride in a car was Vice-President Li Zongren, the recipient of a Buick sedan from the United States. Those serving under General Fu Zuoyi had to make do with military jeeps.

"Open the gate! Salute!" shouted Fang Mengwei, as he strode towards the gate.

The headlights lit up his face. When the car door opened, all the squadron members clicked their heels together and saluted. But the car drove past and into the courtyard through the open gate. Fang Mengwei was stunned.

No Buick at all, this was an Austin bearing the number plate "Central Bank, Peking, A001". His father's car!

The car did not come to a stop until it had reached the middle of the courtyard between the three squadrons and the professors.

Fang Mengwei went over to the right side of the car and opened the back door. "Father."

Stepping out of the car, Fang Buting brushed off his son's helping hand, not even glancing in his direction as he walked straight over to He Qicang. He Qicang remained seated, but his eyes and those of the other professors greeted Fang Buting as he walked towards them.

"Allow me to join you, will you?" Fang whispered to He Qicang.

The estrangement between Fang Buting and He Qicang was hard to fathom, but a tacit understanding still connected them. He Qicang moved to one side. A senior colleague next to him made way for Fang to sit down. As Fang Buting sat on the stone steps next to He Qicang, his son approached and called out: "Father."

"Shut up!" This was the first time Fang Buting had looked at his son. "Call Chen Jicheng. Ask Li Zongren to come here. If he can't make it, call Fu Zuoyi. Tell them that both I, the governor of the Central Bank's Peking branch, and Vice-Chancellor He, economic adviser to the Kuomintang government, are Communists. It's time to escort us by plane to Nanking."

There was no way that Fang Mengwei could make such a call. He stood erect, unmoving, while the army and police squadrons behind him made no sound. Day had already dawned.

Fang Buting raised his left hand close enough for him to make out the time.

"When does the university broadcast begin?" he asked He Qicang.

"Five o'clock," said He Qicang sullenly.

Fang Buting turned to look at Fang Mengwei again. "Let the troops listen to the radio. It seems it's time for your Commander-in-Chief Fu to say his piece."

Fang Mengwei had always revered his father. He clipped his heels and turned to the three squadrons. "Attention, Commander-in-Chief Fu will speak on the radio."

All the soldiers and policemen straightened up and got themselves into formation. Their ears were pricked for whatever news was to be announced. More than a minute passed. Maybe it was too quiet, and time seemed to have been suspended. All of a sudden, a hollow voice came from the loudspeaker. It was so loud that the birds perched above chirped and flew up into the early morning sky. A female radio announcer's voice could be heard: "Attention, everyone! Attention, please! Commander-in-Chief Fu Zuoyi of the North China Headquarters for the Suppression of Communist Insurgency has an important announcement to make."

A few seconds later, Fu Zuoyi began to speak. His heavy Shanxi accent was immediately recognisable.

His statement was made on behalf of the government and the military. He expressed sympathy for those students who had been killed and injured. He tried to appease the wounded and hoped that the students would understand the government's position and take no more extreme action. At the same time, he ordered Peking's military and police forces to impose martial law, and stop arresting or injuring students.

On Fang Mengwei's order, the military and police squadrons turned on their heels as one. He Qicang and the other professors sitting on the stone steps stood up in relief.

Fang Buting stood up with them. He looked at He Qicang and said: "The next issue is money and food. I have to get back to… planning economic reforms, especially the issue of US aid. My dear Brother Qicang, will you put in a good word for us on Peking's behalf?"

"Do you really believe in the reform plan? Trust me, it will never work. With all due respect, I wish you would mind your own business."

Without forgetting his manners, Fang Buting greeted the professors before returning to his car. Fang Mengwei walked by his side and opened his door.

"Ask for leave and come back to see me at once," said Fang Buting as he got into the car.

"I'm afraid I can't take leave right now," Fang Mengwei replied.

Fang Buting looked up at his son outside the car, and asked: "Did you send Cui Zhongshi to Nanking on a rescue mission?"

Fang Mengwei was startled by the question.

"Come home at once," Fang Buting repeated. "We'll talk about it when you're back." Fang Buting closed the door from inside with a loud bang, and the younger Fang watched his car leave the way it had come.

———

Peking had been dry for a month now, but Nanking had been hit by thunderstorms for days.

At dawn, the highway connecting Nanking and Jianqiao airbase in Hangzhou was shrouded in rain clouds. An American jeep followed by two prison vans were travelling with their headlights on full. Despite the difficult driving conditions, the vehicles clattered through the storm at high speed.

The major-general in the passenger seat of the jeep was not too concerned about the weather. His mind was full of the voice of Chiang Ching-kuo, the eldest son of Chiang Kai-shek, with his unmistakable Ningbo accent. In April, Chiang had spoken at the opening session of the Iron and Blood Congress of Nation Saving:

Dear Comrades,

You have always been trusted, capable and committed to the great cause of the Three Principles of the People. At this crucial moment of the battle, I hope that we will become loyal ministers. Though we're not accepted by those in power, we remain loyal to the leader at this moment of struggle between life and death. Prepare to die for a righteous cause even if you know you may not succeed. Currently, while the Communist Party is decaying day by day, the Kuomintang is suffering endemic internal corruption. We are faced with "a revolution and a war fought on both fronts". We should not only oppose the corruption of the Nationalists, but also combat the insurgency of the Communists. The two wars must be fought at the same time and must be won at the same time!

The two-star major-general had a youthful face. It made him look both capable and sophisticated. His name was Zeng Keda, inspector-general of the Ministry of Defence's Bureau of Reserve Cadres and a core member of the Iron and Blood Congress.

"Do you happen to know what's meant by 'loyal ministers'?" Zeng Keda suddenly asked his adjutant who was driving the jeep.

"What, general?" asked the adjutant, not hearing him clearly.

Zeng Keda thought better of asking a subordinate such a question, and switched topic. "How far is it to Jianqiao airbase?"

"Roughly a dozen kilometres," said the adjutant, just before the phone started to ring.

"This is Zeng Keda. Please report."

The voice on the phone was very loud. "Reporting, General Zeng, this is Gendarmerie Team One at Jianqiao airbase. A Curtiss C-46 Commando transport aircraft is taking to the skies despite an absolute flight ban. It is piloted by Squadron Number One captain 'The Eagle' and his co-pilot. Both must be arrested!"

"Hell." Sitting in the passenger seat, Zeng Keda looked up at the storm clouds gathering overhead, his face a ghastly pale. "In the name of the Ministry of Defence and Jianqiao airbase command tower, this is an order. You must stop the plane from taking off."

"The plane has already taken off! I repeat, the C-46 has taken off!"

"Order it to return to base immediately. This instant!" Zeng Keda shouted down the line.

"With weather like this, the command tower is unable to direct its return."

Zeng Keda clenched his teeth and thought hard, before picking up the receiver again: "Fang Meng'ao and his aviation academy cadets should remain where they are for now. Untie prisoner Fang Meng'ao and remain on standby."

"Go! Go!" he shouted at his adjutant who put his foot down on the accelerator. The jeep picked up speed and the two prison vans behind followed suit.

Arriving at Jianqiao control tower, Zeng strode over to the dispatch room with his adjutant, stopping in the doorway. He looked at the staff there with contempt, regarding them as corrupt and useless zombies.

There was a numb stillness inside the dispatch room. Hollow

eyes looked towards the Air Force colonel on duty bent over his command post, calling out: "Control Tower to The Eagle! Control Tower to The Eagle! Come in when you hear me. Respond when you hear me."

Apparently they had lost contact, as there was no response from the C-46. The duty colonel straightened up and in an unhurried voice asked the radar operator beside him: "Shall we carry on our search by radar?"

"Search for what?" came a new voice behind him.

The colonel turned around to find his team suddenly standing upright. The two-star major-general Zeng Keda had surprised him, and all he could do in response was click his heels together.

Zeng Keda looked at the colonel who was clearly discomfited by his presence: "Who gave permission for take-off?"

"Air Force Operations, sir," said the duty officer.

"Which department? Hou Juntang has been arrested. Who else could have given such an order? Take his gun!" Zeng Keda told his adjutant, not waiting for an answer. He took up the microphone at the command post and ordered: "Turn on the loudspeaker."

Zeng Keda's adjutant disarmed the duty colonel while one of the air crew plugged in the loudspeaker.

"This is Zeng Keda! This is Zeng Keda! Gendarmerie! I have an urgent order for you. Team One, Team Two – block the runways. Do not allow any aircraft to take off. Team Three, continue to detain the aviation academy cadets. Have Fang Meng'ao brought here immediately. I repeat, immediately!" These instructions rang through the airbase loud and clear.

Squads of gendarmerie ran over to block the runways. The Air Force ground crew were forced to crouch down and hold their heads in their hands.

Zeng Keda's order even reached the aircraft hangar a kilometre away where the aviation academy cadets had been detained, awaiting punishment. They were young and healthy graduates, handcuffed in a line in the middle of the hangar, and surrounded by gendarmes in helmets clutching carbines.

Everyone was listening attentively to Zeng's orders being broadcast over the loudspeaker. But as his voice died away, all the detainees saw a figure flash past their eyes and straight out of the gate even before the captain of Team Three had time to start carrying out the order.

The captain of the gendarmerie, as surprised as anyone there, took up the chase, shouting: "Come with me, you two!"

The figure sped along the runway towards the control tower, leaving the three gendarmes far behind. There was no point trying to stop him. Inside the control tower, Zeng Keda's eyes brightened.

The figure rushed into the control room and went straight up to the command post. Addressing the radar operator who was still sitting there, he said: "Get out of the way. Give me your headphones." The man was not even panting despite his kilometre-long sprint. This was Fang Meng'ao, a suspect awaiting trial at the Nanking Special Criminal Court. Before being charged, Colonel Fang was an instructor at Jianqiao airbase's aviation academy.

The operator hesitated, waiting for Zeng to issue orders. Fang Meng'ao snatched his headphones and sat down.

Zeng Keda strode over, covered the microphone with his hand and stared at Fang Meng'ao. "You'll still be court-martialled even if you do manage to save The Eagle. Do you understand?"

Fang Meng'ao did not bother to reply, only asking the operator: "Have you searched all the areas?"

"All areas have been searched, but the flight track has completely disappeared."

"Did you search the airspace a hundred kilometres southwest?"

"Absolutely not!" Suddenly, the colonel's whole expression changed. He had been taken into custody by the adjutant. "That's the Nanking city no-fly zone."

Zeng Keda's eyes turned to the colonel and he roared: "If the plane crashes over Nanking, your whole family will be executed!"

Changing his tone, he told Fang Meng'ao: "It's all up to you. Don't think about the military trial. Direct The Eagle to return immediately!"

Fang Meng'ao appeared not to hear Zeng, as he scanned the radar screen.

"Connect me to the Nanking Garrison radar station now. We need to search the city's airspace."

"Nanking Garrison radar station will not follow our orders," the colonel said, panicking.

"Nanking Garrison radar station, over." Zeng Keda gave the order himself, as he walked over to the microphone. The special line was immediately put through to the radar station.

"Nanking Garrison radar station? This is Zeng Keda of the Ministry of Defence. I am ordering you, in the name of Chiang Ching-kuo, to start a search of Nanking airspace and report any aircraft you find."

"Yes sir!"

The name of Chiang Ching-kuo seemed to do the trick, yet the answer from the other end could only be heard through the headphones worn by Fang Meng'ao.

"Give me the headphones." Zeng Keda took another pair from the officer on duty as he shouted to the Air Force ground crew standing in the control tower. "All of you, follow Fang Meng'ao as he guides The Eagle back to base."

All eyes were on Fang Meng'ao, former flying ace of the National Revolutionary Army Air Force.

Fang Meng'ao said into the microphone: "Radar station, conduct a fan-shaped low-altitude search from northeast to southwest. Focus on the airspace between thirty-two and thirty-five degrees southwest."

"Roger!" The voice at the other end came through the headsets worn by Fang Meng'ao and Zeng Keda. No one else in the control tower could hear. They stood their ground quietly. The air was stifling.

"Target identified at low altitude. Thirty-five degrees southwest. Aircraft found in Nanking airspace." The voice of The Eagle's radar operator had become louder.

Fang Meng'ao said to the radar operator beside him: "Mark its tracks, thirty-five degrees southwest."

"Sir!" The operator grabbed the marker and followed the reappearance of the red track on the glass plate, drawing it quickly and accurately.

Fang Meng'ao bent down and approached the microphone: "Radar station, connect me to the target signal. Return under my command."

"Radar station, understood."

There was lots of frequency static, and Fang Meng'ao knew that the signal had been picked up: "Number Two! Number Two! This is Number One. Please come in."

Number Two was The Eagle's code name given to him by Fang Meng'ao after they had both flown over "the Hump", a flying route in World War II between India and China's southwest. He had been Fang Meng'ao's wingman. Fang Meng'ao was invoking his former wingman's loyalty as the comrade who had fought alongside him against the Japanese.

Zeng Keda was momentarily touched, and his cold and scrutinising eyes flashed rare warmth. But this soon vanished as he waited for the other side's response.

The Eagle's breathing came across loud and clear, but no words were spoken. He had not expected to hear from anyone back at base. How could Fang Meng'ao be calling him up here?

The Eagle was startled, Fang Meng'ao realised, and he tried teasing him: "Eagle, this is Fang Meng'ao. Whoever helped you make a fortune, or used you to make their fortune, can't save you now. But I am able to guide you back. Report your plane's condition and flight status."

There was a brief silence, after which the voice of The Eagle finally came through the headphones: "Commander! Who is that son of a bitch in charge of the control tower?"

Zeng Keda picked up the microphone and shouted: "You scumbag! Eagle, listen to me. This is Zeng Keda. I'm in charge now. You're an accomplice in the Peking smuggling case. They'll kill you in order to stop you spilling the beans! As long as you make it back safely and identify the principal offenders, Comrade Jianfeng can protect you from punishment whatever the offence may be. I order you to follow Fang Meng'ao's instructions and fly the plane back to where you took off."

"I hear you, general," The Eagle replied. "I'll follow your orders, but not Fang Meng'ao's. He's a Commie. I'm a Nationalist army officer…"

Pathetic! Making such a devious statement in the hope of exonerating himself! Zeng Keda was disgusted but all the same he still needed to calm him down. Holding the microphone tight, he said: "I know you're a Nationalist army officer. So you must obey my orders! I say it again, hear me clearly – Fang Meng'ao is the only person who can guide you back safely. Never mind if he's a Communist or not. If he were Mao Zedong himself, you'd still have to obey him! Report your flight status immediately."

At this point, he put the microphone back in front of Fang Meng'ao. "Yes sir!"

The Eagle's voice that could be heard in the headphones trembled because of his complex emotions, though he tried hard to stay composed. "The tail of the plane has been hit by lightning, the circuit is seriously damaged, the port engine has failed and the pull of the plane to the right is hard to control. The cloud top is at a height of six thousand metres, with more than ten metres cloud cover, and I'm flying at an altitude of two thousand, two hundred metres. I could crash at any time. Be advised. Over."

"Eagle, listen up!" said Fang Meng'ao. "It doesn't matter whether I'm a Communist, nor does it matter if you're in a thunderstorm. Just remember, you're the pilot who flew over the Hump. There's not a plane in the world you can't command! Maintain your minimum manoeuvring speed, and pay special attention to the port engine. Straight across to the northeast. You'll be over the airbase in ten minutes. Roger."

"Copy that. The starboard engine is working fine. But the pull to the right is increasing. I can't control my path…" Despite the drastic circumstances, The Eagle sounded somewhat calmer now that Fang Meng'ao was guiding him.

The colonel on duty stood up and yelled at Zeng Keda: "General, he can't land here!"

Zeng Keda stared at him coldly. "What are you talking about?"

"If the port engine isn't working, the plane is likely to veer to the right when landing and crash into the hangars. There are three C-46 planes parked there! No matter what, we must be loyal to the Nationalist Party. Fang Meng'ao is a Commie suspect! He's after those C-46 planes!"

Zeng Keda turned to Fang Meng'ao and said: "Fang Meng'ao, did you hear that?"

Fang Meng'ao paid no attention, continuing to speak into the microphone: "Eagle, pedal the right rudder while pressing your joystick to the right. Be careful. Is the right pull decreasing?"

"Answer me!" Zeng said, getting closer to Fang Meng'ao. "Can The Eagle make it?"

"No promises," said Fang Meng'ao, taking off his headphones, "but he must land here. Otherwise, he'll crash in central Nanking. If that happens, General Zeng, it will be you, not me, who'll end up in the military court."

Zeng Keda was momentarily stunned, and had no choice but to wave his hand. Fang Meng'ao put the headphones back on, and he could hear the voice of The Eagle once more. "Reporting! Right glide has weakened, right glide has weakened. The flight gradient is zero. I'm flying northeast."

"All right," said Fang Meng'ao. "Report your speed."

"I'm flying at minimum manoeuvring speed, maintaining a forty-degree gliding path angle."

Zeng Keda also heard the voice of The Eagle, which had now become much calmer. "Maintain your speed, adjust glide angle to thirty degrees," said Fang Meng'ao. "Roger?"

"Copy that. Maintaining speed. Glide angle has been set to thirty degrees."

"Eagle," said Fang Meng'ao, "when you see the airbase, report immediately." All of a sudden, there was dead silence in the headphones.

"Do you see it? Answer me, Eagle!" Fang Meng'ao's voice was not loud, but Zeng's heart began to sink after hearing the question.

There was still no answer in the headphones, only a consistent buzzing noise on the FM tuner setting, followed by a deathlike silence.

Finally, a higher-pitched voice came from the headphones: "We see the airbase!"

"Well done!" said Fang Meng'ao, cheering loudly. "Landing direction, from south to north. Aim for the runway and drop the landing gear at an altitude of five hundred metres. Roger?"

The voice of The Eagle could be heard in the headphones: "Roger that. Drop the landing gear at an altitude of five hundred metres."

"Open the flaps and get ready to land." Fang Meng'ao gave the final order, stood up, took off his headphones and put them back on the navigation platform.

A huge shadow crept towards the airbase. Through the rain curtain outside the window of the control tower, it was just possible to make out that the C-46 had landed safely and was parked on the runway close to the control tower.

Zeng Keda went up to the microphone of the loudspeaker and made the following announcement: "Attention, all gendarmes! Team One, escort Fang Meng'ao and his Youth Aviation Brigade. Team Two, arrest all those from the Air Force's first division involved in the smuggling case."

But what happened next caught him off guard. The colonel on duty, who had been involved in the smuggling case, pulled out a submachine gun from under a table, rushed to the window facing the runway and fired numerous rounds down at the C-46 cockpit.

The two Air Force suspects directly involved in the smuggling case in Peking were dead! The murderous colonel then turned his gun on Zeng Keda, as if he had a death wish for a righteous cause!

"Don't shoot!" But the lieutenant standing behind him had killed the colonel even before Zeng fully realised what was happening.

After two shots were fired in quick succession, the colonel fell through the window with the submachine gun still in his hands.

Zeng Keda turned and slapped his lieutenant on the face: "I said not to shoot, but you went ahead and did it anyway. Why?"

"Indeed!" said the lieutenant, putting the gun back in his holster and straightening up. "I must keep the general safe."

"Would he have dared kill me? You idiot!" He was furious, but it was not until he had finished speaking that he saw Fang Meng'ao standing there. After an inexplicable moment of embarrassment, he told his lieutenant: "Take him away, but don't handcuff him." With that, he left ahead of the others, his face pale with anger.

Fang Meng'ao went up to the lieutenant, glancing at the gun on the floor as he walked. He whispered in his ear: "Learn from General Zeng. That submachine gun was out of bullets."

On their way out, the lieutenant started to comprehend why his majestic-looking General Zeng appeared to look less assured when standing beside the flight instructor.

The killing of The Eagle, the captain of the first squadron of the Air Force Division of the National Revolutionary Army, and the death of the man who had carried out the killing, made Zeng Keda feel guilty. He thought he had failed to live up to the expectations of Director Chiang Ching-kuo because he had been virtually handpicked as the public prosecutor by Chiang himself.

Today's special criminal court had been scheduled to try the espionage case involving Lin Dawei, former staff member of the Air Force Operations Department, as well as the Communist collusion case in which the Flying Brigade of Jianqiao Aviation Academy refused to bomb the city of Kaifeng after it had been taken by the Communist-led East China Field Army, an act in direct violation of military orders. The day before, what would become known as the Fifth of July Incident took place in Peking. Lieutenant General Hou Juntang, deputy director of the Air Force Operations Department involved in the Peking smuggling case, was arrested that same night upon receiving the diplomatic note from the US. On the urgent suggestion of Director Chiang Ching-kuo of the Bureau of Reserve Cadres of the Ministry of Defence, the two cases were to be combined and tried together – Communist rivals and Nationalist traitors – the purpose of which was to implement a strategic decision to "resolutely oppose the Communist Party on the one hand and fight corruption on the other". One of the most pressing issues was how to stop Communist infiltration of the National Revolutionary Army and bring an end to collective corruption within the Nationalist Party in one fell swoop. Today's trial could help crack open both the iron curtain behind which Communist Party undercover operatives penetrated the core of the Nationalist Army and the black curtain behind which the corruption of the Nationalists from top to bottom was running rampant. Fang Meng'ao and The Eagle, one the hammer and the other the drill, would help to chisel them through.

On the drive back to Nanking from Jianqiao airbase, it was still pouring with rain outside. Zeng Keda called the office of Director Chiang Ching-kuo on the jeep's mobile radio: "Is this special line number two? Please transfer me to Comrade Jianfeng."

"Is this Comrade Zeng Keda?" asked the operator. "Comrade Jianfeng is not available."

"I've something important to report to him. It's urgent."

"I'll transfer your call then. Attention, it's special line one."

"I understand," Zeng Keda replied, somewhat in awe.

The number two special line was faster than the number one line. However, after he was put through, he found the operator to be less than helpful. "Director Ching-kuo is in the middle of a meeting. Call again in an hour."

"Please be sure to go in and tell Director Ching-kuo it's urgent. I must report this immediately."

"Who are you anyway? Don't you know the rules? This is the office of the president's assistant." Then he hung up the phone.

Against the backdrop of torrential rain, one could easily see the grievance that was apparent in the eyes of Zeng Keda who felt deeply humiliated by the call. He hung up and looked in the rearview mirror of the jeep, trying to make out the prison van following behind, only to lose it in an expanse of mist. He turned to his lieutenant who was sitting next to him in the driver's seat. "I'm sorry I hit you just now. Please slow down."

It was dark and stuffy inside the prison van that followed the jeep. It had only two small windows that were covered in barbed wire. From outside in the pouring rain, those in the van appeared only as vague shapes.

With a pop, a flip-top cigarette lighter was struck, illuminating a silent Fang Meng'ao and his aircrew, who were seated in the van. Then another lighter was struck, as the first lighter was flipped shut. One by one, lighters were lit as if in a relay race. They flickered in handcuffed hands.

One pilot opened his breast pocket, pulled out a pack of Camel cigarettes and handed it to a small, bald man next to him. The bald man took the pack, tore open the seal, took out a cigarette and put it in his mouth. He lit it and passed the pack down along with the lighter. The cigarette pack passed through the hands of the handcuffed pilots.

The van was shaking as the pack was passed down to Fang Meng'ao. Like his brothers before him, he drew out a cigarette, flicked the lighter and passed the pack to the man next to him. The man who had bowed his head did not take a cigarette, and nor did he pull out a lighter. Fang could not make out his expression.

Meng'ao, along with everyone else there, kept looking at the man in the dim light. The man, however, never raised his head. Fang Meng'ao lit the cigarette himself. Then he took out a wallet from his pocket and opened it, trying to pull something out.

A brother immediately lit his lighter and shone it in his direction. Fang Meng'ao flipped shut the lid of the lighter he was holding, and then took an old picture out of his wallet.

The picture showed a seated woman holding a beautiful little girl in her arms, her daughter happily playing a harmonica. Next to the mother stood two boys. Like their mother, the children were smiling, a rare occurrence in those miserable times. The father was standing, but his face was covered by black tape, giving the impression of a broken family.

Fang Meng'ao glanced at the picture and inserted it into his coat pocket, but he kept hold of the wallet.

"Chen Changwu!" Fang Meng'ao called out to the pilot in the same manner he conducted roll-call with his cadets. Chen was the cadet who had kept his head bowed and refused to light the cigarette passed to him.

Several lighters lit up at the same time.

Only then did the melancholic Chen Changwu look up at Fang Meng'ao who handed him his wallet. He slowly stood up, but instead of taking the wallet, he asked the question that many had been wanting to ask: "Captain, are you really a Communist Party member?"

Still holding the wallet, Fang Meng'ao found all eyes were trained on him, waiting for an answer. He realised he had to say something. "This is bullshit! If I say 'yes', will the Commies accept me? If I say 'no', will Zeng Keda and his gang believe me? Now, all of you, listen up. You followed my order not to bomb Kaifeng. So it's me who's going to be court-martialled and sent to jail. All of you lot can go to Changwu's wedding." As he spoke, he thrust the wallet containing some dollar notes into Chen Changwu's hand.

Everyone went silent, and all lighters were extinguished. It was dark once more in the back of the prison van.

Fang Meng'ao flicked the lighter he was holding, and the familiar smile returned to his face. "Let me sing a song to Changwu. Please think of it as an early wedding present. Come on, be a sport. Light up." Before they could do so, Fang Meng'ao was already beating time by tapping his feet and humming a tune.

The group were stunned. Wasn't this the same tenor voice they heard when the captain performed to packed, cheering houses? And the song. Wasn't it *Blooming Flowers, Full Moon*, sung by Zhou Xuan and popular with countless young lovers?

> *The floating, scattered clouds,*
> *The bright moon shines on the people as they arrive.*
> *Today is the happiest reunion.*

At first, they were surprised, then deeply touched by the authenticity and affection in the captain's voice. Very soon, all the lighters were flicked on.

At first one, then two, then all the pilots, were singing along.

> *Clean and shallow ponds,*
> *Mandarin ducks playing on the water,*
> *Red skirts and emerald caps,*
> *Devoted married couples like two lotus flowers opening.*
>
> *In pairs, the spouses share a mutual love.*
> *This soft wind blows upon the beautiful flowers,*
> *Blowing on the good flowers,*
> *Full of warmth and affection between the people.*

Fang Meng'ao stopped once everyone else had joined in, and he listened affectionately. Of course, they did not know how many secrets and experiences the captain had hidden in his heart. Deep down in the heart of their captain were hidden so many secrets and unique experiences. In fact, the love between man and woman expressed in the lyrics had nothing to do with what the captain cherished in his heart.

———

At the same time, in the governor's office of the Peking branch of the Central Bank, a sleep-deprived Fang Buting, just back from Yenching University Hospital, was sitting at his desk, eyes closed as if in a trance. In fact, he was preoccupied with his own concerns.

Xie Peidong walked in. Knowing that Fang Buting had not managed to sleep, he decided to withdraw quietly.

"What did you make of Fu Zuoyi's remarks this morning?" Fang Buting asked without making mention of any telegram or phone call. He opened his eyes in such a way that it wasn't clear if he was looking at Xie Peidong.

"I didn't have a chance to hear them," said Xie Peidong, who stopped and went back to Fang Buting at the desk where he habitually kept official documents and various account books. "Since drawing up the message to the Central Bank, I've been calling Nanking. I still can't reach Cui Zhongshi."

Fang Buting continued to talk about the speech: "Fu Zuoyi's statement was full of sympathy for the students. The US diplomatic note must have been sent to him the night before. You can't arrest the students even though martial law remains in force. Famine has spread across the entire city, shops are closed, people with nothing to cook are not allowed to leave their houses to beg. When the time comes, it is not just the students who will go hungry. So will the general public. Starving people are more ferocious than tigers. Let's wait and see the outcome of the in-fighting between the young and old Kuomintang factions in Nanking. I expect that some members of the Peking Citizens' Food-Distribution Committee involved in the smuggling case will be exposed, including those from military and political circles."

"Sooner or later, the truth will out. As long as we are honest, we needn't be afraid." Xie Peidong was responding most positively to Fang Buting's comment. At long last!

"I can't afford not to be worried." Fang Buting's eyes were fixed on Xie Peidong even though it seemed that they were looking elsewhere. Finally, he was going to talk about the issue that concerned him most. "Have you had a chance to check out the false financial reporting of the Citizens' Food-Distribution Committee headed by Cui Zhongshi?"

"You've given me instructions that the books were to be kept by Deputy Director Cui alone," said Xie Peidong.

"What a fatal miscalculation!" Fang Buting's voice seemed to have come from deep within his belly. "If the Americans obtained the intelligence from us, what exactly does Cui Zhongshi want?"

Xie Peidong stopped packing up the account books, but before he could answer, Fang Buting continued: "There is only one reason – the Communists. Don't look at me like that. Think about it. Who has been in contact with Meng'ao over the past three years under the guise of reconciling our father-son relationship? That unfilial son of mine is bold, but no matter how bold he is, he would not publicly defy military orders and instruct his brigade not to bomb the Communist occupying army. He would not do so personally unless he was instructed by the Communist Party. Regarding the Air Force, I put a lot of effort into preventing him from flying combat missions and arranging for him to teach at aviation school, out of fear that he would be recruited by the Communists. I have tried to find out by asking the Central Bureau of Investigation and Statistics and the Bureau of Investigation and Statistics of the Military Council. No Communist suspects were found to have contacted him. If anyone is found to have arranged contact between Cui and my son, it's me!"

Xie Peidong listened carefully with an uncomprehending look on his face, shaking his head slightly from time to time in movements that were barely visible.

Fang Buting was mostly talking to himself. He knew that his brother-in-law, who also happened to be his assistant, was good with figures but dull-witted when it came to politics. The only person with whom he could discuss big issues was his younger son, Fang Mengwei.

At long last, as the large clock on the wall struck ten, Fang Mengwei's voice was heard from outside the door.

"Father!" Every time Fang Mengwei went to visit his father, he would call out first for permission to cross over into his father's living room and office on the first floor of the property.

Before responding to his son, Fang Buting instructed Xie Peidong: "Continue to contact Nanking but ask only where Cui

Zhongshi has gone, whom he has met, what he has said and what he has done." Only then did he beckon Fang Mengwei inside.

Fang Mengwei waited for Xie Peidong to leave, politely greeting him with "Uncle" before entering the room and closing the door behind him.

It was a scorching July day. Looking at his son still dressed in a pressed uniform and his face covered with sweat, Fang Buting went to the washstand with a basin of clean water, picked up a clean white towel from the shelf, soaked it in the water and twisted it dry, before handing it to his son.

"Wipe away the sweat," he said.

With so many years of mutual understanding, Fang Mengwei would silently accept such acts of paternal love. He went over and took the towel with both hands, undid the buttons on his collar, wiped the sweat from his face and returned the towel to his father. By the time his father had soaked the towel in the washbasin and dried it, he had added hot water to his father's purple sand teapot and handed it over with both hands.

Fang Buting took the teapot but did not pour himself a cup. He went over to the table and sat down.

Whenever he acted like this, Fang Mengwei knew that his father had more to say, and that he would invariably start with an ancient poem, as had happened since his childhood.

"If you don't learn poetry, you can't speak." For generations, this had always been the way of parenting for the Fang family. Fang Mengwei stood behind his father and massaged his shoulders and back.

Sure enough, Fang Buting began to read the poems of the ancients.

Black clouds loom heavy over the city,
And the city on the verge of collapse,
Armour gleams golden with open scales in the sun.
Battle horns fill the sky of an autumnal hue,
Soldiers' red blood freezes into a nocturnal purple.
Battle banners half-furled over the Yishui River,
Drums go mute from heavy frost and cold.
To return the favour on the Golden Stage,

I tote my Yulong sword to die for the emperor.

After reading the poem, Fang Buting did not stop as he usually did in order to give time for his son to digest the words. Instead, he offered the following observation: "This poem by Li He, I've read many times these past few days. Though written more than a thousand years ago, it still has great relevance today. In particular, the line 'Battle banners half-furled over the Yishui River' seems to explain that the Communist Army are attacking Baoding. What's their next target city? Of course, it's Peking. I'm here to help take care of the Central Bank, but I'm fully aware that Chiang won't be able to attract talented people even though he has the money. Will Fu Zuoyi fight to the last drop of blood in defence of Peking? Even if he is willing, can his troops fend off a Communist attack? Again, how did yesterday's events begin? Were they all really Communists? There is no food to eat, no books to read. Those who were greedy are getting even greedier. Since much of the relief provided to the students from the Northeast is embezzled, they can't even make up the shortfall. Hence, this massive eviction of students from the Northeast. Some have been arrested and forced to conscript, others have taken to the streets. They claim that the constitutional government's in charge, but actually no. It is still the military government! As your father, I'm not sure what to do. Heaven knows what the common folk are meant to think. It's become hard to comment on state affairs."

Fang Mengwei knew that family matters would come up next, and that they would be much harder to solve. The hands that were massaging his father's shoulders slowed down, as he listened to what was to follow.

"You didn't arrest anyone again, did you?"

"No."

"Don't go arresting or killing any more people unless you have to. Especially not students. After all, everyone is beloved by his or her parents."

As if knowing it was time to talk about his older brother, Fang Mengwei solemnly replied: "Yes."

"Your older brother, though he does not recognise me as his

father, is known as my son. I can't believe you kept me in the dark about him being involved in a major Communist collusion case."

Sure enough, Fang Buting cut straight to the quick, his tone harsh.

"My older brother is not a Communist." Fang Mengwei had long been quite sure about this, so he went on: "You know as well as I do that my older brother is a man of integrity. He always does what he wants, and the Communist Party wouldn't want someone like that."

"Who told you that the Communists don't need people like him?" Fang Buting pushed off Fang Mengwei's hands that had been massaging his back and shoulders.

"Since you ask, I'll tell you all about it," said the son. "In Nanking, we've entrusted Director Xu of the Kuomintang's Central Bureau of Investigation and Statistics to act on our behalf. He is in charge of my older brother's case. He has investigated all the circumstances surrounding him over the years, and there is actually no evidence of collusion with the Communists."

"Is Cui Zhongshi still working on the case within the Central Bureau?" Fang Buting's tone was even more severe. Suddenly he turned his head and looked at his son. "Did you take the initiative to ask Cui Zhongshi for help with your elder brother's case during his many trips to Nanking? Or did he go to you to offer his help?"

Fang Mengwei was stunned.

"Think slowly and only answer me when you've figured it out. After working for the Kuomintang's Central Bureau for so many years, let me ask you this – how does the Communist Party recruit its members and how do they contact each other?"

"Most contact each other individually."

"If your brother is a Commie, and that single individual who recruited him works for me, don't you think the people of the Central Bureau of Investigation and Statistics will find out?"

Only then did Fang Mengwei understand his father's tone and the cold expression in his eyes: "Father, do you suspect that Deputy Director Cui is a Communist spy?"

Fang Buting said nothing. He must not tell his son about the bank's secret account for the smuggling and resale of daily necessities. Therefore, he certainly could not confirm his younger son's suspicions that Cui Zhongshi had disclosed economic information.

"If you have forgotten, go back and read your manual issued by the Central Bureau of Investigation and Statistics. It claims that the Communist Party, especially Zhou Enlai, is adept at playing the idle piece in a game of Chinese chess, meaning he is good at planting Communist undercover agents close to the Kuomintang's power centre and making use of them later."

Fang Mengwei was surprised: "Father, do you mean Deputy Director Cui is that idle chess piece planted by the Communist Party next to you, and my brother is a potential piece to be used by Deputy Director Cui?"

"I have my own reason to believe what he is suspected of, which I'll share with you later. Well, it's better to believe that he is than he's not!"

Fang Mengwei raised his head. "If it's really so, let's first cut off contact between Cui Zhongshi and my elder brother. We'll try to save him in other ways. Once we succeed, you can always ask Ambassador Leighton Stuart for help through Uncle He, and send my brother to the United States. I'll call Xu in Nanking and tell him not to see Cui Zhongshi again."

Fang Buting looked over at Mengwei's hand on the phone and said: "No more calls. Whether Cui Zhongshi is a Communist or not, it's between you, me and your uncle, just the three of us. Anyone with this information will surely use it to blackmail us."

In Nanking, inside the building of the National Communications Bureau of the Kuomintang Central Membership Committee, a young secretary dressed neatly in a Zhongshan suit was walking down a long corridor. He was escorting a middle-aged man with gold-framed glasses and wearing a Western three-piece suit. They stopped at the door with a sign that read: "Party Members' Liaison Office".

The middle-aged man waited quietly, and the secretary knocked gently on the door. "Sir, Mr Cui is here."

From behind the door came the director's voice: "Please come in."

The secretary pushed the door half open with one hand, with the other politely stretched out to the middle-aged man: "Mr Cui, please come in."

The middle-aged man was the same Cui Zhongshi whom Fang Buting strongly suspected of being an undercover Communist. Publicly he was known as the deputy treasury director at the Central Bank's Peking branch.

If he was really a member of the Communist Party, the place he was visiting today would surely be highly dangerous. Colloquially, it was known as the Zhongtong, the Central Bureau of Investigation and Statistics, the equivalent of the CIA. In April 1947, the nameplate outside the building was changed to the National Communications Bureau of the Kuomintang Central Membership Committee, although its functions, responsibilities and remit remained unchanged. Chen Guofu and Chen Lifu, also in charge of the Central Executive Committee and the Central Organisation Department of the Kuomintang respectively, were heads of the bureau.

Cui Zhongshi was calm in the presence of the very polite secretary, and he did not hurry to enter the office now known as the "All-China Kuomintang Members' Liaison Office", but instead pulled out of the top pocket of his suit a gold Parker pen and handed it over to the secretary with a smile.

"Mr Sun, please accept this. It certainly doesn't violate discipline, for it is a necessary piece of stationery for a man of culture."

Secretary Sun responded in polite fashion, but there was still no expression on his face. The hand that had previously welcomed him in now pushed away Cui Zhongshi's hand with the gold pen. "It *is* a violation, I'm afraid. Nonetheless, I appreciate the gesture, Mr Cui."

Cui Zhongshi showed a look of admiration and quickly put the pen back in his pocket. "I'm impressed. I will certainly thank your director for having such an upstanding person on his staff."

"Thank you for your kind words," said Sun. He leaned over and let Cui through, gently closing the door from the outside.

Though not spacious, the room was furnished with a desk, but there were no chairs for visitors. The bookshelves against the wall were empty, and packed cardboard boxes were arranged on the floor, each sealed with an official stamp. It was quite evident that the owner of the building was about to leave.

Stacks of documents were piled on both sides of the table, all stamped with the red characters "Top secret". The head of a middle-aged man could be seen in between two stacks of papers. He was working intensely on something at his table.

There was no chair to sit on, and nor was there any greeting from the host. All Cui Zhongshi could do was stand there, waiting quietly.

"Did you have a chance to meet with the people from the Central Bank and the Finance Ministry?" asked the man from behind the desk, his head still buried in papers.

"Yes, I did," Cui Zhongshi replied with a smile. "They all agree that with the director at the helm, everything will be fine."

"Since when did I become so powerful?" The man finally stood up from behind a pile of files. He was neatly dressed in a Zhongshan suit, his hair, half-grey, was side-parted in a very stylish manner. There was the hint of a smile at the corners of his mouth, but there was no warmth in the eyes. His name was Xu Tieying, director of the Liaison Office.

Smiling politely, Cui Zhongshi did not respond, waiting until Xu Tieying spoke.

"Cui, I will set out what I want to say in two parts. You've got to understand me, and then call your boss." With this, Xu Tieying pulled out from under his desk an American-made jacquard box and put it on the desk. "You shouldn't have given me this. Come and take a look at what's inside. I've not opened it yet."

Cui Zhongshi was quite used to the hypocrisy of Kuomintang officials, so he stood there smiling. "I believe you, sir. Go ahead, please, director."

"What's inside?" asked Xu Tieying.

Cui Zhongshi's smile was unchanging. "Our governor has said that it was not for the director, and even if it was, you'd never accept it. But in order to save the young master, you've transferred so much manpower to help with the investigation. Since the bureau did not provide the funding, we'd always be ready to cover the transportation expenses for those out on duty."

Also smiling, Xu Tieying said: "You still haven't told me what's inside."

"To be safe, I withdrew this amount from Citibank in Nanking yesterday. It's just a hundred thousand. Today's exchange rate on the Shanghai Stock Exchange is one to twelve million *fabi*."

Of course he was referring to US dollars, and Xu Tieying's smile slowly disappeared.

CHAPTER 2

The Central Bureau of Investigation was laid out like a Daoist *bagua*.

Being appointed to the bureau required some skills. First, you had to be proficient in not betraying a single feeling or intention. This was the very minimum requirement. Having a poker face was a big advantage. Second, you had to be ready to show leadership when required. Your counterpart would no doubt be a master, so you had to confront this standing up, with verve and genuine self-belief. Yet this skill had to be revealed carefully, and in full awareness. When it came to the third skillset, the capacity to bend without violating the rules, this could only be accomplished by two groups of people. One were the career officers at the Bureau of Investigation, for whom every action was professional, every word proper. Like a mighty wave crashing on a sandy shore, many were washed away by the demands, but the current bureau chief Ye Xiufeng remained afloat.

The other type were leaders in society or Nationalist elders, men of learning who were heavily relied upon by the authorities. Often they would make a mistake such as "obeying the truth instead of the king", yet the authorities couldn't touch them. Zhu Jiahua had once served as bureau chief. Although he had worked for more than ten years and had both the means and experience, Xu Tieying had failed to reach the third rank, having clashed with Xu

Enzeng, a fellow member of the Xu clan and veteran agent who used to be deputy director. Xu Tieying showed too much obedience to his superiors over taking action, and selfishness over hard work. So he had no chance of reaching the third level.

Cui Zhongshi was waiting for Xu Tieying's response in the Liaison Office of the National Communications Bureau. Cui was a veritable god of wealth to someone like Xu. He'd taken bribes for so long, there was no longer any need to hide the practice. Glancing at the stash of a hundred thousand dollars, Xu Tieying stopped smiling but could not hide his avarice.

"If it had been yesterday, I would have accepted it on behalf of colleagues," he said. "But I can't take it today. Cui, if I ask you something, you'll have to tell me the truth."

"Director, I promise to tell you everything I know," said Cui Zhongshi.

"Is your boss implicated in the smuggling and reselling of rations from the Citizens' Food-Distribution Committee?"

"Implicated how, director?"

"Just tell me about any involvement whatsoever. This is of great importance to save your master when the court is in session this afternoon."

"Sir, you're better informed than me. All transactions took place at our bank. Since they all involved TV Soong's China Cotton Trading Company and HH Kung's Yangtze Construction Company, our manager had to assist. However, I can assure you that no one in our branch, let alone our manager, took a penny. By the way, sir, did yesterday's unrest add uncertainty to our master's case?"

"Thank goodness you haven't hidden anything from me. Now listen. The court is in session this afternoon, and your young master's case will be tried alongside the Air Force smuggling case." At this point, Xu Tieying turned serious, and he continued: "It's an outrage that people on the Food-Distribution Committee use such corrupt tricks while our troops fight to the death at the front! They colluded with the Air Force, dispatching combat aircraft to transport smuggled goods! The student unrest in Peking yesterday prompted the Americans to send a diplomatic note. It should have been the Central Bureau of Investigation that took up your master's case. But now it's been taken over by the Bureau of Reserve Cadres.

They're in charge of the prosecution, and we're just meant to assist. One's a smuggling and corruption case involving the Air Force, the other in which your young master is suspected of collusion with the Communists. Directly and indirectly, they both involve your boss. So how can I help?"

Cui Zhongshi bought himself time by passing Xu Tieying a cigarette. Xu didn't move, so Cui lit it for him. "Sir, if things were not at such a critical juncture, I would never say what I'm about to say. But I must tell you now. Do you happen to know how many shares Hou Juntang of the Air Force Operations Department owns in companies affiliated to the Food-Distribution Committee?"

Xu Tieying stared at a stack of blank paper on his desk. Cui Zhongshi immediately understood, pulling out a pencil and writing "twenty per cent" on the paper. Xu Tieying's eyes widened.

"No matter what happens in court, his shares will not be made public. They are registered in all sorts of names. Even if he is sentenced to death, Hou Juntang won't reveal any of them. Tell me this – if the court sentences Hou to death, where would the shares go?"

Xu Tieying stared at Cui Zhongshi, who drew an arrow behind the twenty per cent pointing at Cui!

"Just let me finish," Cui Zhongshi said, rubbing out the arrow. "Our manager does this for his son. Director, it's time for you to think about your children. I know your family is in Taipei, and that your wife is renting. You don't want the children to drop out of school, I'm sure. As I'm in charge of accounts, I know exactly how much has been embezzled and which children and grandchildren will live in material paradise for the rest of their lives. If you trust me and our boss, forget this conversation. Let's just get on with our work, and all will be fine."

"You really shouldn't have told me this," Xu replied. "If Hou Juntang were to be sentenced to death this afternoon, it would look like I was in it for myself. Besides, getting him killed might not even save your master, though it could remove suspicion of him colluding with the Communists. Having said that, Zeng Keda of the Iron and Blood Congress won't let him off for simply having disobeyed orders in battle."

"He can't be convicted of disobeying military orders," Cui

Zhongshi responded. "My master is an instructor at the Jianqiao Aviation Academy. He has teaching responsibilities, but doesn't fly bombing missions himself. The mission instructed by the Air Force Operations Department was for the First and Second Brigades of Air Force One. It was only because Hou Juntang made both brigades airlift smuggled materials that our young master was forced to bomb Kaifeng by instructing the graduating trainees of the academy to carry out his ridiculous command. If you focus on this evidence, my master will never be convicted."

Xu Tieying began to look a little queasy. This refined Shanghai native, a skilled financier, appeared to be equally adept at politics. That said, politeness and courtesy were about to go out of the window: "It seems Hou Juntang must die. Zeng Keda will already be in Hangzhou by now. So I'd better get to court." He busied himself arranging his briefcase. Seemingly forgetting to return Cui Zhongshi's hundred thousand US dollars as promised, Xu pretended to ignore the case.

"Thanks for everything, sir." Cui Zhongshi did not outstay his welcome. He gave a fist and palm salute, and walked swiftly to the door. It opened from the outside, as apparently the secretary had stayed on guard. With the door firmly shut, Xu Tieying closed his court briefcase and opened the smaller case left by Cui Zhongshi.

On top was a fine Western suit, along with a tie and pair of shoes made by a famous French brand. He took them out to have a closer look. Underneath was a neat bundle of cash. By the look of it, one hundred thousand dollars in total.

Without hesitation, he stuffed the money into an envelope addressed to members of the National Communications Bureau of the Kuomintang Central Committee and stamped the envelope with the seal of the Liaison Office. In his own hand, Xu wrote "bribe money" on the front. He put it in his briefcase and off he went to court.

His secretary had been waiting behind the door to his office with head bowed and holding a huge umbrella.

"Raining?" asked Xu Tieying.

"Director, it's been raining for quite a while," the secretary replied as he went to take the briefcase.

"Such awful weather," Xu said, handing him the briefcase. "To court."

It might have still been a military government, but the Nationalists had announced a new era, complete with constitutional law. So although the court was in special session, the Anglo-American model of justice was followed, from case procedures right down to the layout of the building. In the high court, behind the sign stating "Presiding Judge", was a specially appointed judge of the Supreme Court. On the left of the platform, Zeng Keda sat solemnly, the sign in front of him identifying his role as that of public prosecutor representing the Ministry of Defence. The sign on the right side of the platform stated "Jury and Defence Lawyer". Two roles in one? Xu Tieying tried his best to personify the ambiguous position of juror and defence lawyer. It wasn't easy.

Even before the suspects were brought into the courtroom, there was an air of confrontation between Zeng Keda, public prosecutor of the Ministry of Defence's Bureau of Reserve Cadres, and Xu Tieying, defence for the Central Bureau of Investigation.

The expression in Zeng's eyes appeared to warn of his determination on behalf of the Iron and Blood Congress that no favouritism or covering up would save those about to be courtmartialled.

Xu Tieying smiled in return and expressed no hostility towards him. He spread out his documents.

As Zeng Keda pondered the meaning behind Xu Tieying's smile, the judge struck his gavel and announced: "The Nineteenth of June Communist collusion case and the Fifth of July Air Force smuggling case are now in session. Bring in the defendants."

Two helmeted bailiffs opened the double doors into the court.

Fang Meng'ao entered first, and following him, a neat line of pilots. Despite facing court-martial, they remained so disciplined that the bailiffs and police standing guard around the courtroom looked up in admiration.

Fang and his pilots were led to the dock, with Fang leading the way. Zeng glared menacingly at Fang.

Seeing him stare, Fang raised his right leg and stood on his left. Almost in unison, the pilots behind him did likewise.

"Director Xu," said Zeng Keda, addressing Xu Tieying. "What is your defence to the fact that your clients are now in contempt of court?"

"The jury and defence lawyer shall remind parties to this case to accept the trial with humility."

Fang Meng'ao and his pilots remained holding their pose. Zeng Keda and Xu Tieying appealed to the judge.

"The accused will be tried by the court in accordance with all due process. Please respect the court."

The judge's tone and manner were very professional, as might be expected from a man of seventy-odd years having been trained in the United Kingdom and the United States. Fang Meng'ao's wilfulness had never been tested against two particular kinds of people, the professional and the respectful. This judge appeared to be both. He was worthy of respect. Fang Meng'ao could do nothing but agree with his request, and returned his raised leg to the floor. As did his pilots.

Zeng Keda sat sullenly, and Xu Tieying looked down at his files without expression.

Two other defendants should have arrived in court by now, but their entrance had been delayed by Fang's theatrics.

"Bring in the defendants Lin Dawei and Hou Juntang!"

Seats were positioned in the dock to the left and right of Fang Meng'ao. A helmeted marshal walked in through the courthouse doors with a man who had to be supported. The man was in his forties and his hair was starting to grey. He walked slowly in his Air Force khakis, and while the insignia had been removed from his collar, he maintained an air of elegance. He had clearly been tortured and looked ill as well as injured. This was Lin Dawei, a member of the Nationalist Air Force Operations Department and a suspected Communist.

Next came Lieutenant General Hou Juntang in a wide-brimmed hat, and with four gold stars shining on his lapels. The marshals escorted him as if they were his entourage. The aura around this man contrasted sharply with that of Lin Dawei. Hou Juntang was a prime suspect in the smuggling case.

The courtroom doors closed.

The grey-haired Lin Dawei sat on the right side of the dock, while Hou Juntang stood in military pose on the left. Zeng Keda glared at him sternly.

"Honourable judge!" Hou Juntang did not wait for Zeng Keda to grill him, proffering a military salute directly to the judge. "I must protest. I am the current lieutenant general of the Nationalist Army and deputy director of the Operations Department of the Air Force. The Bureau of Reserve Cadres has no evidence for their charge. It is entirely false. By trying me in court with this undercover Communist, you are insulting me, the party and the state. I protest."

"Prosecutor, respond to the defendant."

"I will." Zeng Keda approached Hou Juntang, who was having a hard time hiding his fear from the gaze of such a hostile-looking major general. Of course, it was not Zeng Keda himself who made him fearful, but what lay behind him: the Iron and Blood Congress.

Zeng Keda went to his side and said: "You're right. The Eagle is dead, and so is the colonel who killed him. Therefore, the Bureau of Reserve Cadres has no evidence to charge you of smuggling."

"All this has nothing to do with me," said Hou Juntang.

"Wretched piece of scum!" Zeng Keda roared, grabbing the lieutenant general's wide-brimmed hat from his head, and tearing off his badges.

Before Hou had time to react, Zeng reached for his lapel insignia and tore them off too, shouting: "Shame on you!"

Hou Juntang had worked hard to reach a point in his career whereby his meritorious service and impeccable background would make him impervious to humiliation by a younger major general. Physically, he towered above Zeng, and with this height advantage he reached out to retaliate by grabbing Zeng's collar.

He didn't get far. As he stretched his arms to get hold of his adversary, Zeng Keda pushed his pistol up against his jaw.

Shock echoed around court, reaching the judge, Xu Tieying and the marshals. Even Fang Meng'ao and his pilots were transfixed. Only one person stayed still: Communist undercover agent Lin Dawei seated on the right.

With his pistol pressed against Hou's jaw, Zeng Keda

bombarded him with questions. "Using Nationalist Air Force aircraft to smuggle citizens' goods in the name of the Air Force Operations Department? Nothing to do with you? Of the ten C-46 planes leased by the United States, seven were so overloaded with smuggled goods that they couldn't even take off. Nothing to do with you? Defeat in the battle of Kaifeng on the nineteenth of June? Student demonstrations in Peking? Nothing to do with you, right? You think the party-state will be unable to convict you if you kill witnesses? How wrong can you be. We're not amateurs. And the cheek of protesting about standing trial with Communist agents? This prosecutor declares that you will both be convicted – you for corruption, him for Communism!"

"I'm telling you," Zeng Keda continued, pointing to Lin Dawei, "this man has repeatedly sent secret information to Communist troops. Now, which department does he serve? Who does he report to?"

Zeng then turned to Fang Meng'ao. "In the Battle of the Nineteenth of June, according to the operations department's plan, they called in Brigades One and Two of Air Force One to bomb Kaifeng. Who changed the plans without authorisation to prevent Communist agents in the Aviation Academy having to carry out the mission, thus hindering military operations? Lieutenant General Hou, Deputy Director Hou, we'll deal with two cases today. One is a major case of smuggling and corruption, the other is a case of collusion with the Communists in defiance of military orders. Which one involves you? Whichever it is, we will convict you. We will convict you three times over if necessary!"

Hou Juntang was sweating. Hoarsely, he said: "Your Honour, I wish to make a statement."

"Permission granted. It is not appropriate for a public prosecutor to question the accused in such a manner in court. Please submit your gun to court officials."

Zeng Keda let go of the gun he had been holding against Hou Juntang's jaw and handed it to a marshal on his way back to the public prosecution dock.

"Communist undercover agent Lin Dawei had been serving in the Air Force Operations Department for six years before I was transferred there as deputy director last year. The public prosecutor has implicated me in his case, but I would like to ask the court for clarification."

"Any further statement to make?"

Hou Juntang continued: "Regarding the bombing mission conducted on the nineteenth of June by Fang Meng'ao's Youth Aviation Brigade of the Jianqiao Aviation Academy during the Kaifeng campaign, the Liaison Office of the Communications Bureau has my order on file. The public prosecutor falsely accuses me of ordering Fang Meng'ao not to bomb Kaifeng. I ask the court for clarification."

"I accept the defendant's statement. The jury and defence should be shown the relevant case files," said the judge.

Xu Tieying slowly stood up, opened the first file and briefed the court. "According to our investigation, Lin Dawei, a member of the Air Force Operations Department, enrolled in the Air Force Aviation Academy of the Nationalist Army in 1938 by concealing his Communist Party affiliation. He served in the Nationalist Army for one year after graduating before being sent to the United States by the Ministry of Defence in 1942. On returning one year later, he joined the Nationalist Air Force Operations Department by deception, and since conflict began between the Nationalists and Communists in 1946, the suspect has used his special status as a combat officer to send information to Communist headquarters in Yan'an, and to Communist troops in eastern and northeastern China on twenty-three separate occasions. He acted as an individual and had no accomplices in the Air Force Operations Department. This case does not appear to be connected to that of Hou Juntang, deputy director of said department."

Hou Juntang was unable to express his appreciation of this career summary. He could only cast a grateful glance at Xu Tieying.

"Objection," said Zeng Keda as he stood up. Facing the judge, he continued: "The statement says: 'This case does not appear to be connected to that of Hou Juntang.' This is a speculative way of putting it. The public prosecutor requests clarity from the investigators."

"Objection sustained," said the judge, looking at Xu Tieying. "The investigators should make a clear statement."

"I have no clearer statement to make," said Xu Tieying. "We have not found evidence that Hou Juntang was aware of Lin Dawei's identity as a Communist agent. If Hou Juntang were to be found guilty of sheltering undercover Communist agent Lin Dawei, then both directors and deputy directors of the Air Force Operations Department over the past six years would have to be charged."

The judge looked at Zeng Keda and asked: "Does the public prosecutor agree with this statement?"

"It must, of course, be acknowledged." Zeng Keda turned to Xu Tieying with a sneer. "Does Director Xu have evidence from his investigation to show how Hou Juntang had nothing to do with the twenty-second of June case involving Fang Meng'ao and his collusion with a Communist agent in violation of military orders? Or of him having nothing to do with the case of smuggling and reselling everyday goods by the Peking Food-Distribution Committee?"

Though the judge could hardly approve of Zeng's attitude, Xu Tieying was calmly defiant. "Your Honour, in order to make the evidence supplied by this jury and defence lawyer fair and credible, I'd like to share a piece of evidence of vital importance to me and to this case."

This came as something of a surprise to Zeng Keda, who stared at Xu Tieying. The judge also became serious. "Permission granted. Show us the evidence."

Mr Xu took an official envelope containing one hundred thousand US dollars from his briefcase and walked over to the judge with the envelope in both hands. The envelope could hardly be more incriminating, with the characters for "bribe money" scribbled across it. It contained the cash Cui Zhongshi had given him.

Dark clouds hovered over Nanking, creating an oppressive atmosphere. Heavy rain had been falling all morning over the Qinhuai River, but now it was clearing up. Cui Zhongshi had no wish to be found by his colleagues at the Peking branch. So he neither returned to the Jinling Hotel nor visited the Central Bank or the Ministry of Finance. Instead, he strolled up and down the riverbank holding an umbrella. His watch told him it was two fifty in the afternoon. Time to find a telephone booth.

In 1948, making a call from a phone booth in Nanking was not easy. It used to be that only the caller paid, but now the receiver had to pay too. You also had to use coins and the official *fabi* had no value at all, its coins long having become collectibles. So who would bother to make or answer a call these days? Cui Zhongshi put away his umbrella and waited in the booth quietly. It was three o'clock sharp when the phone rang. Cui Zhongshi picked up the receiver, and heard a female voice from the telephone office: "Sorry, please insert a coin to receive the call." Cui Zhongshi had coins ready to feed into the slot. "I've put you through. Please receive the call now."

"Has the master been admitted to hospital?" came the voice of a man on the other end.

"Yes sir. He was admitted at two o'clock this afternoon."

"Was Dr Xu willing to go to the consultation? Did he accept our gift?"

"He accepted it and will try his best. Rest assured."

"The master's illness may have complications. Wait for the results of the consultation. And don't visit the master yourself to avoid cross-infection. You sound like you have a bad cold."

"I feel well, sir."

"By the time you're aware of it, it can be too late." The tone of the voice on the other end became heavy. "So many things to be dealt with at home. You cannot afford to be ill. Your health is important."

"What's important is that we monitor the young master's situation," Cui Zhongshi replied. "I'm the only one here who can do this."

"Trust us all in the family. Someone higher up is also available to help," said the caller in solemn fashion. "Remain where you are until five o'clock. At five sharp, I will call again." With that, the caller hung up, despite Cui Zhongshi having more to say.

The hospital Cui Zhongshi mentioned referred to the special criminal court, while "consultation" implied that the trial had entered a suffocating period of tension.

"I protest!" a pale-faced Hou Juntang shouted, his voice quivering not at Zeng Keda, but at Xu Tieying. "This is a completely false accusation. It was their collusion to frame the Nationalist Army and the Air Force. I have never given any money to Xu Tieying. Mr Xu, how much money did you receive from the Fang family? Damage me so they won't convict Fang Meng'ao, is that what this is about?"

Everyone in court held their breath. Xu Tieying's sudden submission of the hundred thousand dollars and his accusation against Hou Juntang of bribing him caught everyone by surprise.

The most complicated reaction came from two individuals, one being Fang Meng'ao. He had expected someone to try to save him during the past two weeks in detention. Yet he seemed not to care either way. The countless sorties over the Hump, the countless battles with the Japanese Air Force and the countless comrades lost had put his life in perspective. He felt lucky to have survived with the skin on his back. Meng'ao was done with killing. On 21 June, having received the order to bomb Kaifeng, recently taken over by the People's Liberation Army's East China Field Army, he told his squadron not to drop a single bomb. In issuing the order, he knew that a death sentence in the military court would await him. Yet it warmed his heart to know what Hou Juntang had revealed in court. Whoever came to his rescue reminded him of his mother who was killed in a Japanese raid ten years ago. His mother, whose picture he kept in his breast pocket at all times.

The other person who had felt a mixed reaction to the surprising evidence was, of course, Zeng Keda, who reserved a particular hatred for Hou Juntang and his accomplices. In his mind, they all deserved to be executed. He realised, though, that Fang Meng'ao, exploited by the Communist troublemakers who had brought disaster upon disaster to the party-state, also deserved to die. If the trial could prove that the hundred thousand dollars paid to Xu Tieying was a bribe, it would be hard as hell for Hou Juntang to leave court that day without being convicted. But what about Fang Meng'ao? Hou's conviction was likely to soften the charges against him, because it meant he had not been officially assigned the mission to bomb Kaifeng. He flew the sortie purely because Hou Juntang had personally tampered with military orders.

"Your Honour," said Zeng Keda, consulting the judge with formality before turning to Hou Juntang. "You just said that this bribe presented to the court by Director Xu was a set-up – a framed accusation against you by those who colluded with each other. To whom are you referring? What were their motives?"

The question left Hou Juntang speechless.

"Defendant, you must answer the public prosecutor's question."

Hou Juntang was a ruthless operator in the Nationalist military community, but faced with an inquisition by the elite of the Iron and Blood Congress, a veteran of the Central Bureau of Investigation, he demonstrated the difference between amateur and professional political operator. Out of desperation, he said "they colluded", and the subtext of "they", of course, was Fang Meng'ao's father, Fang Buting. But Fang Buting happened to be *the* person who knew most about his involvement in the smuggling case, and he was backed to the hilt by the Soong and Kung families. Hou dared not mention him by name. In fact, there was another "they": the Bureau of Reserve Cadres representing the prosecutor, and the Central Bureau of Investigation representing the investigating party. But charging the Central Bureau of Investigation with collusion was tantamount to saying it had broken away from the party-state! Still, he had to answer the question.

He forced himself to say: "Fang Meng'ao is a Communist! Whoever gave one hundred thousand dollars to Director Xu planted stolen money in order to frame me. For what purpose? I implore the court and the public prosecutor to investigate Xu Tieying."

Zeng Keda wanted to examine this point, so he asked the judge if the court could "consider the defendant's request".

The judge looked at Xu, while the others glanced at him before turning to Fang Meng'ao. Xu Tieying sighed gently and looked at Hou Juntang with pity. "Hou, you're a prestigious member of the fourth year of graduates from the Whampoa Military Academy, and you were even sent to the German Air Force Academy for training. Both the president and the party-state must have had high hopes for you if they cultivated your talents for such a long period. Now, in times of trouble for the party-state when we are in urgent need of useful people, not only do the president and military wish to save you, but so does someone like me, working for the party's organisation department. But you've gone too far."

At this point, his tone became harsher. "For money, for your wife, for your three concubines, for the sons and daughters they gave you, you completely forgot that you're a card-carrying Nationalist Party member of twenty-one years' standing! I'm in charge of party affairs. Now, let me ask you a question. How do you write the word 'party'? There's no need to answer. Let me tell you. The character is comprised of *hei* meaning 'black', right under *dang* for 'party', and on top there are three 'knife' elements. Whoever dares corrupt the party will have a close encounter with those knives! Let me ask you again – did you use the C-46 without permission, the plane that crashed in Lingnan on the twenty-second of June when it flew smuggled materials to Hong Kong? You can deny it, but we have your personal order. Now, in the battle on the nineteenth of June, for the first two days it was the squadrons of Air Force One's First and Second Brigades that were carrying out the bombing missions, but on the twenty-second of June, what did you reassign them to do? The captain of the Second Brigade died in the plane crash, and the captain of the First Brigade was murdered today. And don't forget, I have a lot of evidence acquired through investigation here at the National Communications Bureau of the Kuomintang."

Hou Juntang was overwhelmed. The whole court was plunged into silence.

For a while, even Zeng Keda was stunned by Xu Tieying's words of righteous indignation. But he quickly realised that Xu Tieying's declamation was a disguise intended to scare Hou Juntang into not talking about the hundred thousand US dollars. Doubt in the heart immediately translated into intention, and of course, the next move was to say it out loud.

"I know what the prosecutor is asking."

Xu Tieying tightly controlled the pace of developments, not giving Zeng Keda any time to ask questions, by continuing: "Let me take the time to answer Hou Juntang's question about the bribe." As he spoke, he took out a tape recorder from his briefcase. "Please play this recording to the court."

A clerk went to insert the tape into in the US-made reel-to-reel recorder. Xu Tieying pressed "play" and the special criminal court quietened down.

"The newcomers in the Bureau of Reserve Cadres are going to attack us old guys this time." The voice on the tape clearly belonged to Hou Juntang.

Hou Juntang's face turned white. The court was silent.

"They want to shoot us so they can take over." It was still Hou Juntang's voice. Xu Tieying was probably just listening quietly. "This is not for you, Director Xu, and even if it were, I'm sure you wouldn't accept it. Many of our brothers are working so hard, but the bureau doesn't seem to have the budget. So, please consider incentivising them with attendance awards and traffic allowances, budgeted by the Air Force."

Finally, Xu Tieying's voice could be heard from the recorder: "Director Hou has yet to tell me what's in it."

"Today, there are twelve million *fabi* to one US dollar, and we can only take out cash. Citibank says our limit is a hundred thousand dollars at a time. I promise I'll make it up to you when the case is done."

With a click, Xu Tieying pressed "stop". "Your Honour," he said, "this piece of evidence is surely self-explanatory."

Before the judge could say anything, Zeng Keda replied: "Director Xu does not seem to have finished playing the recording. Has he completed what he was saying or were the words erased?"

Xu Tieying sighed and pressed the "play" button again. It turned out that the voice had more to say. "No matter who you are, everyone is short of money at some time or another. The party-state is facing its most challenging period." Xu Tieying's words were full of feeling, but he sounded calm. "We should really spend this money fighting the Communists at the front. Deputy director, if you've done anything wrong in the past, now's the time to make up for it." Then came the loud sound of the recorder being pushed forward on the table.

"The Nationalist Army needs money to fight, and so does the Operations Department of the Central Committee's party headquarters. I, Hou Juntang, am also a Nationalist Party member of twenty-one years' standing. Please consider the hundred thousand dollars in lieu of my membership dues, will you?"

"Deputy Director Hou, aren't you concerned that I will hand over your fees to party headquarters?"

"If you do, I'll allow it."

Silence followed, then a deep sigh from Xu Tieying: "Leave it here then."

The tape idled on for a while. No more conversation was recorded. Zeng Keda had nothing more to say, so Xu Tieying pressed the "stop" button.

Everyone turned to Hou Juntang. This time, he neither spoke nor looked up. His body appeared bloated, a pile of flesh and nothing more. Without hesitation, Xu Tieying began to exercise his power as juror of the special criminal court and make his recommendation to the judge for the court decision.

"Currently, we are in a period of national mobilisation in suppression of the Communist rebellion. In accordance with Paragraph Five of Article Five, Law of the Army, Navy and Air Force, Hou Juntang has committed the crime of using the Nationalist Army to smuggle and resell state goods, and the crime of threatening state security as a result of tampering with military orders. The evidence is conclusive and his punishment should be death, carried out immediately. Lin Dawei committed the crime of spying and threatening national security. The evidence is conclusive. He should be sentenced to death and executed immediately. The court is requested to decide in accordance with the law."

"Objection!" said Zeng Keda, standing up at once. "Juror, you seem to have forgotten that you are still their defence lawyer. According to court proceedings, you should defend them, should you not?"

"I want to defend them," said Xu Tieying, "but I find no evidence to support their case. In accordance with the Defence Regulations of the Special Criminal Court, the defence may waive the right to defend if the offender is convicted of threatening national security. Your Honour, I apply for a waiver of the duty to defend."

"Objection null and void. The defence lawyer may waive his duty to defend."

"Fang Meng'ao and his brigade of trainees from the Air Force's Jianqiao Aviation Academy are suspected of defying a military order and colluding with the Communists," said Zeng Keda. "Does Director Xu also give up his duty to defend?"

Fang Meng'ao, who had remained sitting, stood up and said: "Your Honour, my trainee flying brigade and I have no need for a defence lawyer. I'll explain my own actions to the court."

"So many people behind you have spent so much time working for you, but you don't seem to appreciate it at all, do you?" said Zeng Keda.

"Objection!" Xu Tieying persisted. "What the prosecutor has just said was already slander. May I request the court to order the public prosecutor to make a clear statement."

Instead of saying "Objection sustained", the judge asked Zeng Keda: "Is there any evidence as mentioned by the public prosecutor just now?"

"So," said Zeng Keda, "if Xu Tieying goes ahead and kills Hou Juntang, and especially Lin Dawei, then the evidence will naturally be missing."

The judge replied: "Does the public prosecutor mean that there is a chain of evidence associated with Hou Juntang, Lin Dawei and Fang Meng'ao who are suspected of defying military orders and colluding with the Communists? Please make it clear."

"Your Honour, yes. It is a joint trial of the two cases today, which was decided last night by a joint meeting of the Central Military Commission and the headquarters of the Nationalist Party. As a representative of the party headquarters, Director Xu seems to have forgotten this. Since Fang Meng'ao's case has not yet entered trial proceedings, why did he ask the court to close the cases of Hou Juntang and Lin Dawei in advance? And why should the death penalty be carried out immediately? Fang Meng'ao openly disobeyed the military order to bomb Communist forces in Kaifeng. Now, if he wasn't following Hou Juntang's instruction, then whose order was he following? Who else would give him such an instruction besides the Communists? It is this Communist spy Lin Dawei who is directly responsible for issuing such orders from the Air Force Operations Department! Director Xu, don't you want to know whether Lin Dawei secretly gave Fang Meng'ao the order not to bomb Kaifeng?"

"As juror and defender, you're required to answer questions raised by the public prosecutor directly."

"I can only answer with investigatory evidence," said Xu Tieying. "From the twenty-third of June to the fifth of July, on behalf of the National Communications Bureau, I contacted the Confidential Information Bureau and the relevant departments of the Air Force, read a large number of archival materials and found no contact between Fang Meng'ao and the Communist Party, let alone any contact between Fang Meng'ao and Lin Dawei. If the prosecutor continues to suspect that those two are accomplices, you can now question them in court."

"Agreed," said the judge. "Lin Dawei, the defendant, stand up to answer the questions from the public prosecutor."

Lin Dawei, who had been sitting quietly, stood up slowly.

Zeng Keda went up to Lin Dawei. He didn't stare at him the way he did at Fang Meng'ao, nor did he act as recklessly as he did with Hou Juntang. He spoke in a very calm tone: "I understand you when you talk about doctrine. But I also understand you believe in Communism, and we serve our own masters. So I don't intend to entice you to talk about your beliefs right now. I'm talking to you about being a person of integrity. Having joined the Communist Party, you should get paid by your party, and live on that pay and feed your family with that pay. However, while accepting the cultivation of the party-state on the one hand, you also take all the benefits given to you by the party and the state, including medical care. On the other hand, you work for the Communist Party which doesn't pay you a penny. Don't you ever feel guilty about being so disloyal to the party and the state?"

Lin Dawei began to speak, his voice weak, but he was even more calm than Zeng Keda: "Since you don't want to talk about political beliefs, I'll readily comply with your request. Whose belief is the truth, that of the Kuomintang and the Communist Party? History will soon reach its conclusion. Let me respond to your question about being a person of integrity. First, you claim that it's the Kuomintang that gave me a living. My question is how did they do so? Don't give me all that crap about the feudal ethics of being loyal to your monarch because he provides you with food. Don't forget that the last feudal dynasty in China was overthrown in the 1911

Revolution. Did Dr Sun Yat-sen claim to be a monarch? Did he ever say everyone got paid by him? I would counter that all of you, including President Chiang Kai-shek, are funded by the people."

Zeng Keda understood that any sign of temper at this point might prevent him from gaining the upper hand, so he managed to hold back his anger by using his own calmness against Lin's: "You're avoiding my question. Without the government, where do your people come from? Which one of your people paid you your income?"

"Every penny is taken from the people through the government," said Lin Dawei. "But what has your current government thought and done for the people with their money? Here you have Hou Juntang standing trial. It's good to see him being tried today. Yet there are hundreds and thousands of Hou Juntangs. Will you try them all?"

"That's exactly what I want to hear from you, which is also why I especially want you to live, because I want to show you how we take out one Hou Juntang after another and have them all tried. Under the Amnesty Regulations of the Criminal Law on the Army, Navy and Air Force, all members of the Nationalist Army who colluded with the Communists and now wish to repent and turn themselves in will be pardoned. Comrade Jianfeng personally asked about your case. He said that as long as you turn yourself in, we can let you and your family go abroad right away, and the government will cover all your expenses. And you don't have to work for any political party for a living. Look at your grey hair, look at your body. A man like you in his forties, you are worthy of the Communist Party."

Lin Dawei smiled. "Your investigators are too careless. My wife was killed by the Military Council's Bureau of Investigation and Statistics ten years ago, and I've never had the chance to remarry since then. Where did my family come from? As for me personally, I don't want to say how noble I am. Fearing I might die following torture, the authorities of the Central Bureau of Investigation and Statistics gave me an examination and medical treatment. Ask Director Xu, and he will tell you whether a person like me is still worth all the benefits."

Zeng Keda looked at Xu Tieying.

Xu Tieying opened Lin Dawei's file. "According to his medical records issued by the First Hospital of the Air Force on the second of July, Lin Dawei suffered from a variety of illnesses, including a history of duodenal ulcers and gastritis going back five years, years of neurosis that led to severe depression, and insomnia that has been going on for three years. Based on a preliminary X-ray result that showed a large shadow on the lungs, he is suspected of suffering from late-stage pulmonary tuberculosis. According to the medical prognosis, the patient is expected to live for only three to six months."

Zeng Keda's face and tone changed as he addressed Lin: "That's why you violated the espionage work regulations of the Communist Party, and openly used the Nationalist Army's Air Force Operations Department radio to send military intelligence directly to the Communists' East China Field Army! Even if you are going to die, you still want to get Fang Meng'ao involved, the ignorant party member you trained, to act as your scapegoat, and in blatant defiance of military orders, you just sit back and watch the Nationalist Army suffering casualties without dropping a bomb on the Communist troops! Answer me, is all that not true?"

Fang Meng'ao stood up almost immediately. With his knees pressed together and his body erect, he looked at Lin Dawei in the front of the dock as if he were saluting him with his eyes. Lin's hair appeared grey and his back thin and weak.

The pilots behind him also stood up, their knees pressed together while their bodies straightened up. Their eyes followed their instructor Lin Dawei in salute.

Zeng Keda's eyes gleamed. "Well, I admire your guts to act. Fang Meng'ao, admit to whatever you have done. Go ahead."

Fang Meng'ao gave no answer, but instead sat down again. The pilots also took their seats in a neat and orderly manner. Zeng Keda looked to the judge angrily.

"Fang Meng'ao," said the judge, "explain what you just did."

Fang Meng'ao stood up alone and replied: "Your Honour, I've been sitting for quite a while, I just wanted to stretch my legs." With that, he sat down again.

The judge, in fact, had already understood this act of Fang Meng'ao and his pilots through which they tried to show their respect for Lin Dawei, the alleged Communist agent, an act that also served to embarrass Zeng Keda. The judge, who was afraid of letting such entanglements develop, calmly reminded Zeng Keda: "Prosecutor, let the defendant Lin Dawei answer the question you raised just now."

Apparently, Lin Dawei was touched by the reaction of the people behind him. He tried to mobilise the remaining energy in his body, and raised his tone so that the following words could be heard by the pilots who refused to bomb Kaifeng: "As I said earlier, I am not noble, but nor am I as bad as you make out. Now let me answer your question. First, I've been sick for years, so why did you not know that fact until three days ago? It is because I have never enjoyed what you call medical care provided by the Nationalist Army authorities. Every time I'd have to spend my own money seeing a doctor in a private clinic. Second, knowing I don't have long to live, I was desperate and decided to take risks by sending the telegrams using the open code call, violating the confidentiality regulations guiding our party's underground work, thus exposing my identity. I've been thinking about this these days. If I was in good shape, would I have taken such a risk? Not necessarily. So I'm still a selfish person. Third, even if I am selfish, I know I will not live long and I won't let others die with me, whether they're my comrades or those who have worked with me in the Operations Department of the Air Force. Before I joined the Kuomintang's Air Force under a false identity, lurking inside the Operations Department, I worked with Vice-Chairman Zhou Enlai of the Communist Party's Central Committee. His instructions were always crystal clear – in addition to accomplishing the tasks assigned by the party organisation, it is absolutely forbidden to act in an immoral way or do anything that tarnishes our image. This, by the way, will answer your question pertaining to our party and my personal integrity."

In fact, the whole court had very little knowledge of what a true Communist Party member was. At this moment, they regarded Lin Dawei with mixed feelings. Many would ask themselves for the first time: So, is this what the Communist Party is all about?

The pilots who were sitting right behind Fang Meng'ao were particularly impressed. They first looked at Lin Dawei, then at Fang Meng'ao's broad back. Each of them would ask: Could our instructor be a member of the Communist Party of China? It is possible, but really he doesn't much resemble a Communist.

Zeng Keda then recalled *The Complete Works of Marquis Zeng Guofan*, which Comrade Jianfeng had recommended as a must read. He thought of what Zeng Guofan had said on his deathbed: "I'm exhausted, but begging to die as soon as possible." His last question of Lin Dawei was rather unexpected: "Are you from Hunan?"

Lin Dawei smiled calmly. "Like President Chiang Kai-shek, I am from Fenghua, Zhejiang Province."

Zeng Keda was speechless. He turned to Fang Meng'ao and the pilots who were still sitting straight, and then he strode towards Fang.

"It's admirable, isn't it? I admire him, too, but not you. You want to know why?"

"No, I don't," said Fang Meng'ao, still looking ahead. "You should know!"

Finally, Zeng Keda ran out of patience. "You were supposed to command a squadron to bomb enemy troops, but you flew back with all the bombs still on the plane. You worked for the Communists, but let the Nationalists save you when you got into trouble! Do you still want to say you don't want to know it?"

Finally, Fang Meng'ao looked at him slowly: "I do. Go ahead."

"You have a father who is governor of the Peking branch of the Central Bank, which is something I don't admire. Unlike Lin Dawei, you can use your powerful relatives as cover. Isn't that right?"

"Your Honour," said Fang Meng'ao, "may I ask the public prosecutor to step back to his table now?"

"What are you talking about?" asked Zeng Keda.

"May I ask the court to accept my request?"

The judge was confused: "Explain your reasons."

"My file is sitting on his table. Please tell the prosecutor to read it carefully. It very clearly states 'mother died', 'father blank', which means I don't have a father who is the general manager of the bank."

"Funny!" said Zeng Keda. "Well, you surely can't deny his existence! Let me tell you that, from the twenty-third of June up until today, your father's deputy at the Peking branch has flown to

Nanking on four separate occasions, to the Central Bank, the Ministry of Finance and even to the National Communications Bureau of the Kuomintang which is responsible for investigating your case. Actually, Deputy Director Cui paid a visit to Director Xu just a few hours ago. Director Xu, you don't deny that, do you?"

Xu Tieying sat there looking calm and stately without responding to the question. Far from being confused, he clearly did not give a damn about this sudden attack by Zeng Keda.

"Juror and defence lawyer, answer the prosecutor's question," demanded the judge.

Xu Tieying stood up slowly. "Cui Zhongshi, deputy treasury director of the Peking branch of the Central Bank, did come to my office at one o'clock this afternoon."

———

The Qinhuai River in Nanking was usually at its busiest in the evening, when thunderclouds would break and the wind would be cool and refreshing. The food market was bound to be bustling later on. It was just past four o'clock in the afternoon, when a number of snack carts operated by vendors emerged from the shore. Then from the river came the loud sound of oars being rowed by the boatmen who served food on their vessels. The people on shore and on the river were scrambling to prepare for business that evening. Although the Kuomintang-controlled areas had been suffering a major economic depression, some people parading up and down the banks of the Qinhuai still tried to lead an extravagant life as if they were following in the footsteps of Empress Chen in the Southern Dynasty.

Cui Zhongshi skipped lunch for the simple reason that he had to catch up with Xu Tieying before Fang Meng'ao's trial. After the meeting, he spent the whole afternoon walking in the rain on the banks of the river in the hope of finding a place to eat. His stomach was growling when he saw a peddler selling dumplings filled with black sesame. The peddler was still in the process of stoking his coals, but Cui Zhongshi decided it was time for action. As he put up his umbrella and started walking slowly, he saw out of the corner of his eye a rickshaw boy who had parked his vehicle not far away also stand up, slowly pull the cart and follow him at a distance of forty or fifty steps.

As deputy director of the Peking branch vault, he was always vigilant, and he had to resist a desire to buy the dumplings. Cui Zhongshi walked past the dumpling stand, as well as some other snack stalls where local dishes were being prepared, and headed towards a large hotel in the direction of the Confucius Temple. All the while, the telephone booth was receding into the distance.

Xu Tieying continued with his statement in the special criminal court: "Since the matter is subject to confidentiality regulations, that's all I can say. On behalf of the Communications Bureau, today I will not only summon Cui Zhongshi in connection with the incident in Peking yesterday, but will also continue to investigate all suspects involved in the Peking Citizens' Food-Distribution Committee. My meeting with Cui Zhongshi has nothing at all to do with Fang Meng'ao's case."

Zeng Keda felt a helpless desperation in his heart. From Xu Tieying's court performance, he came to realise that Comrade Jianfeng, as well as the two hundred comrades affiliated with the Iron and Blood Congress headed by Comrade Jianfeng, would fail to run the rusty party-state machine. Since it was impossible to further investigate this matter, the only thing that could be done was to make a decision to sort things out.

Quickly, he turned to Fang Meng'ao: "According to Director Xu, no one in your family made an effort to save you, and you denied the fact that your father is bank governor. Perhaps you did sever relations with the family members that are connected with the upper echelons of the party and the state. Of course, you won't admit to your Communist background. But be aware, if the Communists are behind what you've done, you will personally be held responsible for it. If not, your action would have implicated your entire trainee brigade! According to the Criminal Law of the Army, Navy and Air Force, Fang Meng'ao and his flying brigade committed the crime of collective disobedience of military orders and that of espionage and sedition. All prisoners shall be sentenced to death and it shall be carried out immediately. The public prosecutor requests the court to order Fang Meng'ao to make a final statement on behalf of his brigade."

The whole court fell into a suffocating silence.

The judge asked: "Does the defendant Fang Meng'ao wish to make a final statement?"

This time it was Fang Meng'ao who rose up. "I have no final statement to make. I am a Communist."

The first person to look up at Fang Meng'ao was Xu Tieying.

Hou Juntang, who had been sitting there listlessly, seemed to wake up and look back at Fang Meng'ao.

Lin Dawei slowly turned his head and looked at Fang Meng'ao. There was confusion in the eyes of Zeng Keda and in those of the pilots behind him. They all regarded Fang Meng'ao in disbelief.

On the banks of the Qinhuai River, Cui Zhongshi was sitting at the Qinhuai restaurant's VIP table that overlooked the street. He had been served a steamed bun stuffed with juicy pork and a bowl of hot longan jujube soup. But instead of reaching for his chopsticks, he panicked and put his hand into his suit pocket. Out of the corner of his eye, he saw the rickshaw boy across the street outside refuse to take another passenger. Cui Zhongshi took out a pocket watch and opened the cover. It was already five o'clock.

Inside the telephone booth on the bank of the Qinhuai River, the phone that Cui Zhongshi had called at three o'clock started ringing. After it had rung for a third time, it stopped.

At this same moment, the telephone on the judge's table began to ring.

The judge picked up the receiver and after a short pause said: "Yes, this is the special criminal court. Speaking. Who is it, please?

Wait one second." He picked up a pen, spread out the headed paper and spoke into the phone. "Please go ahead, I'll take detailed notes."

Of course, no one else could hear the voice at the other end; they could only see the old judge scribbling away.

The instructions from the other end of the line were abrupt. The judge quickly put down his pen, and said: "I'm done with note-taking. Yes, I'll speed up the trial and complete it by six o'clock today."

After putting down the phone, the judge's attitude changed dramatically. Instead of listening attentively, he began to speak and asked Xu Tieying directly: "Did the National Communications Bureau complete its investigation of Fang Meng'ao and his brigade that refused to bomb Kaifeng on the twenty-second of June?"

"Your Honour, the investigation has been completed."

"Is Fang Meng'ao a member of the Communist Party? Can you draw a clear conclusion based on your investigation?"

"Your Honour, based on our detailed investigation, Fang Meng'ao joined the Nationalist Air Force in 1938 and had no contact whatsoever with the Communist Party since he was transferred to Jianqiao Aviation Academy in 1946 as an instructor. A clear conclusion can indeed be drawn."

"Objection!" cried Zeng Keda.

"Objection not sustained." This time around, the judge simply did not give Zeng Keda any chance to speak further, but instead turned to Fang Meng'ao. "Defendant Fang Meng'ao, on the nineteenth of June, as an active soldier in the Nationalist Army, you commanded the brigade of trainees from the Aviation Academy to drop bombs on Communists in Kaifeng. Why did you and your whole team return without dropping a single bomb? Please make your final statement."

Fang Meng'ao stood up and the pilots behind him rose in unison, looking solemnly brave as if they were about to face death.

"This is none of your concern," Fang Meng'ao shouted. "Sit down!" This time, none of the pilots obeyed. They stood there motionless.

Fang Meng'ao felt a surge of warmth in his heart, so he no longer ordered them to sit, and instead he said to the judge: "Your Honour, the case relating to the failure to bomb Kaifeng on the nineteenth of June was originally handled by the National Communications Bureau. There are two important pieces of evidence in the hands of Director Xu. May I present the evidence? It should explain to the court why we failed to bomb the city."

The judge immediately looked at Xu Tieying, who hurriedly picked up his briefcase. "Which two pieces of evidence?"

"The photographs."

Xu Tieying pulled out two envelopes from his briefcase. The court clerk went over and took them, handing them over to Fang Meng'ao.

Fang Meng'ao drew a stack of photos from the first envelope, and said: "I took these photographs on the nineteenth of June at around a thousand metres, eight hundred metres and five hundred metres above Kaifeng. Your Honour, public prosecutor, juror, please examine them." With that, he handed them to the clerk.

The clerk took the stack of photos and handed them to the judge with both hands. "Permission granted," said the judge. "Let the public prosecutor and the juror examine the photographs."

Both Xu Tieying and Zeng Keda stood up, one willing, the other reluctant, and approached the judge's high table. All three examined the views of Kaifeng from the sky.

The city, with its magnificent sites and quarters wrecked by heavy gunfire and shelling, was in full view. Kaifeng's Iron Tower was clearly visible. Several streets were packed with people running for their lives in panic. They appeared to be ordinary civilians.

"May I know if we Your Honour has finished with the photos?" asked Fang Meng'ao.

"Accused, what are you trying to explain with these photos?"

"I'm trying to explain why I took the decision not to bomb Kaifeng. On the fifth of June 1938, the Japanese Air Force carried out twenty-three sorties over Kaifeng, killing and injuring more than a thousand Chinese compatriots. Many houses were destroyed by heavy bombardment and razed to the ground, leaving hundreds of thousands of residents displaced and homeless. Please take a look at that tower again. It was an ancient pagoda built in the reign of Song Renzong. It was hit by sixty-two Japanese artillery shells on a single day, and its central section was badly damaged. And only three years on from victory in the War of Resistance, our Air Force

Operations Department gave us the same orders as the invading Japanese Army. The bombing of Communist troops was in fact an act of indiscriminate bombing prohibited by the United Nations a long time ago. Now, I must ask, who gave this order? Since when did it become a crime against national security to decide not to bomb our cities and our compatriots? Public prosecutor, which article of the Criminal Law of the Army, Navy and Air Force can convict me of threatening national security? Please answer me now!"

Zeng Keda stood bewildered, his lips trembling slightly. The judge went on to ask: "Present the defendant's second piece of evidence."

By now, the defendant's eyes were moist. He pulled a picture out of the second envelope. The court clerk took the photo and placed it before the judge, on the table. This too was a familiar image. It had made international headlines, featuring the aftermath of the bombing of the Bund in Shanghai by the Japanese Air Force in 1937. The street was in ruins and dead bodies lay everywhere.

Without waiting to be questioned, Fang Meng'ao looked up to the front of the court: "On the thirteenth of August 1937, the Japanese Air Force bombed Shanghai. On that day, my mother and my sister were killed."

There was silence in the courtroom.

Looking at the judge, Fang Meng'ao continued: "That's the reason why I ordered the brigade not to drop their bombs on the city on the twenty-second of June. You can convict me of any crime you like, but you can't do this to any one of my pilots behind me. They are all sons of China, and they shouldn't be convicted of a crime for failing to kill their fellow countrymen! That concludes my statement."

A wailing sound was heard, and it came from Chen Changwu. All the pilots began to weep and wail.

"Silence! Silence!" The judge slammed his gavel on the desk, but he was powerless to maintain order.

"Don't cry!" yelled Fang Meng'ao, addressing the pilots directly for the first time since they entered the courtroom. He softened his tone: "Brothers, is it worth it?" The crying stopped.

The judge struck the gavel again and announced: "The special criminal court of the Republic of China, I now announce verdicts on the three cases presented today. They involve Fang Meng'ao's refusal to carry out military orders on the nineteenth of June, Lin Dawei, a Communist suspected of espionage and threatening national security, and Hou Juntang's case of smuggling and corruption. All rise!"

Zeng Keda and Xu Tieying both stood by their seats. Hou Juntang got up with difficulty, while Lin Dawei was also slow to rise. The judge held the written decision in both hands and pronounced the following: "This court hereby sentences criminal Lin Dawei to death, his execution to be carried out immediately. This court hereby sentences Hou Juntang to death, his execution to be carried out immediately. It is also decided by this court that Fang Meng'ao and his Youth Aviation Brigade shall be released from active service immediately, and he and his team shall be dealt with collectively by the Ministry of Defence. Verdict pending."

Outraged, the whole court was thrown into silence again.

"The executions will be carried out as scheduled."

The two marshals took Hou Juntang by the arms and lifted him from his seat and out of the courtroom. Two other marshals arrived to grab Lin Dawei, but he made a gesture for them to pause, and then he turned around and made a standard military salute to Fang Meng'ao and the row of pilots standing behind him, before he allowed himself to be escorted from the courtroom.

"Objection! Objection!" Zeng Keda shouted to the judge, having finally woken up from his confusion. "It's absolutely perverted for the court to reach this verdict. On behalf of the Ministry of Defence, the public prosecutor expresses his strong opposition."

The judge picked up the phone record and handed it to the clerk, whispering: "Show him the note."

The clerk took the note, went to Zeng Keda and handed it over to him.

Zeng Keda took the note. After reading a few lines, his face turned heavy. One voice, a voice of infinite reverence, sounded in his ears: "Today's judgment is my idea. Please tell Comrade Zeng Keda that I hope he will not object. Chiang Ching-kuo."

CHAPTER 3

Like other departments of state, the Ministry of Defence was located in one place to facilitate personal exchange. As for communicating with other departments and bureaus, this entailed the transfer of telegrams and encrypted texts so the messages could be acted on as fast as possible. For the Ministry of Defence, this also meant being a hub for the troops, ready to fight a war.

There was only one ministerial department that was located in a separate building, and that was the Bureau of Reserve Cadres. It was on its own in a small, two-storey, Western-style building to the rear of the larger building. Those working there did not communicate directly with their counterparts in the other departments and bureaus. And while it was nominally under the auspices of the ministry, the bureau's role was held in high regard by other parts of the ministry.

Zeng Keda parked his car in front of the Ministry of Defence, and walked past the main building to the back. He and his comrades would always walk at a certain pace and with a degree of self-consciousness as they made their way to the small building via a concrete driveway reserved exclusively for Comrade Jianfeng's special car. They did this not only out of respect, but also from a sincere understanding. Comrade Jianfeng was a busy man, working on several different things. He needed a quiet environment.

The bureau was about two hundred metres from the ministry.

At fifty-metre intervals along the driveway were parasol stands, under which young soldiers stood wearing no identifying badge, cap or khaki uniform. Instead, they wore four-pocket uniforms and had pistols in holsters around their waists. They were clearly not ordinary soldiers, yet no one could discern their rank.

Zeng Keda walked by, and at each stand, he briskly saluted the soldier on duty. At the top of the five stone steps leading inside, he was escorted silently to the ground-floor foyer.

The expansive foyer was devoid of furniture except for two wooden benches with backrests, each about five metres long, on either side of the room. Two long clothes rails were set up behind the benches, on which hung a number of badge-less khaki uniforms. Black cloth shoes lay ready, and hooks for anonymous military caps were fixed to the wall. Zeng Keda was familiar with the arrangement, so he walked to the spot where a uniform bearing his name was waiting. He took off his military cap and hung it on a hook, and removed his major general's uniform. The young man who had showed him in took his uniform and Zeng Keda whispered a quick "Thank you". He put on the plain khaki uniform, bent down to untie the laces on his leather shoes and put on the simple cloth shoes. Only then did he head to the staircase in the foyer.

At the top of the stairs was a hallway that led up to an open double door, through which one could see a large hall, the same size as the foyer downstairs. Unlike on the ground floor, there was only one long wooden bench in front of the window against the wall, and the hall seemed more spacious. The two doors to the inner office, deliberately unlocked, were impressive, accentuating the table beside them and the secretary on duty behind the table.

Seeing Zeng Keda standing at the entrance, the secretary stood up, nodded and gave a faint smile.

Zeng Keda strode up to the secretary, enquiring with his eyes only.

The secretary on duty signalled for him to wait. Instead of using the telephone on his desk, he went to pick up the phone on the other side of the door of the inner office: "Comrade Jianfeng, Comrade Zeng Keda has arrived."

A second later, he handed the receiver to the waiting Zeng Keda who put it to his ear, and as if out of habit, looked at the paper taped to the wall above the telephone. Chiang Ching-kuo, known by his working name of Comrade Jianfeng, had written in the Yan style of calligraphy, made famous by Yan Zhenqing in the Tang Dynasty: "Too many things to do, forgive me for not meeting you," while the right side read: "If it's urgent, please call me." Above the door was written: "We are all comrades."

"Is this Comrade Zeng Keda speaking?"

Zeng heard the same message twice, although only one person was actually talking: once through the telephone and once, slightly earlier, through the unlocked door in front of him. He glanced through the door, and could just about make out the back of a person holding the telephone in his left hand, while writing instructions with his right. Sad and warm emotions intermingled as he chose to reply politely: "Speaking, Comrade Jianfeng."

"You don't seem to understand the verdict of Fang Meng'ao and his brigade, do you?"

"I do, Comrade Jianfeng."

"Do you feel imposed upon? Or do you really understand?"

Zeng Keda was silent, but it was possible to reply to Comrade Jianfeng's questions with silence and reflection.

During this brief moment of quiet, the sound of paper being flipped came down the phone line. Zeng Keda could not resist peering through the crack in the door, where he could see Comrade Jianfeng sorting through a pile of documents, pulling out another file and reading it carefully.

"Comrade Jianfeng, permission to report to you," Zeng Keda said. "On some judgments I do offer an opinion, on others not."

"Tell me what you don't understand." The figure held his head low, buried in the document before him.

"It's one thing deciding whether or not to bomb Kaifeng, it's another for Fang Meng'ao to choose to ignore the order. They are different in nature."

"What is the nature of it?"

"A tendency towards the Communist Party, sir."

"What else can you tell me?"

"Apparently, Xu Tieying of the Central Bureau of Investigation and Statistics was instructed by Fang Buting. They had a deal."

"Is there anything else?"

"The Communist collusion case was complicated by corruption at a higher level. We need to crack down on this harder."

"Anything else?"

"No, Comrade Jianfeng, nothing for the time being."

This time the person on the other end of the line was silent. Through the crack, Zeng could see he was writing. Having put down the pencil, it seemed as though he was now ready to focus on their conversation. Zeng Keda brought his attention back to the telephone.

"When seen from both sides, the answer to this question means you may possibly be correct. The key is to determine exactly the two sides of this problem. Which part have you recently been reading in the *Complete Works of Duke Zeng Wenzheng?*"

"I've been reading Zeng's memorial to the throne presented between the fourth and sixth year during the reign of Emperor Xianfeng."

"Well, read more of his diary, and focus on the part where he reads *The Doctrine of the Mean*. It's very important. Zeng Wenzheng devoted his whole life to the practice known as *zhiliang yongzhong* – listening to both sides and choosing the middle path. Everything has its extremes, and whichever way you go, you will make mistakes. Only by keeping to the centre can we keep our mistakes to a minimum and get a little closer to the right way."

"I agree. To avoid going to extremes, President Chiang gives himself a middle name, Zhongzheng, which means to be in the middle and righteous. As his student, I fully understand his desire to achieve the golden means."

"Let's talk about Fang Meng'ao. If you look at him from one extreme, he is a member of the Communist Party. If you look at him from the other extreme, he's the son of Fang Buting. Instead, can we not look at him objectively from the middle? Since the findings of the Party Communications Bureau and the State Secrecy Bureau prove that he is not suspected of collusion with the Communist Party, he should not be subjectively called a Communist. In this regard, we should trust both bureaus. If he was revealed to be a Communist, yet he wasn't charged of the crime because they took money from his family, I doubt Xu Tieying would do such a thing, and no one else would either if he worked for the Party

Communications Bureau and the State Secrecy Bureau. Of course, if the investigators find he is not a Communist, Xu Tieying and many others might as well collect bribe money from his family. But none of this has anything to do with Fang Meng'ao himself."

"Comrade, is it possible that Fang Meng'ao is indeed a member of the Communist Party, yet was recruited in some special way? He stays undercover so that the Communists can use him for special operations, such as ordering him to defect by flying special missions at crucial times. This is of course just an intuition of mine, but it is also my concern."

"Intuition always has a source. Where does yours come from?"

"From Cui Zhongshi, Fang Buting's assistant, also the deputy governor in charge of the vault in the Central Bank's Peking branch. For more than three years, he's been the only person to have direct contact with Fang Meng'ao. They have been socialising in the name of repairing the Fang family's father-son relationship. But although the relationship between father and son has not improved, Cui Zhongshi has become a good friend of Fang Meng'ao. This is very much how the Communist Party's Urban Works Department operates. I suggest we conduct a thorough investigation of Cui Zhongshi's true identity."

———

At around six o'clock on this July evening, the sky in Nanking was still bright. The restaurant where Cui Zhongshi was eating and the Qinhuai River outside were illuminated by twinkling neon lights and the candles from lanterns. Business as usual, although the quiet was somewhat exceptional.

It was dinner time, but Cui Zhongshi had already eaten a late lunch. Occupying the VIP room with his pot of tea, he kept the waiter on his toes for refills. Wearing a fake smile and with coldness in his eyes, the waiter harboured a desire for his guest to leave. If it were not for his gold-framed glasses and three-piece suit, he would have kicked him out already, one way or another.

A man and a woman on stage had already performed several pieces of Suzhou *pingtan*, a mixture of storytelling and ballad singing in Suzhou dialect. Now it was time for the guests to come up with requests. To the waiter's chagrin, Cui Zhongshi neither ordered food nor signalled any intention to leave. Instead, he was quite absorbed in listening to the *pingtan*. The waiter could not help standing next to him and asking with a smile: "Sir, would you like to request a song?"

Cui Zhongshi caught sight of the rickshaw outside the window. By now the rickshaw boy had moved from across the street, and was just five steps away from the restaurant window.

Cui Zhongshi took out a stack of *fabi* from his briefcase. Seeing the notes, the waiter said: "Excuse me, sir. We don't accept *fabi* in our restaurant." But Cui Zhongshi had no intention of paying in that currency. He just put the *fabi* on the table, then pulled out a stack of US dollar bills from his briefcase.

The waiter's eyes brightened at once.

Cui Zhongshi drew out a ten-dollar note: "How about *Blooming Flowers, Full Moon*, but make sure it's in Zhou Xuan's original style."

The waiter grabbed the money. "Sir, you have great taste. The singer we hired in our restaurant is known as Golden Voice. I can't guarantee she sings better than Zhou Xuan, but she is certainly her equal." With that, he took the ten dollars to the counter where he paid on Cui's behalf. Immediately the cashier went up to the stage and gave some instructions.

A man wearing a long gown and playing the *sanxian*, switched to *Blooming Flowers, Full Moon*, while the woman swiftly changed style from *pingtan* to this popular tune:

The floating, scattered clouds,
The bright moon shines on the people as they arrive.
Today is the happiest...

Cui Zhongshi liked the song so much that his eyes filled with melancholy on hearing this rendition.

On the first floor of the Bureau of Reserve Cadres, the lights were on both in the hall where Zeng Keda stood and in the inner office. It was supposed to be dinner-time, but Comrade Jianfeng was in the middle of giving important telephone instructions, so Zeng Keda politely listened, while the secretary glanced at his watch again and made a 'chopsticks' gesture. Zeng Keda shook his head seriously, and the secretary had no choice but to attend to his papers again.

"The party and the state are in a bad way at present. However it is not the Communist Party, but the Nationalists that have made it so. From top to bottom, how many people are working for the party, how many people are working for the state, how many people are not working for personal gain? The Communist Party does not have an air force, we do, but ours is busy airfreighting smuggled goods! There are few brigades that can fly combat missions. People like Fang Meng'ao, as well as the trainee pilots he has schooled, I've read all their files. They're a class apart in terms of combat technique and discipline. Such a man, such a brigade, however, has always been curtailed by the likes of Hou Juntang. If it were not for the Battle of Kaifeng where insufficient brigades were available to fly bombing missions, Fang Meng'ao and his brigade would have still been on furlough. It would be strange if the Communist Party did not have their eyes on him. His value is obvious, but what is abnormal is that we don't value such talent ourselves."

"Yes. It's our fault that Fang Meng'ao and his brigade were not discovered earlier, or nurtured in time. We should be held responsible for that. But it's too dangerous to redeploy them now. Comrade Jianfeng, please reconsider."

"What are the hidden dangers? Those suspicions you cited just now?"

Zeng Keda was stunned, still waiting for follow-up questions, but the voice in his receiver fell silent. "My suspicions are just one of the reasons."

"What else is on your mind?" asked Jianfeng, quickly this time. Zeng Keda seemed hesitant. "Say whatever is on your mind."

"Yes, Comrade Jianfeng. It is clear that Fang Meng'ao and his brigade should not be trusted to fly combat missions. Now, if sent to Peking to investigate the smuggling and corruption case as well as to transport goods, it's quite certain they would not engage in smuggling that may damage the reputation of the Air Force. But regarding the corruption case involving the Peking Citizens' Food-Distribution Committee, Fang Buting is the key figure behind the scene. Though he has fallen out with him, I have grave doubts as to whether Fang Meng'ao would investigate his own father. Moreover, both the commandant and Comrade Jianfeng have instructed us that a man's loyalty primarily depends on whether or not he is filial. We all have fathers, yet we can check on Fang Buting, while Meng'ao may not. I agree that he's an ace pilot in the Air Force, daring and talented, but I don't approve of the fact that he severed relations with his father ten years ago."

There was silence at the other end.

Zeng Keda seemed to remember something, but he managed to curb his enthusiasm and instead whispered into the telephone: "If what I have said is wrong, please feel free to say so, Comrade Jianfeng."

"You're quite right. Young people tend to be silly and petulant. I opposed my father once."

"I'm sorry Comrade Jianfeng, that's not what I meant."

"That's what you should have meant." Sweat broke out on his forehead. "He who has faults should not fear to correct them. I didn't acknowledge my father for the simple reason that I was too young and unable to understand how people should behave. Fang Meng'ao is different. For him, his father has committed a wrongdoing. The invading Japanese Air Force bombed Shanghai on the thirteenth of August, and Fang Buting abandoned his wife and children, trying to curry favour with the Soong and Kung families by sending their belongings out of danger to Chongqing, leaving his wife and daughter behind to die in the bombings. Fang Meng'ao witnessed the death of his mother and sister when he was seventeen and had to take care of his brother who was four years younger. For a time, they were destitute refugees. If this had happened to you, would you acknowledge your father?"

Zeng Keda was sweating, overwhelmed by what he was hearing. It was rare to hear Comrade Jianfeng so emotionally involved, and it was even more unexpected to learn that he had delved so deeply into the life of this Air Force colonel. He swallowed and replied: "I did not investigate Fang Meng'ao thoroughly enough. I should be held responsible for this."

"As I said, we have plenty to learn from the Communist Party. Their idea of 'criticism and self-criticism' is one I appreciate. But you haven't eaten since early this morning. Eat first. After supper, think about whether Fang Meng'ao and his brigade should be used or not, and if so, how?"

Zeng Keda stood to attention. "Comrade Jianfeng, I'd like to hear your instructions now so that I can set out to adapt the brigade and reassign them to work in Peking."

"Well, in that case, I don't think I have any more instructions. Remember this: an employed man should be suspected, while a suspected man may still be employed. The crux of the matter is how to use him well. Yesterday's student protest in Peking was just the beginning, and the situation is likely to deteriorate to the point where it affects the whole country. The joint meeting has decided to set up a team to conduct a thorough investigation in Peking. You're on the team, and so is Xu Tieying. You can deal with the Communist Party, but none of you can deal with Fang Buting. He has the Central Bank and the Ministry of Finance behind him. For this reason, making good use of Fang Meng'ao is key."

"I agree with your suggestion," said Zeng Keda, standing to attention once more. "Let me carry out an in-depth investigation into Cui Zhongshi."

Inside the Qinhuai restaurant, Cui Zhongshi was still listening to the music. According to the going rate, one *pingtan* ballad cost one dollar, and since Cui Zhongshi had paid ten dollars, he was entitled to listen to ten ballads, even though he had selected only *Blooming Flowers, Full Moon*. With the same ballad sung ten times, how could one expect other diners to be patient? At the moment, few could remember exactly how many times the ballad had been sung:

In pairs, the spouses share a mutual love.
This soft wind blows upon the beautiful flowers,
Blowing on the good flowers,
Full of warmth and affection between the people.

Other customers were starting to complain. Yet Cui Zhongshi remained calmly seated. The waiter came running over: "This is the third time. Could you select a different song? Please, I beg you."

Cui Zhongshi stood up while holding his briefcase and said: "No more. And there's no need to refund me the seven dollars." As he spoke, he walked towards the door.

The waiter followed him closely. "Have a good night. Let me call a cab for you, sir."

Cui Zhongshi stopped at the door. "Are you after a tip?"

"No, sir. Absolutely not."

"Then thank you for showing me out." With that, he left the establishment.

Outside the Qinhuai restaurant, the rickshaw boy was standing, looking at Cui Zhongshi as he appeared at the door. His work could now begin.

Cui Zhongshi walked calmly to the rickshaw boy and asked: "How much to the Jinling Hotel?"

"Hop in, sir. It's no bother."

There seemed an open hostility between the two.

"As a rickshaw boy, money surely matters. What's wrong with you?"

The rickshaw boy remained defiant, yet not rude. "If you choose to ride in my carriage, I'll pull it to wherever you wish to go."

"All right, then I'm not going to the Jinling Hotel." Cui Zhongshi got into the rickshaw calmly. "Take me to the National Communications Bureau of the Kuomintang Central Membership Committee."

"At your service. Please sit tight." The boy did not look like an amateur. As soon as he began to run, he turned the rickshaw round, neither too fast nor too slow.

"I said the National Communications Bureau. Where on earth are you taking me?"

The rickshaw boy kept running, but he was still not panting. "No one's working at the Communications Bureau at this hour of the day. Let me first take you to the Jinling."

Cui Zhongshi stopped arguing, leaned back, closed his eyes and thought quickly.

The boy began to talk again. "Sir, rest assured, the master is well now. He was discharged from hospital at six this evening, and may go to Peking in a few days for a family reunion."

Cui Zhongshi looked astonished as he stared at the back of the boy in front of him. "Did you pick up the wrong person?"

"It hardly matters if *I* got the wrong person, but it matters if *you* did, sir." The pace quickened, as the rickshaw sped even faster with its passenger Cui Zhongshi holding tight.

―――

The Ministry of Defence's so-called Honourable Army Guesthouse was where Chiang Kai-shek entertained those he considered loyal and honoured, people who he felt could be drawn into his inner circle. Generally speaking, it was a venue reserved for field officers, such as generals and graduates from the Whampoa Military Academy. It was where they were accommodated when reporting for duty in the capital before being sent on missions by army headquarters to fight Communist troops. Of course, graduate field officers from the newly established Air Force's Aviation Academy who were promoted to the ranks of general and colonel were also entitled to stay there.

Being prisoners an hour ago and guests of honour now, it was arranged for Fang Meng'ao and his fellow pilots to stay at the guesthouse. They took a bath and changed into newly issued shirts and shorts. But as there were no more pilot jackets, they had to keep wearing their filthy old ones. The glowing faces of the rehabilitated pilots and the brilliant white of their shirt collars and sleeves, contrasted markedly with their grubby jackets.

An officer took them to the mess hall. He ordered them to march, but found their discipline left much to be desired. Walking into the dining room in twos and threes, they completely ignored his words of command. Four places were set at each table. The twenty trainee pilots were soon seated around five tables, tucking into four dishes plus soup and helping themselves to the bottle of red wine placed on each table. An additional table was set for two, meant for Fang Meng'ao and one other person. The officer had been instructed to be pleasant so he pretended to enthusiastically welcome the group of rowdy pilots.

"You must be starving. We provide accommodation for honourable members of the Revolutionary Army, and my instructions are for you to be treated as colonels. One table for four, food will be served according to rank. Everyone of the same rank will receive the same food. Please feel at home."

The twenty pilots crowded by the door, all looking towards Fang Meng'ao.

"Captain Fang will be seated at a separate table. A special guest will join later. Comrades, please take your seats. Captain Fang, please."

Fang Meng'ao queried the rationale: "The military court has ruled that we have been relieved of our duties. You must have been given the wrong instructions if we are to be treated like colonels. Please, ask again. We wouldn't want you to be disciplined later."

The officer smiled and replied: "No mistake. This was an order from the Bureau of Reserve Cadres."

"Did the bureau say we were to be treated as colonels?"

"Not in so many words, Captain Fang."

To spare him the embarrassment, Fang Meng'ao turned to the pilots: "Since we've been dismissed from active duty, please consider this royal treatment by the ministry's Bureau of Reserve Cadres a blessing. Let's eat!"

At Fang's order, the pilots rushed to the tables. It took a while for them to settle.

Fang Meng'ao went up to his place, but did not sit down. With his left hand, he stretched out to pick up a bowl plus chopsticks, along with a cup and spoon. He tucked a bottle of red wine under his arm. Picking up his chair with his right hand, he walked over to Chen Changwu's table, and asked him to make some space.

Chen Changwu immediately picked up his chair and was ready to move to the left and sit with another pilot. But Fang Meng'ao stopped him with his foot.

"Don't you want to sit with me?"

Within the course of a single day, Chen Changwu, who had been expecting to be a bridegroom, had witnessed the court commute his death sentence, and now was more than willing to regard his captain and instructor as his own blood brother. With the formalities over, all he now felt for Fang Meng'ao was familial love.

"Why do I have to sit with you since you're not the one I'm about to marry?" Chen shot back.

The people in the dining room roared with laughter.

"Shit!" blurted Fang Meng'ao, a favourite curse of his that he had not uttered for ten long days.

The pilots loved it. Everyone knew that their instructor and captain was in the habit of speaking English with the American pilots of the Chennault Flying Tigers. They would frequently swear together. In class or during pilot training, Fang Meng'ao would often swear, and they knew it was somewhere between criticism and praise. The good old days.

"Lots of beautiful college students are chasing me, I'll pick them one at a time. When will it be your turn, Chen Changwu? Just sit down on that seat." Fang Meng'ao forced Chen Changwu's chair back to the floor, as he urged his pilots to eat freely.

The men at all five tables rushed out to grab the food. There were five dishes and a bowl of soup already laid out on Fang Meng'ao's table. Each of the other four tables had an extra dish, but unfortunately all Chen Changwu brought back was a bowl of soup. There was only a set of cutlery left on the table and an empty chair reserved for the special guest.

After the initial excitement was over, the pilots returned to their seats and began to eat. They displayed impressive table manners unmatched by any other unit of the Nationalist Army.

The pilots were quite adept at opening the wine bottles, and knew exactly how much to pour into each glass. Hands resting on the stems of their glasses, they swirled the wine, examining its quality. Then came the ringing sound as glasses chimed, before everyone took a sip.

After putting down their glasses, they ate the food, but without making any vulgar sounds. The guesthouse employee in charge of this group was embarrassed to be left out of this show of manners. Unwilling to serve them again, he moved towards the door. As soon as he got there, he found himself face to face with an unknown man.

Zeng Keda was not dressed in the attire of a general, yet he still looked imposing. Wearing that khaki uniform without collar badges, he strode over in his black cloth shoes.

Outside the door, Zeng Keda and the officer stopped. It was so quiet inside the mess that he looked at the officer and asked in a low voice: "How are they behaving?"

The officer whispered: "As soon as they arrived, they played tough with me, pretending they had been served without permission. And now they're pretending to be as civilised as Americans. Aren't they just a bunch of disciplined pilots? Proud as peacocks with their tails stuck up in the sky? General Zeng, we've received senior generals at this guesthouse before, but for heaven's sake, I've never seen anything like this."

Zeng Keda smiled bitterly and said: "I haven't seen this kind of a show either. Now, remove everyone else and position sentries outside. No one is to approach the canteen."

"Yes sir," replied the officer. He waved his hands, and hurried away with some soldiers at the door.

The officer of the guesthouse had been humiliated a moment before, and now it was Zeng Keda's turn to be embarrassed. He walked in all alone and stopped at the door, wearing his distinctly plain uniform, a neutral expression on his face. He was no longer the condescending and domineering figure he had been in court. Almost shyly, he glanced at the young pilots. As if by mutual agreement, none of them looked at him, each busy working on the food and wine. Zeng Keda cast his eye on Fang Meng'ao.

Fang was watching Zeng with contempt evident in his eyes. His expression epitomised everything Zeng stood against. Yet Zeng Keda himself was too small and too weak, just like a grain of sand or a leaf.

These were the eyes that had flown over the Himalayas, these were the eyes that had flown over the Hump in extreme weather conditions. Here was the man who was able to distinguish between army troops and civilians on the ground at an altitude of thousands of metres, was sincere and gentle to women and children, could discern those who took away lives and property by force or trickery. What these eyes showed was a unique kind of vacuum, as pure and clean as the air up there in the sky. The pilots felt it too.

They saw Fang Meng'ao at that moment and they looked at

Zeng Keda timidly. All were waiting, knowing that their captain and instructor was tailing an enemy plane and was ready to open fire.

The enemy aircraft, however, apparently refused to engage. Instead of taking the seat at the table that had been arranged for him and Fang Meng'ao, Zeng Keda walked over to Fang's table with the empty chair and crockery. Sitting opposite Fang Meng'ao at the opposite end of the table, Zeng Keda said to the pilot: "It's a big day today. I haven't had supper either. May I sit beside you?"

The fact that he was so polite and willing to sit at the lower end of the table helped reduce the degree of hostility between these proud men. The pilot nearby readily shifted his chair, giving up his position to Zeng Keda.

"It looks like I won't be able to enjoy this meal," said Fang Meng'ao, putting his chopsticks on the table. "How is the bureau going to punish us? Go ahead, tell us."

"There's no punishment, but a new assignment," Zeng Keda replied. Then, addressing all the pilots, he said: "Everyone, feel free to continue. I won't say anything while you eat. No, not a word."

At this point, he was about to fill his glass with some boiled water from a nearby kettle when a tilting wine bottle stretched out in front of Zeng Keda, with the mouth of the bottle facing the rim of the glass. Zeng Keda sat there with an empty glass, looking at the mouth of the bottle, while Fang Meng'ao held the bottle, looking at the mouth of the glass. All eyes were on the two men, on the bottle and on the glass.

The voice, the one that came from the phone and from behind the door, rang again in Zeng Keda's ears: "An employed man should be suspected, while a suspected man can still be employed. The crux of the matter is how to use him well."

Zeng Keda held the glass to the mouth of the bottle. Fang Meng'ao poured the wine very slowly, all the way to the top of the glass. Zeng Keda, holding the glass full of wine, appeared rather embarrassed and shook his head.

Fang Meng'ao filled his own glass, and downed it in one. He refilled the glass, put it on the table and sat down. He did not look at Zeng Keda; instead, he stared at the glass of wine in front of him.

Everyone else looked at Zeng Keda.

No longer hesitating, Zeng Keda put the glass to his mouth and in three gulps, he drank it all. His face flushed.

Fang Meng'ao looked at Zeng Keda again, with sincerity in his eyes. He was not faking it. This man could not drink, yet he's showing forgiveness, at least more than might be expected.

So when Zeng Keda handed over his glass again, Fang Meng'ao took it and said: "I'm sorry, I forgot you have your own rules. I didn't mean to break them. Changwu, General Zeng is part of the New Life Movement that requires him to abstain from smoking or drinking. Go get him a glass of water."

He passed the empty glass to Chen Changwu, who took the glass and went to look for a kettle. Chen Changwu returned with the boiled water in the wine glass and handed it over to Zeng Keda with both hands. Zeng Keda was surprised to see that the glass had been washed before it was filled with water.

Zeng Keda looked at Chen Changwu with admiration. He appreciated him as a young person who could be shaped for future use.

———

Another two glasses of boiled water, this time in Room 209 of the Jinling Hotel. One glass was placed in front of a young man sitting at the table, while the other was held by a man standing by the window facing the street. Both were dressed in white, long-sleeved shirts and they were wearing headphones.

A new US-made bugging device was placed on the large table in the next room against the wall.

The two young military agents assigned by Zeng Keda were ready to monitor Cui Zhongshi's every move and every word next door.

"Here he comes," the young man in front of the window whispered.

"OK," the young man sitting near the recording device answered softly. He clicked the button to switch on the machine.

The two parallel spools on the device began to rotate. At the same time, the man in front of the machine picked up a pen and got ready to write shorthand in his notepad.

Next door in Room 210, the lock in the door was turning. Clearly, someone was opening the door with a key from outside. The door opened and in came Cui Zhongshi.

On entering the room, Cui Zhongshi made no attempt to look for bugs, nor did he sigh or show any sign of relief after experiencing the tension out there on the street. He opened the wardrobe door, put his briefcase down, and took off his suit and placed it on a hanger before putting it in the wardrobe. He then took off his tie and hung it on a rack, closed the door and walked into the bathroom.

In Room 209, the sound of water running could be heard in the headphones of the young man. The noise soon stopped, indicating that the man next door had just washed his face. Sure enough, the sound of footsteps followed.

All of a sudden, the young man at the listening device became alert, and so did his colleague standing by the window. The sound of a phone dialling in the next room came through their headphones almost simultaneously. The young soldier in charge of eavesdropping picked up the pen.

"Biyu," said Cui Zhongshi in his strong Shanghai accent.

"Have you forgotten you've got a family, you dead ghost!"

Using shorthand, the young man quickly scribbled the following words in his notepad: "Cui called his wife in Peking at 8.15pm."

As he was writing, in Room 210 next door, Cui Zhongshi seemed to have become transformed; in fact he had completely reverted to his former self, a man from Shanghai patiently listening to his wife nagging with the rapidity of a soldier firing a submachine gun.

"You've been travelling to Nanking constantly these days. I dare say you keep a mistress and want to bring her back to Peking."

"Actually, it's business. Are you all right? Have the children been behaving themselves?"

"What do you mean by 'all right'? We're almost out of rice. I can't buy any groceries with those *fabi* notes, and when I went to pay the children's tuition fees today, it turns out the school doesn't accept them either. I've looked right through the drawers. Where have you put all the US dollars?"

Cui Zhongshi was stunned and looked at the wall that separated his room from the next, as if he could see the huge listening device on the other side.

"Like I told you before, I made some investments with all our dollars."

"People live in Western-style apartment buildings and buy cars with the money they made from their investments. I don't see any of the money you've made as a result of your investments, do I, Mr Deputy Director?"

"I'll be back in Peking tomorrow," Cui Zhongshi responded. "Let's discuss it when I'm home." With that he hung up.

In Room 209, the following words were written in shorthand: "Deputy director of the Peking branch of the Central Bank, family suffering financial difficulties?"

In the mess of the Ministry of Defence's Honourable Army Guesthouse, the meal was still going on in a subdued atmosphere.

Headed notepaper bearing the name "Bureau of Reserve Cadres" at the top and its official seal at the bottom was clearly visible on the empty table covered with white cloth.

No one knew when Fang Meng'ao and Zeng Keda sat down at the empty table. Fang Meng'ao was still sitting at the head of the table, leaning against the back of his chair, looking at the document. Zeng Keda, sitting opposite, stared at him, trying so hard not to get upset by the defiant look on the man's face. It was an arrogant face, full of disdain and contempt for the party-state represented by that handwritten signature of Chiang Ching-kuo at the bottom of the document.

At the other tables, the pilots sat silently, having finished their meals and with the empty cups and plates strewn about in front of them. They were looking at Fang Meng'ao and Zeng Keda.

"Your mother died in the Japanese bombing. Director Chingkuo's mother also died in the bombing at the hands of the Japanese Imperial Army. He knows you very well. He asked me to say hello," said Zeng Keda, initiating the conversation.

There was the fleeting look of a child in Fang Meng'ao's eyes.

He gazed at Zeng Keda, and then over to the three characters written below: Chiang Ching-kuo.

It worked. Zeng Keda continued to read in a soft and emotional tone, starting with some lines written by the Tang Dynasty poet, Meng Jiao: "'Who would say that the heart of inch-high grass could repay the sunshine of deepest spring?' Director Ching-kuo also said that he could understand if you did not forgive your father."

Sitting in the governor's office of the Central Bank's Peking branch, Fang Buting looked confused and lost. Xie Peidong was reading a secret telegram just sent by the Central Bank headquarters in Nanking:

> The investigation team is composed of Du Wancheng, general auditor of the Ministry of Finance of the Republic of China, Wang Benquan, chief secretary of the Central Bank of the Republic of China, Ma Linshen, deputy director of the national government's Central Commission on Citizens' Food Distribution, Zeng Keda, inspector and major general of the Bureau of Reserve Cadres, and Xu Tieying, the new chief of the Peking Police Bureau and director of the Department of Criminal Investigation of the Peking Garrison headquarters. The specific inspection tasks and the subsequent transportation of materials in Peking shall be carried out by the Youth Aviation Brigade assigned by the Bureau of Reserve Cadres of the Ministry of Defence. Captain Fang Meng'ao, former colonel and instructor at the Air Force Academy in Jianqiao, will serve as captain. The Central Bank's Peking branch that replied by telegram on the sixth of July, claiming it had nothing to do with the Fifth of July Incident, should cooperate closely with the five-member team. Negligence of duty is subject to disciplinary punishment. Governor Fang Buting should reply as soon as he reads the telegram. Sixth of July, Central Bank, Nanking.

Holding the telegram, Xie Peidong looked tentatively at Fang Buting who happened to be staring out of the south-facing window that appeared shrouded in dark. Xie Peidong gently placed the telegram on Fang Buting's table and said: "Their investigation has been directed at us. And the worst part is that they asked the son to investigate his own father. How malicious can you get?"

Fang Buting was continuing to stare out of the window, when suddenly he turned around, looked at Xie Peidong and said: "You haven't seen Meng'ao for five years either, have you?"

"More than five years."

"At long last. We'll meet each other, even if it means we end up dying together!" Fang Buting smiled and continued: "This is happy news. Don't let Mulan know just yet. See if Mengwei has finished his meal and ask him to come up."

In the mess of the Honourable Army Guesthouse, Zeng Keda was still conveying Director Ching-kuo's instructions. "First, you're assigned to fight corruption and punish those involved in corruption. Second, you will not be flying bombing missions but only transport missions. Third, although it involves your father, you work on the case and don't work against him. You have no reason to reject Comrade Jianfeng's three instructions, do you?"

Zeng Keda was trying to sound as sincere and serious as possible. "By the way, you do care about the students you trained yourself, don't you? At the aviation academy, they studied for three years, and trained for bombing for three years. Do you want to see them end up being forced to retire like this? Don't you think about the future of these young people?"

"You can share this document with them," Fang Meng'ao said. "They all deserve a future. But please don't mention my appointment until after you make the announcement."

Zeng Keda was starting to lose his composure. "If you don't want to be captain, there is no need to set up this brigade. They won't be entitled to such good arrangements. The special criminal court concluded that you must wait until further notice."

Fang Meng'ao looked at him in silent protest.

Zeng Keda softened his tone again: "We all know you were a hero in the War of Resistance. So many people died flying the

Hump, you're lucky to be alive. You've got your life back. As a survivor, you should think more about these young people."

"Did you give me sufficient time to think about it?"

Only then did Zeng Keda realise that he was to blame for his impatience, while at the same time, he also saw some room for compromise. He immediately responded: "OK. I'll announce it to them first. By the way, your family still cares about you. Deputy Director Cui has been filing petitions on your behalf. He's staying at the Jinling Hotel. It'd be fine for you to go and visit him."

Fang Meng'ao stood up and said: "General Zeng, sorry, I haven't had the chance to salute you since our courtroom encounter more than ten days ago." Clipping his heels, he gave a standard military salute to Zeng Keda.

The gesture caught Zeng Keda by surprise, and he found that, wearing casual clothes, he was not appropriately dressed to return the salute.

The eyes of the pilots brightened. Fang Meng'ao, however, was striding to the door, and this made the pilots look confused again.

"Here we go," murmured the young man standing by the window to his colleague working at the table. Looking out of Room 209, he could see a military jeep was parked at the gate of the Jinling. Fang Meng'ao got out from the rear door and walked to the hotel's main entrance.

In the governor's office of the Peking branch of the Central Bank, the door opened and in came Fang Mengwei. Taking off his police uniform and changing into casual clothes, he now looked more like his actual age of twenty-three. And he also more closely resembled a son in front of his father.

Fang Buting had already seated himself in one of the two armchairs on the other side of his desk. "Sit down," he said to Fang Mengwei.

Fang Mengwei sat down in the armchair by the door opposite his father, his body leaning forward.

This time it was Fang Buting who picked up the purple sand teapot and poured tea into the cup in front of his son. Fang Mengwei raised the cup with both hands and took a sip. By now, his father had already poured tea into another cup.

"May I ask my uncle to come up?" he asked.

"He's busy with bank business," said Fang Buting.

"Are you expecting any guests?"

"Yes. An important member of our family is set to return."

Fang Mengwei stood up quickly. He looked at his father with his eyes wide open: "Is my older brother coming back?"

"He won't make it today. But perhaps he will tomorrow or the day after."

"Director Cui can certainly get things done when he wants to," Fang Mengwei replied, genuinely excited. "Dad, I think he's still one of us."

"I'm also inclined to think that way." The heavy tone of Fang Buting had the immediate effect of cooling his excitement. "Cui Zhongshi is one of us, and he saved your elder brother again, who I still expect to change his mind by recognising me as his father. I'm almost sixty years old, my subordinates are loyal, and my two sons are supposed to be filial to me. Do I deserve such blessings?"

Slowly, Fang Mengwei sat down, waiting for his father to tell a truth he could not possibly know.

"Do you want to know which high-ranking government official saved your brother?" asked Fang Buting.

"Is it not Director Xu?"

"He's not high-ranking enough."

"Is it the Communications Bureau chief?"

"Could Ye Xiufeng become head of the Central Bureau of Investigation and Statistics by working on a case like this?"

"Did Mr Soong or Mr Kung personally intervene on our behalf?"

"I don't seem to deserve their intervention. Though I'm valued by Mr Soong and Mr Kung, I know my place in the scheme of things. There's no point in speculating. There are only two kinds of people who can really save your elder brother – one is the Communists, the other should be those within the Kuomintang who work against the old guard."

Fang Mengwei's face paled with confusion, and his question became heavy: "Dad, who on earth was it that saved my elder brother?"

"The Bureau of Reserve Cadres!" Fang Buting said each word slowly and deliberately. "He was not just acquitted, but also re-appointed as captain of the Youth Aviation Brigade for publicity purposes. Internally, he is captain of the Peking Economic Inspection Brigade of the Bureau of Reserve Cadres, and he's entitled to inspect the materials and accounts of the Peking Citizens' Food-Distribution Committee. And Cui Zhongshi is in charge of these accounts. You should understand by now why your father suspects Cui Zhongshi, right?"

Fang Mengwei sat there bewildered, as if someone had poured water over his head. He thought long and hard, but still could not figure it out.

"What's Cui Zhongshi's hotel and room number in Nanking?" asked Fang Buting.

"Room 210, the Jinling Hotel."

"Call Director Xu, ask him to consult the operator at the Jinling and see if Cui Zhongshi is back in his room yet, and if your big brother is in the same hotel room now. But remember to say thank you to Director Xu before you ask."

Fang Mengwei stood up at once.

At the table in the Jinling Hotel's Room 209, the young man wearing headphones listened attentively to the conversation that was taking place next door and quickly scribbled down a few lines in his notebook:

"Fang Meng'ao arrived at 9.05.

Cui, surprised, remained in expectant silence.

At 9.06, Fang sang two lines from *Blooming Flowers, Full Moon*."

In Room 210, there was a stack of paper on the table. Cui Zhongshi sat at the table and was writing quickly with a pencil, while talking at the same time: "It's up to you to decide whether

85

you want to do it again. No one can force you. But since you have consulted me, I will advise you again. For ten years, you've been living without any communication with your own father. Now you've quit your job, what will you do to make ends meet? Without family or employment, are you expecting to make a living solely by flying? You'd hardly deign to work as a porter on the Huangpu River, would you? Come to think of it, you'd go crazy if you couldn't afford your beloved red wine or cigars, even for a single day."

Fang Meng'ao stood next to Cui Zhongshi, listening to him while looking at what Cui had written. At this moment, Cui Zhongshi became silent, but he wrote down the words on the paper that he wanted to say: "Given what I know about your character, you won't accept the appointment from the Bureau of Reserve Cadres. But please accept it before approval by the party organisation. Accept the appointment in your own style. It's important."

"You should insist I tell you if the money I gave you was from your father or brother!"

Fang Meng'ao frowned. He felt compelled to lie when normally he would never do such a thing. Instead, he chose to be silent.

Cui Zhongshi looked up at him with encouragement and understanding in his eyes.

At the same time, the young man sitting at the table in Room 209 stopped writing and listened carefully through the headphones.

"I understand that Governor Fang pays for the wine and cigars you bring along every time you visit me!" Fang Meng'ao refused to tell lies.

Cui Zhongshi showed no sign of nervousness or tension even though he was secretly surprised. At this time, he had no choice but let Fang Meng'ao go on talking in this manner.

Fang Meng'ao continued: "I won't recognise him, but I drink your wine and smoke your cigars, which were supplied by the Americans. Whether I choose to drink or smoke or not, they still won't end up in the hands of the people."

"So, have I been wasting my time visiting you these past three years?" Cui Zhongshi naturally became angry. "A decade has passed, and we won the War of Resistance three years ago. It was the Japanese who killed your mother and little sister, after all, not your father. Now that we've forgiven the Japanese, why can't you forgive your own father?"

"The Japanese are now on trial. But what about him? And you, at the Central Bank. What are you up to here? Deputy Director Cui, we used to be friends, but I don't have friends in Peking, and nor do I have a father. Do you still want me up there?" Fang Meng'ao was speaking in a somewhat different manner than usual, but he was telling the truth nonetheless.

Cui Zhongshi immediately wrote two words on the paper: "Well said."

Fang Meng'ao was silent again. Then he took out a cigar, struck a match and lit it. It was the kind of long match provided exclusively by hotels. Fang Meng'ao held the match in his hand, gesturing to Cui Zhongshi whether he should burn the paper. Cui Zhongshi shook his head and motioned Fang Meng'ao to blow out the match.

The shorthand note on the table in Room 209 read as follows: "Fang was angry, and when it came to going to Peking, he stopped. (Perhaps he was faking the silence.) Then he struck a match (smoking or possibly burning something)."

―――

Back in the governor's office of the Peking branch of the Central Bank, Fang Buting's face was grim, his eyes fixed on the private telephone on the table.

"We can't allow them to be seen together in that room! Call Cui Zhongshi's room at the Jinling Hotel right away."

"Shall I call from here?"

"Of course, I'll speak to him here."

Fang Mengwei went to pick up the phone and dialled the number. In Room 209, the sound of a ringing telephone could be heard in the headsets. The young man who was listening at the table got excited. The tip of his pen was already poised over the notepad.

In the room next door, Cui Zhongshi looked at Fang Meng'ao and slowly picked up the phone.

"Hello, governor." Hearing Cui Zhongshi's greetings, Fang

Meng'ao stopped smoking and turned his head towards the window.

"Yes. That's what I should do." Cui Zhongshi covered the mouthpiece and said in a lowered voice: "He came to visit me. Yes, he's here. I'll try to put him on."

In Room 209, the stenographer quickly wrote the following words in shorthand: "At 9.38, Fang Buting called. He thanked Cui, who wanted the father and son to talk. But Fang Buting did not utter a word."

A loud bang sounded in the young intelligence officer's headphones, and he immediately turned to his colleague by the window: "Watch closely. Has Fang Meng'ao gone?"

He continued to listen attentively to the sound coming from the headphones. Through them, he knew that the phone in the next room was still off the hook, but no sound came out of it for some time.

Fang Buting did not hold the phone close to his ear, nor did he put it back on the rack. Instead, he held it in his hand which was frozen in the air. He heard Fang Meng'ao slamming the door.

For ten years, father and son had been so estranged that those who knew them were very secretive about this troubled relationship that stemmed from Fang Meng'ao's refusal to recognise him as his father and Fang Buting's own insistence on maintaining his image as a Confucian-style father figure. He felt reluctant to make that call. It was also the first time he had placed such a long-distance call, fully aware that his son was listening to the phone conversation. However, Fang Buting had never expected that his son would leave in this manner, even though all kinds of possibilities had flashed through his mind. In fact, Fang Meng'ao's slamming of the door felt like a punch to his heart.

Fang Mengwei had never seen his father act in this manner before. He tried to walk over to him, but he did not dare. Instead, he stood some distance away and continued to hear Cui Zhongshi's thick Shanghai accent down the line.

And all of a sudden, he came to recognise the foreboding that was apparent in hearing that voice.

Cui Zhongshi continued on the phone: "Don't think too much about it, governor. He'll be all right. Actually, Meng'ao was already on his way out when you made the call. He was about to leave, in fact. He had said he wanted to go."

There was no response from the other end of the line.

"Governor, I'll just hang up if you have no more instructions," Cui Zhongshi said. "I'll be arriving in Peking the day after tomorrow by train. I'll report to you in detail when we meet up."

Now it was Cui Zhongshi's turn to hang his hand in the air, before he gently put the receiver back on the hook. He looked over to the window facing the street, though he did not walk over to it. Silently, he went to the bathroom with the piece of paper on which he had scrawled those words.

Standing by the window in Room 209, the young man said: "Fang Meng'ao has got into in the jeep."

The stenographer wrote the following: "At 9.46, Fang Meng'ao slammed the door and left. Cui did not see him out. (During the telephone conversation, he tried to initiate a reconciliation between the father and son. They are deeply estranged.)"

Downstairs came the sound of the jeep driving away, and the young man let go of a corner of the window curtain and looked back to his colleague who pointed at the reel-to-reel tape recorder.

There was not much tape left. The young man strode up to an iron box and took out a handful of blank tapes.

Outside the dining hall of the Honourable Army Guesthouse, the soldiers who were following Fang Meng'ao stopped outside the gate of the compound.

Fang Meng'ao walked into the dining hall alone, and was stunned at the sight of his fellow pilots. All twenty of them were now dressed in brand new flying jackets. Even though there were no collar or cap badges, each one wore a round badge on his left chest. Standing in two rows in the middle of the dining room, they all saluted him after he entered.

Fang Meng'ao regarded these very familiar yet strange faces.

With five fingers pressed together against the right side of the brim, all were looking to Fang Meng'ao with great anticipation.

Fang Meng'ao could not bear to stare into these eyes again. He looked to one side, and found that the tables and chairs had been tidied and lined up against the wall. The table where he was sitting was covered with a clean cloth. A number of flying jackets were arranged neatly on the table, together with an officer's hat without a badge.

Zeng Keda was still dressed in unofficial uniform and stood quietly to one side. Just an hour ago, he had managed to inspire the young squadron by conveying the trust on behalf of the Bureau of Reserve Cadres. He personally handed out the uniforms to the pilots and pinned a badge on each one. However, the appointment documents had not yet been read out; he must wait for Fang Meng'ao to return.

Now, he either could not or dare not touch the military uniform on the table, and he was expecting Fang Meng'ao to put it on himself. But Director Chiang Ching-kuo's high expectation could be seen in the eyes of Zeng Keda who managed to pass it on to the twenty pilots.

On entering the dining hall, Fang Meng'ao stood all alone by the door, somewhat like Zeng Keda. He began to move his feet, with his eyes panning across the twenty-one people whose eyes were following him. He went up to his uniform. The air seemed to have solidified.

All eyes were on Fang Meng'ao putting on his uniform, putting on his officer's hat, pinning a badge on his jacket.

"Salute!" The two lines of pilots performed a neat quarter turn under Chen Changwu's command. All of them were facing Fang Meng'ao, who was now looking resplendent in his new uniform.

Fang Meng'ao, gently clicking the soles of his shoes, had no choice but to raise his hand and return the salute.

"Now, permit me to read this announcement!" Zeng Keda picked up the appointment documents and to the best of his ability began to read them out in a calm and serious tone. "From the twenty-fourth of January 1949, the former Eleventh Graduating Class of the First Trainee Squadron of the National Air Force at

Jianqiao Aviation Academy is redesignated as the Peking Transport Squadron and Economic Inspection Brigade of the Ministry of Defence. Known as the Youth Service Squadron of China Airlines based in Peking, the squadron is directly affiliated to the Bureau of Reserve Cadres. Fang Meng'ao is appointed colonel and squadron leader. All members of the squadron are to be awarded the rank of captain of the Air Force. The specific mission shall be conveyed to Fang Meng'ao by Zeng Keda, major general and inspector of the Bureau of Reserve Cadres. Twenty-fourth of January 1949.'"

The C-46 transport plane parked at an airbase in the Nanking suburbs looked huge. The soldiers standing guard next to the plane were dwarfed by the monstrous giant.

A motorcade arrived, headed by a military jeep and followed by a black Austin sedan and a large bus. The three vehicles stopped side by side near the steps leading to the C-46.

A guard opened the front door of the jeep and out came Fang Meng'ao, dressed in a flying suit. Another two guards opened the rear door of the jeep, with Zeng Keda stepping out on the left, and Xu Tieying on the right. Zeng Keda was wearing a major general's uniform while Xu Tieying was in the official uniform of the chief of the Peking Police Bureau.

The door of the bus opened, and twenty trainee pilots in Fang Meng'ao's squadron disembarked. They lined up and boarded the aircraft in neat fashion ahead of the three officers.

Finally, the guard opened the doors of the car. Emerging from the front was Du Wancheng, general auditor of the Ministry of Finance of the Nationalist government. In his thirties, Du was dressed in a Western suit and was wearing thick glasses. He looked very scholarly and there was a certain panache about him.

From the back seat on the left side of the car emerged Wang Benquan. In his forties, he was also dressed in a three-piece suit. But unlike his fellow travellers, he was wearing a pair of sunglasses.

The last man to alight the car was in his fifties and dressed in Zhongshan attire. His collar was fastened tightly, his face lathered with sweat. He kept patting the folding fan in his hand. His name was Ma Linshen, deputy director of the Central Commission on Citizens' Food Distribution of the Kuomintang central government.

All five members of the Investigation Team into the Fifth of July Incident and the Peking Citizens' Daily Necessities Investigation Team were flying to Peking on the same plane.

Zeng Keda obviously did not want to talk to the three sedan passengers, so he chose instead to stand with Fang Meng'ao even though they did not strike up a conversation. A clearly divided camp.

A smiling Xu Tieying came forward to say hello.

Perhaps due to the heat, the other three looked very serious. They just politely nodded their heads at one another. The guards showed their way up the passenger steps.

Xu Tieying looked up at the sun and said: "How incredibly hot it is!"

"Don't worry," said Zeng Keda. "Peking's much cooler than Nanking. It's also much cooler to be the police chief than the director of the liaison office."

Xu Tieying did not rise to the bait, so he turned to Fang Meng'ao and said: "Meng'ao, you are our pilot today. I trust my life is in good hands."

Occasionally, Fang Meng'ao was able to reveal the smile hidden in his heart: "Director Xu, are you asking me to repay you for saving my life?"

Xu Tieying and Zeng Keda both looked embarrassed.

"That's not what I meant," said Xu Tieying, quick to explain himself. "After working for more than ten years, I'm still afraid of flying."

Fang Meng'ao decided to respond in a more polite, sympathetic manner: "Director Xu, please sit in the front. You're more likely to get airsick in the back."

"I'm not afraid of getting airsick, I'm afraid of this thing crashing."

Fang Meng'ao took offence, and was quick to show his anger at the hypocrisy: "Then wait for the plane to crash. I can always parachute to safety!" With that, he went straight to the staircase.

Zeng Keda looked at Xu Tieying and said: "Scared or not, we'll have to go. Director Xu, after you, please."

Xu Tieying now noticed the young secretary who was standing about five metres away. It was Sun who worked for him in the liaison office. Sun had also changed into police uniform and was holding two leather suitcases, one bigger than the other.

Zeng Keda walked in front, followed by Xu Tieying and Secretary Sun carrying the suitcases. The three climbed the staircase on their way to boarding the plane.

The huge propellers began to turn.

Zeng Keda walked briskly into the cabin. Xu Tieying, however, was buffeted by the airflow, and he hurried to hold the staircase railings. From this position he could see the side of Fang Meng'ao who was piloting the aircraft. Would he actually use a parachute!

CHAPTER 4

In Peking, there were only a handful of small, Western-style buildings like the one in which Fang Buting lived. These elegant and luxurious homes belonged to the princes and princesses in the Qing Dynasty. By 1945, after victory in the War of Resistance and the takeover of Peking by the Nationalists, it had become a priority for military and political agencies of the state to seize these well-preserved residences. The one owned by Princess Hejing was among the finest in the city. It was seized by Chiang Kai-shek's Eleventh Army and turned into its headquarters.

It was 7 July, the eleventh anniversary of the Marco Polo Bridge Incident – a minor skirmish that led to a full-scale war between the Japanese invaders and China. The Nationalist authorities in Peking did not dare hold any commemorative activities on that day. Two days earlier, General Fu Zuoyi had publicly stated that no students should be arrested, but the repressive martial law against exiled students from the Northeast had not yet been fully lifted. The military and police were somewhat embarrassed by this half-lockdown. Several small groups of students gathered to protest, yet the gatherings were all peaceful, supported by citizens who joined them on the streets. Both the Peking Police Bureau and the Peking Garrison headquarters had roadblocks set up, fire engines deployed, and the gates of important military and political organisations guarded.

This was the situation outside Princess Hejing's residence on

Zhang Zizhong Road. Early in the morning, a number of exiled students from the Northeast with nowhere else to go were out on the street. Soon the student associations of Peking University, Tsinghua University, Yenching University and others organised in large numbers to lend their support.

The Peking Police Bureau and Peking Garrison headquarters were sufficiently nervous to deploy troops to guard the main entrance.

It was strange to find students separated by barbed wire a hundred metres from the gate to the east, while to the west the street was empty and eerily silent, with not a roadblock in sight. But it was heavily guarded and no pedestrians were allowed. Clearly the road had been closed. A VIP convoy coming from the west must have been expected.

A large sign was hanging on the gate of the residence announcing the identity of those VIPs: Fang Meng'ao and members of his squadron. Local officials from the Peking municipal government had decided to treat him and his team like royalty. Not so much in flattery, but more in fear.

On this side of the roadblock, the army and police were armed with shields and batons. Fu Zuoyi must have prohibited the use of firearms against the students. On the other side of the roadblock, many students still had their heads and arms covered in bandages; they were all students from Manchuria in the northeast of China.

Beside them, and behind them, were local students, all wearing their university badges. They were silent, but it was the silence of expectation – when would the crash of thunder come?

In the student crowd from Yenching University, Xie Mulan and her fellow classmates were visibly excited.

"When the convoy arrives, are you going to jump over to join your big brother?" one girl asked Mulan.

All eyes were trained on her. Wild with joy, Mulan pretended to be calm and whispered: "When he arrives, you have to lift me up. I'll jump over there!"

Their eyes fluttered and they kept turning their heads as they whispered. Their voices were low, not in fear of the police on the other side of the roadblock, but of the people standing behind them.

Standing behind the girls was Professor Liang Jinglun, his piercing eyes casting a familiar light. It was Liang who had been standing behind the glass door of Yenching University Hospital on the night of 5 July. He Xiaoyu was standing beside him, while Xie Mulan was with the students.

Professor Liang read the minds of the female students in front of him, whispering to He Xiaoyu: "Tell Xie Mulan it's a peaceful protest today. There must be no conflict with the military or police. This is not the place for her to greet her elder brother."

He Xiaoyu nodded, and she was pushed forward by several sturdy male students so that she could squeeze her way through the crowd to Xie Mulan.

Liang Jinglun's eyes followed He Xiaoyu, observing the protective actions of the male students surrounding her.

Xie Mulan was flushed from having made the exciting promise to her classmates: "Trust me, you'll get my big brother's autograph," she said.

At that very moment, she stopped. He Xiaoyu had pushed her way up to her side and gave her a nudge. "Professor Liang says you shouldn't contact your big brother here. Do you hear me?"

"That's a shame," said Xie Mulan, her eyes flashing. "Your instructions or Mr Liang's?"

He Xiaoyu could sense her defiance, and she held her. "Go ask for yourself."

Xie Mulan hesitated. "No need. I'll save my greetings for another time. Perhaps you can welcome him on my behalf?"

He Xiaoyu blushed, and she turned away, trying to leave.

Xie Mulan called her back. "Don't worry, I'll be obedient. Come on, stay with me. I promise to be good, all right?"

"Enough now." Xie Mulan nodded, seeing a police officer heading in their direction. He pointed his baton at her.

"Why point that thing at us!" yelled Xie Mulan, even though she had just promised not to utter a word. "Come and get me if you can!"

Several police officers approached her.

He Xiaoyu gently pulled Xie Mulan back, and stood in front of her.

This irritated Xie Mulan: "I dare them to arrest me. Let go of me!"

He Xiaoyu held her tight.

This was all that was needed for the officers to soften their attitude. It was a turbulent time, and the children of many military and political dignitaries were involved, picking fights with the government in all sorts of ways. They could be found in every student movement. From where the police stood, here was a girl with a Yenching University badge pinned to her chest, shouting at them. Smartly turned out, this pretty girl could be the daughter of any of the big shots.

A police officer, apparently the head of the team, said politely: "Miss, please tell everyone to keep order."

"Aren't the pilots coming?" Xie Mulan looked over the crowd to the road ahead of them, now separated by the police cordon.

On the road from Nanyuan airbase to central Peking, two military trikes were leading a convoy, followed by a black sedan that for some reason contained no passengers. The bus behind was full.

The twenty-seat bus was just big enough to accommodate the entire Youth Aviation Brigade. But with Fang Meng'ao choosing to join them, they were short by one seat. One member of the team sat in the front passenger seat and Fang Meng'ao took a seat near the door.

A man in a neatly pressed Zhongshan suit stood near him holding the handrail. With a skinny face, greenish bags under his eyes, blackened teeth and a smile hidden in the wrinkles and folds of his jowls, here was a classic example of officialdom. His name was Ma Hanshan, deputy director of the Peking Citizens' Food-Distribution Committee, and director of the Civil Affairs Bureau of Peking Municipality.

With war looming large over the city, municipal maintenance had long been suspended. The road was dilapidated and repairs were on hold. It was a bumpy journey, which Ma Hanshan endured without much complaint. Fang Meng'ao had chosen to take the bus, so he had to join him. Since no one would give up their seat, he was forced to stand, but this seemed to suit him. Having spent half his life as a Nationalist official, he didn't enjoy being idle. Instead, his energy was spent getting out of trouble by any means possible. It always worked out in the end. This was a habit that died hard, and would once again be put to the test.

Fang Meng'ao was looking out of the window when he turned to him and said: "Deputy Director Ma, Director Ma. We're soldiers. You don't have to keep us company. Please ride in my car."

"I am here to escort you, Captain Fang," Ma Hanshan said most sincerely. "I'll be damned if I ride in your car."

"Let me give you my seat then. I'm happy to stand." Fang Meng'ao made to get up.

"No need," said Ma Hanshan, holding out his hand to stop him. "I'll get off and walk if you insist."

"Pull over!" Fang Meng'ao called out to the driver who slammed on the brakes. Ma Hanshan almost toppled over as the bus came to an abrupt halt.

"Open the door," said Fang Meng'ao. "Director Ma would prefer to walk."

The pilots laughed under their breath.

Ma Hanshan was stunned, but he was thick-skinned. He laughed along with the pilots. "Well, seeing is believing," he said. "Captain Fang, you're a funny guy. Driver, our guest appears to be joking."

The driver's face was wet with perspiration. He stepped on the accelerator and the bus began to move. It was the first time that Director Ma had boarded his bus, and the driver could not offer him a seat. To make things worse, he had almost got him injured when he braked abruptly just a moment ago. Ma was still laughing when he looked in the rearview mirror. Would he be able to keep his job at the end of the day? His mind was in turmoil. One hundred metres west of Princess Hejing's residence, Ma Hanshan called out: "Stop the bus!"

The driver had learnt his lesson by now, allowing the bus to glide to a stop. Ma Hanshan approached the driver and bent to look forward from behind his seat. Far away, he could see two big-character banners put up by the student crowd who had gathered to the east side of the gate. One read "Welcome the patriotic Air Force pilots who chose not to bomb Kaifeng!", while the other read "Welcome to the anti-corruption Youth Aviation Brigade!"

Ma's eyes rolled. "Reverse the bus and go in via the back entrance," he whispered to the driver.

"Director Ma," said Fang Meng'ao, now standing behind him, "we never go through the back door. Why be afraid of some students?"

Ma Hanshan straightened up, concern written all over his face. "They're just a bunch of trouble-making students from the Northeast. Clearly, they're against you. And I'll be held responsible should anything happen to you. Besides, Captain Fang, you and your band of brothers have had a long journey. No matter which gate you use, you'll need to shower, eat and rest."

Fang Meng'ao smiled as he also bent down to look at the crowd in the distance. "Indeed, but they aren't against us, are they? Take a look at the banners. Let's go."

The driver was in a difficult position, looking back to Ma for instructions.

Fang ignored them and went to open the bus door. "Attention everyone! Exit the vehicle!" he ordered as he led his pilots off the bus and into formation.

With Fang Meng'ao by their side, the twenty pilots formed into two rows. All dressed in bomber jackets, they marched as if conducting a military parade. The Youth Aviation Brigade walked past the main entrance of the residence towards the crowd of students gathered to the east.

The students' eyes shone as they watched the team of pilots approach, unidentified by lapel badges or insignia.

"Salute!" Fang Meng'ao ordered, at which they all raised their right arms in unison, paying tribute to the crowd in front of them.

The police made way for the marching pilots and stared at them in amazement.

The students beamed with excitement. Xie Mulan and several other female classmates jumped with joy.

"Mulan!" He Xiaoyu called out to stop her. The students all had to stop, including He Xiaoyu, but their eyes shone brighter than ever.

One of the girls could not help whispering in Xie Mulan's ear: "Is that the leader of the team?"

Xie Mulan eyed her "older brother" who was walking in her direction. She was so excited that she could not utter a word.

"Yes," He Xiaoyu whispered. "Don't talk any more." Her eyes had long been fixed on Fang Meng'ao, as if she were searching for his childhood image.

"Stand by!" instructed Fang Meng'ao. The marching pilots stopped and stood neatly in front of the roadblock.

"Stand in rows!" The two columns quickly turned into two rows, and stood straight, facing the chanting students.

"Salute!" Fang Meng'ao ordered again. With that, he and the pilots made a salute to the students.

All the female students responded by clapping their hands with great excitement. Then the boys reacted, and some began to clap their hands as hard as they could.

What Fang Meng'ao showed on his face was not sympathy, but empathy, as if he were one of them. He took a big step forward, standing right in front of the barbed wire fence.

The applause from the student crowd faded until all was quiet again.

"Hello, students of Peking!" said Fang Meng'ao. "We are the Peking Youth Aviation Brigade. We're here to investigate the Fifth of July smuggling case. I am Fang Meng'ao, captain of the investigation team. Please note the badges on our chests and inform us if you have anything to report."

A tall student representative elbowed his way out of the crowd opposite the roadblock. With a strong northeastern accent, he asked: "Excuse me, Captain Fang, are you going to stay in this compound?"

"Why do you ask?"

"This is where the senior officers of the Eleventh Army Corps stayed. In April, they turned it into the headquarters of the Peking Citizens' Food-Distribution Committee. It was supposed to be their office, but they were actually here to engage in corruption! They vacated the premises last night. Are you still planning to stay here?"

The students were well organised and experienced. With their spokesperson up front, everyone else looked to Fang Meng'ao for answers. They were a united bunch. Some were especially curious to hear his response. One of them, of course, was Xie Mulan, and another was He Xiaoyu. And behind them was Liang Jinglun.

Fang Meng'ao was in no hurry to oblige. He looked back and shouted: "Director Ma?"

Ma Hanshan had also had plenty of exposure to this kind of situation. This time, he could hardly avoid it, so he had made an effort to get out of the bus. He followed Fang Meng'ao's team and was standing apart from them, next to the policemen on the roadside. With Fang Meng'ao yelling his name, Ma Hanshan had no choice but to come over, pretending to be calm. First, he smiled at Fang Meng'ao, and then he spoke loudly to the students: "Well, well, folks! You're all decent, intelligent people with a good education. Captain Fang and his fellow pilots have just flown in from Nanking. They've had a long flight. Please be considerate and let them have a good rest. His team and me, and each member of the Citizens' Food-Distribution Committee, will provide answers in due course. Now, please go home, go!"

The student representative was outraged and countered: "We don't even have a place to live. Tell us where to go!"

"Don't speak to him!" another student in the crowd shouted. "We'll only talk to Captain Fang!"

The students began to chant: "Corrupt officials, go away! Corrupt officials, go away!"

Ma Hanshan's thin face turned an even darker hue.

The soldiers and policemen became nervous and ran towards the crowd from both sides, holding up shields. The head of the police stood next to Ma Hanshan with a few of his men.

Fang Meng'ao looked back at Ma Hanshan and glanced at the policemen. "I'm speaking with the students now. Can you step back?"

The policemen were truly afraid of the captain. Still facing the students, they took a few steps back, thereby distancing themselves from the crowd.

Ma Hanshan took up position next to Fang Meng'ao again. Sensing he had more to say, the students fell silent. "Director Ma, is this compound solely reserved for us?"

Ma Hanshan swallowed and replied: "Yes. You'll have the whole compound to yourselves. And, of course, there will be the logistics staff at your service."

Fang Meng'ao smiled and replied: "It'll be too big and cold for us, just twenty-one people, don't you think? Besides, we don't need any of your logistics staff. That said, since the city authorities have put this residence in our hands, we have the power to share it, don't we?"

With that, he turned around and looked at the students in the crowd, noticing the bandages that covered their heads and bodies. Of course, these were scrutinising eyes, eyes full of eagerness and yearning. They were naturally also eyes of scepticism. Suddenly, Fang Meng'ao saw something that melted his heart. It was a pair of familiar eyes, sparkling with affection, excitement and incomparable enthusiasm – those of Xie Mulan!

Then Fang Meng'ao saw another pair of familiar eyes, in which there was also affection of a slightly more subtle nature. The excitement in them was more restrained – those of He Xiaoyu.

Two pairs of beautiful big eyes! Fang Meng'ao had guessed correctly. These were his cousins, the two girls who were like his blood sisters eleven years ago! Fang Meng'ao's eyes flashed the way an ace pilot's eyes do when seeing stars on a night flight. He failed to catch another pair of eyes, though, eyes that were like stars hidden in the distant darkness of the galaxy – those of Liang Jinglun.

It was not the right time to talk, so Fang Meng'ao just winked at them, and turned to the student representative, asking: "How many people need a place to stay? We'll accommodate as many students from the Northeast as we can."

"That would be most inappropriate," said Ma Hanshan, becoming desperate. "The Peking municipal government won't allow it."

Fang Meng'ao gave him a look out of the corner of his eye and walked alone towards the entrance of the princess's former residence. He commanded the armed guards at the gate to listen: "I'm here to take over the compound. Attention! Off you go!"

The guards were deployed by the Peking Garrison headquarters, so they were not subject to Ma Hanshan's command. However, they all knew about Fang Meng'ao. With Fang Meng'ao having taken such an aggressive stance, they had no choice but to obey. Clipping their knees together in salute, the group retreated from the gate.

Fang Meng'ao strode to the east of the roadblock, and said to the students: "You were asking me whether we would live in this princess's house. I'll tell you now, on the record, no we won't! I just learnt that the students from the Northeast don't have anywhere to stay. So, on behalf of the Youth Aviation Brigade, I will give up this compound to these students."

Overjoyed, the crowd took up their chanted slogans: "Long live the progressive youth!" and "Long live the Youth Aviation Brigade!"

Fang Meng'ao found himself in front of the police chief. "Remove the roadblocks and let the students in."

The police chief was hesitant: "Captain Fang…"

"Director Xu came to Peking on the same flight as me. I'll hold myself responsible for any trouble. Remove the barricades!"

"Yes sir." The police chief pressed his knees together. "Captain Fang! Director Xu is also my superior…"

He clearly wanted to rub shoulders with Fang Meng'ao, who had no such plan. "Just remove them."

The police chief agreed once more, before directing his officers to move the roadblock. There was a hubbub of voices as Fang Meng'ao turned to the team members and said: "Back to the bus! At the double!"

The men turned back and ran to the bus. Ma Hanshan, all skin and bone, followed on behind.

One voice behind them sounded louder than the others: "Long live Elder Brother!"

Despite the hubbub, Fang Meng'ao picked out the words, and glanced to see who it was. Chanting excitedly, there was Xie Mulan and he waved to salute her in a rather American style.

More female students joined in: "Long live Elder Brother!"

The roadblock was removed, and many students, especially women, were shouting, trying to catch up with Fang Meng'ao's brigade.

Fang Meng'ao, the pilots and Ma Hanshan all got on the bus.

"Go! Go!" Ma Hanshan yelled at the driver. The driver stepped on the accelerator, turned the bus around and drove westwards. Xie Mulan, together with many other students, followed for quite a while. More students from the Northeast had flocked to the main entrance of Princess Hejing's former residence.

There were not many students left in the place where they had originally assembled. He Xiaoyu and several others from Yenching University surrounded Liang Jinglun.

One piped up: "Mr Liang, the students from the Northeast, they just can't move in like this. They have to be organised about it."

"You're right," said Liang Jinglun. "Please go and tell them to leave separately and register themselves based on which school they represent. Make sure they are not arrested."

"All right." Some of the students went to the crowd at the door, leaving only He Xiaoyu behind with Liang Jinglun.

Liang Jinglun turned to He Xiaoyu and instructed her: "Find Xie Mulan and escort her to the Fang mansion. Wait for Fang Meng'ao there."

He Xiaoyu made no reply, nor did she make a move. She just looked at Liang Jinglun.

Liang Jinglun whispered: "Try to approach him. We should win him over to our side." Having said these words, He Xiaoyu ran towards Xie Mulan.

Liang Jinglun looked at the back of He Xiaoyu, then to the crowd of students who swarmed towards the princess's compound. His deep eyes suddenly seemed even deeper.

The Yenching University Foreign Languages Bookstore in Peking was rarely visited by Nationalist agents. One reason was that all the books on sale were foreign. Another was that the owner was an American woman who used to specialise in theology at the university. Not being able to speak a foreign language, or having no affiliation with Yenching, would soon give one away in front of the American shopkeeper.

This is why it became Liang Jinglun's chosen spot. To be exact, it was where he secretly met people from the organisation.

"Good morning, Miss Sophia." Liang Jinglun knew the lady very well. As he greeted her in English, he lightly kissed the back of her outstretched hand.

"Good morning, Professor Liang," the woman replied in English. She was in her early sixties, full of vigour and enthusiasm, yet without having lost any of her grace. "I've got all the books you need. They're on the second floor. There's no one else there. It's very quiet."

"Thank you very much. Mr Yan from the library will bring me some material. Could I trouble you to show him upstairs when he arrives?"

"Sure, no problem."

"Thanks." Through the door to the inner room he was familiar with, he went straight up the stairs to the reading room. It was lined with economics books, some written in English and German, others in French.

Liang Jinglun read carefully, taking notes and making index cards.

The stairs creaked and Liang Jinglun stood up. With a bag under his arm, the new arrival motioned for Liang to sit down. He took a seat opposite.

"Professor Liang, here's the collection of the latest foreign papers on finance."

Liang Jinglun stretched across the table and took the bundle with both hands. "Thank you, Mr Yan."

Liang Jinglun opened the package and began to read the papers one by one, then raised his head and whispered: "Are there any instructions from the boss?"

Yan Chunming became serious and spoke softly: "They were sent yesterday. There are strict requirements that instructions be conveyed through oral communication."

Yan was in charge of the Yenching chapter of the Communist Party's Student Committee.

Liang Jinglun nodded seriously, closed his eyes and applied his extraordinary memory to record Yan Chunming's oral instructions.

All instructions were conveyed in an atmosphere of peace and quiet. As Yan Chunming looked out of the window, he saw the clouds speeding across the sky. He closed his mouth gently.

Liang Jinglun opened his eyes and said: "How visionary." In just two words, Liang Jinglun summed up the spirit of the instructions as he understood them. "Comrade Chunming," he continued, "can I share my understanding of the spirit of the instructions in the light of our roles in the current student movement?"

Yan Chunming nodded his agreement.

"According to the superior's instruction," explained Liang Jinglun, "we've made good progress with the Peking student movement, and the wave-like campaigns have had a major impact. However, the general policy is to hide our capacity and build our strength. It is not our main aim to confront the Nationalist Party. We understand that the vast number of students have spontaneously launched several waves of protests because of their disenchantment with Nationalist reactionaries. Yet we should neither use force nor intervene to stop them, should we?"

"You can understand it that way," said Yan Chunming. "However, the party's leadership in the student movement remains essential. As a result, you're not supposed to interpret the spirit of the instructions negatively. My understanding is that one can neither ignore the revolutionary enthusiasm of most of the students, nor let the young ones make pointless sacrifices. The Fifth of July Incident is a lesson. Now that the reactionary authorities have arrested a large number of students, we must do our best to mobilise people from all backgrounds across the community, including opposition forces within the Nationalists, and put pressure on them to release the students."

That was exactly what Liang Jinglun seemed to want as a guideline, so he gave a quick nod of approval. "So the important thing is to mobilise all the forces that can be mobilised, but the priority is that we should be clear in our message about the Fifth of July Incident. The embezzlement of goods by the Peking Citizens' Food-Distribution Committee triggered the student protests. In response to the protests across the country, as well as the US intervention, the Nationalist authorities have investigated the incident. I think we can work on one person on their investigation team."

"Who?"

"Fang Meng'ao, captain of the Nationalist Party's Youth Aviation Brigade stationed in Peking." After saying the name, he looked closely at Yan.

The other man clearly attached great importance to the name, but held back from saying anything.

Liang Jinglun continued: "Comrade Chunming, I know you have concerns." At this point, he paused before reciting the following words: "Article Two of the instructions stipulates that those who tend to work as double agents as well as those with a particularly complex political background, we can ask other comrades to work on them. Generally speaking, it is better for the Urban Works Department not to engage in these tasks. Even if we do so, we should use special people, and we should not recruit special party members, either. If anyone wants to join the party, we should explain our constitution to them, explain the conditions and qualifications for joining the party honestly. Do not arbitrarily recruit special party members or deceive others."

Yan Chunming had always appreciated the talent and ability of his subordinate. In fact, he admired Liang for being able to recite his instructions almost word for word. He continued in an encouraging manner: "Share your ideas with me."

"Fang Meng'ao is clearly one of those with a particularly complex political background referred to in our instructions," said Liang Jinglun. "Therefore, the Urban Works Department should not carry out this task. However, this situation needs to be dealt with specifically. Fang Meng'ao has a very special relationship with the progressive students we have been working on, and no other department has such an advantage. According to the first article of the instructions, 'certain activities can only be conducted by a certain organisation, that is, to do what is permitted in the circumstances'. In spirit, I think we can make use of the special relationship with the Urban Works Department to approach Fang Meng'ao."

This suggestion got Yan Chunming's attention. After thinking about it, he replied: "I'm afraid I'll have to consult my superior."

"Comrade Chunming," Liang Jinglun said, "of course we should consult our superiors, but it is not necessary at the moment. Just because we'll appoint someone to get to know Fang Meng'ao, we won't be recruiting him as a special member just yet. Our policy demands that we don't lose any opportunity to access core Nationalist intelligence. This policy doesn't run counter to the spirit of the new instructions given by the superior."

Yan Chunming suddenly became very serious: "Who are you planning to send to contact Fang Meng'ao?"

"He Xiaoyu."

In Xie Mulan's room on the first floor of the Fang mansion, the latest model desktop fan was set to maximum power.

"It's cold in here!" said Xie Mulan in her rusty Peking dialect. She deliberately spoke with a heavy southern accent. Her mother, and for that matter Uncle Fang, were both from Wuxi.

She was rocking Fang Buting in the chair, directly in front of the fan that was blowing cold air. "Uncle, you shouldn't wear so much if you're don't like the heat. I'm going to turn it down."

Fang Buting smiled, which was what he always did in the company of his niece. She was as dear to him as any child of his own. With his mandarin jacket worn over a gown, he sat there smiling, allowing her to rock him in the chair without complaint.

"Really, I'm going to turn it down." Xie Mulan walked away with her hands pressing down her skirt to prevent it from billowing up. She saw He Xiaoyu sitting by the bed and smiled at her.

The Fang family was rich and powerful, and they lived in a Western-style building with modern bathrooms complete with showers and a toilet.

The first thing Xie Mulan and He Xiaoyu did when they came back from Princess Hejing's residence was take a bath. He Xiaoyu often stayed overnight at Xie Mulan's house, and she even kept her own clothes there to change into. Now, both were in identical summer school uniforms.

He Xiaoyu sat on the edge of the bed, her hands on her knees. She looked very demure, always smiling – a sharp contrast to the noisy Xie Mulan.

The closer Xie Mulan got to the fan, the higher her skirt blew, and she quickly pressed her hand against it. She squatted by the fan and looked up at He Xiaoyu: "What do you think, Xiaoyu?"

He Xiaoyu continued to smile. "It all depends on whether you really love your uncle or not."

"You're cunning," Xie Mulan responded as she paused with her hand on the fan dial, "for you're the only one who can please the old man."

He Xiaoyu remained smiling, and so did Fang Buting.

Xie Mulan looked straight at him. "Uncle, am I right in saying that you like Xiaoyu better? Go on, admit it!"

Fang Buting continued to smile.

"Out with it!" Xie Mulan huffed.

"I like you both," Fang Buting answered.

Xie Mulan jumped to her feet, allowing the wind to catch her skirt. She ran to Fang Buting and demanded: "Who is she to you? Why do you like her so much? Honestly, no more lies."

"I like all girls as long as they're good."

"Liar! Many of my classmates are good girls. Have you ever liked them as much?"

He Xiaoyu regarded Xie Mulan. Knowing that she was going to say something unpleasant, she ceased smiling, glaring at her in a way that was designed to cut her short.

Xie Mulan ignored her, sat next to Fang Buting and whispered into his ear: "I'll just say three words, and if I'm right, just nod."

"Mulan," said He Xiaoyu, "if you are going to say something frivolous, I had better go."

"You must have a ghost in your heart. Otherwise, you wouldn't choose to leave."

Xie Mulan now uttered those three words: "Marry them young!"

He Xiaoyu stood up with her hand pressed against her skirt, but she did not step away.

Not only did Fang Buting fail to nod, but the smile disappeared from his face, and his eyes filled with melancholy.

Xie Mulan nervously but gently whispered into Fang Buting's ear: "Uncle, all our classmates saw my elder brother today. Guess what they said about him?"

At that moment, even the melancholy in Fang Buting's eyes disappeared. Though appearing aloof, he was still eager to hear her out.

Xie Mulan plucked up courage and continued: "Everyone says that my big brother is a real man! Guess what I said in response? I said, of course, like father like son, my uncle is a real man, and so is my big brother." With that, she paused, observing his reaction.

A bitter smile played on the corner of Fang Buting's mouth, which was quite a natural response. He had been so preoccupied by both girls, especially He Xiaoyu, that he hardly wished to embarrass her.

"I'm telling you the truth." Again, Xie Mulan began to shake Fang Buting's shoulder. "When two real men meet, they compete with all their might. I greeted him in the street and he saluted me. I guess the first thing he'll do when he gets home is salute you. If he continues to defy your authority, Xiaoyu will join me in helping you deal with him, and demand that he salute you. Then you'll make peace with him, yes?"

Fang Buting stood up, and turned to He Xiaoyu with a forced expression on his face. "I'll call your father and ask his permission for you to stay for dinner. Will you join us?"

He Xiaoyu gave him a soft nod that concealed the extent of her eagerness. What was apparent was her sincerity and consideration. To outward appearances, her visit had nothing to do with what Liang Jinglun had instructed her to do.

———

State and family affairs can never be settled simultaneously. The more you try to settle them, the messier they become.

What Fang Buting was about to face was more than just his elder son. In fact, by choosing to sit in his niece's room, he wanted to avoid his younger son who had just returned home after picking up Xu Tieying at the police station.

His arrival coincided with the return of his second wife who had been staying away from the family, and had needed to come home to finish a piece of business assigned by Fang Buting.

Fang Mengwei obeyed his father in every way possible, but he had nothing but disdain for his stepmother. He saw her as his mortal enemy. Fang Buting did not wish to choose one over the other, so he decided to be evasive instead.

Of course, another reason why he joined Xie Mulan and He Xiaoyu was to listen to them talk about his elder son whom they had just seen. The dilemma, however, was that he wanted to hear about his son, but not too much. He thought that his wife should have left after finishing her business, so Fang Buting went out of Xie Mulan's room, and got ready to go downstairs.

As soon as he reached the corridor near the ground floor living room, he heard something he did not want to hear. It was Fang Mengwei angrily calling out: "Where are the servants? Are you all asleep?"

Fang Buting stood stock still in the corridor.

Fang Mengwei stood in the doorway with his back to the living room. Had he not been wearing a summer police uniform, he would have looked exactly like a young master of the house. As he yelled, two middle-aged maids in short, white blouses made of thin fabric of foreign origin stood outside the room. They looked at a raving Fang Mengwei without responding. Though silent, they did not seem to be scared.

"Mrs Cai and Mrs Wang,-did you hear me?" Fang Mengwei softened his tone when he spoke with them face to face. Obviously, his anger was not directed at them.

"Mengwei," said Mrs Cai, using his first name instead of "Young Master". This had been a rule of the house, in which servants were allowed to call younger members of the family by their given names. "The master gave the instruction that these photos can only be laid out by the second wife."

On hearing this, Fang Mengwei's face became pained. He was about to burst out with even angrier words when he heard another woman's voice coming from the living room. "There's no need for the young master to be angry. I'll set up these pictures and leave straight afterwards."

Hearing her voice, Fang Buting felt a complex mixture of emotions: affection, indifference and helplessness, all wrapped up in one.

The woman who responded to Mengwei's tirade was trying to place a framed photo on the cupboard against the north wall. From behind, her hair looked neatly combed, her dress smart and her overall appearance elegant. She looked to be in her early thirties.

Her name was Cheng Xiaoyun, and she was the second wife of Fang Buting. "Where is the young master of the Fang family?" she asked.

Finally, Fang Mengwei uttered these terrible words: "My mother died ten years ago. What do you mean by 'young master'?"

Cheng Xiaoyun did not respond, and she stopped wiping the glass frame of the photo with her handkerchief.

In that photo, a woman's eyes were looking at her, as she looked back. The photograph, taken eleven years ago, now came into view. Next to the woman sat Fang Buting, hugging a little girl who was happily playing the harmonica. Next to her stood a boy of sixteen or seventeen, who was more than 1.7 metres tall. Next to Fang Buting stood a boy who was about twenty centimetres shorter, aged eleven or twelve. The taller boy was obviously Fang Meng'ao, the shorter one was Fang Mengwei; both of them were wearing foreign suits and braces, and they were brimming with energy.

This photo was exactly the same as the one Fang Meng'ao pulled out of his wallet in the prison van, except that this one was enlarged. In addition, Fang Buting's face was not covered with adhesive tape. The absence of tape revealed his black hair parted to one side, and an expression on his face that showed he was in high spirits.

Fang Mengwei could not deal with the silence. He turned to the table in the living room. Without bothering to see what was inside the large suitcase, he closed the lid with all his strength.

He made such a loud noise that Fang Buting, standing in the corridor on the first floor, was momentarily stunned. He paused and expected his right-hand man come to his aid.

Fang Mengwei lifted the suitcase and walked to the living room door.

"Mengwei!" said the man who should have come forward long ago. His name was Xie Peidong and he had stepped out from the left side of the living room.

Fang Mengwei stopped.

Xie Peidong came over and said: "That's way too heavy." He took the suitcase from Mengwei.

Tears welled up in Cheng Xiaoyun's eyes.

Xie Peidong put the suitcase back on the table, stood behind her and whispered: "Sister-in-law, let me do it. Please go home."

Cheng Xiaoyun nodded.

Xie Peidong called out to someone outside the living room: "Get the car ready. Drive the lady home."

Cheng Xiaoyun turned around and walked towards the main entrance in a respectful manner. She stopped before Fang Mengwei and said: "Please tell your elder brother that I married your father after your mother died in the bombing."

Fang Mengwei did not look at her and nor did he make any response.

Cheng Xiaoyun took a small step and stopped, but she did not look back. "On the way to Chongqing," she added, "your father was very kind to me. We happened to meet each other by chance. Please also share this fact with the master." With that, she strode out of the courtyard, followed by Mrs Wang.

Xie Peidong went on to rearrange the photographs around the living room, which soon radiated with images of Fang Meng'ao and Fang Mengwei, along with their mother and sister.

While this was happening, Fang Mengwei had chosen to sit by the table. "I don't know what Dad was thinking. Why does the sad past have to be displayed at this time of reunion? Did he really mean to make it so heart-wrenching for my big brother?"

Fang Buting stood looking out of the corridor window on the first floor. Who could know what was on his mind and how he felt at this moment?

"Your big brother may not be the person you think he is." Xie Peidong's voice came from the living room on the ground floor. "On the contrary, it's you who is messing things up. Don't embarrass the governor any more. Actually, he was hiding in Mulan's room early in the morning because he was afraid you would argue with your stepmother. If you are to observe filial piety, Mengwei, you should abide by the old rules today."

Facing the window, Fang Buting's back shook a little in response to the touching words he had just heard.

"Yes," answered Fang Mengwei respectfully. He admired his uncle greatly. He went to the phone in the living room and dialled a number.

"Can I speak to Mr Li?... Did you find out where they put up the Peking Youth Aviation Brigade?"

On the other end of the line, someone spoke.

"Well, that sounds good," said Fang Mengwei. "Thanks for the hard work. I told Commissioner Xu I can't make it tonight. You guys just enjoy the dinner party and make sure he's well entertained."

Fang Buting gazed out of the window at the night skyline of Peking. He saw rooftops all around.

He searched for Princess Hejing's former residence, but saw only rooftops hidden among the trees. Where was the brigade staying? When could he meet that elder son of his who had been sent to investigate the corruption case?

A train whistle in the distance brought him back to the present. It was a passenger train enshrouded in black smoke pulling into Peking railway station. His eyes radiated with a frightening and precipitous chill.

On the platform of Nanking railway station, a passenger train billowing white smoke was about to depart. A sign on the side of a central carriage read "Nanking-Peking". Amid the hustle and bustle, two pairs of menacing eyes were fixed on Cui Zhongshi who was ready to board the sleeping carriage with his suitcase. Cui was followed by two boys also carrying suitcases, and wearing student uniforms made of quality material. They looked like the schoolchildren of rich families.

The two men handed tickets over to the conductor in order to be assigned their seat numbers. It turned out that they were the two young agents monitoring Cui Zhongshi in Room 209 of the Jinling Hotel.

All the passengers were now on board, and as the conductor boarded too, the doors were closed. As the train whistle blew, its huge wheels began to turn.

"Which train did Cui Zhongshi take?" asked Fang Buting from behind his office desk. He was wearing a traditional Chinese robe and mandarin jacket.

"Train Number One. It departs from Nanking at two-thirty this afternoon and arrives in Peking at five-thirty tomorrow evening." Fang Mengwei might normally be a filial son while alone with his father, but today it looked as if he was a little agitated.

Fang Buting sighed as he looked out of the window, before bursting out: "When a disciple asked him how to be filial, Confucius replied: 'Be submissive to your parents.' This means one must obey one's parents from the bottom of one's heart. Since you are unhappy in your own heart, you do not have to pretend to be filial in front of me."

"Father," cried Fang Mengwei, no longer able to suppress his grievance. "For ten years, your own son could not see you, and I could not see my own brother. And now he's become a Communist suspect, to be investigated by the Iron and Blood Congress! I also work against the Commies as part of the paramilitary police force. Aren't you making things too complicated? I simply find all this hard to accept. You had that woman bring home pictures of my mother and sister today and set them up in the living room. Are you doing this to fight the Commies, the Iron and Blood Congress or my elder brother? You're right to teach me about filial piety. I'm not a good son. But who can be a good son in the current circumstances?"

Fang Buting looked at his younger son in a strange way, but his tone was surprisingly peaceful: "Yes, I've had to fight the Commies, the Nationalists and even my own son at home. I earned a Ph.D. in Economics from Harvard University, and wrote my thesis on Marxist economics. Who could have predicted I'd be applying my economics studies to factional fighting in China!"

Fang Mengwei lowered his head and said nothing more.

"I love my country," Fang Buting continued. "I love my hometown of Wuxi. I've been dreaming about fishing in Taihu Lake these past few days. But it's all dreams. Mengwei, this country and this family won't accommodate us. Go to America. After all, my alma mater and former classmates are there. I don't want to fight anyone over those photos, but I must tell you that my biggest wish is to take you to America. The biggest regret of my life is that I couldn't take your mother and sister to America. That's all." In saying these words, the man whose heart was deeper than the sea had tears in his eyes.

Fang Mengwei knelt on the floor and tried to hold back his own tears. He said: "As long as my beloved father can enjoy his twilight years, we'll be quite all right. Don't you think?"

Fang Buting looked at the son he loved most. "I've lost your mother and your sister. I can't afford to lose my sons. Without them, what is there to enjoy in my old age? Your stepmother has been living outside this house to avoid conflict with you. Moreover, for the sake of you and your brother, your stepmother has had two abortions. You should not have treated her that way. Now your big brother has arrived in Peking, and Cui Zhongshi will also return tomorrow… God only knows what kind of old age I'll end up enjoying."

Almost immediately, Fang Mengwei stood up and said: "Dad, I'm going to the barracks. I must bring my elder brother home today. Let's have a reunion dinner."

With that, Fang Mengwei picked up his hat from the tea table and strode out.

"Younger Brother!" said Xie Mulan as she saw Fang Mengwei make his way out. She ran up to him and went on: "Are you going to pick up my elder brother?"

Fang Mengwei saw He Xiaoyu standing next to the living room table. He greeted her while trotting downstairs, but ignored Xie Mulan.

"We're coming, too!" said Xie Mulan, chasing after him.

Fang Mengwei stopped by the living room door. "Why do you have to get involved in everything? When can you stop giving me trouble?"

"You want to see my big brother, and so do I. How is that giving you trouble?"

"Let me remind you again. Don't think your connection to me will exempt you from punishment for getting involved in the student protests. And don't even think about using my elder brother's name. You'll regret it because no one can save you when you get in trouble again." With that, he left Xie Mulan behind and stormed out of the front yard.

"We represent justice! It's not trouble we're making," she called out in the direction of the disappearing Fang Mengwei. "It's a cry for justice!"

Xie Mulan stamped her feet in anger.

"Mulan," He Xiaoyu whispered behind her, "he's your cousin, not the police chief. We do not fight him at home. Let's think how to help your uncle reconcile with your big brother when he comes back." At this point, she lowered her voice even more. "We'll have a lot to ask, too."

At the long, narrow table on the west side of the living room leading to the kitchen, Xie Peidong was still quietly wiping the photo frames. He did not bother to turn around when he heard his daughter arguing with her cousin. Then he walked quietly to the kitchen with the dirty white handkerchief, as if the disagreement had nothing to do with him.

Ma Hanshan had never before suffered from the consequences of his own poor decision-making.

Since Fang Meng'ao had given up Princess Hejing's residence to the exiled students from the Northeast, Ma Hanshan had shown the pilots two other decent compounds. But Fang Meng'ao did not get off the bus; instead, he insisted on staying at a warehouse located between Yenching University and Tsinghua University.

Luckily, he remembered an army barracks where a battalion of the Fourth Corps of the Nationalist Army used to be stationed. The barracks had recently been vacated because the battalion was deployed in another location. Ma Hanshan had no choice but to accommodate Fang Meng'ao and his brigade there.

With his pilots assembled behind him, Fang Meng'ao stood at the door, looking at the interior of the deserted barracks that was more than a hundred metres in length. It contained a large space with bunk beds for soldiers on both sides and a separate bedroom in the rear. It was a good fit and a ready-made place for his brigade to stay.

"Director Ma," demanded Fang Meng'ao, "didn't we agree that we'd be put up at the warehouse belonging to the Citizens' Food-Distribution Committee? Why did you take us here?"

The warehouse to which he referred happened to be a sub-supply unit under the supervision of the Peking Citizens' Food-Distribution Committee for the college students. Since there was so much deception going on at the warehouse, Ma Hanshan wouldn't let them stay in the deserted barracks.

Seeing Fang Meng'ao so insistent, Ma Hanshan pretended to have a guilty conscience: "These barracks are hardly an ideal place for you and your brigade members to stay, let alone that shabby warehouse. Captain Fang, I feel deeply ashamed. You're all national heroes and valiant soldiers of the party-state. I have specific orders from my superiors that you're entitled to royal treatment. They'd hold me accountable if you were poorly accommodated, say, in a warehouse!"

Guo Jinyang, the pilot with the shaven head, snapped: "Isn't it outrageous, Director Ma? We all attended the aviation academy after victory in the War of Resistance. How come you call us national heroes?"

"There's no doubt your captain is a real national hero! Since you follow him, it's natural that you'll be treated as a heroic national brigade."

"The Japanese surrendered three years ago," Fang Meng'ao interjected. "Who has the guts to call themselves national heroes? Besides, we were just tried by the military court yesterday. How come you, Director Ma, now regards us as war heroes of the party-state? Who gives you the power to rehabilitate us?"

With that, he turned to the pilots. "Here we are, close to both Tsinghua and Yenching! And it shouldn't be far from the warehouse of the Citizens' Food-Distribution Committee. Go pick your own spot and clean it up. Let's get started."

Fang Meng'ao went in first, followed by other members of the brigade.

Ma Hanshan stamped his feet at the door again. Addressing the driver who followed him, he asked: "Where are the logistics people? Where's the bedding for everyone? And the office supplies for

Captain Fang? By the way, the food, why hasn't it been delivered yet?"

The driver of the car, part of his close entourage, replied: "I've called the Distribution Committee's Logistics Department. They'll deliver it right away."

Fortunately, the phone in the guard room at the gates of the barracks had not yet been taken away. Ma Hanshan picked up the phone and dialled an important number.

The person at the other end was Ma Linshen, who was responsible for the day-to-day running of the Peking Citizens' Food-Distribution Committee, and deputy director of the central government's Citizens' Food-Distribution Committee and one of the five-member working group.

Since early in the morning Ma Linshen had been feeling unfairly treated, and now he resorted to whining: "I've been dealing with the Ministry of Defence, the Iron and Blood folks, Director Dai of the Central Bureau of Investigation and Statistics, and Madam Chiang. None of them were so arrogant! Look at what they did out there on the street today. It was directed against not only the Citizens' Food-Distribution Committee, but also the party-state. If you ask me, Fang Meng'ao is a Commie! The Ministry of Defence is employing a Commie. You must speak up, I mean, report to Mr Soong, to Mr Kung..."

"Shut up! Shut your fucking mouth!" The voice at the other end was so sharp and loud that Ma was shocked. Clearly, this mysterious person was rather annoyed by what Ma Hanshan had just said. Ma had no option but to continue listening, even though his eyes glared with anger and he pretended to spit into the microphone, knowing full well that the person at the other end could not see him.

The voice at the other end said: "You can't even handle a bunch of kids. Mr Soong and Mr Kung would be ashamed of you. Do you think they can be bothered to deal with a trivial thing like this? If you can't get the job done, hand over the accounts. I've got an endless stream of people ready to take over from you."

The person at the other end of the line slammed the phone down. An equally angry Ma Hanshan also hung up. He stood there wondering who to pin the blame on.

It happened that a jeep had just made a turn into the compound followed by two military trucks covered in camouflaged fabric. Ma Hanshan stomped out of the guard room and stood in the middle of the road before the main entrance. The jeep stopped with a screech, and so did the two trucks behind.

Ma Hanshan burst out cursing: "You motherfucking bastards! Why are you so fucking late? Have you been drinking or sniffing around brothels!"

There was no response from inside the jeep. Instead, the two section chiefs of the Citizens' Food-Distribution Committee jumped out from the cab of the trucks behind and walked hurriedly towards him.

One of the section chiefs said: "Director, it makes no sense for you to get so angry. It did take us a while to find this location, to place a call for supplies and to put everything together. We managed to get the supplies delivered in an hour. Has the delay really caused any problems?"

It seemed that there was no proper discipline at the Citizens' Food-Distribution Committee, where the superiors could scold their subordinates, only for the subordinates to talk back in defiance.

Ma Hanshan was shocked by the sharp response, wondering how to scold him in return. The other section chief tried to restrain him by pulling his shirt.

"Mr Li, no more talking back. The director has not eaten anything since early morning."

"No more meals for either of you tomorrow!" It was a sharp and authoritative bark. "Two million people in Peking are starving! Now it's your turn. You and your families. What gives you bastards the cheek to talk back to me? Li Wuzhi, if you can't do your job, submit your resignation letter. I've got plenty of people queueing for your position!"

Surprisingly, Li continued to defy him: "Director Ma, you're the director of the Civil Affairs Bureau, while I've been transferred from the Social Security Bureau. In fact, I was appointed by the director of the distribution committee on which you serve only as deputy director."

"Well done! Well said!" said Ma Hanshan, whose face had turned even darker with anger. "Deputy Director Ma of the Central Commission on Citizens' Food Distribution has arrived today. I'll meet him later. Let's see who it is you're going to listen to. Is it this lowly local official or the deputy director of the Central Commission I'm about to meet? I swear I'll strip you of all your positions."

Li had become so scared that he stopped talking back. Even so, he felt reluctant to apologise.

The other section chief came to his aid: "I say Comrade Li, why is it so hard for you to take Director Ma's criticism? Just say 'sorry'. The Youth Aviation Brigade is expecting our supplies."

"Director," Li said to Ma Hanshan apologetically, "it's all my fault. If you want me to resign, just give me one last chance to carry out your instructions before I go."

Ma Hanshan felt half relieved now that he was done with his scolding and Li had made his apology. "Go ahead," he instructed. "Get the trucks in and distribute the supplies." He then looked at the jeep that was blocking the way. Again, he was about to release his pent-up anger at the man still sitting in the jeep.

Ma Hanshan walked up to the jeep and said: "You bloody son of a bitch! Get your arse out of there, and out of the way. Move! Move! Now!"

The back door of the jeep opened, and a man got out. He quickly walked up to Ma Hanshan and asked: "Director Ma, who are you referring to as 'a bloody son of a bitch'?"

Ma Hanshan was dumbfounded. How could he have expected the man in the jeep to be Fang Mengwei!

CHAPTER 5

Another reason why Ma Hanshan failed to recognise Fang Mengwei when he was cursing was that Fang was out of uniform. Instead, on his way to the army barracks, he had changed into his work clothes, that of the secretary general of the Peking chapter of the Youth League of the Three Principles of the People. Through the window, Ma Hanshan mistakenly assumed he was a staff member of the Citizens' Food-Distribution Committee.

Although Fang Mengwei was young, his personal experience was quite unique, unmatched by his peers. He joined the Three Principles of the People early, before being transferred to its Peking chapter to become secretary general of the Youth League. In 1947, the league was abolished and incorporated into the Nationalist Party. As a result, he was transferred to the position of deputy director of the Peking Police Bureau and simultaneously, deputy director of the investigation department of the Police Garrison headquarters. As he stood in front of Ma Hanshan, a towering young man about 1.8 metres tall, it was more than just his physical stature that made him remarkable. His eyes shone with a determination that was a product of his years as a member of the Nationalist Party, the government, the military and the police that Ma Hanshan sensed would be unwise to test. Indeed, it took him quite a while to recover his poise. Moreover, he happened to be Fang Buting's son, and Fang Meng'ao's brother!

"Really! What a son of a bitch!" Ma Hanshan was quite adept at finding himself an excuse. He immediately turned to his two subordinates and scolded them again. "You quarrelled with me as soon as you arrived without reporting to me about Deputy Director Fang's visit. It doesn't look like you're qualified for the positions at all! Submit your letters of resignation when you're done here!"

The other section chief called Wang protested: "Director, I find your criticism unacceptable. You gave us a severe reprimand for being late as soon as we arrived. How could we interrupt you and report to you about his visit?"

"Yes you're right, it's all my fault. Both of you are such hardworking officials," Ma Hanshan replied sarcastically. "But remember this, you'll be subject to disciplinary punishment when you get back to the bureau."

Ma Hanshan spluttered with indignation in saying these words. Then his voice became an angry roar: "Now, go drive the trucks and give the supplies to Captain Fang. You can't expect me to reward you now, can you?"

The two section chiefs were sweating, confused and resentful, but had no choice but to go to the trucks.

Wang walked over to Fang Mengwei's jeep to greet the driver and ask him to move the truck to one side. Li went up to the two military trucks and shouted at the driver of the one in front. The truck started. Li, instead of sitting in the cab, jumped on to the running board. He stood there firmly, his hands grasping the wing mirror. As if to vent his spleen or simply to show his loyalty and diligence, he rode into the compound on the truck, his short-cropped hair standing erect against the wind.

Wang was too fat to leap onto any truck and did not have Li's skills, so he had to motion to stop the second truck. With a bitter expression on his face and one eyebrow raised, he climbed into the cab.

The second driver slammed on the accelerator to follow the first truck. Without his subordinates alongside, Ma Hanshan began to explain to Fang Mengwei the misunderstanding that led to his act of rudeness. In fact, by seriously reprimanding his two subordinates, he had completed more than half of his mission tonight. His remaining goal was to turn the negative into a positive, and that involved securing the help of Fang Mengwei.

Ma Hanshan pulled out a Cuban cigar tube from his bulging Zhongshan suit pocket. He opened it to reveal a single cigar of the highest grade. Knowing that Fang Meng'ao liked smoking cigars, he planned to offer it to him when they met. He was afraid to show it to anyone on his way to the barracks. Now, he was ready to hand it to Fang Mengwei.

"My mind has been really messed up. How could I possibly not have thought Deputy Director Fang would come to visit his elder brother? You see, I totally forgot the fact that I was planning to give the cigar to Captain Fang of the brigade. Deputy Director Fang, please give it to Captain Fang on my behalf when the two of you meet."

Fang Mengwei deeply respected his parents. To him, uttering a profanity against them constituted a serious offence. Just now Ma Hanshan's use of the phrase "son of a bitch" implicated his parents. Although he tried to explain that he was not referring to his parents, it was clear that Man Hanshan was certainly addressing him at that moment. So he must settle accounts with him. Without looking at the hand that was holding the cigar tube in front of him, he stared into his eyes and said: "Director Ma, were you born to your parents?"

Ma Hanshan did not expect Fang Buting's younger son to be even more stubborn than his elder one. He found himself speechless.

"Why curse like that?" Fang Mengwei continued. "Are you really a son of a 'bitch'?"

By now, Ma Hanshan had figured out that Fang Mengwei had actually long been regarded in the police headquarters as a filial son. Had he realised earlier, he would have known how to calm him down. "That's my stupid fault. My parents died early. Please excuse my poor breeding. Deputy Commissioner Fang, please don't take it to heart."

"You parents' early death doesn't mean you were destined to be raised badly. My mother also died early, so does that mean I'm a man of poor breeding, too?"

Ma Hanshan stamped his feet in frustration. "Deputy Commissioner Fang, if you're angry, just feel free to vent it on me. A fortune teller advised me on the first day of this year that I might have bad luck in the months ahead, so just do whatever you want to take it out on me."

Since Fang Mengwei was quite a reasonable man, and having been used to dealing with all kinds of Nationalist party members, he could not very well continue his reprimand. But he had to let Ma Hanshan know the disgust he felt deep in his heart.

"I have to be straight with you. I'm here on business, there's no 'family' dealings here. We also have an obligation to investigate the shady business of your Citizens' Food-Distribution Committee. By the way, our new Director Xu is on the five-member investigation team. I'm here to complete the task he assigned me. Put away your cigar."

With that, he turned to his jeep. The engine started and the jeep drove off in the direction of the military trucks.

Standing in the sun, Ma Hanshan suddenly remembered something. He ran to the guard room at the gate, and went straight to the phone and dialled the number. He held the receiver for just a few seconds before the operator picked up his call.

Ma began with his customary profanity: "You son of a tortoise! Why's there no operator on duty? Find out who's going to host the dinner party this evening on behalf of Director Xu, the new chief of the Peking Police Bureau, and which restaurant they're going to. Tell me now!"

There was also an awkward situation in the Youth Aviation Brigade's barracks.

Eight years of fighting the Japanese followed by three years of civil war had resulted in a severe shortage of goods thanks to a failure on the part of the Nationalist government to rebuild the economy. By 1948, many cities were running out of food, so the Citizens' Food-Distribution Committee was set up. By "citizens' food", what was actually meant was everything needed for living, including special supplies allocated to the military, government and education. They were all distributed by this committee. The trucks were loaded not only with bedding and daily necessities, but also items rarely seen now in China such as tobacco, alcohol, coffee, radios, jukeboxes and aftershave. This is how it came to be known that Captain Fang enjoyed a Western lifestyle. And this was why the bribes offered by two section heads were certain to be rejected.

Fang Meng'ao was in a separate bedroom in the rear part of the barracks when the two section chiefs, together with a number of his subordinates, started carrying in boxes. It was hard work and their heads were dripping with sweat. Stopped at the gate, the boxes were examined by Chen Changwu and Guo Jinyang, who refused to accept most of the items.

"Apart from sleeping, bathing and cleaning items, please take everything else back," Chen Changwu said with a firm tone.

Li knew that if he took these items back, he would not escape a severe scolding even if he managed to retain his post. He responded without thinking: "These are to be given to the brothers in the brigade. We are instructed by our superiors to do so. It's absolutely not possible to take them back."

The pilots looked at each other mischievously. Apparently, they were thinking of how to make fun of this greedy bunch.

"Really, it is making things difficult," said Guo Jinyang, coming up close to Li. "Sir, please look at my hands." As he spoke, he stretched out his hands for him to check.

Li did not know what he meant, and just stared at his hands.

"Do you think my ten fingers are clean?" asked Guo Jinyang.

Mistakenly thinking that he was referring to corruption, Li hurriedly replied: "Our aviation service brigade is widely known as strictly disciplined. It has always been clean."

"Don't make things complicated. I'm just asking you if my fingers are clean. Just tell me if they're clean or not!"

Embarrassed, Li checked his fingers once again. He found that the index finger of his left hand and the tip of his middle finger were a little yellow. But he could not very well say as much.

"Of course they're clean."

"Brothers, all of you, show this gentleman your hands!" Guo Jinyang called out to the pilots.

Everyone from all corners of the barracks cooperated by stretching out their hands.

Again, Guo Jinyang asked Li: "Are the hands of our brothers clean?"

Li looked at Wang as if for help, but could not help wondering what those arrogant pilots were up to. He was reluctant to make a quick response.

"Are our hands dirty?" said a usually expressionless pilot with a deep, mellow voice, his face cold with impatience.

Li looked at Wang who replied with a smile: "Sorry, sorry, all of you have clean hands."

The pilot who challenged Li continued to stare at him.

"What did you say?" asked the pilot.

"Of course, they're clean," Li answered reluctantly.

The pilots looked at Guo Jinyang, who nodded in return. Everyone put their hands back.

Guo Jinyang said to Li again: "Let me take another look."

Li held out his hands uncertainly. The index and middle fingers of both hands were yellow and black.

"Look, all our ten fingers are clean, sir, whereas four of your fingers are stained as a result of smoking," said Guo Jinyang. "You must be a chain smoker, right?"

Li understood this was a set-up, but replied: "It may be a bad habit, but having a little addiction doesn't harm anyone else, does it? None of you smoke at all?"

"That's something we can't accept," said Guo Jinyang, becoming angry. "Our hands are clean because none of us smoke. You just said these items were given to us according to the rules, and that we could throw them out if we had no use for them. You're more than generous with daily necessities for the people. But we won't blame you for that. Now that these items are in such short supply, you must be running out of cigars. Since none of us smoke, we'll give these cartons to you. We're not breaking any rules, are we?"

"OK," said Li, realising that he could not fight them. "We'll take back these cases."

"I've told you to take them all back except for the daily necessities," said an impatient Chen Changwu. "Why make such a fuss?"

Guo Jinyang stared at Li in disgust. "Do you want my brothers to take off their clothes and let you inspect them before you take those things away?" As he spoke, he began to take off his jacket and reveal his impressively firm stomach muscles.

Standing where they were, the other pilots were poised to take off their clothes.

Li and Wang looked at each other. Wang would never take the initiative to speak up.

"It would be no big deal getting scolded again back in the office," said Li, who was also a man of determination, quite capable of making a prompt decision. "Why are you standing there doing nothing? Do as you're told. Take what they don't need back to the trucks."

Fang Meng'ao was having a smoke in the single room in the rear of the barracks. He was lost in thought when his attention was drawn to events taking place outside. He laughed along with the pilots who were making a scene. Before finishing the cigar, he pulled out another and lit it. As he smoked, he listened to the conversation outside and laughed.

Laughing accentuated his good looks. His team members laughed like he did, that is, they laughed to be handsome.

Sure enough, laughter could be heard once more from outside his bedroom. Fang Meng'ao stood up and was ready to walk out of the room.

All of a sudden, the laughing stopped, and so did Fang Meng'ao. All eyes were on the man in the doorway. Though wearing different facial expressions, the pilots shared one sense in common, which was a strong sense of disgust.

The man in the doorway, whom the pilots identified as a member of the Citizens' Food-Distribution Committee, was carrying two large boxes. The writing was all in English, but it was still easy enough to make out that one case contained red wine and the other cigars.

"Excuse me, is Captain Fang Meng'ao here?" What set this young man apart from the former group was the dignified manner in which he behaved. However, what surprised them was that as soon as he opened his mouth, he demanded that the bribes be given to their captain.

The pilots looked at each other in disbelief. How strange that this practice had become the new normal in Peking.

Standing in the room, Fang Meng'ao flashed his eyes, which was something he only did when he was extremely excited. He heard the question that came from outside his room. Although it was not the childish voice of the thirteen-year-old he last saw ten years ago, he was quite sure it belonged to his younger brother. His eyes turned to the doorway. The way he wrung his hands and stretched his legs were reminiscent of the figure who dashed to the control tower at Hangzhou Jianqiao airbase. But this time around his power was concentrated between the thumb and index finger of his right hand – the burning cigar was pinched out, the ash falling to the ground.

He stood there listening, curious to see how his younger brother interacted with the pilots. After all, it had been ten years.

Fang Mengwei stood in front of the doorway for two or three minutes. He gave a shout, yet they responded by giving him the cold shoulder as if they were under instructions. Didn't he want to see me even though he knew I was in the room? Holding the two boxes, he twisted his body as if intending to go back. Then, he turned around and strode into the barracks.

He was instantly blocked by three or four brigade members, as Guo Jinyang stretched out his hands and showed him his fingers. The other pilots who blocked his way did the same.

Not knowing the meaning behind their actions, Fang Mengwei looked at those cold eyes in surprise.

"Don't you understand? Or do you think you're smarter than we are?" Guo Jinyang demanded.

Fang Mengwei put the boxes down on the floor. "No, I really don't. Just tell me if my brother wants to see me."

At this, Guo Jinyang and his fellow soldiers gazed at one another in disbelief. It now occurred to them that the captain had a younger brother who served as deputy director of the Municipal Police Bureau, someone whom the captain occasionally referred to as "the most dearly loved".

Chen Changwu sized up Fang Mengwei and asked: "Excuse me, are you Deputy Director Fang Mengwei?"

"I am Fang Mengwei, younger brother of your captain."

Trying hard to find a way to make amends, Guo Jinyang shouted: "Salute!" He raised his arm and saluted.

Standing where they were, the other members of the brigade raised their hands and saluted him. It was this gesture that made Fang Mengwei's eyes slowly moisten with tears. His heart was aching. Yet within this brief moment of silence, Fang Meng'ao's figure appeared from the door of the single room. It was so absurdly sad that they had failed to bridge their divide over a period of ten years. As Fang Meng'ao walked towards his brother, he noticed the tears in his eyes.

Just three metres away from Mengwei, Meng'ao stopped abruptly to look at the brigade members who were saluting with their palms pressed to the sides of their heads. "Put them down. He's just a kid. Stop it."

"Yes sir!" said Guo Jinyang, and they all stood at ease. Fang Meng'ao then went up to Fang Mengwei once more. As if to size him up, he looked him up and down from head to foot, and then from foot to head. His eyes narrowed, and he smiled in a way that his brigade members had never seen before: "Look, who is taller, him or me?"

No one answered, and a few of the more sentimental brigade members already had tears in their eyes. Fang Meng'ao bent down and opened a case containing twenty-four bottles of red wine arranged in four rows. He pulled out a bottle and inspected it. "Yes, French. The real thing." Then he tore open the other box which was full of metal cigar boxes.

Fang Meng'ao took out four bottles of wine and handed them over to Fang Mengwei. "Take them for me," he said.

Fang Mengwei took the bottles without thinking.

Fang Meng'ao took out four boxes of cigars from the other box. "One bottle of wine per person, one box of cigars. Let's share them." With that, he picked up four boxes of cigars along with a military blanket and a mat, and walked towards his single room in the back.

Fang Mengwei was so overwhelmed that he remained standing with the wine in his hands. Chen Changwu smiled at Fang Mengwei and motioned him to follow his elder brother into the separate bedroom.

The pilots looked at the two open boxes. It was Guo Jinyang again who was the first to rush up to snatch the cigars and wine. The rest of them piled in and caused a commotion.

As soon as Fang Meng'ao threw his roll of bedding on the bed, he took out a cigar from one of the boxes, lit it and started smoking. Then he took out another and handed it to Fang Mengwei.

"Brother," said Fang Mengwei, "I do not smoke, and nor do I drink."

"New Life Movement?" asked Fang Meng'ao.

"No, I'm not following the herd. At first, my father wouldn't allow me to smoke or drink. Then, later, I found it all quite a drag. I feel bad when I drink and cough if I smoke."

"Then why did you repeatedly ask Mr Cui to bring me cigars and wine?" Fang Meng'ao continued.

Fang Mengwei became silent. When he looked up again at his elder brother, he turned quite emotional: "With you down there all alone, I was hoping that the wine and cigars might help beat the loneliness, especially over the past three years when you were suspended from flying. As for Dad, he felt a little guilty about his previous actions although he had some legitimate concerns."

When the discussion came to their father, the look on Fang Meng'ao's face changed. Fang Mengwei decided to stop speaking about what was on his mind.

Fang Meng'ao strode to the door of the room and instructed the pilots: "Make the beds and clean up! For supper, let's eat biscuits washed down with cold water."

Fang Mengwei's heart saddened. As soon as his brother turned around, he went to open the bed roll and spread it out on his bed.

Fang Meng'ao did not stop him. He sat in his chair, smoked the cigar and watched his brother make the bed.

Fang Mengwei seemed to have grown into a decent person, at least not like the incumbent corrupt deputy director of the Peking Police Bureau. After making the bed, he wrung out a wet rag and scrubbed the mat diligently.

"Nationalists can't accomplish anything, yet they do have a clear sense of how to categorise people in a hierarchy," said Fang Meng'ao. "This bed used to belong to a battalion commander in the Kuomintang's Central Army. Strangely enough, it was a bronze bed, two metres wide at least. I don't know how many women that guy slept with here. Clean it up. You can sleep here tonight, too."

Fang Mengwei stopped scrubbing the mat, and then started

again. He replied softly: "All right, I'll spend the night here talking with my big brother."

Fang Meng'ao grew silent. He knew what his brother had come for and intended to say so in order to stop him from making the request. However, he didn't expect his brother could be so obedient. Like the events that occurred ten years before, a wave of love emanated from his heart.

Fang Meng'ao stubbed out his cigar in the ashtray, stood up and spoke to his brother for the first time with a smile. "This bed is not where you'll sleep. I've been sleeping alone for ten years and have never shared a bed with another man. If I'm going to share a bed with anyone, that person must be your future sister-in-law. Now, are you going to keep talking all night? Stop making the bed. Let's go home. I'm starving."

Fang Mengwei stood up and turned around. He looked at his elder brother in disbelief.

"Well, haven't you come here to pick me up?" asked Fang Meng'ao.

"The car is waiting outside," said Fang Mengwei, quickly coming to his senses.

"Shall I drive? Sit next to me. Let me take the opportunity to familiarise myself with the streets of Peking." Fang Meng'ao picked up his cigars from the table and walked out of the room.

Fang Mengwei smiled for the first time after meeting his elder brother and quickly followed him out.

After arriving in Peking, the five-member investigation team into the Fifth of July Incident chose not stay in any military or political building. Instead, they selected a courtyard mansion on Zhang Zizhong Road. They were allowed to set up base there by the property's owner, Gu Weijun, then the Kuomintang's ambassador to the United States. There were three reasons: first, since Gu himself and his family were in America, the home was vacant; second, by living there, they could be free from any interference from the relevant authorities involved in the case; third, and most important, Dr Sun Yat-sen died here in 1924, and by selecting the residence as the headquarters for the investigation, it demonstrated a determination to carry the mission out until its end in order to assuage the spirit of the former prime minister.

The mansion and its grounds covered ten acres and contained more than two hundred rooms, complete with gloriettes, pavilions, halls and buildings, all covered in the shade of towering trees and surrounded by fragrant flowers and chirping birds. Each of the five members stayed in a separate courtyard house. All meetings were arranged in the conference room next to the bedroom where the former premier died.

Of the five members, one stood out, and that was Xu Tieying. He had officially taken over as head of the Peking Police Bureau and director of the Investigation Department of the General Command of the Peking Police. Although allocated a courtyard house, as police chief he had to stay in a special residence most of the time. Of course, he also had to attend tonight's working dinner and meeting.

The five men sat around the conference table eating their dinner. Each had a bowl of congee, two small white steamed buns and two cornbread rolls, a plate each of salted and fried vegetables, and a boiled egg. At Zeng Keda's repeated request, all the relevant documents and major newspaper reports had been put on the dinner table. As a result, Zeng Keda could read while eating, while the other four members felt obliged to follow suit.

The investigation had not yet begun, and it was clear that the key note had been set by the Bureau of Reserve Cadres of the Ministry of Defence. It would be impossible for any person to work half-heartedly with Zeng Keda overseeing the whole process.

A soft voice came from outside the conference room window: "Director Xu, Director Xu." Everyone looked at Xu Tieying.

Zeng Keda chose to say nothing. He was slowly chewing the steamed cornbread, his eyes fixed on a document.

Xu Tieying stood up quietly, nodding to everyone to apologise for his temporary absence. He walked away and went out through the half-opened door.

The man who had called him was Sun, the secretary Xu Tieying had transferred to Peking from the Liaison Office of the Communications Bureau. He was standing under a tree near the staircase, about five metres from the conference room.

Xu Tieying stopped in the hallway by the door. "Come and speak to me here," he said.

Secretary Sun came up and whispered: "Director, the police bureau called, saying that cadres below deputy director level are waiting for your instructions. Since martial law has not yet been lifted, the Communist Party instigators and students are about to make more trouble according to our sources of information. They're expecting your instructions about how to respond."

Xu Tieying listened. This was exactly what he wanted – to let Sun speak near the conference room so that the other four participants could also hear. A few seconds later, he pushed open the door and went back in.

Before Xu Tieying could say anything, Ma Linshen, deputy director of the Central Commission on Citizens' Food Distribution spoke: "It's quite a serious matter. Go ahead, Director Xu."

Wang Benquan, chief secretary of the Central Bank, nodded his head. Du Wancheng, general auditor of the Ministry of Finance, remained impassive and looked up at Zeng Keda.

Zeng Keda continued chewing his cornbread and reading his papers without making a response. Xu Tieying addressed him: "Comrade Keda, please complete your review of the papers. I need to leave since the Communist Party may incite students into making trouble, and I'll have to make some arrangements back at the police bureau."

Zeng Keda finally looked up and said: "Of course, we can't allow them to cause any trouble, Director Xu. Please share with us all the information and brief us when you get back."

"I promise," Xu Tieying replied. "Everyone, please excuse me."

Zeng Keda finished his bowl of congee and bread. He then stood up and announced: "I'm afraid we won't be able to convene tonight's meeting. I suggest we split up and read the materials individually."

Ma Linshen and Wang Benquan concurred, while Du Wancheng, who was nominally the coordinator of the five-member group, thought about it, and then had to agree as well.

"In that case, let's do our homework first," he said, before turning to Zeng Keda. "I heard that the Youth Aviation Brigade spoke directly to the students as soon as they arrived in Peking, and gave up the accommodation that Peking Municipality had arranged for them to the students from the Northeast. Inspector General Zeng, they are under the command of the Bureau of Reserve Cadres. Please have someone look into the matter. It's better not to give the impression that we are divided over the issue."

Wang Benquan was a member of the Central Bank, while Ma Linshen was directly under the leadership of the Central Commission on Citizens' Food Distribution. Both of them were also aware of what the Youth Aviation Brigade had done upon their arrival in Peking, and while they were rather unhappy about it, they did not dare say anything. But when they heard Du Wancheng, the coordinator affiliated with the Ministry of Finance, describe the matter in the way he did, they began to wonder who he was referring to. They looked at each other, and then up at Zeng Keda.

"Let me investigate it first," said Zeng Keda. He left the conference room with the case file under his arm.

The two brothers stood by the gate and studied the family mansion. Since Fang Meng'ao did not approach any closer, Fang Mengwei had to wait patiently.

A middle-aged servant opened the door. He stood quietly waiting inside the compound gate, from which there were only a few tall trees that lined the pebbled driveway leading to the building, around which there was a large lawn. All the servants were under instructions not to greet the returning son, yet many eyes were looking out from distant windows.

Instead of standing in front of the window, Fang Buting remained sitting at his large desk, staring blankly ahead. He seemed to be listening to what was going on outside. All was relatively quiet.

Fang Meng'ao's eyes lit up all of a sudden. He saw two umbrellas patterned with peach blossoms appear to float out of the building. The umbrellas, however, were not being used to provide protection from the glaring sun; instead they were tilted towards the front to hide the identity of the people underneath. But the skirts and shoes of the girls were visible; they came gliding towards him with the umbrellas.

A smile could be detected at the corner of Fang Mengwei's mouth. Sometimes Xie Mulan was a source of wind and rain in this dry and lifeless house.

Fang Meng'ao realised that the faces behind the umbrellas belonged to Xie Mulan, a cousin whom he had already met but only talked with briefly in front of Princess Hejing's former residence, and He Xiaoyu, with whom he had spent his childhood. He revealed his signature grin.

Suddenly, Fang Mengwei felt something flash past in front of him. It was his elder brother who was quickly disappearing into the distance. When he looked more closely, he could see his brother already standing in front of the two approaching umbrellas.

The girls' feet came to a stop as they were confronted by a pair of military shoes, which were visible under their umbrellas.

Underneath the two umbrellas, Xie Mulan looked at He Xiaoyu and He Xiaoyu returned the gaze.

"My fair ladies, present your flowers as well as your treasures," said a smiling Fang Meng'ao, who had seen through their tricks.

"You're awful! Such a killjoy!" Xie Mulan lowered the umbrella to reveal a bouquet of flowers that she had intended to give him. She jumped into Fang Meng'ao's arms, put her hands around his neck and wrapped her legs around his waist. "Big Brother!"

Fang Meng'ao supported Xie Mulan's back with one hand. The other umbrella also lifted in front of him, as He Xiaoyu handed over her bouquet with a smile.

Fang Meng'ao took the flowers with his other hand and looked at her eyes that seemed so full of expression. But he did not know how to address her. It would be odd to call her "Miss", while impertinent to call her by her first name "Xiaoyu".

"Thank you," said Fang Meng'ao, getting round the problem by speaking in English with a heavy American accent. "So beautiful."

Xie Mulan refused to come down from Fang Meng'ao. Supported by his large hand on her back, she sat up straight and looked at him with her face almost pressed against his. "What is beautiful? Me or the flowers?"

"The flowers are beautiful." Fang Meng'ao's respect for women, especially for young women, had always been expressed in a subtle and considered way. Knowing that it was impolite to praise the beauty of a woman in a direct and straightforward manner, he would instead compare her favourably to the beauty of another object like a flower. With that, he looked most sincerely into the eyes of He Xiaoyu.

He Xiaoyu's reaction somewhat confounded Fang Meng'ao. His personality was such that many girls were shy but happy in his presence, so shy that they could no longer dare look at him. However, He Xiaoyu smiled back and offered a "thank you" in return.

"What a pleasant surprise! You're giving her the glad eye as soon as you meet her!" Xie Mulan had always been inclined to take a scene to the extreme. Obviously, she had been quite carried away by the fact that she was in Fang Meng'ao's arms. "What about me? Am I not pretty?" She let go of one hand and tried to put the flowers next to her face.

"Pretty, of course." Fang Meng'ao was never tired of making fun, and the smile on his face was full of mischief.

"But it had to be dragged out of you! I'm not coming down!" Xie Mulan became even more excited, because no boys ever teased her like her cousin.

Fang Mengwei appeared and asked: "Aren't you going to show my brother into the house?" Then he came up and admonished Xie Mulan the way he had done in the past. "And do please come down, you're no longer a small child."

Xie Mulan's enthusiasm was dampened. Just as she was about to slide down, Fang Meng'ao hugged her tight and said: "Don't listen to him. I'll carry you in." With that, and while still holding the flowers in one hand, he carried her with the other hand around her waist and walked with ease to the building entrance.

Xie Mulan loved being so close to her "big brother". She smiled cheekily at He Xiaoyu who was following behind, and looked at Fang Mengwei who was pretending to be serious. "Long live Big Brother!" she shouted.

The eyes hidden behind the windows around the compound were startled, because there had never before been such a day in the

Fang family. The sun was coming out, and the house would be full of vitality again.

Behind the lace window curtain in the governor's office, a pair of eyes witnessed all these events. The eyes had never before shone so bright, and they were fixed upon the strong arms of the elder son who was holding his niece, and upon his firm and powerful steps as if they were treading on his heart. By then he realised that the arm was not only holding Xie Mulan, but also his daughter who died in the plane crash ten years ago, as well as his wife who perished in the same disaster, and the countless people still suffering in this country. His eyes slowly dimmed again. He loosened his grip on the lace curtain as he saw his elder son turn and look in his direction. That pair of eagle eyes seemed to penetrate the curtain and see him standing there.

This elder son of his was an ace pilot that even the Americans admired. What could escape his gaze?

Among those who stepped into the hallway, the first to become nervous was Fang Mengwei. He held his breath, and quietly appraised his big brother. From where he was standing, he could see all the photos positioned around the living room.

He Xiaoyu also held her breath. Standing behind Fang Meng'ao, she was actually looking at Xie Mulan, who was still in the arms of her elder brother.

Xie Mulan was quiet and motionless in her brother's arms. Fang Meng'ao's arm loosened, and Xie Mulan carefully slid down from his embrace. Having lost some of her previous audacity, she now looked at him in a rather timid way.

Fang Meng'ao reached into his breast pocket and pulled out a piece of folded paper. He then took out the small picture originally hidden in his wallet, and went straight to the large photo frame on the cabinet in the centre of the living room.

All eyes were looking at him nervously.

Fang Meng'ao inserted the small picture in the lower left corner of the frame and turned around.

Fang Mengwei, Xie Mulan and He Xiaoyu all looked at the small picture. It was indeed the same image, except that the face of Fang Buting in the upper corner of the small photo was still covered by a piece of adhesive tape.

"Big Brother…" pleaded Fang Mengwei. Fang Meng'ao glanced at his younger brother and reached out to tear off the adhesive tape that had been attached to the little photo for so many years.

Fang Mengwei became so desperate that he lowered his head without uttering a word. Xie Mulan was also at a loss as to what to do. The same was true of He Xiaoyu, who was standing quietly to one side.

"Uncle!" Fang Meng'ao called out affectionately. All eyes were on Xie Peidong, who appeared at the kitchen door on the west side of the living room with a large plateful of steamed buns and cornbread.

Xie Peidong's eyes showed not only a familial look of care, but also the affection of the older generation towards a prodigal son.

Carrying the plate of steamed bread, Xie walked to Fang Meng'ao. He put the plate on the table, then took down the small picture inserted in the frame and went back to Fang Meng'ao. Fang Meng'ao wiped his clothes as if brushing away the dust that had gathered over the past ten years, then inserted the small picture back into the pocket of his jacket.

Xie Peidong carefully examined his nephew's face. "Don't say anything. You must be starving. Let's eat first." He turned to Xie Mulan and demanded: "Why don't you go to the kitchen and get the dishes out on the table? The only thing you can make is trouble."

Xie Mulan did not feel close to her own father, certainly not as close as to her uncle, but she was still quite obedient. "All right, Dad." She walked briskly to the kitchen on the west side of the building.

"Let her go alone," said Xie Peidong, preventing He Xiaoyu and Fang Mengwei from following her to the kitchen. "Why don't you two join Meng'ao in washing your hands?"

A porcelain basin was attached to one of the living room walls. There were several taps above the basin, including one in the shape of a lotus, which was specially designed for hand washing. Fang Meng'ao was very much like a child responding to his elders. He walked over to wash his hands. Fang Mengwei always felt awkward in He Xiaoyu's presence, and had to gesture in order to get her to wash her hands.

He Xiaoyu felt quite at ease. She walked over and washed her hands in the basin next to Fang Meng'ao. Fang Mengwei went over and washed his hands in another basin. Xie Peidong stood to one side, as if supervising his own children.

"It's so hot!" cried Xie Mulan, even before she emerged from the hallway leading to the living room. Xie Peidong quickly walked over and took the bowl from her.

"Why don't you use a towel? Really, you're not much use, are you? Wash your hands." Xie Mulan immediately went to join the others who were washing their hands.

"It smells so delicious," said Fang Meng'ao. "It's one of your specialties, isn't it?"

Xie Peidong smiled and said: "You may have forgotten plenty, but I'm sure you remember my braised meatballs with bamboo shoots."

"I've dreamed of eating that dish so many times." Xie Peidong smiled and went back to the kitchen.

The food and chopsticks had been set on the table, but the four youngsters didn't sit down, since one person was still absent. Or to be exact, it was the person they were most worried would not show up.

So a moment of silence ensued. Xie Mulan secretly looked at the east staircase and the door that was half open on the first floor.

From the kitchen, Xie Peidong carried a large pot of porridge to the dinner table. On the pot cover there was also a large plate of radish in soy sauce mixed with beans. "Why are you all standing? Sit down and eat."

Fang Meng'ao finally said what everyone else was afraid to hear: "There should be another person?"

Xie Peidong's eyes radiated a frightening quality as if he had the power to stop anything improper from happening. He looked at Fang Meng'ao firmly, and said: "Your father and I have already had our afternoon tea. Please go ahead. All of you, sit down and eat."

Fang Mengwei took the initiative by being the first to sit down. "Big Brother, let's eat first."

Xie Mulan chose to sit down opposite him. "Xiaoyu, let's sit on this side."

He Xiaoyu walked over, but stood by the chair waiting for Fang

Meng'ao to speak. Fang Meng'ao remained standing and said: "I insist. There should be another person."

The three young people stood gazing at one another, feeling confused.

Xie Peidong smiled. "You mean your stepmother?"

"Uncle, perhaps you're mistaken," said Fang Meng'ao. "Mother is mother, there's no such a thing as a stepmother."

The other three realised that Fang Meng'ao was referring to Cheng Xiaoyun, Fang Buting's second wife.

Fang Buting was alone in the governor's office on the first floor, sitting on the sofa by the door. The conversation between Fang Meng'ao and Xie Peidong just now made him stand up in disbelief, but what was revealed in his eyes was not gratification, but loss. The elder son was proving to be the most formidable fighter he had ever encountered. He sat back again, listening attentively to what might come from the living room beyond the door.

"Mrs Cai, Mrs Wang!" Xie Peidong shouted in the direction of the kitchen.

Mrs Cai and Mrs Wang, both wearing aprons, rushed out and looked at Fang Meng'ao with a smile of surprise. Mrs Cai, typical of a servant working for a rich family, followed convention by bowing slightly before Fang Meng'ao. "Hello, master," she said. "Our lord has made it a rule that the Fang family servants can only call the younger family members by their first names. What shall we call you in future?"

Fang Meng'ao immediately pressed his knees together and bowed to the two women. "Hello, Mrs Cai and Mrs Wang! This is not just the rule of the Fang family, we're all equals in this society. Call me Meng'ao in future, and I'll call you Cai Ma and Wang Ma."

Both servants smiled.

"Get the driver," said Xie Peidong, "and tell him to pick up the lady. Tell her Meng'ao is inviting her back for dinner. We're all expecting her. The sooner the better."

"Don't bother," said Fang Meng'ao, stopping Cai Ma and Wang Ma. "Mengwei, drive your car. Let's pick her up ourselves." With that, he went over to the living room door.

Not expecting this intervention, Fang Mengwei felt rather confused.

Xie Peidong threw a sidelong look at him and said: "Hurry up!"

Fang Mengwei had no alternative but to follow his brother out.

Xie Mulan ignored her father's presence and jumped with joy, while holding He Xiaoyu's hand. "He's such a good man. You'd be hard pressed to find better."

The Nationalists established their political and military centres in Nanking, their economic centre in Shanghai and their cultural centre in Peking. The first two centres were located in the south, while most of the liberated areas controlled by the Communist Party were situated in the north. Therefore, northern China, northwestern China and especially a large area in northeastern China had to be administered by a relatively strong local government in a major city, and Peking happened to be that major city. As a result, Peking had become something of a political and military centre in the north of the country. By the same token, Peking was heavily guarded by a massive military and police gendarmerie. Therefore, it was easy to understand the importance attached to the Municipal Police Bureau in Peking.

The former chief inspector should have stepped down long ago. Allegedly, he had been involved in various cases of corruption and public malpractice. He was regarded by the Nationalist authorities as irreplaceable because he was ruthless in the fight against the Communist Party, and especially because of the strong repression of progressive students and Communist sympathisers. In spite of strong public opposition, the man remained in power. The Fifth of July Incident shook the country, and the United States also intervened, so the chief inspector had to be removed from office. After a complicated election process, Xu Tieying was chosen. First, he had a long experience of combating the Communist Party, and second he was a member of the Central Bureau of Investigation and Statistics. As the new superintendent, Xu was also put in charge of a fresh campaign to preserve property owned by the Nationalist Party in the north where the ownership structure of the state, party and private individuals had become problematic.

Appointed at a time of crisis and amid much hardship, Xu

Tieying met with the five-member investigation team upon his arrival in Peking, and in the early evening he assumed his position as head of the Municipal Police Bureau.

One of the two deputies, Fang Mengwei, was at home and unable to show up due to special circumstances. Xu was accompanied into the conference room by the deputy inspector in charge of personnel matters. The deputy walked Xu Tieying and his secretary into the inspector's conference room.

"Chief Commissioner Xu!" the deputy chief announced when he was still outside the door. The directors, chiefs and captains, who were sitting on both sides of the long conference table, immediately stood up.

Xu Tieying smiled, went to the head of the long table and stood in front of the single empty seat. "Deputy Commissioner Shan, I'm expecting a proper introduction now."

Shan smiled humbly and said: "Sir, I don't know why, but Deputy Commissioner Fang hasn't arrived yet. But someone has sent for him."

"Deputy Commissioner Fang has another mission," explained Xu Tieying, "so there's no need to wait for him."

A trace of jealousy flashed across the face of Deputy Commissioner Shan. "Sir," he said, "you've already met Deputy Commissioner Fang, haven't you?"

Xu Tieying stopped smiling. "He's the first deputy inspector. He was the one who picked me up from the railway station. Is there a problem?"

Shan was stunned and replied hastily: "Of course not. No problem, absolutely no problem."

Xu Tieying sat down and stopped looking at Shan Fuming and his subordinates standing in two rows. Instead, he stared down at the table and said: "Introduce yourselves to me."

In the order of where they were seated, the director, section chiefs and captains began to introduce themselves.

The meeting ended half an hour later. Xu Tieying was unwilling to say any more before he was in a position to size up his subordinates, but asked them to carry out their tasks according to their original deployment. Then he went into his own office.

The commissioner's room, which was next to the conference

room, had two more rooms inside: an outer room that served as the office and an interior one that was his living quarters.

The office of the commissioner covered an area of more than sixty square metres. The desk of the secretary was opposite the door. In order to see the commissioner, one must first pass through Secretary Sun. Xu Tieying worked behind a screen that one must also navigate in order to see him.

Only the deputy commissioner remained in the office, sitting in a chair on the other side of the screen, with Secretary Sun sitting at his own table, right opposite him.

The sound of running water could be heard inside. At first the noise was very feint, probably it was the commissioner taking a pee; then the sound level increased, indicating that he was taking a shower.

The deputy was by nature an extremely patient person; now he was simply taking advantage of this opportunity to get close to the secretary. It was just chit-chat between two strangers.

"Judging by your accent, you must be also from Jiangsu, right?"

"Actually, I'm from Wuxing, Zhejiang Province," said Secretary Sun.

"Sorry, sorry," said the deputy, standing up. "Secretary Sun, it turns out that you have the same hometown as Chen Lifu and Chen Guofu. Well, how rude of me to mistake your accent! Though close to Jiangsu, Wuxing is on the other side of Lake Taihu. Yet it is home to some of the greatest men of our age!"

Secretary Sun stood up respectfully. "Deputy Commissioner Shan, you're a very knowledgeable man."

"I'm humbled," said Deputy Shan. "Those who work for the central party headquarters of the Nationalists should be as knowledgeable as Chief Commissioner Xu. Otherwise they wouldn't be qualified for a position at the Communications Bureau. Minister Chen has written so many books. What a learned man he is! And so wise of him to pick Mr Xu as director of the Liaison Office of the Communications Bureau. He's got to be an erudite person. Mr Xu also values you and relies on you so much that I'm sure I'll need to consult you often in future."

"I'm flattered, Mr Shan." As usual, Sun managed to keep a poker face. "The commissioner said he was very tired, and he will need to read the material after his shower. Do you have any other business to conduct here?"

This was almost a polite request for him to leave. Hurriedly, the deputy came a step closer and lowered his voice: "There is a very important person who wants to meet the commissioner right now. Of course, it's up to the commissioner himself to decide whether to meet with him or not."

"Who is this important person?"

"Ma Hanshan."

Not only did Secretary Sun manage to keep a poker face, but he was also adept at feigning ignorance. "And who is Ma Hanshan, please?"

The deputy was taken aback. How could the secretary possibly not know the identity of Ma Hanshan having been the one who had escorted Xu and the five-member investigation team to Peking? He thought about it and replied, pretending that he was addressing someone who knew nothing about Ma Hanshan: "He's the director of the Civil Affairs Bureau of Peking City. He also serves as a deputy director on the Peking Citizens' Food-Distribution Committee which was set up in April. This person can be of great help to the chief commissioner in understanding the situation in Peking."

Sun was silent. The sound of running water stopped, and was followed by soft footsteps from the bathroom to the living room. He reckoned that Xu Tieying had just got out of the shower.

Secretary Sun did nothing but look at Shan.

Deputy Director Shan seemed to be quite anxious. "Please, if I may, can I ask you to pass along the request to the chief commissioner?"

Secretary Sun reckoned that Xu Tieying would have changed into his clothes by now and replied: "Just a second."

Sun walked around the screen towards the interior of the office. Shan seemed to have a habit of pacing around. He shuffled from one foot to the other in the small area outside the screen.

Fortunately, Secretary Sun came out soon after entering Xu's office.

"Well?" asked Deputy Commissioner Shan.

"The chief commissioner said that he could meet with him if

he's here to explain the case regarding the Citizens' Food-Distribution Committee."

"Of course, we need to report the case," the deputy commissioner replied.

"Then please show him in," said Sun.

"I don't know what to say, apart from two words, 'thank you'," the deputy said incoherently on his way out.

Sun, that poker-faced secretary, smiled stiffly.

Clearly, there were three Chinese characters in that "thank you". Why did the deputy say that there were only two? The political officialdom in Peking seemed quite beyond his comprehension.

In fact, the situation was entirely comprehensible. As the saying goes, a cannon is worth a thousand taels of gold. If Generalissimo Chiang Kai-shek was going to fight the civil war, it was a good time for them to take advantage of the chaos to make a fortune. The chaos of the war had addled the minds of many people and even messed up their language. In less than two minutes after he had uttered the two words, the deputy commissioner came back with Ma Hanshan. The man had apparently been waiting in his deputy's office.

"Brother Xu! Brother Tieying!" Ma Hanshan called out on entering the room.

"Excuse me," said Secretary Sun standing in front of the screen, blocking Ma Hanshan's way.

Ma Hanshan turned around and asked Deputy Commissioner Shan: "Is this Mr Sun, the secretary?" The deputy commissioner had been so embarrassed at the failure to introduce him properly that he slipped away even before he came in.

Ma Hanshan, however, continued to behave as if everything was normal. He turned his head again, and smiled at Secretary Sun. "Hey, I've heard so much about you. Don't you know that due to the shortages, your chief commissioner and I were sharing jackets while we were in Chongqing, though not trousers I should add."

Secretary Sun still stood in his way. "Are you Director Ma Hanshan?"

"Yes, I am."

Secretary Sun stretched out his hand and said: "Have a seat, please."

"Where's your boss?" Ma Hanshan refused to wait, and tried to peer around the screen.

"Director Ma," said a stony-faced Secretary Sun, "we have regulations at the Communications Bureau for party members in Nanking. Our superiors must be informed before meetings. Please don't make things difficult for me."

Only then did Ma Hanshan start to curb his excessive enthusiasm. He stood there, not knowing what to do next. Perhaps he was reminded of the "unlucky year" predicted by the fortune-teller in the first month of the lunar new year.

"Sun," came Xu Tieying's voice from behind the screen.

"Yes sir," Sun answered.

"Has Director Ma arrived?"

"Yes sir."

"Show him in." Xu Tieying's tone was not cold, but it was certainly not warm either.

Ma Hanshan had been itching to enter the room, but stopped at the invitation, thinking that he had been rudely treated, and upset that the word "please" had not been uttered. It looked like the day would not be as easy as he had expected.

"Director Ma, please." At least Secretary Sun was being polite, but Ma Hanshan was still far from enthusiastic as he stepped inside.

Secretary Sun left the room holding a file and a pen, and closed the door behind him. He sat down at the conference table to work, while at the same time guarding the door.

Standing to one side of the screen, Ma Hanshan felt the sun shining on his head once more. Mr Xu, fresh out of the shower, looked radiant. With a slight smile, he extended his right hand powerfully.

"It's been three years since we last met in Chongqing. Time's passed in the twinkling of an eye, hasn't it?"

Ma Hanshan stretched out his hand which Xu Tieying held and shook forcefully a few times.

"Sit down, let's talk."

Ma Hanshan suddenly felt moved and stood there with tears in his eyes. "Brother Tieying, if you hadn't come to Peking to take over, I'd no longer want to continue in this job. It's hard to accomplish anything for the party-state."

Naturally, Xu Tieying tried to comfort Ma who had become quite emotional. "Have you forgotten what we said in Chongqing during the eight-year War of Resistance? Sit, sit. Let's talk things over."

They sat down on a sofa beside the tea table. "Tea?" Xu Tieying pushed a cup in front of Ma Hanshan.

It was so considerate of Xu to have tea prepared for him. Ma Hanshan picked up the cup, lifted the lid and took a large gulp.

"It's hot!" Xu Tieying warned, but too late to prevent Ma Hanshan from burning his mouth.

"It's nothing," said Ma Hanshan as he put down the cup and placed the lid back on. He got straight to the point. "The Fifth of July Incident was a Communist conspiracy. At first, more than ten thousand students from the Northeast surrounded the City Council, followed by tens of thousands of students from various campuses in Peking. Later, even the Senate speaker's house was smashed. Nine students were killed during the riot, plus two of our police officers. Only a few hundred of them have been arrested. The government has been quite restrained. Why has an investigation team been set up to investigate us at the Citizens' Food-Distribution Committee? It's unbelievable."

"The real incident didn't occur on the fifth of July, did it?" Xu Tieying looked intently at Ma Hanshan. "How could the Peking City Senate come up with such a proposal? Allowing the students from sixteen universities in the Northeast to enter central Peking? Was it approved by the Ministry of Education? No matter how much food you were running short of at the distribution committee, there should have been enough for more than ten thousand people, since each person consumes only fifteen catties a month. Why was there such a big shortage?"

Ma Hanshan stood up to see if it was safe to speak.

"Go ahead," urged Xu Tieying. "No one would dare bug me here in my office."

Ma Hanshan sat back and lowered his voice. "I'll be honest with you, sir. If everything is distributed strictly in accordance with the provisions of the Ministry of Finance, the Ministry of Civil Affairs and the Ministry of Social Affairs, no one would go hungry. However, the funds allocated by the Treasury, together with the US dollar aid money, dictates that we distribute food from those designated companies. I won't complain about the two companies controlled by Soong and Kung giving short measures. But the real issue is that even if the money was remitted, they wouldn't transport the grain. I mean, the whole shipment of food and grain was not delivered. We made inquiries, and they replied that the ships had sunk in stormy weather. Brother Xu, tell me who we should talk to?"

"It is indeed a shame," said Xu Tieying with a look of anger on his face.

"They're so corrupt, they have the gall to claim that we're even more corrupt!" Ma Hanshan became so animated that his naturally dark-complexioned face began to sweat. Strangely, as he spoke, the sweat on his face also appeared black.

Xu Tieying looked at his face and could not help laughing. He got up and turned on the fan. "Don't get excited. Calm down and cool off first."

As the wind from the fan started to blow, Ma Hanshan did indeed calm down. Xu Tieying sat back again and said: "Go on, indulge me."

Ma Hanshan picked up the teacup again and blew on it a few times before taking a sip. "Currently, all of these companies are bigger than the party-state," he said. "I made the proposal several times at meetings of the Distribution Committee – for example, whether grain and cloth could be purchased from some of the companies affiliated to the party headquarters of the Central Committee, but they immediately rejected them. Brother Tieying, my chief grievance is that we're all members of the Nationalist Party. Why is it that we can't make our own contributions to the party headquarters of the Central Committee as if it has nothing to do with us?"

Xu Tieying became serious. "Have you got all your minutes of the meetings?"

"Don't worry. I always bear in mind the interests of the party. I know what to do. I made a copy of all the minutes."

"That's good. If they want to turn all party property into private hands, they should be expelled from the party!"

Ma Hanshan leaned over and said: "These days, we all have to feed our families, so we need our share of the money. Fighting against the Communists represents the biggest proportion, the expenses of the party department come next, and the smallest proportion is for private individuals. It's only human to work for some personal gain. I put forward a 'six-three-one' proposal at previous meetings, with six for the state, three for the party and one for private. They didn't approve it, but nor did they object. However in reality, they all messed up. Brother Tieying, there is a figure I have to reveal to you today because it involves the Police Bureau of Peking Municipality.

Xu Tieying became very serious and stared at Ma Hanshan.

"Do you know what proportion of shares your predecessor took in those companies?" asked Ma Hanshan.

"How much?"

Ma Hanshan stretched out four fingers, indicating four per cent!

Xu Tieying listened without expression. He was waiting to hear more.

"He told me to transfer his four per cent of the shares to Shanghai, which I rejected," Ma Hanshan continued. "Brother Tieying, since you've just assumed office, please be informed that many brothers will be under your command and depend on you in the bureau. If he took the four per cent, all of the brothers would go hungry with that scale of depredation!"

Xu Tieying nodded, and suddenly changed the subject. "Let me ask you this. If we are brothers, then tell me the truth."

"Sure, I promise."

"Were all the transactions conducted at the Peking branch of the Central Bank?"

Ma Hanshan hesitated for a second before nodding.

"Are any of these transactions being withheld by the Peking branch?"

"As far as I know," said Ma Hanshan, "Governor Fang is aware of the big picture. He just helped facilitate the transactions for various stakeholders. The branch wasn't interested in making money from it."

"Is Mr Fang personally in charge of the accounts?"

Ma Hanshan subconsciously glanced out of the window. "Mr Fang is such a formidable character that he would hide behind a screen. All the accounts are put in charge of his deputy, Cui Zhongshi."

"And what about Cui Zhongshi?" asked Xu Tieying.

"A very smart guy. Quite capable of delivering what he promised!"

Xu Tieying nodded slowly and stood up. "Don't rush, remain cautious. Also, don't stay in my office long. And one more thing, don't say anything to anyone else. As long as you keep quiet, I can help you."

Ma Hanshan also stood up, and stretched out to shake hands with Xu Tieying. "Understood."

Xu Tieying walked Ma Hanshan to the door of the conference room. He did not go back until his figure disappeared from sight.

Sun, his secretary, had been waiting for him. He opened the door to his office for him. Xu Tieying stood by the door and whispered to him: "Arrange for some reliable people to go to the railway station tomorrow and report to me as soon as you see Deputy Director Cui get off the train."

"Of course," said Secretary Sun.

———

It was nine o'clock in the evening on 7 July when Cui Zhongshi's train arrived at Dezhou station. It was a large station where the train would stop for ten minutes.

Cui Zhongshi sat on a lower-level hard seat. He looked out of the window at the platform. The lights were dim and only a few passengers were boarding.

A middle-aged man holding a suitcase stopped at the carriage opposite Cui Zhongshi. He looked at the number on his ticket, then checked the number on the iron plate on the carriage. As if struggling with poor eyesight, he asked Cui Zhongshi: "Excuse me, sir, is this lower berth number seven?"

Cui Zhongshi looked at the passenger and replied: "Yes, it's number seven."

The passenger still seemed a little unsure: "Sir, are you number six?"

"Mine is number six," confirmed Cui Zhongshi.

Apparently relieved, the passenger put his suitcase on the luggage rack, and fixed a lock over the suitcase handle and around a metal bar on the rack. He went to sit down on the lower level of berth number seven, took out a copy of *Ta Kung Pao* from his briefcase and put it on the table.

"Today's newspaper, sir. You can read it if you're interested." The passenger seemed to be solicitous and enthusiastic.

"Thank you," said Cui Zhongshi. "As soon as the train departs, all lights will be turned off." He continued to look out of the window.

At one of the seats numbered eleven and twelve, not far away from seats six and seven, a pair of eyes were pretending to read a newspaper, but they were actually monitoring Cui Zhongshi. The eyes belonged to the young man who was assigned to eavesdrop on Cui in Room 209 of the Jinling Hotel.

CHAPTER 6

The seventh of July 1948 was the first day of June according to the lunar calendar, the start of a period known as "Slight Heat". At this time of year in Peking, all the hutongs at night would normally be crowded with men wearing only shorts, cooling themselves with cattail-leaf fans and playing chess boisterously. But since the imposition of martial law earlier in the year had not been lifted, and it was almost nine o'clock at night, everyone was indoors. With the family abroad, the Gu compound appeared large and empty, giving the impression that the whole city was like a ghost town.

Zeng Keda changed into a short-sleeved satin shirt, escorted by his adjutant, who was also in plain clothes. They walked out of the courtyard towards the back door.

It was a moonless night, and dim yellow streetlights illuminated the meandering street. The adjutant led the way as if they were intending to take a stroll. They were getting closer and closer to the rear door of the Gu compound.

"Who's there?" came a shout in the dark from a guard deployed by the Peking Garrison headquarters.

The adjutant rushed over and said: "The general needs to take a look outside. Open the door!"

There were several guards, all standing in different positions, all silent. A platoon leader came by. He knew Zeng Keda and saluted him. "Sir, orders state that officers in residence are not allowed to go out at night for safety reasons."

The adjutant was about to lose his temper, but Zeng Keda made a gesture for him to stop. He decided to address the platoon leader himself: "Martial law troops are deployed out on the streets, aren't they?"

"Yes sir, of course," the platoon leader replied.

Zeng Keda smiled. "Then there should be nothing unsafe. I'll take a quick look around the neighbouring streets. Open the door, please."

The platoon leader felt compelled to open the door. "Yes sir." He took the key and unlocked the gate, and then removed a large cross door latch and opened the door. "Sir, how many men do you need to escort you?"

Zeng Keda shook his hand and said: "It is your duty to ensure that the officers in residence are protected from danger." Then he sauntered off.

Sure enough, guards and troops were posted along all the streets in the neighbourhood. They belonged to the security forces and were equipped with helmets and armed with guns. On seeing the two men emerge from Gu's residence, they all stood erect and saluted. Zeng Keda nodded his head and stopped at the intersection of the hutong and the street.

Zeng Keda did not smoke, but his adjutant took out a cigarette and handed it to him and lit it with a match. Zeng took a puff and spluttered. He took another one and did the same again; he started choking and coughing on the third puff. The adjutant took the cigarette, threw it on the ground and put it out.

Not far away, the driver of a military jeep recognised Zeng Keda's face illuminated by the glow of the cigarette and drove over to them.

The adjutant opened the rear door, and Zeng Keda hopped in followed by the adjutant who closed the door behind him.

The jeep carried the number plate of the Peking Garrison headquarters, and also had a flag of the Central Army affixed to the front bumper. The jeep looked rather majestic, and the martial law troopers saluted the general on his way.

It was a real curfew imposed under martial law. With the jeep driving out of town into the distant suburbs, they could see that almost every section of road was posted with troops, though not as densely as in the centre. With both Tsinghua and Yenching university campuses not far away, the jeep pulled over on the shoulder of a cold suburban road.

They saw six bicycles parked beside the road, four of them belonging to students, the other two unattended. The adjutant got out of the jeep, opened the door and Zeng Keda followed.

The two young men pushed the bicycles to Zeng Keda, to whom they saluted. One of them whispered: "General, we're all from the Chiang Kai-shek Student Society."

Zeng Keda smiled. "Thanks for coming along." He took one of the spare bicycles, with the other one for his adjutant.

The two young men went back to their bicycles, kicked off the feet supports and jumped onto their steeds.

Zeng Keda got on the bike with one foot supporting himself, and the adjutant followed. The other two young men also got on their bikes.

Two bicycles were leading the way, twenty or thirty metres ahead, and two bicycles followed the same distance behind, escorting Zeng Keda and the adjutant in the middle. They were heading to Yenching University.

Although the street lights were dim, something protruding from the back of two of the young men could still vaguely be seen; they appeared to be armed with pistols.

Cheng Xiaoyun was driven to the Fang mansion at around seven o'clock. Dinner was served in the first-floor living room at nearly eight, and now it was just past nine. Xie Peidong had long explained that both he and Fang Buting had eaten in advance.

There were only five people at the dinner table. On the left sat the two brothers, Fang Meng'ao and Fang Mengwei, while on the right sat He Xiaoyu and Xie Mulan.

Cheng Xiaoyun sat alone at the head of the table. For the first few months following the family's move to Peking, she lived in this residence. The whole family used to eat dinner together, but Cheng Xiaoyun had always been forced to sit at the far end of the table. Later, she went to live alone in another courtyard residence because of a rift with Fang Mengwei. She rarely returned to the mansion, although Fang Buting did visit her on a regular basis.

Today was the first time in a long while for Cheng Xiaoyun to come back and eat with the Fang family, and she was forced by Fang Meng'ao to sit at the head of the table. She ate her porridge one small spoonful at a time, barely moving the chopsticks to eat the dishes. She made almost no eye contact with anyone in front of her.

After dinner, Fang Meng'ao glanced at his Omega watch. "It's after nine already," he said.

"Not quite. Look, Big Brother, the clock hasn't chimed yet." Xie Mulan's eyes flashed, pointing to the tall clock nearby.

The clock said eight forty-five.

Fang Meng'ao gave a thin smile, but it was tinged with fatigue. "When I was a child, I always liked to play with the clock. My watch is designed for combat. It says nine fifteen."

Xie Mulan stamped her foot and stood up. "What a killjoy!" she said. "Why does everyone in this family try to outsmart everyone else? It takes the fun out of everything."

Fang Meng'ao stood up. All eyes were on him.

"I have to go back to the barracks."

Everyone remained impassive. Xie Mulan looked at the stairs leading to the first floor and the door that remained half closed.

Fang Buting had been sitting in the armchair in his first-floor office and must have fallen asleep. Suddenly he opened his eyes, like a child who had just woken up, looking around, without focusing on anything in particular.

"Big Brother, you'll have to go up and say hello to our father, won't you?" came Fang Mengwei's voice from downstairs. Fang Buting's gaze was fixed as he listened.

"This is not the Peking Police Bureau," was the surprising response from Fang Meng'ao. "Mengwei, you have no right to interfere in family affairs." Fang Buting rolled his eyes up and looked directly at the chandelier on the ceiling.

Fang Meng'ao continued: "Mother should stay here from tonight on." Everyone looked at Cheng Xiaoyun.

Cheng Xiaoyun stood up and said: "Each generation has its own way of living. Mengwei, you remember what I told you earlier this evening?" Reluctantly, Fang Mengwei nodded.

Fang Meng'ao looked at Xie Peidong, who was walking towards them. "You've had a hard day, Uncle. I wonder if there are any more steamed buns and cornbread left. My men back at the barracks would appreciate them, for sure. They only had biscuits for supper tonight."

"Do I need you to remind me of this?" said Xie Peidong. "Mrs Ma, give him the basket of food."

The housemaid came out with a large bamboo basket.

Fang Meng'ao addressed his younger brother: "It's better if you drive me back to the barracks." He then turned to Xie Mulan, and finally, his eyes fixed on He Xiaoyu. "Thank you for what you've done today. Please give my best to Uncle He."

He Xiaoyu looked back into his eyes. "It's very chaotic in Peking these days. You and your brigade members should pay attention to your own safety."

Fang Meng'ao, who did not expect to receive such an entreaty from her, resumed the mischievous energy he had displayed in the barracks in order to liven up the atmosphere. "Yes ma'am! Adieu!" he said, his knees pressed together. With that, he walked towards the door.

Fang Mengwei glanced at the empty staircase and followed him out with a feeling of melancholy. Cai Ma was close behind, the basket of food in her hand.

Cheng Xiaoyun stood in front of the table and watched the backs of the two tall men as they left the living room. Not knowing what to do, He Xiaoyu and Xie Mulan observed Cheng Xiaoyun with great concern.

"Sister-in-law," said Xie Peidong, "according to Meng'ao, you must not go back to that home today. I'll have everything brought here tomorrow morning. Go up and accompany the governor, please."

Cheng Xiaoyun nodded and thanked He Xiaoyu and Xie Mulan.

"Auntie, you're always welcome," He Xiaoyu replied politely.

"Auntie, do you need me to go with you?" asked Xie Mulan.

Xie Peidong answered instead: "That's not necessary."

Cheng Xiaoyun bowed slightly before leaving the table for the first floor.

At nearly the same moment, the clock chimed, its sound reverberating nine times, as if to accompany the footsteps of Cheng Xiaoyun as she walked into that room on the first floor.

He Xiaoyu looked at Xie Mulan. "I'm going back, too."

"Didn't you say you'd spend the night here?" Xie Mulan asked, becoming upset. "Why are you going back? It's so late anyway!"

"Dad's had another asthma attack," He Xiaoyu explained. "I have to return. Uncle Xie, please arrange for the driver to give me a lift."

"Of course," Xie Peidong replied. "Given the circumstances, I'll happily arrange the car."

"Thank you, Uncle Xie."

Xie Mulan stamped her feet again. "That's ridiculous. If you insist on seeing Mr Liang, you don't have to be in such a hurry."

He Xiaoyu's face was serious. "What did you just say?"

Xie Peidong also gave Xie Mulan a hard stare. She turned around and dashed towards the staircase leading to her first-floor bedroom.

On a road near Yenching University in the northwestern outskirts of Peking, six bicycles, with two in the front, two in the middle and two in the rear, were moving at a moderate pace due to the fact the road was bumpy and it was dark. The two cyclists in front stopped pedalling abruptly but did not dismount. Instead, they stood straddling their bikes, waiting for Zeng Keda and his adjutant to catch up. Zeng stopped in front of them, and the adjutant followed. Soon, all six bikes were congregated in the same spot.

The young man leading the way pointed to the barracks a few hundred metres away on one side of the road. It seemed even darker over where the barracks were located.

The young man said to Zeng Keda: "Those barracks are home to the Youth Aviation Brigade."

"How far is it from Yenching and Tsinghua?" asked Zeng Keda.

"Less than a kilometre," the young man replied.

"How far is it from the warehouse in the university area under the supervision of the Citizens' Food-Distribution Committee?"

"About two kilometres. General, would you like to go there first?"

"Not tonight. Let's go to our agreed destination."

"Yes sir," the four young men answered in unison and they started pedalling once more.

Maintaining their original formation, the men continued their journey towards the east gate of Yenching University. Although it was dark, the façade of the institution was recognisable. This was also the location of the bookstore where the Communist Party spy Liang Jinglun reported to his contact point Yan Chunming, who headed the Yenching chapter of the Student Committee of the Communist Party of China (CPC).

The six bicycles stopped about a hundred metres from the bookstore. "Sir, may I show you the way?" asked the young man who had been the vanguard on their journey.

"Do you happen to know the bookstore owner?" asked Zeng Keda.

"Yes sir," the young man said, and as soon as Zeng Keda had dismounted the bike, another young man wheeled it away. Zeng Keda walked briskly to the bookstore. The young man who had led the way followed him with his bike.

"Remember, don't call me 'sir' again," said Zeng Keda softly.

"Yes, Mr Zeng," replied the young man.

Upon arriving at the entrance of the bookstore, the young man knocked on the door.

"Who is it?" asked a woman from inside.

"I studied under Professor Liang. I'm here with a friend of the professor," the young man replied in fluent American-accented English.

"OK. Come on in," the American woman answered, opening the door.

"Professor Liang is a dear friend. It's so nice to meet you." Zeng

Keda surprised the American lady by also being able to say "hello" in perfect English.

"Nice to meet you as well Mr Liu," she replied, using Zeng Keda's cover name. "Mr Liang is waiting for you upstairs." The American lady let Zeng Keda into the store.

Liang Jinglun watched Zeng Keda climb the stairs in much the same way he had regarded Yan Chunming at the entrance only a few hours ago. The difference was that Yan Chunming took the initiative to shake Liang Jinglun's hand earlier on in the day, while at this moment it was Liang Jinglun who was striding into the room taking light footsteps and stretching out his hand to Zeng Keda.

Liang Jinglun warmly clasped Zeng Keda's hand with both hands. "Thanks for coming all this way, Comrade Keda."

"Thank you, too, for your hard work, Comrade Liang Jinglun." Zeng kept his voice low, but his tone betrayed a certain heaviness.

Mr Liang sensed that Zeng Keda was not shaking his hands as enthusiastically as he had hoped. "How is Comrade Jianfeng?"

"What can I say?" Zeng Keda withdrew his hand and continued: "He asked me to say hello."

Liang Jinglun felt a coldness and sense of dissatisfaction coming from Zeng Keda. He said: "Please pass on my thanks to Comrade Jianfeng when you get the chance to speak to him next." At that moment, he was not a professor of Yenching, nor was he He Qicang's assistant, but the true Liang Jinglun, the core member of the Iron and Blood Congress. Zeng Keda had already taken the place where Yan Chunming had been sitting earlier in the day, while Liang Jinglun also went to sit down in his familiar place.

"How did it happen, the riot on the fifth of July?" asked Zeng Keda. "Why didn't you submit a report in advance?"

Liang Jinglun stared at the table, before looking up at the other man. "The Northeast student protest on the fifth of July at the Peking Senate was not instigated by the Communist Party… there was no CPC involvement in its organisation."

Zeng Keda became more concerned. "They managed to amass tens of thousands of people, so very large in scale. The whole nation couldn't help being shocked. The United States government sent a diplomatic note to the Nationalist government that very evening. Are you saying it was all spontaneous, that there were no Communist instigators behind it? Even if I were to believe that, our superiors wouldn't."

Liang Jinglun's face did not reveal any objection, nor did he feel intimidated after being criticised, despite the sense of suspicion he may have felt. Instead, he looked calmly at Zeng Keda.

"Comrade Keda, the senior leadership of the Communist Party of China issued new instructions yesterday. May I first brief you about them?"

Zeng Keda's eyes brightened and his attitude softened a little. "Go ahead."

Liang Jinglun recited, almost verbatim, the most important content: "'The task of our work in the city is to be prepared to cooperate with the field army to seize the city and prepare to manage it after the takeover. The task of capturing the city was primarily the responsibility of the field army. Based on our existing urban workforce and expansion in the near future, it is impossible to seize the cities through armed uprising. By the same token, it remains impossible to seize any city in northern China through combined efforts. So let us not carry the burden of organising an armed uprising, which is impossible in terms of condition and time…'"

"The Communist Party seems to be poised for victory!" Zeng Keda was more shocked than fascinated when listening to Liang Jinglun. He stared at Liang as if he were a Communist Party member. "What else?"

Liang Jinglun intentionally emphasised the following words to express his opposition to Zeng Keda's criticism and scepticism: "Comrade Keda, here are the key words: 'Regarding the strategy of our struggles, we've made better progress with the student movement in Peking, and the wave-like campaigns have far greater impact. However, the general policy is to hide our capacity, to accumulate our strength and avoid head-on collision with the Kuomintang, this is the main principle. To launch a struggle we must achieve the following. First, to win over the large majority, we must avoid waging conflict that would fail to win over the majority. Second, avoid confrontation during adverse conditions. The idea is to accumulate strength and get ready to cooperate in seizing and managing the cities.'"

With that, Liang Jinglun stopped. Zeng Keda didn't urge him to continue. Instead, he was thinking fast and sharp. Silence hung between them.

"When did the Communist Party issue these instructions?" Zeng Keda asked, raising his head.

"They were urgent instructions issued on the sixth of July," Liang Jinglun replied. "I heard them today. Not everything, though. The Communist Party is disciplined, and at our level, the instructions were only communicated verbally and restricted to the section pertaining to the student movement. Comrade Keda, the protest by the refugee students from the Northeast on the fifth of July was not organised in advance by the Communist Party. So I didn't expect things to get so out of control. Nevertheless, I still bear responsibility for failing to grasp the dynamics of the student movement in time. I will conduct a profound self-criticism to Comrade Jianfeng."

"There's no need," replied Zeng Keda, who's mood was now much improved. "This confirms Comrade Jianfeng's judgment from another aspect. He said at the joint meeting in Nanking that the Fifth of July Incident in Peking was, to a large extent, a case of official depredation and civil disobedience. To put it bluntly, it was caused by the unscrupulous embezzlement of basic goods for the public by corrupt groups within the Kuomintang. The Communist Party document you reported today is very important. Put down in writing as much as you can remember. I'll report it to Comrade Jianfeng."

Liang Jinglun stood up, went to the bookshelf beside the wall and drew out an economics textbook in English. Walking back to his seat, he removed two folded sheets of paper from the book and handed them to Zeng Keda. "It's already here in writing. Because it was communicated orally, a few characters may be wrongly transcribed. But the main content is all here."

Zeng Keda stood up, too, and took the abstract of the Communist Party's "Seventh of July documents" with both hands. There was a look of jubilation on his face. He was about to say something when Liang Jinglun handed over the book in which he had hidden the note.

Zeng Keda looked at him doubtfully.

"This is my analysis of the national economic situation over the next month," Liang Jinglun explained, "based on the price differences between the five major cities and the daily depreciation of the *fabi* over the last fortnight. It's all written in English in the margin of every page. It's a task that Comrade Jianfeng gave me two weeks ago. I hope it will be of some value to the currency system reform to be carried out by the party-state."

On taking the book, Zeng Keda started to regret his critical feelings towards Liang when they first met. His tone was now more sincere: "Comrade Jinglun, before I came here, Comrade Jianfeng asked me to pass on a message. I'm sorry, I forgot to share it with you before now."

Liang Jinglun stood quietly, waiting intently to hear the message.

"Comrade Jianfeng said that if our party had a hundred people of the calibre of Comrade Liang Jinglun, there would be hope for the success of the national revolution," said Zeng Keda.

The words ought to have brought joy to Liang Jinglun, but all Zeng Keda could make out was deep melancholy in his eyes.

"I would like to thank Comrade Jianfeng for his trust," Liang Jinglun replied, "but in the current situation, even if we had ten thousand Liang Jingluns, that may not be enough. I'm just doing the best I can."

"Have some faith," said an increasingly excited Zeng Keda. "At present, our most important task is to crack down on the economic corruption within the party-state and launch the currency system reform as soon as possible. As long as these two tasks can be vigorously accomplished, our allies' confidence in us will be restored. If the national government stabilises the city and prices, the president will be able to command the whole army to defeat the Communists on the front line. Within a year, Comrade Jinglun, you can go to Nanking to take on more important work. I would also add that Comrade Jianfeng is very interested in knowing more about your personal life. How is your relationship with He Xiaoyu developing? Comrade Jianfeng said you make a good pair. Besides, her father is a much-valued talent that the country needs. He is looking forward to hosting your wedding and to having you and your professor and future father-in-law working in Nanking. We cannot allow comrades who have made special contributions to live a spartan life all the time."

Liang Jinglun could no longer be indifferent, even though his smile of gratitude was a little reluctant: "'Ancient nights and distant music are eternal, but they don't belong to me.' That's from a favourite poem of one of my CIA friends. It's not one of my favourites, but I believe in the message. Let me report to you about my work. I've sent someone to do the job you assigned me yesterday."

Zeng Keda stared at him for a while, then he remembered and asked: "Monitoring Fang Meng'ao?"

"Yes. He Xiaoyu's been sent to contact him."

Zeng was stunned. "Couldn't you have sent someone else?"

Liang turned slowly to avoid looking into Zeng's concerned face. "She's quite fit for the job. Her father and Fang Buting were former classmates at Harvard and have maintained a good relationship. She actually lived for a time in Fang Meng'ao's house when she was a child. I also heard their parents had agreed for them to marry once they were older." Surprisingly, a faint smile appeared on Liang Jinglun's face as he spoke.

Zeng Keda began to ponder the meaning of this smile, which soon disappeared.

"It's all been agreed. Comrade Keda, He Xiaoyu is a radical youth affiliated to the fringes of the Communist Party. She might be a good choice to test or recruit Fang Meng'ao, though we need to be flexible if circumstances change over time. Permission to ask you to approve my action plan."

Fang Buting's car took He Xiaoyu to the front gate of He Qicang's courtyard residence in Yenching University's Yannan Garden.

Yenching University was originally a missionary school run by Americans. It followed the tradition of famous universities in the United Kingdom and the United States by setting up a residential quarter in the south of the campus, where several small Western-style houses with courtyards were built for the chancellors, vice-chancellors and senior Chinese and foreign professors. Hence the name Yannan Garden, *yannan* meaning "south of the Yenching campus". He Qicang was awarded a PhD in Economics by Harvard. Upon returning to China, he was hired by John Leighton Stuart as Yenching's vice-chancellor and given a courtyard house in the quarter.

The driver stepped out of the car and opened the door for He Xiaoyu, who said to him: "Would you like to come in for a cup of tea?"

"No, thank you, Miss He," the driver replied respectfully, and he got back into the car and started the engine.

He Xiaoyu politely waited until the car disappeared before stepping into the courtyard. She looked around and noticed that the ground floor lights were still on. Without ringing the doorbell, she took out her key, unlocked the courtyard door and went in.

Zeng Keda, sitting in the Foreign Languages Bookstore, was obviously quite touched by the idea of using He Xiaoyu to recruit Fang Meng'ao. "Comrade Jinglun, Fang Meng'ao is key to digging deep into Peking's corruption cases, while Fang Buting is essential in carrying out the currency system reform. Using your observation and analysis, do you think it possible that Meng'ao is a special member of the Communist Party? If so, what can He Xiaoyu do to find out the truth?"

Liang Jinglun did not answer immediately; instead, he looked back at Zeng Keda, his eyes full of expectation. He thought for a second before asking: "Comrade Keda, I want to know why Fang Meng'ao and his aviation brigade are entrusted with such an important task since he is suspected of being a Communist. What does Comrade Jianfeng think of him?"

It was Zeng Keda's turn to be silent. He thought for a while before replying: "On the issue of using Fang Meng'ao, my thinking is somewhat different to Comrade Jianfeng's. However, you know, with regard to Comrade Jianfeng's instructions and arrangements, we can only implement what we are told, irrespective of whether we understand it. The key is to do it well."

"I see." Liang Jinglun fell into contemplation again.

He Xiaoyu walked into the living room. She thought her father would be asleep, but He Qicang was sitting under the floor lamp reading, obviously waiting for his daughter.

"Dad, it's ten o'clock already. Why haven't you gone to bed?" He Xiaoyu walked over to her father and picked up the folding fan spread on his knees. She gently fanned him.

He Qicang closed his book. "Did you have a chance to see Meng'ao?"

He Xiaoyu nodded.

"Did he say hello to his father?"

He Xiaoyu lowered her eyes and continued to fan her father. "No, Uncle Fang stayed in his room. They didn't even see each other."

"Oh dear. Uncle Fang has been strong all his life, but he won't even dare to see his son in his later years. What is that being strong for?"

He Qicang sighed and pondered for a long time. Then he looked at his daughter and asked: "Did you want to visit the Fangs today, or were you invited, or did someone tell you to go?"

"Dad, what do you mean by that?"

"Of course, if you were invited, it must be the Fangs. If you were told, it must be Jinglun. Tell me the truth."

Faced with her father's questioning, He Xiaoyu felt an unexpected sense of dejection given what had been weighing on her mind these past few days. Only then did she realise that, no matter what the issue was – something she tried to suppress in her mind, or the assignment given to her by the organisation – nothing could be confessed or shared with her father.

"I met elder brother Meng'ao in the morning when we took to the streets to support the students from the Northeast," she replied. "Mulan just dragged me to the Fangs. She said I could be of some help to Uncle Fang. Dad, don't make things complicated."

Half of her account was true. He Qicang couldn't very well ask for more. He changed topic: "Mr Liang lives more off-campus now, so the apartment I've arranged for him is left vacant. I know you're not members of the Communist Party or the Kuomintang, but Yenching is a place for learning after all, so don't involve yourself in politics because you don't know anything about the subject. Of course, I don't either. But your father bears in mind these two adages of Mr Chiang and Mr Mao. Mr Chiang states that 'It's better to kill a thousand by mistake rather than to let one go unpunished', whereas Mao's adage is 'Revolution is a riot, a violent action by one class to overthrow another.'"

"Dad," said He Xiaoyu, interrupting her father, "I don't agree with you. In any case, the Communist Party and its army will not arrest the people, let alone kill them. But as of now, hundreds of innocent students from the Northeast are locked behind bars in Peking. You were trying to protect them from harm, weren't you? You, and so many other progressive leaders, should speak up against the status quo."

"When it's time to speak, absolutely I will." He Qicang's eyes shone with a sense of helplessness. He looked at his daughter fondly. "Alas, I'm only a scholar after all. I do have some friends in powerful positions in the Kuomintang, but I've never been their friend politically. I am old, you're my only family. I do have many students, but there is only one I consider my son, and that is Jinglun. With my fame and connections, I should be able to keep you two safe from trouble."

―――

"I fully understand Comrade Jianfeng's instructions about double agents, but the key is to make good use of them."

"Comrade Jianfeng's instruction about how to use Fang Meng'ao is both sound and open-minded." Liang Jinglun's heart was full of admiration. "I also agree with your analysis, Comrade Keda. Even though he was not a special member of the Communist Party, it's very likely that Fang Meng'ao would be recruited as a special member after arriving in Peking. As for the former point, I think Comrade Keda can come to a conclusion as soon as you give Fang Meng'ao a task to carry out."

"Please…"

"Fang Buting has assigned Cui Zhongshi to conduct all illegal transactions on behalf of the Citizens' Food-Distribution Committee. Comrade Keda can directly entrust Fang Meng'ao with the task of reviewing their existing accounts. As soon as Fang Meng'ao begins to check out Cui Zhongshi's accounts, we can quickly identify whether they are members of the Communist Party. In view of this, I would like to make a suggestion."

"Please, indulge me," said Zeng Keda.

"Fang Meng'ao and his brigade are Air Force pilots, and not one of them understands finance. I can arrange for progressive students, those not affiliated with the Communists at Yenching University, to help review the accounts. This way I can be informed of every single detail."

"Good, very good." Not only did Zeng Keda begin to appreciate him, but he was also starting to get excited. "Tell me about the last piece of advice you've been thinking about."

"That relates to the fact that Fang Meng'ao was not previously a special member of the Communist Party," said Zeng Keda. "Today, I came to form an insight of him at the front gates of Princess Hejing's mansion. It's very likely that he became a target of recruitment for the CPC's Urban Works Department in Peking or even the Enemy Works Department of the CPC Central Committee. Today, I sent He Xiaoyu to reunite with Fang Meng'ao to prepare her for a particular purpose. The idea is to make use of the special relationship between the two families so that we can propose to the Urban Works Department in Peking that the Yenching chapter of the CPC's Student Committee be assigned to convert Fang Meng'ao."

By now, Zeng Keda had fully understood Liang Jinglun's idea. Both men stood up and Zeng Keda went up to Liang Jinglun. Zeng Keda said with the utmost sincerity: "Comrade Jinglun, I admire you for sending Miss He Xiaoyu to contact Fang Meng'ao, but I also sympathise with you for it. On behalf of both the party organisation and Comrade Jianfeng, I would like to express my thanks."

Liang Jinglun felt grateful and genuinely touched, but behind these feelings was a sense of eternal loss. "It's my own choice. Comrade Keda, I still believe that line from the poem – ancient nights and distant music are eternal, but they don't belong to me."

Zeng Keda was concerned. "You shouldn't think that way. Comrade Jinglun, you should trust the party and Comrade Jianfeng!"

"I believe in my choice. Comrade Keda, please pass along the message to the party and Comrade Jianfeng that since I have decided to stop thinking about my personal love interests, there is absolutely no alternative."

Those were intriguing remarks, but Zeng could quickly understand Liang Jinglun's mood. After thinking about it, he came up with some advice that he barely believed himself. "Stop reading Sartre. *The Complete Works of Marquis Zeng Guofan* are a much better read."

———

"Jinglun will not be back tonight," said He Qicang, standing up. "Go to bed now."

Her father made to go upstairs. He Xiaoyu followed and helped him climb the stairs. "Dad, have you taken your medicine?"

"Ms Li has already helped me with it." He Qicang went upstairs with his daughter's assistance, but after two steps he stopped again. "You should go to bed, too."

He Xiaoyu was still supporting him. "Let me help you to your bedroom. I'll go to bed once you're asleep."

He Qicang resumed climbing the stairs. "Well, sing me *Blooming Flowers, Full Moon*."

"Dad, what a stale piece! When Uncle Fang visited us, he also asked me to sing that song. I'm sick and tired of it. May I sing you something new?" Although she said this smilingly like a naughty child, He Xiaoyu had developed a profound sense of sadness in her heart. She could not tell whether it was sadness for her parents or for her own generation.

"Then don't sing anything at all," said He Qicang.

"OK, shall I hum it instead?" Smiling, He Xiaoyu helped her father upstairs slowly, while humming *Blooming Flowers, Full Moon*, a song that had been wildly popular among elderly folk in regions south of the Yangtze River.

He Qicang smiled, a smile radiating a contemplative quality. Behind the smile was the story of his youth. He hoped that his daughter could turn the various imperfections in his own story into "a perfect reunion".

The vice-chancellor of Yenching University was gone, the famous economist was also gone. What was left was an old child who was being coaxed into his bedroom by his daughter.

Zeng Keda had left.

It was late at night on 8 July 1948, or 2 June according to the lunar calendar. A thin crescent moon appeared outside the window. Liang Jinglun stood in front of the window for quite a while. People were watching the moon, while the moon was watching the people.

He went to the bookcase and pulled out *The Wealth of Nations* by Adam Smith, the noted British economist. He spread the book on the table, sat down and arranged a stack of lined paper. He took out a pen and wrote the following:

"A report on recruiting Fang Meng'ao as a special member of our party."

Standing by the window, He Xiaoyu looked at the quiet courtyard below. On the east side, two bungalows were illuminated by the crescent moon just rising in the southwest. He Xiaoyu's voice had been widely admired in Yenching's student drama club. Whether singing on stage or just crooning at home, she could always intoxicate her audience. Just a moment ago, though reluctantly, she hummed *Blooming Flowers, Full Moon* to her father, but now she sang directly to her own heart, words that only she could hear:

The floating, scattered clouds,
The bright moon shines on the reunited people.
Today is the happiest reunion.

Clean and shallow ponds,
Mandarin ducks playing on the water,
Red skirts and emerald caps.
Devoted married couples like two lotus flowers opening.

In pairs, the spouses share a mutual love.
This soft wind blows upon the beautiful flowers,
Blowing on the good flowers,
Full of warmth and affection between the people...

Once she stopped, the voice she could hear in her mind faded away. Who was she singing to? Liang Jinglun? Fang Meng'ao? Or herself? Maybe only the crescent moon knew.

―――

At 8am on 8 July 1948, in the conference room of Gu Weijun's residence, the five-member investigation group of the central government of the Republic of China held its first meeting on the Fifth of July Incident.

Due to the involvement of the Citizens' Food-Distribution Committee, Du Wancheng, an inspector at the Ministry of Finance, was chosen as chief coordinator of the group. At this moment, he was sitting in the front row opposite the door of the conference room.

Thanks to the Air Force's involvement in the transportation of smuggled everyday materials and the suppression of the students by the military and police forces, Zeng Keda, a representative of the Ministry of Defence, sat on the left as a key member of the group.

Whether it involved the finance ministry or the military authorities or the police department, Xu Tieying, sent by the National Communications Bureau of the Kuomintang, was authorised to carry out the investigation on behalf of the Kuomintang's central party headquarters. Though not holding a senior position, he was seated to the right of Du Wancheng.

As a result of the diplomatic note from the United States and the impeachment of the members of the Senate in Nanking, the Peking Citizens' Food-Distribution Committee and the Peking branch of the Central Bank were both targets of the investigation. Representatives from both the Central Bank and the Central Commission on Citizens' Food Distribution were put in a somewhat awkward position. Both of the agencies practised top-down management and were suspected of a dereliction of duty. Wang Benquan, director and secretary of the Central Bank and Ma Linshen, deputy director of the Central Commission on Citizens' Food Distribution, were sitting at opposite ends of the table.

The respondents or interviewees were sat near the door on the opposite side of the conference table to take questions from the members of the investigation group.

A chair was placed at each end of the long table. Fang Meng'ao sat in the chair at the top next to the bedroom of the late Dr Sun Yat-sen. He was in attendance as an observer, but he was more visible than the other participants because a portrait featuring Dr Sun was hanging on the wall just above his head.

Sitting at the opposite end of the table was the conference notetaker, who was neither from the Ministry of Finance, nor from the party headquarters of the Kuomintang Central Committee; instead, it was Zeng Keda's adjutant who had followed him to Peking. This left everyone with the impression it was the Bureau of Reserve Cadres that directly organised this investigation. To put it bluntly, all the investigators were responsible to only one person – Comrade Jianfeng.

"Shall we start now?" Du Wancheng asked Zeng Keda in a low voice. Zeng nodded his head.

Du Wancheng turned to look at Xu Tieying, who uttered his approval.

Unexpectedly, Du Wancheng did not solicit the opinion of either Wang Benquan or Ma Linshen. He loudly proclaimed the meeting open.

The first person to be investigated was Ma Hanshan, deputy director of the Citizens' Food-Distribution Committee in Peking Municipality.

The door of the conference room was pushed open from the outside. Ma Hanshan came in with a pile of documents. He nodded and smiled at the five people in the front row, but immediately found something amiss.

Du Wancheng, Zeng Keda and Xu Tieying all looked at him. Ma Linshen and Wang Benquan, whom he regarded as his backers, both wore gloomy faces. They stared at the table.

Ma Hanshan did not know that the reason for their downcast appearance was Du Wancheng's failure to offer any greeting to them before opening the meeting. There was no time to think things through, however, so he went straight to the chair in the middle across from the investigators. As he moved the chair to sit down, he nodded and smiled at Fang Meng'ao who was sitting at the top of the conference table.

"No one's asked you to sit down yet." Zeng Keda stared at Ma Hanshan. Ma Hanshan froze, his body half seated. He looked at Zeng Keda in disbelief.

"You're facing the five-member group sent by the central government," said Zeng Keda. "First, report your name and position."

Zeng Keda was clearly trying to cow him into submission

Ma Hanshan rose slowly and straightened himself up. He was known for his capacity to swallow insults and humiliations, yet he found it unacceptable to be judged and treated like a prisoner. Because this also involved Peking's Food-Distribution Committee, it naturally also involved the Central Food-Distribution Commission. He looked at Ma Linshen.

Ma Linshen, who had been in a sombre mood, suddenly looked up and said: "This is a five-member investigation group, not a special criminal court. Director Ma, you're only a person of interest. There's no need to give your name or position. Sit down."

Now, the confrontation could begin. Ma Hanshan put the pile of documents on the table and prepared to sit down.

"Get out!" Zeng Keda pounded the table with his fist, then stood up abruptly, his eyes burning with rage. Pointing to the door, he shouted at Ma Hanshan: "Get out of here right away if you refuse to give your name and position!"

Ma Hanshan froze again.

"I protest!" Ma Linshen also pounded the table and stood up. "This is an insult to the Citizens' Food-Distribution Committee! Mr Du, as group leader, aren't you supposed to implement conference norms on behalf of Nanking?"

Du Wancheng, a PhD in Finance from Oxford University, was appointed chief inspector of the Ministry of Finance because he was a protégé of Wang Yunwu, the current finance minister. He was valued for his expertise and sense of justice as a scholar, which is why he was recommended to the joint meeting as coordinator of the five-member group, or in Ma Linshen's words, "the group leader". He hated the corruption that prevailed in the party-state from top to bottom as much as Zeng Keda did, but he didn't expect that all was set for a showdown as soon as the meeting started. Put simply, he couldn't deal with such conflicts.

Du Wancheng was at a loss and looked to Zeng Keda for help. Zeng Keda, now wearing a conciliatory look, nodded at him and said loudly: "Everyone has a copy of the documents of the joint meeting of the Central Committee. Read Article Two of Section Two. What attitude should the respondents adopt when being investigated by the working group? If anyone in the group of five hasn't even read the documents, I suggest they go back to do the necessary homework before coming to the meeting!" With that, he stared directly at Ma Linshen.

Fortunately, Ma was sitting next to Xu Tieying, and there were still two people separating him from Zeng Keda. But his face was dripping with sweat. Being an official at vice-ministerial level of the central government, he could not tolerate today's public reproach by a major general whose position was much lower than his own.

Xu Tieying was quick-witted and picked up the glass of boiled water in front of him and handed it to Ma Linshen. Ma's hands were still shaking slightly as he held the glass. He managed to take a sip of water and inhale, but could no longer speak. All he could do was look down at the red-letter-headed document before him.

Ma Hanshan stood, his mind blank. Although the large ceiling fan was turning, the sweat rolled down his face.

Zeng Keda squinted at the top of the conference table where Fang Meng'ao was seated. It was the nearest seat to Ma Linshen.

Fang Meng'ao had a sinister smile on his lips, as he raised his hand to show both the index and middle finger. Some might have thought that he was making a smoking gesture, but anyone who had dealt with the US military would understand that it was a rebuke in response to Zeng Keda's rage just now.

The smile that Zeng Keda returned was unnatural. He sat down again and turned his attention to the documents. Wang Benquan, sitting next to Zeng Keda, was full of defiance. He belonged to the Central Bank and had no interest in fighting the people under Jianfeng. However, he felt it necessary to help bring about a compromise. He turned to Ma Hanshan and said: "Since it is stipulated by the joint meeting protocol of the Central Committee, Director Ma, why don't you give us your name and position?"

Ma Hanshan managed to muster up courage and stated: "I am Ma Hanshan, male, fifty-three years old. Director of the Civil Affairs Bureau of Peking Municipality, I have also served as deputy director of the Peking Citizens' Food-Distribution Committee since April, the thirty-seventh year of the Republic of China." After stating these details clearly, he stared straight at Zeng Keda, who was still reading with his head lowered. "Might I take my seat now?"

"Sit down," said Zeng Keda without even looking up.

Ma Hanshan plopped himself down in the chair, but the humble expression he wore on first entering the room was gone; his face was ablaze with fury, waiting for the worst to come, and preferring death to the alternative of living in humiliation.

The person who should have begun the questioning was Du Wancheng, but Du did not know what to say in a situation like this. So he looked around at the other four members of the group.

Zeng Keda was still reading the papers he had in front of him, while Xu Tieying looked ahead with a solemn face; Wang Benquan gazed out of the window.

Although appearing to read the papers, Ma Linshen was still panting as if he were about to be afflicted with a serious illness.

Only Fang Meng'ao, who was attending the conference as an observer, smiled kindly at the bespectacled Du Wancheng.

Du looked at Ma Hanshan, and said: "Deputy Director Ma, can you brief us on the progress you've made since assuming this post in April?"

"If you want me to report in a comprehensive way, you should summon the director of the Peking Citizens' Food-Distribution

Committee. I must make it clear to the five-member group that I am only a deputy director, I'm not in charge of the overall situation."

Du Wancheng was taken aback by Ma's response. However, his remarks seemed to improve the health of Ma Linshen, who took a long breath of relief. He looked up and cast an approving look at Ma Hanshan.

Zeng Keda slowly raised his head and asked: "Who is the director of the Peking Citizens' Food-Distribution Committee?"

Ma Hanshan was stunned by the question, but he could not provide a straight answer: "Everyone knows that Mr Liu Yaozhang, the mayor of Peking, acts as the director."

"When did Liu Yaozhang begin to serve as director of the committee?" Zeng Keda asked.

Ma Hanshan swallowed his phlegm and replied: "The twenty-third of June."

Zeng Keda raised his tone abruptly: "General Inspector Du asked you to report the overall situation since April, but you tried to divert our attention by naming someone who was appointed to this additional post on the twenty-third of June. Ma Hanshan, do you think it appropriate to use what you picked up at the Bureau of Investigation when dealing with us?"

At this moment, Du Wancheng managed to muster a little strength. He pushed up his thick glasses and demanded: "Answer Inspector Zeng's question."

By now, Ma understood the group's main objective today. If he succumbed during the first investigation, the people behind him would abandon him, so he had to put up a fight at all cost. "Well, let me answer you this way. First, the committee has more than one deputy director. Each one is in charge of their own area. I don't know all their specific responsibilities. Second, although Mr Liu succeeded his predecessor not long ago, he has all the reports, not me. Third, He Siyuan, the former mayor of Peking, was also the director before June. You can always ask the former director what the current director does not know. Fourth, Inspector Zeng has just mentioned the Bureau of Investigation. Yes, I have a part-time position at the bureau. Do you also want to investigate the bureau on this occasion, may I ask? If you're going to investigate the material supply of the Military Committee, Inspector Zeng, you can always ask Director Zheng Jiemin in Nanking. Director Zheng is now vice-minister at the Ministry of Defence. Since you're also from that ministry, it should be easy enough to ask him directly."

Though Ma Hanshan was expected to come up with all kinds of confrontational moves, no one had thought he would respond with a list of four points. He also mentioned Zheng Jiemin, who was head of the Bureau of Investigation as well as deputy defence minister and deputy director of the Military Material Supply Committee.

The atmosphere in the meeting became tense. Du Wancheng's confidence deserted him once more, and he looked to Zeng Keda for help. Xu Tieying appeared even more expressionless than he did before.

When it came to the military, especially the secret service, Wang Benquan found it hard to come up with the right words. But he was now wearing a cheerful expression. By contrast, Ma Linshen looked askance at Zeng Keda. It was time for him to vent his outrage.

Physically, Zeng Keda could easily deal with Ma Hanshan. But now he was calm, and he looked at no one but Fang Meng'ao. He didn't care about Ma Hanshan. But in reality, he was secretly observing Fang Meng'ao's reaction. It was Fang Meng'ao and his background in which he took a profound interest. Now was the ideal time to test him. If this man had no connection with the Communists, he must be the person to rely on when it came to handling Ma Hanshan, especially Fang Buting, whom he found hard to deal with.

Fang Meng'ao's indifferent manner, which he had maintained since the start of the meeting, had now gone and the eagle-like eyes that Zeng Keda had previously witnessed, re-appeared, and he stared at Ma Hanshan in anger.

"Captain Fang," demanded Zeng Keda, "you're the leader of the Economic Inspection Brigade dispatched to Peking. You will be responsible for carrying out specific tasks in the future. We'd like to hear your response to the four rebuttals put forward just now by Director Ma Hanshan."

Fang Meng'ao immediately resumed his indifferent manner and

said: "I'm attending the meeting just as an observer. Am I allowed to share my opinion with you?"

"Of course you can," replied Du Wancheng. "You've every right to share your own views and perform any tasks. This is clearly stated in the documents of the joint meeting."

"Then, might I continue?"

"Please indulge us," said Zeng Keda.

Fang Meng'ao looked at Ma Hanshan. "Director Ma, allow me not to address the four points you just raised, because I don't have a clue how to respond."

For unknown reasons, Ma Hanshan had always been in fear of Fang Meng'ao, even more afraid than he was of Zeng Keda. He started his career as an agent at the bureau and served as its director in residence in Peking. As director of the local Commission for the Suppression of Traitors, he had executed many people, leaving their families broken. Over a period of time, he had developed a justifiable reputation for ruthlessness. But he did not know why, yesterday, when he saw Fang Meng'ao, he had had an ominous sense of the cynicism of this young man who made Japanese pilots tremble with fear, who was valued by the American allies, who dared to disobey the orders of the War Department and who even daunted Fang Buting. His experience suggested that such people were afraid of no one. If you refused to cooperate with him, he would beat you in the same way he shot down a Japanese pilot, then went to drink his foreign wine, smoke his foreign cigars and in the twinkling of an eye had forgotten the people whom they had beaten in the first place. This might be the root cause of his fear.

The selfish fear those who are not selfish, in the same way that the calculating fear those who are not calculating. Ma Hanshan understood that. Now he was experiencing exactly this feeling when listening to what Fang Meng'ao had just said. As a result, he retracted from his confrontational attitude towards Zeng Keda, and answered Fang Meng'ao gently: "Captain Fang, you're a hero of the Chinese Army and a national hero against the Japanese invaders. I have great respect for you, as does everyone. I appreciate your disdain for doing many things. Indeed, you don't even bother to think about them. So I empathise with you when you say you didn't understand what I just said. Didn't you once work for another faction, the Military Bureau? Since you have been kept in the dark, is it fair to use you as a stooge?"

The first half of what he said was fairly accurate, although the second was rather off the mark. As soon as he finished, Ma Hanshan himself felt he might have struck the wrong note, but it was too late to retract his words.

" I understand what you just said," said Fang Meng'ao, standing up. "Let me ask you this – who actually used me as a stooge?"

Ma Hanshan explained by reverting to type and replying with a forced smile: "A soldier's duty is to obey. That's all I mean."

"Again, I don't understand you." Fang Meng'ao's eyes narrowed. "Tell me if I should obey or not? To obey is to serve as someone's tool, while to disobey is not to serve, yes? No, you don't have to answer me, I'll answer the question myself. You were thinking I'm a person who can give up self-interest because I was capable of defying the orders of the War Department. That's what you mean. But let me make it clear to you. I ordered my brigade not to bomb Kaifeng because I had no intention of bombing our own cities or killing our compatriots. But Director Ma, you're different. Last night I looked into some of your background. I found out that not long ago, you used your position in the bureau to dispatch hundreds of undercover agents to kill students. What laws did those students break? They just wanted to get the food rations to which they were entitled. He Siyuan, the former mayor of Peking, who was also the former director of the Citizens' Food-Distribution Committee, firmly opposed what you did. Today, we asked you about the situation. You, however, shirked your responsibility in front of He Siyuan, the former director who has been removed from his post. How can we get hold of him? Liu Yaozhang, the incumbent director, doesn't even know what this committee is all about. What information do you think we can extract from him? Deputy Director Ma, you're directly in charge of the allocation and transfer of everyday materials to the public. My brigade is specially assigned to investigate materials transfer and make an audit of all the items. From now on, I'll ask no one but you!"

"Captain Fang..." Ma Hanshan said, getting heated.

"I'm not finished yet. I have fought countless battles in the air, and the pilots I've gunned down were all Japanese. Not a single shot was fired on my fellow pilots' planes. If you don't believe me, check my file. That's all I have to say. Go ahead!"

Zeng Keda was the first to clap his hands. Very loudly. Du Wancheng subconsciously clapped a few times, only to find none of the other three were joining in. He realised that it might not be appropriate for him to applaud, so he stopped.

Zeng Keda also stopped and looked at Ma Hanshan. "All your four rebuttals are refuted by Captain Fang Meng'ao, right? Do you want me to add anything else?"

Ma Hanshan stood up and said: "I solemnly propose to correct the five-member investigation group in that the Peking Municipal Citizens' Food-Distribution Committee is not placed under the leadership of Ma Hanshan. It's not my committee. There's so much food and material to purchase and allocate, I couldn't manage it even if I had a thousand hands. If I'm to be the only person to audit the materials and items just as Captain Fang said, I would like to resign as deputy director of the committee right away. Unless you also investigate the relevant Central Bank agencies and the procurement agencies abroad, I will refuse to answer any questions."

This was typical of Ma Hanshan. He was always ready to implicate other government organisations with joint responsibilities.

The first group member to get upset was Wang Benquan. He stared at him in anger: "What has the Central Bank to do with your committee's purchase and transfer of everyday materials? Director Ma, you'll be held responsible for what you said!"

Ma Linshen felt impelled to support Ma Hanshan at this critical moment: "Chief Inspector Du, I think Ma Hanshan's proposal is reasonable. There are so many departments involved in the procurement and allocation of everyday materials for the public. We can't put all the blame on the committee, let alone on Ma Hanshan himself."

"Who else do you want to investigate at the same time?" asked Du Wancheng.

Having presided over the meeting for quite a while, Du's words had everyone baffled, including Ma Hanshan.

But Zeng Keda remained attentive and alert. First, he gave Fang Meng'ao a deep look, hoping that he would understand what he was going to say. Then he turned to Ma Hanshan: "Are you suggesting that the investigation group should ask the governor of the Central Bank's Peking branch to tell us his side of the story?"

Ma Hanshan hesitated, before replying: "I don't have a say in who to invite. Just do everything by the book."

Zeng Keda turned to Du Wancheng and said: "Chief Inspector Du, then we'll ask Governor Fang Buting to come. Otherwise, the committee will not cooperate with the investigation."

Du Wancheng represented the Ministry of Finance, but the Central Bank managed the fund, much to the resentment of almost everyone under Minister Wang Yunwu. One of the daunting tasks of this mission was to investigate how the Central Bank had managed the funding. Therefore, he looked to Wang Benquan and said: "I agree with this proposal, Director Wang. Since the Peking branch is under your supervision, can you please make a phone call and invite Governor Fang to present himself here?"

There was no reason to refuse. Wang stood up angrily and said: "OK, I'll place the call."

Zeng Keda subconsciously looked up at Fang Meng'ao out of the corner of his eye. Fang returned the look and said: "General Zeng."

Zeng Keda seemed unprepared to respond. Fang Meng'ao took out a cigar and lighter and asked: "Can I smoke here?"

"Certainly." Zeng Keda sensed that Fang Meng'ao was starting to become a little confrontational.

Fang Meng'ao flicked the lighter loudly and lit his cigar. He took a big puff. After he exhaled, a layer of smoke clouded the meeting room.

Once more, when observing Fang Meng'ao through the smoke, Zeng Keda found that Fang was looking out of the window. He imagined the smoke magically turning into a cloud of heavy smoke issuing from a locomotive train.

―――

Clouds of smoke were spewing out of the Nanking-to-Peking train on which Cui Zhongshi was travelling with the two agents in tow. The train was already in Hebei Province. In a few hours, it would reach Peking.

Cui Zhongshi was still sitting in seat six, carefully reading the *Ta Kung Pao* that his fellow passenger had brought along. In those days, the newspaper contained many pages, but Cui Zhongshi did not know which page he was looking at.

The passenger in seat seven put his hand on the window, which seemed unintentional, yet a finger of that hand was gently tapping where Cui Zhongshi could see. Sometimes he stopped after five taps, sometimes after eight.

On the page that Cui Zhongshi was reading, the fifth word of the first sentence of the first article was the word for "we", corresponding with the number of taps made by the passenger. His fast fingers continued to tap the numbers. The words on that page that corresponded to the tapping at intervals were quickly unfolding before Cui's eyes, into a combination that read as follows: "We must ensure that Comrade Fang's identity is not exposed. Be sure to protect yourself..." The train slowed down as it arrived at the next station.

The passenger in seat seven got up, went to the rack, pulled out a key and opened the lock. He then took the trunk off the rack.

Not far away, the two young men looked at each other. The train came to a stop.

The passenger in seat seven stood before Cui Zhongshi. "Excuse me, sir," he said. "I'm about to disembark. Are you done with the newspaper?"

Cui Zhongshi raised his head and gave him a knowing look. "I'm done with it. Thank you." He rolled up the paper and gave it back to him.

Not far away, the two young men stretched out their arms. It looked like they were preparing to get off the train for a break. They parted ways, one moving up to the head of the carriage, while the other went to the end of the compartment.

The passenger in seat seven carried his suitcase and took the newspaper to the exit near seat one. Only a few people got off the train. The passenger in seat seven had just reached the door and was about to disembark when suddenly someone put his hand on his shoulder. The passenger turned around and saw a young man's shining eyes. The young man whispered: "Excuse me, could you leave your *Ta Kung Pao* for me?"

CHAPTER 7

It had been the rule that every time he went out on business, Fang Buting would carry his bag and walk out into the front courtyard alone. The guard would open the gate to let him leave quietly where his car would be waiting.

Today, the rules had changed. Not that Fang Buting had come up with a new idea. It was because Xie Peidong, the recently returned Cheng Xiaoyun and Fang Mengwei who stayed home to keep him company, all three quietly followed him out of the house.

Half way down the front yard, Fang Buting seemed to realise that they were on his tail. He stopped and slowly turned around. "Why are you all following me?"

No one knew what to say, so none of them replied at first. Xie Peidong was the first to speak: "Sir, let me escort you there. You don't have to say anything. Let me do the talking."

One could see the usual trust in Fang Buting's eyes, but he shook his head. "Don't get yourself involved in this. I don't need your company, especially when it comes to dealing with these people."

"Governor, please allow Uncle Xie to escort you." Cheng Xiaoyun had always respectfully called Fang Buting "governor" and Xie Peidong "uncle" in front of others. "It's not that we're saying you're afraid of these five people. It's just that Meng'ao will listen to you a bit more if his uncle is present."

Fang Buting's face darkened. "Who do you think you are? Since when have you been allowed to interfere in my official business?" Though what he said was directed at Cheng Xiaoyun, his eyes were watching Fang Mengwei's reaction.

"Father," Fang Mengwei said, "don't say too much when you're there. I'll go to the Peking Telephone Office and see to it that they connect you to Mr Gu overseas. With that, you can call Ambassador Gu directly."

Fang Buting looked much relieved. He took great comfort in the filial loyalty and sagacity demonstrated by this younger son when major events occurred. But he soon became serious again and turned to Xie Peidong: "What's that famous line by Xin Youan? 'You should have a son like Sun Zhongmou', right?" The remark was a compliment, but it was obviously over the top. Fang Buting had always been reluctant to praise his son so that he should not become complacent.

Xie Peidong was very tactful: "Governor, don't praise him like this. Mengwei might not be worthy of the name."

Fang Mengwei understood his father's mood at this moment, and also his father's true intention behind these words. He glanced at his uncle and father with a grateful expression.

"Father, Uncle. I'll see you soon." He strode briskly out of the gate.

Fang Buting and Xie Peidong followed. Cheng Xiaoyun remained standing there. Fang Buting stopped again and looked back at Cheng Xiaoyun, who had no choice but to go up to him.

Fang Buting told her: "In the future, when Mengwei's around, please speak less. I'm saying this for your own good."

"Yes," replied Cheng Xiaoyun in a low voice. Fang Buting turned and strode towards the gate.

Xie Peidong followed him there and instructed the driver: "Go to Ambassador Gu's residence on Zhang Zizhong Road. Drive safely!"

"Yes sir," said the driver and two plainclothes guards in unison. Fang Buting got in the car, along with the driver and guards. The car drove smoothly out of the alleyway.

Xie Peidong and Cheng Xiaoyun watched the car until it made a turn. The two looked at each other, eyes full of concern. They silently went through the gate.

There should have been eight people in the meeting room in Gu Weijun's residence, but only seven were seated at this moment. The seat for Zeng Keda's adjutant was vacant.

The seven men were silent. They were all reading the files to distract them from the embarrassing moment that would surely follow.

Fang Meng'ao had stopped smoking his cigar, and looked so intense that his eyes were fixed ahead as if he were piloting a fighter plane.

Ma Hanshan was chain smoking. He lit up his second cigarette with the butt of the previous one.

"Permission to report!" came the voice of Zeng Keda's adjutant from outside the door. All five members of the group raised their heads.

Ma Hanshan took the cigarette from his mouth. But Fang Meng'ao was unmoved, remaining in his original position.

"Governor Fang, please!" The adjutant announced his arrival loudly outside the door.

Zeng Keda stood up swiftly with the bearing of a soldier. Du Wancheng reacted slowly, and as he stood up, he said to the other three: "Will you get up?" The three men obeyed.

In acting this way, the five-person group was showing considerable respect and courtesy to the governor.

Ma Hanshan was so distraught that he wondered why he was being treated in a different manner from Fang Buting even though this was the same investigation. Of course, he felt obliged to stand up, yet he couldn't refrain from looking at Fang Meng'ao.

At the same time, Zeng Keda was also looking at Fang Meng'ao. Seeing that the young man was sitting there without making a move, he said under his breath: "Captain Fang, please stand up."

Fang Meng'ao stood up.

The door was pushed open slowly. Was the adjutant being too

careful or were the people in the room imagining things? It seemed to take an age for the door to open.

The only person in the meeting room who had never seen Fang Buting before was Zeng Keda. The only other person in the meeting room who had not seen Fang Buting in the past ten years was Fang Meng'ao.

It was as if Zeng Keda was capable of watching two people at once, with one eye looking at Fang Buting emerging from behind the door, and the other secretly observing Fang Meng'ao to his right.

Fang Buting stood outside the door. Although it was midsummer, he was neatly dressed in the formal panache that made him look like a real gentleman. Waiting until the door was fully opened, he took off his hat, pressed it against his chest and made a slight bow to everyone in the room.

Once again, Zeng Keda raised his hand to salute him. The other four in the group followed and then bowed. Zeng Keda looked sideways at Fang Meng'ao.

Fang Buting felt the presence of the tall figure in the flying jacket standing to the left at the door.

Fang Meng'ao was still standing straight, looking ahead, without any reaction. There were mixed feelings in Zeng Keda's eyes as he looked at Fang Buting.

There was no expression on Fang Buting's face, before he smiled and bowed to the group of five. "Thank you all." He then walked slowly into the meeting room.

The group of five straightened up and waited for Fang Buting to be seated. The issue was where to sit. The place next to Ma Hanshan was the one designated for those being investigated. But if not there, where else could he sit?

Fang Buting did not embarrass the group of five and went straight to Ma Hanshan. Ma was impressively quick-witted, and moved the chair beside him so that Fang Buting could stand close to the table. He waited for Fang Buting to take his position at the table. And then he moved the chair straight so the governor could sit down.

"Governor Fang, please sit down," said Du Wancheng. Fang Buting obliged, and the group of five also took their seats.

Fang Meng'ao sat down with his eyes still looking ahead. Ma Hanshan was the last one to sit down.

Since Fang Buting was placed directly under the supervision of the Central Bank, Wang Benquan made the introductory remarks: "Most of you here are old friends of Governor Fang. Perhaps only Chief Inspector Zeng has not had the pleasure of meeting him before. Allow me to make a quick introduction. Governor Fang has a PhD from Harvard University and has long been a member of the Nationalist government's Central Bank. He is highly respected by both Mr Soong and Mr Kung. Inspector-General Zeng serves in the Bureau of Reserve Cadres. He's a young general held in high regard by the president."

The two looked squarely at each other.

"I've heard so much about you," Zeng Keda said politely.

Fang Buting responded appropriately: "Delighted to meet you."

"Captain Fang," Zeng Keda said, suddenly looking at Fang Meng'ao, who stood up in a military posture. "Governor Fang, since we're all here, I'd like to introduce you to your son, Fang Meng'ao. He serves as leader of the Peking Economic Inspection Team and Youth Aviation Brigade of the Bureau of Reserve Cadres."

Everyone else in the room was acting evasively, reading documents or simply looking elsewhere.

Fang Buting had no option but to look at his son and his head moved slowly to the left.

Of all the events in his life, this was even more perturbing than his first meeting with his mentor in the United States and being introduced to Chiang Kai-shek after returning to China. He had no idea how this "treacherous" son of his would respond when their eyes met.

There was also another pair of eyes that remained very focused on this first meeting between father and son in a decade. They belonged to Zeng Keda. He was keen to see whether Fang Meng'ao would recognise his father. As for whether this was out of sincere care or simple curiosity, even he himself was not sure.

At long last, Fang Buting met the son whom he hadn't seen for ten years! Sitting down, Fang Buting had to lift his head to see his son standing at his full height of 1.8 metres. A huge picture of Dr

Sun Yat-sen, the father of the nation, appeared on the wall above his head.

Fang Buting's eyes were hollow, waiting for some kind of response from his son. Bang! Fang Meng'ao clicked his leather shoe heels, the sound almost deafening in this quiet room. All eyes were trained on him.

Fang Meng'ao hadn't saluted up to this point, so it was somewhat surprising to see him raise his right hand to the brim of his hat and salute in the standard military way. Indeed, he was saluting to some unknown person right in front of him!

Fang Meng'ao turned forty-five degrees to the right, his body facing Fang Buting. All eyes now turned to Fang Buting.

Fang Buting's empty eyes appeared to brighten, but only fleetingly, because his son's eyes only looked at a place somewhere above his head.

To stand up or remain seated? Fang Buting sat there firmly and said to his son: "Sit down, please."

Fang Meng'ao put down his hand in the same military manner, his body relaxed and he sat down.

All the other participants in the room remained very concerned. They knew enough about Fang Meng'ao's background to understand why he had been granted amnesty. Party affairs should never be handled the way state affairs are handled, but when state business was conducted by private hands, they were always inseparable from these two words: gratitude and resentment. Those who had been grateful to the party would have their crimes reduced to nothing; while those who were resentful of the party would have their crimes inflated, or something more serious would be conjured out of thin air. However, it was beyond everyone's expectation for Fang Buting's son to be pressed to work against his own father. It sent a strong signal that the young would be tough on those who were decrepit or behind the times.

In his forties, Du Wancheng was at an age that some regarded as embarrassing. He was neither old nor young. If he were to be classified at all, he belonged to the middle-aged and the erudite, and the scrupulous who abhorred corruption yet lacked the courage to participate in the factional strife within the Kuomintang. Now it was his turn to preside over the meeting again.

After mulling the matter over, he said: "Governor Fang, we hope you understand why we asked you to present yourself here. The government attaches great importance to the 'Fifth of July' student unrest. There has been much speculation. To make things worse, our US allies sent us a note, and many members of the parliament also raised concerns. The war is straining the government's budget, the supply of military materials has been stretched to the limit and the budget for people's everyday materials has been kept to a minimum. If there is corruption and smuggling, the Ministry of Finance will be in a lot of trouble. Everyday materials purchased by the Peking Citizens' Food-Distribution Committee are done in strict accordance with the budget allocation of the Ministry of Finance. Why is there always such a big gap between physical goods and the accounts? In July, the Ministry of Education officially reported the budget to the Ministry of Finance for the relocation of more than fifteen thousand students from sixteen Northeastern universities. The Ministry allocated special funds for the relocation. Why was there a motion by the Peking Senate to dismiss students from the Northeast on the fourth of July? The Peking branch of the Central Bank is in charge of the accounts of the Citizens' Food-Distribution Committee. Has the Central Bank's money been transferred to Peking? Has the Peking branch transferred the money to the committee? If all the money is in place, then the branch will not be held responsible. Governor Fang, this is the main reason we asked you to come here."

Du Wancheng was not politically well-versed, but he was competent in meticulously analysing the economics of the situation. Consequently, Fang Buting had no choice but to respond.

The other four members of the group were all burying their heads, pretending to read the documents while waiting for Fang Buting's answer.

Fang Buting replied: "Since the representatives of the Finance Ministry and the Central Bank are here, might I take the liberty to ask first whether the money Mr Du referred to was US dollars or *fabi?*"

The question caught Du Wancheng off guard because cash transfers had always been conducted by the Central Bank. How could the Ministry of Finance know? He looked to Wang Benquan for help.

Wang responded: "The US Mission of Assistance to China signed the Law on Assistance to China on the third of July. As to how much the bill agreed to help us, it is a state secret and I cannot disclose it here. But what I can share with you is that about two thirds of the aid in US dollars is spent on the military, while the remaining one third goes on people's everyday materials. It's not clear how much and how useful it will be. The money, it's just words written into the agreement between the two countries. When it comes to *fabi*, I think the Ministry of Finance knows better than we do, that even if you were able to mobilise all the planes and trains to transport it, you still couldn't buy all the goods and materials with it. Governor Fang, let me explain this to you: all banks need reserves. However, there's no gold in the vaults, and the dollars are still in the United States.

"But why is the Central Bank and the Peking branch involved in material purchase, allocation and distribution? Governor Fang, you can write your resignation to the headquarters of the Central Bank now, and I will help to have you removed from the position so that you won't be their scapegoat."

This was not what the members of the investigation team sent by the Central Committee were supposed to say, since they were meant to be impartial. This first meeting seemed to be over now.

But one man felt this was unfair: Ma Linshen, deputy director of the Central Commission on Citizens' Food Distribution. When such an outrageous incident happened, should the Central Bank shirk all its responsibility? Why was the committee singled out to bear responsibility?

Ma Linshen stood up and said: "What Director Wang has just said is quite true, I have no objections at all. Just one quick question, however. The Central Commission and the Peking Committee for the Distribution of Citizens' Food were both established in April, with all their members coming from the Ministry of Social Affairs, the Ministry of Civil Affairs and their lower-level counterparts. Neither ministry prints money, nor can they produce food or other materials. If the Central Bank does not allocate funds or the government does not allocate materials, how can the commission purchase and allocate the materials? If you don't make this clear, Director Ma, I also agree that you should write your resignation letter and I will help you to resign as deputy director of the Peking Citizens' Food-Distribution Committee so that you won't be their scapegoat."

Ma Hanshan stood up and made a deep bow to Ma Linshen. "Please," he said, "it would be better to let me resign right now. Please, Director Ma, please!"

What an outrage! Du Wancheng turned pale with anger, pushed his glasses up a little and stuttered: "You're working against this group, aren't you? No, you're actually working against the decision made by the joint meeting of the Nationalist government! If the representative of the Central Bank and the representative of the Central Commission on Citizens' Food Distribution share similar ideas, I will report to Minister Wang Yunwu right away!"

Sitting at both ends of the same side of the table, Wang Benquan and Ma Linshen leaned back simultaneously and uttered the same words: "As you please."

Du Wancheng's lips quivered with anger. "Phone! Get me the phone!" Zeng Keda's adjutant was attending the meeting to take the minutes, and it was his job to fetch the phone. He looked to Zeng Keda who gave him a nod of approval.

The adjutant rose and picked up the telephone on the table behind him. Fortunately, the cord was long enough to reach Du Wancheng.

Because it was a special line, a phone with a ring handle was required. Du Wancheng stood up, with one hand pressing on the phone, and the other turning the handle. Because his hand was still shaking, he could not grasp the handle properly. When he picked up the receiver and prepared to talk to the operator, a hand reached over and pressed down the phone.

It was Zeng Keda. "Mr Du," he said, "will calling Minister Wang resolve the issue?" Du Wancheng looked up at him.

"Give me the phone, please," Zeng Keda continued softly. Du Wancheng was obedient and handed the receiver over. Zeng Keda picked up the phone and put it in front of him. He turned the handle, quickly and powerfully. Speaking into the receiver, Zeng sounded as if he was commanding thousands of troops at the front line. "This is Zeng Keda from the Ministry of Defence. Please connect me to number two special line in Nanking. Do it right away."

Wang Benquan and Ma Linshen, who were still leaning back in their chairs, straightened up like springs. Ma Hanshan also looked transformed. He was no longer the dead mouse that felt no cold.

Xu Tieying, who had been keeping a poker face, was also slightly shocked. He looked at Fang Buting.

Fang Buting managed to keep his countenance during the confrontation. Like his father, Fang Meng'ao had been sitting there all along, looking straight ahead.

The phone call seemed to connect. Du Wancheng looked at Zeng Keda with great anticipation. "Yes, it's me. This is Zeng Keda." Zeng was standing upright. "Yes, might I ask Director Chiang Ching-kuo to answer the phone right away? OK, thank you."

Apart from Fang Buting and Fang Meng'ao, everyone else was looking at the receiver pressed against Zeng Keda's ear.

"Yes. I'm fine. How are you, Comrade Jianfeng?" Zeng Keda asked with a pious face. "As you correctly predicted, Wang Benquan, the Central Bank's representative, said the bank has no responsibility for the Seventh of July Incident, and so did Ma Linshen, the representative of the Central Commission on Citizens' Food Distribution."

Director Ching-kuo apparently said something at the other end. Zeng Keda listened attentively, and then replied: "Yes. I'll ask them on your behalf right away." With the phone in his hand, he looked at Wang Benquan and then at Ma Linshen. "Director Ching-kuo asked both of you – whose responsibility is it? Is it his responsibility? Please reply now."

Ma Linshen looked at Wang Benquan from a distance, and Wang Benquan returned the stare. Neither of them dared say anything; they each wanted the other to speak first.

Zeng Keda's eyes fixed on Ma Linshen, and he held the phone's mouthpiece out to him: "This is number two special line. Do you intend to keep Director Ching-kuo waiting?"

Ma Linshen had to reply. With his body leaning on the table, across from Xu Tieying and Du Wancheng, he tried to put his head close to the speaker and said loudly: "Director Ching-kuo, permit me to report to you that I absolutely did not say that the commission bore no responsibility. We will check carefully..."

Zeng Keda grabbed the phone and listened to the short instruction given by Director Ching-kuo: "Yes." He then extended the phone slightly to the left.

Sitting beside Zeng Keda, Wang Benquan stretched out his hand for the phone.

Zeng Keda's hand tightly held the mouthpiece and he ordered: "Speak."

"Hello, Director Ching-kuo," said Wang Benquan. "Perhaps it was General Zeng Keda who misunderstood me. The Central Bank's headquarters is certainly responsible for such a mass incident, and so is its Peking branch. We'll look into it, improve our work and put an end to it in a satisfactory manner."

Zeng Keda took the phone back and pressed it to his ear again. "Yes. Mr Du, Director Ching-kuo wants to speak to you."

Du Wancheng had been growing increasingly excited, and he grabbed the phone: "Thank you very much, Director Ching-kuo. Yes, I'm listening... OK... Totally agree... OK, OK, I'll put him on straight away."

Du Wancheng looked at Fang Meng'ao. "Captain Fang, come here quickly. Director Ching-kuo has praised you. Come here to speak to him."

This was a little beyond Fang Meng'ao's expectation. He stood up, but did not make as if to answer the phone.

Zeng Keda was quick in his response. He took the phone and grabbed the cord from Du Wancheng, and walked briskly to Fang Meng'ao.

Fang Meng'ao took the phone, but instead of saying hello, he waited quietly before making his reply: "It's what we should do. We're soldiers, and soldiers should live in barracks..."

Nobody knew what the director had said at the other end, and Fang Meng'ao became silent. Zeng Keda, who was standing by, was anxious: "Feel free to speak to Director Ching-kuo."

"I know," said Fang Meng'ao on the telephone. "I can tell the difference between public and private." With that, he returned the phone to Zeng Keda.

Zeng Keda snatched the phone, went back to his original place and listened attentively. "Yes. Please rest assured, Comrade Jianfeng, I'll ask Mr Du to announce it."

Back at his seat, Zeng Keda did not put the phone down until the director on the other end had hung up. Looking at Du Wancheng, he explained: "Chief Inspector Du, Director Ching-kuo said that he had told you what he wanted to say. Please announce it to everyone."

"Good." Du Wancheng was now full of confidence, and he stood up. "All rise." Everyone in the meeting room stood up, including Fang Buting and Ma Hanshan.

Du Wancheng now assumed a very serious expression. "Two instructions," he said. "Instruction one. During the investigation process initiated by the current five-member group, any person under investigation is allowed to resign. But after resignation, he shall be transferred to the central government's special criminal court and be subject to the court's investigation and a trial. Instruction two. The Economic Inspection Brigade dispatched by the Bureau of Reserve Cadres to Peking shall have the power to investigate the materials in any warehouse used by the Citizens' Food-Distribution Committee and check the accounts of the Peking branch of the Central Bank. The investigation results shall be reported directly to Inspector General Du Wancheng and General Zeng Keda. Commissioner Xu Tieying of the Peking Police Bureau must fully cooperate with the inspection team in conducting the investigation."

It was all quiet in the meeting room.

Du Wancheng broke the silence: "Deputy Director Ma, and Director Ma, do you still need our help to resign now?"

Ma Hanshan replied in an unexpectedly loud voice: "I must confess to the panel of five that what I said previously was outrageous. I take it back."

Du Wancheng's eyes slowly turned to Fang Buting. Everyone became nervous, despite trying to give the appearance of remaining calm. They all looked at Fang Buting, except for Fang Meng'ao. He was looking at Du Wancheng!

Du Wancheng's heart thumped. Fang Meng'ao was staring at him like an eagle. What did he mean by glaring in this manner?

"Governor Fang didn't say anything about resigning just now," said Zeng Keda. "If I remember correctly, it was Director Wang Benquan who uttered those words. Is that right?"

Wang Benquan felt obliged to reply right away: "I did say that. Governor Fang did not mention anything about resigning."

"When the time comes, I will step down," Fang Buting said. "But not now. The country is in crisis, and if I resign, I will have a guilty conscience." He looked to Zeng Keda and continued: "Inspector Zeng, can I use your phone, please?"

Zeng Keda hesitated before agreeing to the request and handing the phone over to Fang Buting. Everyone held their breath again, having only just recovered from that recent phone conversation. Who was Fang Buting going to call now?

Fang Buting had been put through: "Is that Ambassador Gu? Brother Weijun, sorry to bother you. This is Fang Buting."

Everyone was taken aback by Fang Buting's decision to call the owner of the mansion, the ambassador to the United States of America, Gu Weijun!

Fang Buting acted as if there was no one around. "Yes, I think you're also fully aware of what went on. The 'Seventh of July Incident' should not have happened. It makes it more difficult for you to ask for American aid. But I still want to plead for help. It's imperative to ensure the continued provision of military supplies to fight the Communist troops. But so many people in so many cities have no food to eat, especially those in Peking. If everyday materials for the public from the US don't arrive soon, we'll lose the battle at home before we lose it at the front. Since the main battlefields are in the north, please get more to Peking."

No one had expected Fang Buting to utter these remarks so forcefully. Everyone was deeply affected.

Fang Meng'ao cast his eyes on his father for the first time.

Fang Buting seemed so busy with the call that he forgot the people assembled around him: "Thank you. On behalf of all my colleagues in the party-state, as well as the two million residents of Peking, a tremendous thank you! Say hello to your wife. Take care of yourselves. Goodbye."

Fang Buting put down the phone. Everyone looked at him in admiration.

He now turned to Fang Meng'ao. "Captain Fang, the Citizens'

Food-Distribution Committee account is handled by the Peking branch. The person in charge is my assistant, Cui Zhongshi, deputy treasury director of the branch. He'll arrive in Peking this afternoon. You're welcome to come to check the accounts at any time."

Nobody uttered a word. Fang Meng'ao no longer avoided his father's eyes.

The two who had not met for ten years looked directly at each other.

Fang Buting nodded his head and turned to Du Wancheng. "General Inspector Du, can I leave now?"

"We'll see you off," Du Wancheng said hastily. "Come on, everyone. Let's walk Governor Fang out."

The Peking Youth Aviation Brigade had drawn up orders to prohibit soldiers from leaving its barracks. As a result, members of the brigade were all staying put indoors. Some were reading, others were writing. There were also two groups of pilots playing poker.

Chen Changwu's group were playing according to strict rules in which the losers had to stick a slip of paper on their face. Chen Changwu had stuck multiple slips on his face, leaving only his eyes uncovered.

Guo Jinyang's group seemed somewhat out of control since the rules of their game stated that losers should carry items on their backs. There was nothing in the barracks for them to carry except for what was on their beds. They started with pillows, then military quilts. The most unfortunate guy was the tall, rather taciturn Shao Yuangang. Although a trusted member of the brigade, Shao was rather slow-witted and easily manipulated by Guo Jinyang. He had three pillows and two army quilts strapped to his back.

On a hot day in the height of summer, even the shirtless felt the burning heat. The sweat was running down Shao Yuangang like raindrops with all that bedding on his back. To make things worse, he had become muddled-headed. As he wiped the sweat away, he tried to figure out how to continue playing cards.

The only man not to lose a game was Guo Jinyang. Standing with one foot on a bed, he demanded loudly: "Shao Yuangang, if you have the guts to mess with me, you'll be sure to have another quilt on your back!"

The two pilots who were reading and writing by the door stood up immediately at the sight of their captain.

Fang Meng'ao came in holding a large cardboard box and made a gesture to the brigade members who saw him, signalling them not to say anything.

Fang Meng'ao crept up behind Guo Jinyang, glanced at his cards and quickly walked behind Shao Yuangang.

Everyone saw him and was ready to collect the cards to end the game.

"Don't stop," said Fang Meng'ao, anxious not to be regarded as a spoilsport. "Shao Yuangang, show me your hand."

Shao Yuangang spread out the cards for Fang Meng'ao to see.

"Guo Jinyang," said Fang Meng'ao, "what did you say just now? If Shao Yuangang has the guts to mess with you, he'll have another quilt on his back?"

Guo Jinyang was quite downhearted, but his voice remained firm: "Captain, you stole a glance at my cards, it's not fair."

"You talk too much," said Fang Meng'ao. "Yuangang, just hit him!" Shao Yuangang immediately discarded all his cards.

Guo Jinyang mingled the cards in his hand with those on the bed: "Winning in that manner is not really winning."

Shao Yuangang didn't care. He took down the army quilt tied to his back and placed it on Guo Jinyang right away.

"Aren't you embarrassed to win a game like that?" Guo Jinyang retorted. Shao Yuangang was too honest and timid to hang the quilt. He glanced up at Fang Meng'ao. Everyone else had stopped playing, and was looking at Fang Meng'ao.

"Go hang it up," said Fang Meng'ao, "hang it up and I'll tell you all the truth." Shao Yuangang went to hang the quilt up again and Guo Jinyang didn't protest any more. He let the quilt be placed on his back.

Fang Meng'ao glanced at all his subordinates and said: "From today on, everyone who is supposed to see the cards will get to see them in an open and above-board way, anything but stealing a look. Our opponents never obey the rules, all their cards are hidden, like a triad gang. Is it possible to win such a game? Jinyang,

I've nothing against you. Do you understand who I'm referring to?"

All the pilots replied in unison: "Yes sir!"

"Do you really?" asked Fang Meng'ao with a heavy heart.

All the members of the brigade looked at him.

"I just came back from the meeting," Fang Meng'ao continued. "We've been assigned the task of checking the accounts of all the warehouses of the Peking Municipal Citizens' Food-Distribution Committee, as well as those of the Peking branch of the Central Bank."

Hearing this, everyone stole a glance at each other. Was the captain willing to follow orders and investigate his own father who happened to be governor of the Peking branch of the Central Bank? Chen Changwu winked. The men took off their pillows and quilts and lined up in two rows.

"Captain," said Chen Changwu, "when we were in Nanking, Inspector Zeng told us to investigate the materials of the Central Commission on Citizens' Food Distribution, and we were also responsible for the transportation of everyday materials in Peking. Why did they add another duty? We can't manage this, can we?"

"No," Guo Jinyang continued, "we're all pilots. It's too much to ask us to check the warehouses. Besides, how can we check their accounts without understanding them? We simply can't do it."

"We will not accept this task!" all the pilots said.

Fang Meng'ao looked at them. He was moved, but could not show it. "Well, checking the warehouses or banks won't happen for a few days. Let me first show you something. Jinyang, you're from Shanxi, and your ancestors were natural born businessmen. Now, do me a favour, open the box."

A doubtful Guo Jinyang untied the cord and opened the box, which was full of abacuses.

"Please distribute them among yourselves," Fang Meng'ao said. "Guo Jinyang, you can be the head instructor, while those of you who can use an abacus should be tutors. Those who can use an abacus will coach those who can't, and those who can count will tutor those who can't. I'll give you three days to learn."

"I can't learn in three days!" complained Shao Yuangang.

"Neither can we!" echoed many of his fellow pilots.

"If you can't, you can sweep the barracks and do the laundry for everyone else," Fang Meng'ao said as he went to his room.

All eyes were on the captain's back. For the first time they discerned that he was walking without his previous air of virility. The pilots looked at each other again, yet no one went to reach for an abacus.

Several people pushed at the door of the warehouse controlled by the Peking Municipal Commission on Citizens' Food Distribution. It opened reluctantly.

"Sons of bitches!" Ma Hanshan screamed on entering the building. "Why haven't you turned on the ventilation fans? Are you expecting a fire to break out here?"

He had good reason to utter these words. It was a scorching day in the sweltering heat of summer. Piles of goods and materials were strewn all over the warehouse. It was like entering a food steamer. No wonder he broke into curses as he seethed with rage.

Chastened by the criticism, the two section chiefs who followed Ma Hanshan, Li and Wang, turned to scold the warehouse caretakers.

"You bastards!" said Section Chief Li. "It's clearly stated in the warehouse regulations that ventilation must be guaranteed. Who turned off the fans?"

"The city is short of electricity," Wang said. "We were told to control electricity consumption..."

"Then why is our electricity bill so high? Wang Yixing, you must be corrupt!" said Ma Hanshan. "Which department dared to cut off the power to a warehouse? Damn you for embezzling money meant for paying electricity bills! You'll have your family electrified because of your greediness!"

It wasn't clear if Wang had a guilty conscience, or if he was accustomed to receiving a scolding, but at any rate, he stopped talking back. Instead, he turned to the two junior officials: "Come on! Turn on the electric fans right away!"

A member of his office ran to press the switch. The ventilators fixed to the walls around the warehouse started to turn.

Ma Hanshan continued his inspection resentfully. Li and Wang followed him at some distance.

"Has the ten thousand tonnes of rice from Yangtze Construction Company been put into storage?" Ma Hanshan asked as he walked.

Li and Wang were silent. Ma Hanshan stopped abruptly, and turned around. He glared at the two men.

"You know, Director Ma, we couldn't even get through the door of Yangtze Construction Company's office in Peking," Li replied. "The goods should have been delivered five days ago. We've made dozens of phone calls, which were all answered by this rather impatient woman. We didn't dare to rush her."

"Good, good," Ma Hanshan gasped. "Fang Meng'ao's brigade is going to check the warehouse soon. Yet we still have ten thousand tonnes of rice undelivered and due to arrive in the warehouse today. Prepare to get shot by his firing squad!"

"Director!" said Li, unable to restrain himself. "We paid the money, but they didn't deliver the rice. And you tell us that we'll get shot! Isn't there a law in the party-state preventing us from being shot?"

"Stop threatening me with the law!" Ma Hanshan almost roared. "Li Wuzhi, as transfer section chief, your accounts are so messy that you can't even make sure it'll stand examination by legal experts. You're dead meat already!"

Li Wuzhi did not dare to say anything more.

"Where's the phone?" Ma Hanshan continued to growl. "I'll place the call, and you, get the trucks ready and have the rice delivered tonight!"

As he barked, he found the phone himself. Chief Wang stammered: "Director, the telephone cord was bitten by rats."

Ma Hanshan shuddered with anger and glared at him. This time around he didn't bother scolding them; perhaps he felt he'd be wasting his breath, cursing these stupid sons of bitches. So he spat a thick ball of phlegm in front of Wang's feet and strode out of the warehouse.

Li and Wang looked at each other, and neither of them followed him out.

After arriving at his office from the warehouse, Ma Hanshan

started dialling. He waited on the line, but no one answered. "Sons of bitches! Those folk from Yangtze Construction Company, are you all dying out? Don't piss me off, otherwise I'll submit a report directly to the president! He'll come and curse you himself. You motherfuckers!"

As he was muttering away, he found himself put through by the operator. It was a young woman: "Who is speaking? How did you get our number? Do you know who we are?"

The arrogance! Ma Hanshan could hardly stand it, but he tried to suppress his anger and fall in with the tone of the woman at the other end: "This is the Peking Municipal Citizens' Food-Distribution Committee. Your phone number was given to me personally by General Manager Kung. I know you're the Peking office of Yangtze Construction Company! OK? Now, put Mr Kung on the line!"

The woman's tone was not as shrill as it had just been: "General Manager Kung is taking his lunch break. With so many people on the committee, how can I know who you are? Besides, Mr Kung doesn't take unscheduled phone calls."

Ma Hanshan was so angry that he raised his voice: "Let me tell you what, go tell Mr Kung that none of the five members on the investigation team sent by the national government is taking a lunch break! The inspection team of the Bureau of Reserve Cadres will be checking on you! Understand?"

The woman remained hopelessly ignorant: "What five-member investigation group? What do you mean by 'inspection team'? Have they reported to Mr Soong and Mr Kung? How dare you approach us in this manner."

Ma Hanshan almost lost his breath. Massaging his chest, he tried to speak in a calmer voice: "I'm telling you now that the people who sent the five-member group and the inspection team are more powerful than both Mr Soong and Mr Kung. Do you want me to spell it out?"

The woman seemed a little nervous now, but she still maintained her original tone: "How do I know if what you said is true or false? Who are you anyway?"

Ma Hanshan literally spelt his name syllable for syllable: "Ma Han-Shan! Just ask him if he can take the call!"

"What's Ma Hanshan's position?" The woman at the other end obviously had no idea who he was.

"Ma Hanshan is the deputy director of the Peking Municipal Citizens' Food-Distribution Committee, director of the Peking Municipal Bureau of Civil Affairs and former head of the Peking Committee for Combating Japanese Collaborators! Do you understand? If you don't act now, you'll be in serious trouble. Just wait for Kung to sack you!"

At this, the woman lowered her voice: "I didn't know you were Director Ma. You should've told me earlier. I'll get Mr Kung for you."

The sound of the phone being put down on a table followed. There was no engaged tone, so obviously she had not hung up.

Ma Hanshan pulled out a handkerchief and wiped away his sweat. Then he picked up his cup of Longjing tea and took a big gulp. He was waiting for Mr Kung. He seemed to hear the sound of footsteps approaching down the line. Ma Hanshan pressed the receiver to his ear.

Back in his room from the conference, Zeng Keda was also answering the phone. After listening for a short while, he whispered: "I agree to organise students to assist Fang's team in checking the accounts. Don't get the students from Peking and Tsinghua Universities involved. Only those from the Department of Economics at Yenching University. They must be under your control. You can arrange some students from Northeastern universities... Of course, we need to plant our own people in the group... Agreed. Don't get Miss He involved in the account-checking team. It would be better to ask her to continue her contact with Fang alone... OK. After asking your superiors for instructions, pay attention to their reactions. If they don't agree, something must be wrong. Ask for instructions right away."

On the first floor of the Foreign Languages Bookstore near the east gate of Yenching University, Liang Jinglun was on the phone with Zeng Keda.

"Good. I'll contact them right away. Will report to you in detail."

After hanging up the phone, he thought for a while and dialled another number. The call apparently connected, but no one answered. Liang Jinglun's eyes flashed a trace of suspicion. He waited for a moment and dialled the number again.

The telephone rang in the rare books section of Yenching University library. Yan Chunming heard the phone ring, but didn't answer it. At the opposite end of the table, a middle-aged man was sitting next to a mirror. Yan Chunming looked at the ringing phone, and then at the person with his back turned to him.

"Take it," the figure said, "and don't promise anything. Tell him you'll meet in half an hour and talk to him face to face."

Yan Chunming picked up the phone. "Professor Liang. Sorry, a professor wanted to check out a rare book just now. I'm processing his request. Please go ahead."

Liang Jinglun's voice came down the line. It was very weak and could not be heard clearly by anyone else in the room.

"It's very important," said Yan Chunming. "Well, I'll see you in half an hour. The old place." With that, he hung up the phone.

Yan Chunming's face turned serious, and he looked at the back of the person across the table.

The figure whispered: "The message relayed to you on the sixth of July should ring in your ears. Why did you turn a deaf ear to it? Each department has its own work. There are other departments that are actively encouraging defections from the Youth Aviation Brigade. You've no role in this. This is a serious violation of the rules of the organisation!"

Yan Chunming replied in a low voice: "Minister Liu, it's just a proposal, we haven't carried it out yet. If you don't agree, I'll stop her."

"Just a proposal?" came the stern voice. "He Xiaoyu has already contacted Fang Meng'ao. How could you stop her anyway? By taking a sudden decision to prevent He from making any further contact, you've reduced the rest of us to passive spectators."

Yan Chunming lowered his head in silence. Suddenly he raised his head again. "I accept your criticism. But please trust us and Professor Liang. We did this because we didn't want to miss the opportunity to conduct the struggle against the Kuomintang. What shall we do next? Please give us your instructions."

The figure was silent for a brief moment. "It's not that we distrust you," he said after a pause. "Fang Meng'ao's Youth Brigade has a very complex background, and we don't know much about it. Go meet with him. As long as it's controlled within the scope of the students' peripheral organisations, you can make contact first. Remember, don't endanger the lives of these progressive students."

"How do you explain the scope of peripheral organisations?" asked Yan Chunming. "Please clarify."

"No comrades in the party should take part in it. No confrontation. With these two principles upheld, the Kuomintang authorities will not be able to make further arrests. The students will not make any unnecessary sacrifice."

"Understood. I will report to you after I have shared the new instructions with Comrade Jinglun."

The figure stood up and responded: "Don't contact me. I'm leaving Peking today. In the future, someone else will be appointed to contact you. Also, don't break ranks. Don't tell Comrade Jinglun that you report to me."

Yan Chunming also stood up, with a trace of grievance and worry on his face. "If the organisation doesn't trust me, you can always review my portfolio."

"I take issue with your way of thinking," said the figure. "Is it true that the closer we get to the victory of revolution, the more you'll worry about your personal gains and losses? I've communicated the spirit of the Central Committee message to you. So make more effort to digest it."

"Of course," replied Yan Chunming.

"If the organisation doesn't trust me, you can review my portfolio at once." Surprisingly, Liang Jinglun repeated what Yan Chunming had just said, but adding the words "at once" to reinforce the message.

"Comrade Jinglun, the organisation approves of your work. But I take issue with your way of thinking. The closer we get to the victory of revolution, the less you will worry about personal gains and losses."

Liang Jinglun was silent. After a short while, he raised his head again. "I accept your criticism, but I don't admit to being worried about any personal gains or losses. If I worry about anything, I worry about the revolutionary work. Peking is the cultural centre of all China. Progressive youth yearn for revolution and the establishment of a New China. There is no reason for us to curb their revolutionary enthusiasm. Revolution is not just about fighting a battle, it's about mobilising everyone to resist the Kuomintang, imperialism and the oppressors. Long ago, Chairman Mao said that revolution is the conscious resistance by all the oppressed and exploited Chinese people to imperialism and Kuomintang reactionaries! Now, the revolution involving the struggle between the people and the reactionary regime has reached a decisive stage. I agree with the spirit of the 'Sixth of July Instruction' of the senior leaders. But this instruction only advised us to pay attention to the strategy of struggle. It did not tell us to reject the masses, especially the progressive students. Now the Kuomintang regime has engaged us in a decisive battle with our troops in northern and central China. But their economy is on the verge of collapse, relying mainly on American aid. Because of their fear of losing US aid and the huge wave of opposition in cities across the country, they sent a five-member investigation team to Peking as a mere formality. Fang Meng'ao's brigade represents our best opportunity. If we can take advantage of this brigade to carry out a real investigation of corruption within the Kuomintang, we'll be able to create a new revolutionary climax in Peking. This will provide the strongest support for our field army to fight against the Kuomintang army at the front!

"Comrade Chunming, I'm fully aware of the need for strict discipline and that, as spies, we must obey our superiors. However, as a party member, we should understand the true spirit of the Central Committee independently. Chairman Mao is our shining example. He never believed in dogmatism, including the arbitrary orders of the Comintern, at all critical moments of the revolution. As a party member, I solemnly propose to the organisation again that we should immediately organise a group of peripheral, progressive students, mostly from the Department of Economics, to help Fang Meng'ao's brigade fully investigate the corruption case, namely the smuggling and reselling of the people's everyday materials by the Kuomintang. If we are afraid of making mistakes and lose this opportunity, we will allow the Kuomintang to use this five-member group to deceive people across China. That's what we refer to as worrying about personal gains and losses! That's all I want to say, Comrade Chunming. It's up to you."

Yan Chunming was equally excited. He stood up and paced back and forth in the small reading room. All of a sudden, he stopped and said: "Tell me all the details. As long as we can contribute to a successful revolution, I will bear responsibility for any mistakes. We'll prove ourselves with the fact that we never seek personal gain."

Liang Jinglun was very moved. "I will report to you in detail right away."

Outside the office of the commissioner of Peking Municipal Police Bureau, Secretary Sun was sitting once again at a table near the meeting room, dealing with official documents.

Xu Tieying was secretly meeting with important guests in the office to discuss urgent matters. "Brother Tieying! Director Xu!" said Ma Hanshan, looking worried this time. The blue veins on his dark, skinny face were clear to see. "If you don't believe me, I'll just smash the pot. I might act hastily!"

Xu Tieying obviously didn't demonstrate the same enthusiasm when he first met him here. As a long-term agent of the Central Bureau of Investigation, his face looked a little fearsome. "What do you mean by smashing the pot? Why do you want to write yourself off?"

Ma Hanshan belonged to the Kuomintang's Military Bureau. He knew that once the people of the Central Bureau of Investigation and its military counterpart split openly, it would be a life-and-death struggle. Seeing the way Xu Tieying responded, he didn't dare do anything more than stamp his feet. "How about this? If it would please you, I'll borrow your phone and place a call from here. Then you can personally have a real feel for how these royal relatives, the folks at Yangtze Construction Company communicate with me!"

"What do you mean by 'royal relatives'?" said Xu Tieying. "Are you vilifying the president or Madam Chiang by insinuation? Director Ma, you're a veteran of the Kuomintang. Don't act as if you were part of the underworld. If he didn't have a stake in your Citizens' Food-Distribution Committee, would Hou Juntang have deployed so many Air Force planes to help you smuggle? Don't forget that Hou Juntang was executed, a case that I investigated! I regard you as a friend. So why do you treat me like this? When I tried Hou Juntang, I could have easily implicated you as an accomplice in the case. Do you want me to submit the letter you wrote me at that time to the Bureau of Reserve Cadres?"

Ma Hanshan collapsed on the sofa. He picked up his cup of tea and took a sip. "For what you did, I should never again call you 'Brother Tieying'. From now on, you will be my father, all right? I'll share this with you – Hou Juntang has twenty per cent of the shares in those companies."

Ma Hanshan picked up his cup again, but there was no water. To Xu's surprise, Ma drank from Xu's cup and then became silent.

Xu Tieying now looked relaxed – twenty per cent! Before his eyes appeared the words that Cui Zhongshi had written in his office in Nanking: the pencil, the letterheaded paper of the Kuomintang Party Members' Communications Bureau, twenty per cent and that line of words, dash and then a big character "You"!

That made sense!

Xu Tieying got to his feet, picked up a thermos bottle, filled the cup for Ma Hanshan, but didn't add any water to his own cup – given the state of Ma Hanshan's black teeth, he vowed not to drink from his own cup any more.

"I think you're to blame," said Xu Tieying. "You need to have at least one or two real friends when you are a party official. If you discard friends when they are no longer useful, you'll end up with no friends at all. I appreciate the fact that you told me Hou Juntang owns twenty per cent of the stock, which means that you still treat me as a friend. But even if you hadn't told me, I would still have found out the details. Of course, this is not all the shares Hou

Juntang owned. Now that Hou is dead, those subordinates of his in the Air Force dare not raise the issue any more. But you have to explain the twenty per cent of the shares, right? That's left behind by a dead lieutenant general, a colonel and several ace flyers. You can't steal them, can you? Now, what did Mr Kung say?"

"Really, that's exactly what I just said," said Ma Hanshan. "Ten thousand tonnes of rice has not yet been delivered. Also, no one dares claim Hou Juntang's twenty per cent of the shares. They are indeed rotten!"

"What do you think?"

"Brother Xu, my mind is blank. What can I think about? I can't tell Du Wancheng and Zeng Keda all I know, can I?"

Xu Tieying nodded in an understanding way. "How can you make General Manager Kung a little afraid? You certainly know how to do this."

Ma Hanshan began to say to himself: Of course, they do have their concerns. For example, the Peking branch of the Central Bank, they are in charge of all their accounts, but Governor Fang will not work against the Kung family.

"Then try to make them understand that if they continue to be so corrupt in this matter, the Peking branch of the Central Bank will not take the blame! Two people, one is Cui Zhongshi and the other is Fang Meng'ao. Give the Kung family a crumb of information, that is if they continue to ignore the message, these two will get tough on them."

"But Cui Zhongshi and Fang Meng'ao will not listen to me," Ma Hanshan protested.

Xu Tieying smiled pitifully and responded: "Of course they won't listen to you. I just want you to pass on the message. You can at least do that, can't you?"

Ma Hanshan sprang to his feet. "I'm going to do it right away. That son of a bitch! He was scolding me on the phone just now. I don't have a way out anyway."

"It's not worth getting angry at them," said Xu Tieying. "Just pass on the message exactly as it is. Secretary Sun!"

Sun opened the door and appeared from behind the screen. Xu instructed him: "Inform Deputy Commissioner Fang Mengwei immediately that the train from Nanking arrives in Peking at five o'clock. Tell him that you'll go to the railway station on my behalf with Deputy Commissioner Fang to meet Deputy Director Cui of the Peking branch."

"I'll do it right away," Secretary Sun replied, before leaving.

When Ma Hanshan heard this, it all clicked. He looked at Xu Tieying and said: "I'm now certain of what I'm going to do! Brother Tieying, I'm going to straighten things out with those people at Yangtze Construction Company!" He strode out.

Xu Tieying glanced at the two empty cups, frowned, held them with two fingers of each hand, and walked to the bathroom while keeping the cups a good distance from his body.

He Xiaoyu had been "invited" once more by Xie Mulan to the Fang mansion.

With Cheng Xiaoyun in their company, Fang Buting appeared less amiable and comfortable than when he was in Xie Mulan's room the previous day.

Xie Peidong was busy as usual, running from one place to another, taking care of the tea, and preparing dinner with Mrs Cai and Mrs Wang in the kitchen.

"Auntie," said Xie Mulan, breaking the somewhat awkward silence. "I heard that you once studied the Cheng school of opera with Mr Cheng Yanqiu. My father said you sang better than those performing on stage. How come I've never heard you sing?"

Cheng Xiaoyun gave a modest smile and slowly turned towards Fang Buting.

"It's Uncle who won't let you sing. Isn't that right?" Xie Mulan said, turning to Fang Buting.

Fang Buting was impassive. He had no interest in answering her question. "Aunt Cheng," He Xiaoyu said, "my father is also a fan of the Cheng school of opera. Can you teach me?"

He Xiaoyu looked to Fang Buting. Put on the spot, Fang Buting felt obliged to express a view: "If Xiaoyu has the passion, I will take you to visit Mr Cheng Yanqiu one day and ask him to teach you personally."

"Uncle Fang, my father can easily arrange for Mr Cheng to

teach me," said He Xiaoyu, keen to join in the effort to enliven the atmosphere. "I just want to learn with Aunt Cheng. I want her to tutor me. The idea is that in the future, my father and you will no longer ask me to sing the old songs of Shanghai. Uncle Fang, you won't say no, will you?"

Fang Buting looked at He Xiaoyu with deep eyes and a smile on his face. "If you really want Aunt Cheng to teach you," he said, "you should invite her to your home. She teaches by singing and you learn by singing, and your father will be happy to hear that. All right?"

"Can I ask Aunt Cheng over to teach me today?" He Xiaoyu was normally quiet, but she was unusually animated today.

"Not today," said Fang Buting as he stood up. "Mengwei will be back soon. And Deputy Director Cui will talk to me about work once he returns from Nanking. Mulan, why don't you take Xiaoyu for a stroll in the garden? Also, tell your father to come to my office and ask your auntie to go to the kitchen to arrange dinner."

Everyone stood up and watched Fang Buting climb the stairs leading to the first floor.

Xie Peidong was in the office, and so was Fang Mengwei even though nobody knew when he had come home. They were both standing at Fang Buting's large desk in his office.

Fang Buting was meditating in his office chair. Slowly he looked up and said: "Peidong, why do you think Xu Tieying asked Mengwei and his secretary to pick up Cui Zhongshi from the train station?"

"He has ulterior motives."

Fang Buting turned to Fang Mengwei and asked: "Do you understand what your uncle means?"

"Why don't you explain?" Fang Mengwei said.

Xie Peidong looked at Fang Buting, who beckoned him to go on.

"First," Xie Peidong explained, "to protect the party's asset, which is the task he must complete, and the main purpose of this trip to Peking as demanded by the Kuomintang central party headquarters. Second, well, who doesn't need a route of retreat in the current political situation? Xu is short of money, too."

Fang Buting nodded.

"Sooner or later, the party-state will perish at the hands of these people," said a furious Fang Mengwei. "If I can't stop him from embezzling the party's assets, and if he ever wants to take advantage of the opportunity to make money, I won't recognise him as my chief, even though I'm his deputy!"

Fang Buting looked at his son. "It's not about money. Xu Tieying does not yet suspect Cui Zhongshi. The most important thing now is to discover whether Cui Zhongshi is a Communist or not. This is a matter of life and death to us!"

"Mengwei, do you understand what the governor said?" said Xie Peidong. Fang Mengwei remained silent.

"Calm down," Xie Peidong interjected. "Don't confront Xu Tieying. Take Cui back home and treat him the usual way when you meet him. Whether he is a Communist or not, the governor and I will find out."

"Did you hear what your uncle has just said?" Fang Buting thought deeply, while looking at his son in an intense way.

"I know what to do," Fang Mengwei replied, looking at his watch. "It's five o'clock. Dad, Uncle, I must depart for the railway station."

CHAPTER 8

It was called the express train, but it still took 27 hours to get to Peking from Nanking. Most of the passengers scurried off the train as it arrived at the terminal. In the sleeper compartment, Cui Zhongshi remained sitting in seat number six, looking out of the window at the platform. The two secret service agents in seat numbers ten and eleven were very embarrassed. They could hardly leave the train ahead of Cui but lingering on board like this was awkward. One of them opened a suitcase and pretended to sort out its contents.

The other pretended to hurry him up: "Everybody's disembarked now. Get a move on, OK?" All the while he was keeping watch on Cui Zhongshi out of the corner of his eye.

Cui rose abruptly, carrying a suitcase in one hand and a briefcase in the other, and he sped towards the carriage door.

"He's off the train," said the agent who was standing. Ignoring his colleague who was still sorting out his suitcase, he followed Cui with his own luggage. The other agent rushed to catch up.

When the two young agents got out of the carriage, they were dumbfounded by the sight of a police jeep and a black car driving over from the far end of the platform. Several passengers scattered in fright.

The two vehicles drove straight in front of Cui Zhongshi and stopped with a screech. The jeep doors opened, and several officers jumped out and stood guard around the jeep.

When the car doors opened, the first person to emerge was Fang Mengwei, followed by Sun, Xu Tieying's secretary. Both men's faces were wreathed with smiles.

Two police officers went to help Cui Zhongshi with the suitcase and briefcase.

Fang Mengwei came up and greeted Cui Zhongshi: "You must have had a long journey, Uncle Cui." The pair shook hands.

"Hello, Deputy Director Cui," said Secretary Sun, who also went up to shake hands.

"Thanks for coming to pick me up," said Cui Zhongshi. "I appreciate it very much."

The two young agents had to pretend to be regular passengers, and they headed out of the station, returning occasionally to monitor the convoy.

Fang Mengwei and Secretary Sun accompanied Cui Zhongshi to the car. "Our director wanted to pick you up in person," said Secretary Sun, "but he's busy with official business, so he entrusted me to represent him. I hope you don't mind, Deputy Director Cui."

Cui Zhongshi stopped at the door and replied: "Director Xu is very kind. I'll pay a formal visit to him straight after I've finished my report for Governor Fang."

"Uncle Cui, get into the car, please." Fang Mengwei opened the rear door for Cui Zhongshi. At this moment, Fang Mengwei was being sincere. After all, Cui Zhongshi had travelled to Nanking a few days ago in order to save Fang Meng'ao.

Cui Zhongshi got into the car without formality. Fang Mengwei walked around the car and got into it from the other side. Secretary Sun hopped in through the front passenger door.

During the civil war, all passengers who exited Peking railway station were subject to police surveillance. Those who appeared suspicious would be checked on the spot. That made it rather slow for anyone wanting to leave the station.

"Xu Tieying's secretary has also come," one of the young agents said. "That's a little weird isn't it?"

"Let's report it immediately," said the other agent.

The two became impatient waiting for the passengers to leave the station, so they elbowed their way towards the exit and jumped the queue.

Two policemen approached them and demanded: "What's up? Come to this side."

One of the agents took out his ID card and flashed it in front of him. Paying no attention to the policemen, the two agents strode out of the station.

Still confused, one of the two policemen asked: "Which department did they work for? Did you see it clearly?"

"Looked like the Ministry of Defence," said the other.

Leaving the railway station, Cui Zhongshi, who was sitting in the back of the car, took out his pocket watch and opened the cover. He cast a quick glance at Secretary Sun in the front seat and at Fang Mengwei. "It's six o'clock. The governor must have been waiting for a while?"

Fang Mengwei looked at Cui Zhongshi and felt that his eyes were still loyal and reliable. They switched their focus to Secretary Sun. Suddenly, Fang Mengwei felt a burst of pain and sadness. "Secretary Sun," he said, "would you please join us for dinner in our humble house in honour of Deputy Director Cui?"

Secretary Sun turned around and replied: "I'm sorry, I'm just about to report to Deputy Commissioner Fang and Deputy Director Cui. According to Commissioner Xu's instructions, we should take Deputy Director Cui home first. After all, the family haven't seen each other for many days. At nine o'clock this evening, Commissioner Xu will come to visit Governor Fang. Deputy Director Cui, could you come and join us? He has something important to discuss with you."

Hearing this request, Fang Mengwei got very cross. Cui Zhongshi took Secretary Sun's hand and said to him: "OK, I'll go home first. Mengwei, tell the governor Mr Xu's instruction. If the governor has new instructions, I'll wait for his call at home."

Fang Mengwei was still a subordinate of Xu Tieying. Besides, Xu Tieying's arrangements must have been deliberately planned.

He had no choice but to say: "Then use the jeep in the front to drive Mr Cui home."

It was Fang Buting's car. The driver accelerated, overtook the jeep in front and came to a stop.

The jeep also stopped. Fang Mengwei, Cui Zhongshi and Secretary Sun all emerged from the car. The officers in the jeep got out in a rush.

Fang Mengwei said to the police officers: "Get some people to take Deputy Director Cui home in your jeep."

The driver of the sedan car brought Cui Zhongshi's suitcase and briefcase which the driver of the jeep had put inside his vehicle.

Cui Zhongshi sat in the jeep, with Secretary Sun following him into the car. Fang Mengwei stood by the door and looked at Cui Zhongshi gratefully. "You've had a busy few days," he said. "My apologies to Aunt Cui. Please say hello to her."

Cui Zhongshi smiled wearily. "Of course I will. Please also remember me to the governor and Mr Xie. I'll be with you at nine o'clock."

Fang Mengwei closed the door for him. "Go ahead please." The jeep carrying Cui Zhongshi and Secretary Sun headed to Cui's house.

Fang Mengwei stood in the street with mixed feelings as he watched the jeep disappear into the distance.

The Peking branch of the Central Bank of the Nationalist government was located in Dongzhong Hutong in the eastern section of the Legation Quarter in the western part of the city. Since its establishment in 1928, the branch had purchased many properties in Peking. Especially in the area close to the Legation Quarter, many Siheyuan-style houses both large and small were bought for bank staff.

Being deputy treasury director of the Peking branch, with Fang Buting himself serving as director, Cui Zhongshi was entitled to a large courtyard house in the neighbourhood. But Cui always kept a low profile. Over the years, he developed a reputation as the gold key and iron bolt in the entire Central Bank system by keeping the bank's money tight. As for himself, he never coveted a single penny. Because of this, he was promoted from a junior clerk in the Shanghai branch to his present position. After arriving in Peking, he stayed in a small courtyard house about two *li* from the bank. He and his family of four dispensed with the need to employ a nanny. His wife took care of the housework herself.

Dongzhong Hutong was very narrow. The police jeep squeezed into it, leaving barely enough space for bikes to pass on either side.

"Reverse, please," Cui Zhongshi instructed the driver.

The driver stopped the jeep.

"Let's walk Deputy Director Cui to the front entrance," suggested Secretary Sun.

"The lane's very narrow," said Cui Zhongshi. "If we proceed any further, it will be hard for anyone else to enter. Let's reverse and park on the street. It's not a long walk anyway."

"Let's back out then." With Secretary Sun's order, the jeep reversed and parked on the street at the end of the alleyway. Cui Zhongshi got out first, followed by Secretary Sun with Cui's suitcase and briefcase.

"Thank you for looking after me while I was in Nanking," Cui Zhongshi said, "and also for helping me in Peking. Secretary Sun, I'll save expressing my thanks until later. For the moment, do you want to come in for a snack?" As he was talking, Cui Zhongshi picked up his suitcase and briefcase. Cui, the generous deputy director in the Central Bureau of Investigation building in Nanking, disappeared. In truth, he couldn't afford to treat him even to a light meal. He wanted no one to eat at his house.

Secretary Sun remained true to his character, smiling: "We have rules to follow, I'm afraid. Deputy Director Cui, please go home to bathe and eat. I'll wait here and then let's go together to the governor's house at eight-thirty."

"Why the rush?" asked Cui Zhongshi.

"The commissioner specifically entrusted this task to me. Deputy Director Cui, please return home."

"Well then, I'll treat you to some Peking duck at Quanjude on a separate occasion." With no more exchange of formalities, Cui Zhongshi carried his bags and walked towards the hutong.

Secretary Sun looked from the entrance of the hutong at Cui

Zhongshi who by now had walked more than ten metres. He stopped and knocked on the second gate.

Cui lived at No. 2 Siheyuan in Dongzhong Hutong.

"Are you all right?" Cui Zhongshi asked his wife, Ye Biyu. He smiled apologetically as she took his suitcase and briefcase.

"Stop talking, take a shower and eat."

He was not put off by the absence of a smile on his wife's face. What made him nervous was her failure to utter a single word of complaint. What made him scared was that his wife went straight into the courtyard. Cui Zhongshi was stunned for quite a while. Looking at the back of his wife, he felt more uneasy. She would typically have started nagging him by now, and would only stop once they entered the house. Indeed, she would go on so much he frequently compared her to a moneylender bleeding him dry with extortionate rates of interest.

This loyal member of the Communist Party of China would find himself continuously scolded by his wife at home like many men from Shanghai because he strictly abided by the inherent secrecy of the organisation.

Cui Zhongshi smiled bitterly, closed the courtyard door behind him and turned around, eyes brightening once more.

"Daddy! Daddy!" cried his two children.

His elder child was the ten-year-old Cui Boqin. His hair was parted in the middle, and he was wearing a Western suit popular at that time in Shanghai, a white, Hawaiian-style short-sleeved shirt, and khaki, knee-length trousers.

His daughter Cui Pingyang was six-and-a-half years old. She had two small ponytails, and was wearing a little dress of blue flowers against a white background.

The children were dressed neatly and in the Western style, yet the materials were relatively modest. Standing in front of him, Cui Zhongshi found their voices soft, but sweet and amiable. It appeared that both his son and daughter were closer to Cui Zhongshi than to his wife, who dominated the household.

Remembering something, Cui Zhongshi searched his pockets hastily, but did not pull out anything. He looked apologetically at his children. "Dad didn't have time to go shopping on this trip, I'm afraid. I wasn't able to get you any White Rabbits."

"We still have a couple left from the last batch you bought us, Dad. Look!" The son and daughter were each holding a sweet.

Cui Zhongshi squatted down. "Since you've both had a bath, I won't hug you just yet. Dad's been sweating rather a lot."

With that he held out both of his hands. His son took one hand, his daughter the other, and the three of them went to the north-facing room. His wife Ye Biyu was cutting watermelon on the table in the same room. The children looked up at their father and Cui Zhongshi pretended to look frightened. The daughter stopped her father and asked softly: "Daddy, will Mum scold you again?"

The son looked at his younger sister and then at his father. "If she does, it will only last a few minutes. That'll be all right. If it goes on for any longer, we won't be able to eat or do our homework. I don't think she'll scold you again."

"I dare not..." began the daughter.

"What were you saying?" Ye Biyu asked.

The three no longer dared utter a word. As if treading on thin ice, they walked gingerly towards the door.

Outside Cui's house, near the Dongzhong Hutong entrance, the well-disciplined Secretary Sun was standing on the street in his long-sleeved Zhongshan suit. The suit being fully fastened, sweat was streaming down his face.

The driver had bought some pancakes. Secretary Sun took the pancakes and looked around. Finding no one in sight, he began to eat them. Suddenly, he stopped, and hastily swallowed the food in his mouth. He was staring at a military jeep that was now about five metres away from his own jeep.

The jeep was slowing down, and sure enough he saw clearly that the driver was Fang Meng'ao. The jeep stopped at the entrance of the hutong opposite Sun's vehicle.

Chen Changwu got out from the passenger seat. Fang Meng'ao turned off the engine and approached him with the key in his hands.

Secretary Sun handed the remaining pancakes to the driver and walked briskly to Fang Meng'ao. He raised his hand and saluted. "Good evening, Captain Fang."

Fang Meng'ao returned the salute. "Does Deputy Director Cui of the Peking branch live here?"

"Yes," Secretary Sun replied, "he's just arrived in Peking. Got in only a moment ago."

"Did you pick him up?"

"Yes. My boss said that, according to a decision made at the five-member group meeting, the Peking Police Bureau will assist Captain Fang in checking their accounts."

Fang Meng'ao looked at him intently and said: "Do the best you can. What's Deputy Director Cui's house number?"

"Captain Fang, it's Number Two Dongzhong Hutong, second gate on the left."

Fang Meng'ao walked to the hutong, but stopped after only a few steps. He looked back at Secretary Sun, who hurried over.

"How long has Deputy Director Cui been home?"

Sun glanced at his watch. "About a quarter of an hour."

Fang Meng'ao walked back to his jeep and took out a cigar. Chen Changwu lit it for him. Fang Meng'ao puffed on the cigar and said: "Let him take a bath and have dinner. We'll go in and question him after he's eaten."

Hearing what he said, Secretary Sun looked at his watch again.

"One more thing," said Fang Meng'ao, "who else is expecting to talk to Deputy Director Cui?"

Each of the five-member group was assigned four guards. Outside Zeng Keda's courtyard residence in Gu Weijun's sprawling complex, two guards were positioned at the steps near the gate, and the other two at the intersection leading to his property.

A Central Army officer, the one who had picked up Zeng Keda in his car the previous night, came with four guards. The four guards saluted spontaneously.

"Time for a change of guards," the officer said. "Go back to the barracks and have supper."

The four guards put down their hands and goosestepped away.

The officer winked and two new guards stationed themselves at the east-west intersection. The officer then looked at the other two guards. "Come with me," he said, "the general is waiting for you." These two guards turned out to be the two agents who had followed Cui Zhongshi on his journey.

The officer was standing guard at the door. A large ceiling fan in the living room was motionless.

Upon entering the room, the two young agents saw Zeng Keda sitting on a sofa reading some documents, with a folding fan in his hand.

The young agents saluted him as they walked in. "Comrade Keda, good evening."

Zeng Keda raised his head and saw the sweat streaming down their hat brims. "Thanks for your hard work. Turn on the fan if you find it hot."

"Comrade Keda, we're fine," one of the two young agents replied. "We fight waste and strive for economy."

"Good for you," said Zeng Keda, standing up. "But the fan won't consume too much electricity." He switched it on himself. The blades rotated, creating a continuous motion that cooled the room. "Sit down."

Zeng Keda returned to the sofa. The two young agents, each grabbing a chair, put them down in front of the tea table opposite him and sat bolt upright.

"OK, then tell me about your trip." Zeng Keda gathered up the materials, using a cup cover as paperweight. He listened to their reports.

One of the young agents took out the *Ta Kung Pao* and handed it to Zeng Keda. "When the train arrived at Dezhou station, a man came up and gave this newspaper to Cui Zhongshi. Cui read it from cover to cover. We suspect it's the way they communicated. All the answers can be found somewhere in this newspaper."

Zeng Keda only glanced at the first page of the newspaper without reading it. "Have you tried to crack the secret?" he asked.

"We've read every single page," the other young agent replied. "No words underlined, nor any marks whatsoever."

"Then you need to give up," said Zeng Keda.

"We believe that if Cui Zhongshi is a Communist, the instructions of the Communist Party must be hidden in this newspaper. Please advise us, Comrade Keda."

Zeng Keda looked at the two and said: "Let's work it out together." He spread out the newspaper on the tea table.

The two young agents stood up, walked to Zeng Keda's side and looked down at the paper.

Zeng Keda examined a news report on the front page. "Look at this report. Remember the numbers I'm going to say. Make a note of every word by my number."

With their eyes wide open, the two young agents read the report attentively.

"Seven, thirteen, fourteen, twenty-six, thirty-two, fifty-four, fifty-nine, sixty." Zeng Keda stopped.

The two young men looked at each other and began to comprehend. "Read aloud the words," said Zeng Keda.

"*Fang, tong, zhi, ming, tian, dao, bei, ping*. Literally, it says: Comrade Fang will arrive in Peking tomorrow."

The two young men read quietly, and immediately showed their admiration. "They connected with each other using ciphers in the indexing system!"

"That's right," Zeng Keda exclaimed. "If you did this randomly, you wouldn't get this result in ten thousand years."

The phone rang. Zeng Keda stood up, and almost self-consciously the two young agents made to leave.

"Sit, please," Zeng Keda said as he walked over to answer the phone. He listened for a while. "Captain Fang has the right to visit Cui Zhongshi at his house. You are not allowed to stop him. Just keep your eyes on Secretary Sun." He put the phone down having given these instructions.

"Comrade Keda," said one of the agents, "just when we were about to report to you after the train arrived at the station, two vehicles drove to the platform to meet Cui Zhongshi. One was a jeep belonging to the Peking Police Bureau, the other was an Austin, its number plate being quite similar to the Peking branch vehicle. Fang Mengwei and Xu Tieying's secretary personally met Cui Zhongshi at the station."

Zeng Keda stood there, thinking about what he had just heard. "Let me plan tomorrow's work for you."

"Can I help you?" Ye Biyu opened the door and looked at the tall pilot officer standing in front of her, with suspicion and caution written all over her face.

Fang Meng'ao knew that Cui Zhongshi's wife would open the door for him, yet his eyes were full of surprise. He'd imagined she would be well-educated, but what he saw in front of him was a typical woman from a Shanghai alleyway.

Fang Meng'ao managed to stay polite. "Excuse me, are you Mrs Cui? My name is Fang Meng'ao. Deputy Director Cui often visits me in Hangzhou."

"Oh!" Ye Biyu's voice was a little bit affected, but it was heartfelt. "So, you're Mr Fang! Come on in. Zhongshi, Master Fang's here to visit you!"

Ye Biyu's movements seemed slower than usual as she closed and bolted the courtyard gate. Fang Meng'ao strode over to Cui Zhongshi, while Cui approached him more cautiously.

"Come on inside," said Ye Biyu. "I'll cut some watermelon." As she spoke, she walked past Cui Zhongshi into the north room.

Fang Meng'ao and Cui Zhongshi stopped in the middle of the courtyard. They were lost for words.

Suddenly, Fang Meng'ao's attention was distracted and his eyes brightened. He walked past Cui Zhongshi, straight to the north room door.

At the entrance, the two children were leaning on the doorframe. Two pairs of curious eyes were looking at this uncle who seemed even taller than that locust tree in the courtyard.

Fang Meng'ao stopped at the door and bent down. "So you're Pingyang, and you're Boqin."

Still leaning on the doorframe, the two children nodded their heads in succession.

Cui Zhongshi came over. "This is Uncle Fang. Say hi to him, will you?"

The son, Boqin, and the daughter, Pingyang, stood up straight and bowed the way they were taught at school. "How are you, Uncle Fang?"

Fang Meng'ao put his hands into his trouser pockets. When he pulled them out, he spread out his hands to the two children, revealing a handful of American chocolates in each palm.

This was way too extravagant! The children's eyes sparkled with excitement, but they didn't take the chocolates at once. Instead, they looked to their father, Cui Zhongshi. "Come on, say thank you to Uncle Fang," he said.

"Thank you, Uncle Fang!" The two children scooped the chocolates from Fang Meng'ao's palms.

"Now, you'll need to go back to your room and do your homework," said Cui Zhongshi.

Again, the two children thanked Uncle Fang, and they trotted happily away.

Ye Biyu had apparently completed preparing the watermelon and came to the door. "Mr Fang, please make yourself at home. I'll make a pot of West Lake Longjing. It's the new tea made this very year. Zhongshi has been dying to drink it several times, but I told him to wait since I knew a guest of honour would soon visit us."

As expected, the nagging had just begun.

Fang Meng'ao was in a good mood today. "Thank you! Thank you! Thank you..."

"Why not show Mr Fang into the house?" Ye Biyu continued. "Where are the manners of a deputy treasury director?"

Cui Zhongshi looked at Fang Meng'ao and grinned bitterly. Fang returned with a hearty smile. Only then did they enter the north room.

As twilight turned to a deep blackness, shadows appeared and several crows came back to roost in the courtyard tree.

As dusk fell, crows were also returning to their nests in the courtyard of Princess Hejing's mansion. In the small yard of Cui Zhongshi, they were settling in their nests in the locust tree, but here they were hovering over a large, shady tree in the grounds of the mansion.

The refugee students from the Northeast gathering at the former royal residence were more miserable than ordinary folk. Even though Fang Meng'ao had given up the mansion to them, they still yearned to return to school. Besides, the problem of food remained unresolved.

Under public pressure, the Peking Municipal Citizens' Food-Distribution Committee delivered several truckloads of biscuits, but each person ended up with only two packs. Many people had assembled in the courtyard because Liang Jinglun had arrived. A number of students from Yenching University's Students' Union also came.

He Xiaoyu and Xie Mulan were also summoned by the students of Yenching University. They stood quietly in the corner of the yard and hid in the crowd.

Liang Jinglun was standing on some stone steps next to a rather grand, gated entrance. He was surrounded by several tall and sturdy male students, several of whom were familiar. They turned out to be the young students who escorted Zeng Keda on his cycle ride the night before. They were the undercover student spies who belonged to the Chiang Kai-shek Student Society.

"We are very sorry," Liang Jinglun said to countless pairs of eager eyes. "We still can't give you the legal status to continue your education in universities in Peking, nor even half a *jin* of rice a day."

There was a moment of silence, apart from the sound of the crows cawing in their nests. The students were waiting to hear more.

Liang Jinglun went on: "There are no saviours. All of you, you must fight for your own rights and interests, all by yourselves."

"Fight against corruption!" a student chanted, followed by many in the crowd. "Fight against corruption!"

"Fight against corruption!"

"No civil war!"

"No more persecution! No more persecution!"

The crows and sparrows in the tree took fright and flew up into the sky.

Liang Jinglun pressed his hands to signal the students to be quiet. Silence returned.

"But we still have to believe that there are more people with a conscience who care about you," Liang Jinglun said. "Many highly respected, non-partisan individuals care about you, along with many righteous officials. The reason why you're able to stay in this mansion is because the Peking Youth Aviation Brigade has a sense of justice. If they are true to their mission to eliminate corruption and stop persecution, we should welcome them with great sincerity. And help them."

"Excuse me, Mr Liang, how can we help them?" asked the student who was speaking that day with Fang Meng'ao on behalf of the refugee students.

"We're economics majors, we can help them to check the accounts!" exclaimed Xie Mulan. Many people looked at her.

It was too late for He Xiaoyu to stop Xie Mulan. Liang Jinglun was also surprised. He glanced at the two young women and winked at a student beside him.

The student didn't move, but he was ready to protect He Xiaoyu and Xie Mulan. Liang Jinglun turned to face the student crowd again: "As for how to fight for our legitimate rights and interests, there are several important things to consider. First, you can't use your own flesh and blood to fight against bullets. Second, we need to work out how to help the Peking Youth Aviation Brigade expose the real corruption of the authorities. Please discuss this among yourselves. Choose a representative from each school. Let's meet in the back room in ten minutes."

Immediately, there was a great deal of noise.

The student who received the hint from Liang Jinglun had quietly wormed his way into the crowd and squeezed towards He Xiaoyu and Xie Mulan.

In the corner of the north room of Cui Zhongshi's house, a gramophone was positioned on a tall table. A record had been placed on the turntable. Cui Zhongshi grabbed the handle and wound it up. Then he lined up the needle over the rotating disc.

With the turn of a hand, Zhou Xuan's original voice could be heard:

The floating, scattered clouds,
The bright moon shines on the reunited people

Cui Zhongshi looked at Fang Meng'ao in a sentimental way. Fang Meng'ao's eyes closed. The song had obviously prompted his thoughts to drift away to an unseen space and a past that had soon disappeared.

Today is the happiest reunion.

"Isn't it annoying?" said Ye Biyu. "It's always the same song, over and over." Holding a tea plate supporting a pot of well brewed Longjing tea and two cups, she came into the room.

Zhou Xuan was still singing:

Clean and shallow ponds,
Mandarin ducks playing on the water,
Red skirts and emerald caps,
Devoted married couples like two lotus flowers opening...

"Thank you, Mrs Cui." Fang Meng'ao rose to take the tea.

"Captain Fang, sit down," said an overly attentive Ye Biyu. "You know what, he listens to that song whenever he comes back home from a two-week business trip. Mr Fang, let me confide this with you. I'm not being suspicious. After a trip to Nanking three years ago, he began to like the song. I've no idea which pretty woman sang it to him. Even though he's home, his heart is far away with some beauty."

Cui Zhongshi was embarrassed and looked at Fang Meng'ao. Fang was quite moved.

The scene when they first met at the Air Force Academy in Jianqiao, Hangzhou, three years ago reappeared before his eyes. Cui Zhongshi pictured Fang Meng'ao holding photos of his mother and sister, singing *Blooming Flowers, Full Moon* in a sad, soft voice. Cui Zhongshi's eyes flashed with tears and he sang along with him.

At the end of the song, Cui Zhongshi grasped Fang Meng'ao's hands, his voice shaking with sincerity. "Comrade Meng'ao, on behalf of the party and the organisation, I hope your future life is long, with blooming flowers and a full moon!"

"Master Fang! Captain Fang!" Ye Biyu's words brought him out of his reverie. "Are you feeling all right? Do you have heatstroke? Shall I bring you some herbal liquid?"

Fang Meng'ao smiled. This young man looked so handsome when he laughed.

Cui Zhongshi joined in the laughter, and he said to his wife: "Fortunately, Captain Fang's my friend. It would ruin my career if your suspicions were to be leaked."

Fang Meng'ao looked at Ye Biyu sincerely. "Madam, I think I've done the right thing in coming here today. In Director Cui's defence, he came to Hangzhou to visit me three years ago. I liked this song, and so did he. I gave this record to him. The 'beauty' you referred to is me."

Ye Biyu was stunned. "You dead ghost. Why didn't you tell me earlier? I hope you didn't take offence, Master Fang."

Fang Meng'ao smiled again. "No, I won't since I'm not that pretty woman."

Ye Biyu gave him an embarrassed smile. "Tea is ready, please. Go on with your conversation. I'm sure you two good friends will have plenty to discuss."

With that, she hurried out of the room. Zhou Xuan was still singing.

Cui Zhongshi said seriously: "Comrade Meng'ao, you shouldn't have told her about the song."

Fang Meng'ao looked at Cui Zhongshi in a rather confused manner.

"This is a party secret," Cui Zhongshi whispered. "Tell no one about it."

Fang Meng'ao smiled and waved away his concern. "What kind of secret is that? Everyone knows you came to visit me on behalf of the family. We happen to enjoy the same song. Who dares make such an accusation?"

Cui Zhongshi became even more serious: "This is what I want to tell you today. The Kuomintang's Central Bureau and Military Bureau, as well as the Chiang Kai-shek Student Society that was recently founded by the Iron and Blood Congress, they're all professional secret agencies. Even the smallest detail may give them a clue that later on has serious consequences. Don't say a word about our previous meetings. Given your current status, you can defy anyone's attempt to question you, but watch out for those who try to obtain information through small talk. Remember this."

Fang Meng'ao nodded earnestly, then asked in a low voice: "What should I do next? Earlier today, the Nanking authorities officially assigned me to check the accounts of the Peking's Citizens' Food-Distribution Committee, as well as those of the Central Bank's Peking branch. I'll be fine checking the accounts of the Food-Distribution Committee, but if I do the accounts of the Peking branch, I'll be investigating you."

"No, I'm not a target of your investigation. Check me out if you must, but you won't find anything. I'll let you know when it's time for you to find out. Remember, when you investigate me, you must make me feel upset. Make things really difficult for me. Because both sides are now investigating your relationship with me."

Fang Meng'ao saw him pause, but he did nothing. Zhou Xuan was still singing.

Cui Zhongshi edged closer to him, his voice low but very clear: "One is Zeng Keda. On the train journey to Peking, their agents followed me all the way. The other one happens to be your father."

Fang Meng'ao was stunned.

"I can't tell you the specific reason," Cui Zhongshi went on. "Your father has been suspicious of my affiliations, and therefore yours too. He'll give us a hard time. You must be aware of that. You, Fang Meng'ao, pretend you have never been a member of the CPC. Continue the way you are and the way you do things. As long as you forget you're a member of the Communist Party, no one can hurt you. The party has specific instructions that you are free to do whatever you want without asking for approval. Protecting you is our most important task!"

Nobody knew how often Zhou Xuan had sung the last line of that same song.

Full of warmth and affection between the people.

The image of Cui Zhongshi as that big brother gradually blurred in Fang Meng'ao's eyes. A handsome, gracious and smiling woman slowly emerged in his mind – it was his mother.

"Please rest assured, I'll remember that," Fang Meng'ao said gently.

To Cui Zhongshi, Fang Meng'ao looked exactly the same as when he said those words as a teenager ten years ago. It was the promise that a child makes to his mother.

"What time is it?" Cui Zhongshi asked. He went to get the pocket watch from the table.

Fang Meng'ao looked at his wristwatch. "It's twenty past eight."

"I've got to go now. Xu Tieying has scheduled a meeting with the governor and me at your house at nine. Go back to your barracks."

"So Xu Tieying has an appointment with you, does he?" Fang Meng'ao raised his eyebrows. "What's he up to?"

"It's none of your business. Remember, do what you have to do. Take no interest in what I do."

Fang Meng'ao was silent for a short while, before saying: "Take care of yourself. Let me know if there's anything I can do. I can handle them."

Cui Zhongshi stamped his foot gently. "How can I make you understand what you need to understand? My priority is to protect you! Now, get back to your barracks."

Fang Meng'ao looked at Cui Zhongshi affectionately again, and resolutely turned around and walked out of the room.

"Madam, bye-bye!"

Cui Zhongshi glanced up at the disappearing figure of Meng'ao in the courtyard with a look of concern.

Four small eyes behind the window of the house's west wing were also looking at Uncle Fang in the yard, full of admiration.

Ye Biyu dashed out in quick, short steps. "Aren't you staying longer? Come and visit us often!" She made the remarks with genuine affection, with no intention of flattering him.

In the living room on the ground floor of the Fang mansion, all the servants had been banished. Xie Peidong was standing alone in the hallway. Cui Zhongshi was waiting outside the door, ready to enter.

After a brief eye contact, Cui Zhongshi bowed slightly. "Good evening, Mr Xie," he said.

"Let's go upstairs," said Xie Peidong. "The governor and Commissioner Xu are waiting for you." Cui Zhongshi entered the hallway and walked up to the staircase on the left.

In the governor's office, a round rattan tea table had been placed in front of a high window facing the south. Fang Buting was sitting in a rattan chair to the right of the table, while Xu Tieying took the one on the left.

The unoccupied chair was reserved for Cui Zhongshi. "Good evening, governor." Cui Zhongshi bowed slightly at the door, before stepping inside.

"Come on in and meet Commissioner Xu." Fang Buting looked amiable, though he was secretly displeased with Cui for not greeting the commissioner.

"Director Xu, how are you?" Cui Zhongshi was all smiles. "Look at me, I'm still calling you 'director'. I should instead be calling you 'Commissioner Xu'."

Fang Buting sat still, but Xu Tieying stood up politely. "Hello, Cui. We've been friends so long, can't you call me 'brother'?"

"Commissioner Xu," said Fang Buting, "please take a seat. In terms of seniority, he is a junior to both of us. We still have to follow our rules. Take a seat."

Xu Tieying remained standing until Cui Zhongshi came to the chair. He even politely reached out his hand to invite Cui Zhongshi to sit first. Feeling unable to do that, Cui Zhongshi looked up to Fang Buting.

"It's very respectful of him. Perhaps it's better to be obedient than respectful." Fang Buting knew Xu Tieying's style too well.

"Respectfully, thank you." Cui Zhongshi felt obliged to take his seat.

"This is the way things are," said Xu Tieying, who sat down with a smile and poured some tea into the empty cup before Cui Zhongshi.

Again, Cui Zhongshi was about to rise to take his tea.

"Sit still." Xu Tieying was good at befriending people even when there was an ulterior motive.

Cui Zhongshi had to sit with his hands cupping the teacup.

When Xu Tieying had finished pouring the tea, he took a sip and put the cup down gently. "Mr Xu, I'm humbled," he said.

"Wrong," said Xu Tieying, still smiling. "It is Governor Fang who thinks highly of *you*. You should owe this to Governor Fang, on whose behalf you've been trying your best to take care of us. Cui, let me propose a toast with this tea instead of wine, to the respectful governor."

Both men held up their teacups.

Fang Buting also raised his cup. "Xiao Cui, Mr Xu is so kind to say those words. We're grateful to him for helping out Meng'ao. His wisdom helps turn calamities into blessings. Hold on! Let me drink to Commissioner Xu first." With that, he took a sip.

Xu Tieying didn't drink his tea in return, but said most sincerely: "Brother Buting, I'm not worthy of your praise. When you said those words, I feel like I am regarded as an outsider. Besides, your son Meng'ao is widely known as a military hero. So if you take back what you said, I'll drink to you also."

"OK, I will."

Xu Tieying finished his tea. Instead of waiting for Cui Zhongshi to pick up the teapot, he grabbed it first, refilled it for Fang Buting, then for himself. He held up his cup with both hands and looked at Fang Buting: "I envy you tremendously, Brother Buting. For decades, I've had multiple assistants working for me. In terms of loyalty to you, no one can match Cui. Let's propose a toast to Cui."

Cui Zhongshi subconsciously lowered his head slightly so he could evade Fang Buting's gaze.

Fang Buting held up his teacup: "Brother Tieying, don't spoil my subordinates. But when it comes to loyalty, sometimes the subordinates you trained yourself are more reliable than your sons! Cui, raise your cup."

Cui Zhongshi quickly processed Fang Buting's comments in his mind. He held up his cup and said: "Governor Fang, it's so kind of Director Xu to say so. You may not praise me like that. I've done so little, I don't live up to your evaluation."

"Was I praising you?" Fang Buting looked at Xu Tieying. "You see, sometimes a superior doesn't say what's supposed to be correct. They simply don't believe you!"

"Come on, finish the tea!" said Xu Tieying, pretending to reprimand him. "Do you really want the governor to think you don't believe him?"

Cui Zhongshi raised his cup and drank the contents slowly. Xu Tieying smiled and waited for Fang Buting to finish his tea simultaneously. There was a silence after the three cups were set down. A moment's silence often follows the formal rituals before it is broken by the real business.

Fang Meng'ao's Youth Aviation Brigade had always been highly disciplined. Usually, a bugle call sounded in the barracks for the men to retire for the night at nine o'clock in winter and ten o'clock in summer. But today, the captain had issued an order that restricted pilots to two hours sleep a day so they could learn how to use an abacus.

So the barracks were ablaze with light. Some men were one-to-one, others were one-to-two. Squatting or sitting beside their beds, those who could would teach those who could not.

The sound of men working on their abacuses rang out loud. Suddenly, those located near the barracks door stopped working. All calculations ceased. Their eyes were fixed on the entrance to the barracks. Surprised by what they saw, a few stood up, and soon everyone was standing.

Fang Mengwei took off his hat, smiled with embarrassment and looked to Chen Changwu, who was nearest to him. "Sorry for interrupting you. Is the captain in?"

Chen Changwu did not reply, but nodded to the single room at the rear.

"Please continue," Fang Mengwei said, nodding to those who were eying him. He walked over to Fang Meng'ao's separate bedroom. Once again, loud noise emanated from the abacuses behind him.

"Did Dad ask you to come, or Commissioner Xu?" Fang Meng'ao asked as he grabbed a thermos bottle to make coffee for his brother. "This coffee is good. Where did you get it?"

Two questions. Fang Mengwei sat at his desk, and for some

reason he responded to the second question first: "Some people from the Central Bank bought it from the US."

Fang Meng'ao handed the coffee to Fang Mengwei. "You haven't answered my first question."

"I came by myself. I was upset, I wanted to see you."

Fang Meng'ao looked into his younger brother's eyes. "There's been no proper explanation of the Seventh of July Incident to the students. They may take to the streets again at any time. Why are you, as deputy commissioner of the police bureau, so free to visit me?"

"Elder Brother, don't regard me as deputy chief of the police department." Fang Mengwei looked intently at his elder brother.

Fang Meng'ao suddenly remembered his brother as the smart and agile person of his youth, someone who always put others first. This was also like himself, or more accurately, like their mother.

Fang Meng'ao sighed very rarely, but he sighed at this moment. "I guess what you want to say is that I stop functioning in the capacity of chief of the inspection team?"

"Yes," Fang Mengwei replied.

"In that way, I'll have good reason not to check the Peking branch accounts."

Fang Mengwei was silent for a moment, then raised his head again. "Elder Brother, you really don't feel like doing this, do you? Because you know nobody here is qualified to make sense of the accounts when they are in such a mess."

"Go on."

"Many from the Iron and Blood Congress are Economics and Finance majors. Why didn't the Bureau of Reserve Cadres recruit them to check the accounts? Instead, they asked you guys in the Air Force to do it."

"Go on."

"That means they would use you to check on Dad. But Dad has seen through the whole situation. Since the very beginning, he refused to take charge of the accounts of the Citizens' Food-Distribution Committee. It's Cui Zhongshi who is assigned to take care of them."

Fang Meng'ao was taken aback. "Don't you call Deputy Director Cui 'Uncle Cui'?"

"I always call him Uncle Cui."

"Well, go ahead."

"Then you'll have to investigate Uncle Cui," said Fang Mengwei. "Elder Brother, what kind of person do you think Uncle Cui is?"

Fang Meng'ao's eyes narrowed into a line. "What do you mean?"

"Are you supposed to check on Uncle Cui?"

Fang Meng'ao did not answer. Instead of pressing his brother to continue, he picked up a cigar from the table. He lit it and exhaled a big puff. Fang Mengwei did not usually smoke himself, and he started coughing. Fang Meng'ao quickly stubbed out his cigar in the ashtray.

Discussions continued in the governor's office on the first floor of the Fang mansion.

"No distinction has ever been made between property owned by the state, the party and private individuals, no distinction whatsoever." Xu Tieying looked at Fang Buting and then at Cui Zhongshi. "The government has always been aware that the accounts of the Central Bank are not easy to manage. It's a tough call for Governor Fang in Peking."

Fang Buting did not respond to the remarks. Neither did Cui Zhongshi, who only looked at Xu Tieying.

Xu Tieying was a little unhappy. He picked up the teapot and refilled his cup with water even though he did not take a drink. He turned to look out of the window. "You've got a nice place here. What are those flowers? They're so fragrant, aren't they?"

Cui Zhongshi stole a glance at Fang Buting. Xu Tieying continued to gaze out of the window. This was no longer the time for small talk.

Fang Buting felt obliged to respond: "Zhongshi, did you promise Director Xu something while you were in Nanking? Tell me now. At the Peking branch, we mean what we say."

"Yes, I did." Cui felt he had to tell the truth.

But the truth was hard to explain. In Nanking, Cui Zhongshi promised to transfer the twenty per cent of shares owned by Hou Juntang and his Air Force officers to Xu Tieying. Originally, he planned to act on his own initiative back in Peking, but Xu Tieying was so impatient that he had him followed by his operatives as soon as he got off the train. Now, he was so desperate he called at Fang's house in person to finalise the transfer of shares in front of Fang Buting. He felt so very disgusted and embarrassed that he remained silent, apart from saying "yes".

Xu Tieying kept watching the night view outside the window. What was so appealing about this view?

"Commissioner Xu," said Cui Zhongshi as he now called him.

"Hmm?" Xu Tieying pretended to be awakened by Cui and slowly turned his head.

"Governor Fang has put me in charge of many things at the Peking branch. For some issues, I need to request his instructions, while for others I don't. Might you allow me to put it this way?"

"Do you have such an established practice at your bank?" asked Xu Tieying, pretending to be astonished. "You have to hide things from your superiors? I need to be advised."

He was not only forcing Cui Zhongshi into a showdown, but also pressing Fang Buting to clarify his position.

"I am humbled." Cui Zhongshi was showing the bright and capable side of his character. "With regard to how to manage and use state and party property, I have to ask the governor for his approval regarding the use of every single penny. However, I don't have to consult him if it involves the various aspects of private property. Some of the transactions can only be conducted off the table. And it would be my responsibility were someone to have the misfortune of being cracked down on some day. It has nothing to do with my governor. Commissioner Xu, do I make myself clear?"

Xu Tieying had taken money from Cui Zhongshi on multiple occasions. He found Cui Zhongshi pleasantly warm and genial, but now he discovered that behind this gentle exterior, there was a ruthless character inside.

Xu Tieying was made speechless and looked slowly at Fang Buting. It was Fang's turn to watch the night view. He looked out of the window and ignored Xu Tieying's gaze. Xu Tieying had to look at Cui Zhongshi instead.

"Commissioner Xu," Cui Zhongshi began, "just now our governor said that we mean what we say in the Peking branch. So you can rest assured that I will fulfil my promise. But please don't embarrass me, let alone our governor."

"Nothing can embarrass me," said Fang Buting suddenly. "The night view here is wonderful. Commissioner Xu, sit down and enjoy the conversation. Please, if you will excuse me."

To their surprise, Fang Buting left the two men behind and walked to the door alone. What was going on? What the hell was the matter? Xu Tieying, the veteran spy at the Central Bureau, was starting to get irritated by Fang Buting. He stood up without thinking, feeling confused.

Cui Zhongshi walked quickly to the door and opened it for Fang Buting. Fang walked out.

Cui Zhongshi closed the door gently and came back alone. "Commissioner Xu, regarding the twenty per cent shareholding, please take a seat. Let me explain it to you."

"No more tea, no more," said Fang Buting in Xie Peidong's room on the first floor of his mansion. "I won't be able to sleep if I drink any more." He sat down on a cane chair almost out of habit, looking at the photograph on the long table.

A much younger Xie Peidong could be seen in the left of the picture. On the right was a beautiful and dignified woman. This was Xie Peidong's wife. On close inspection, she was wearing an identical look to Fang Buting. Standing in front of the pair was a little girl, Xie Mulan, who was now quite grown-up.

"Ten years and eleven months?" Fang Buting sighed. "I always feel Buqiong is still with us. How could there be no news of her?"

Xie Peidong put down his rattan chair in front of the photo, thereby blocking Fang Buting's view of it as he sat down. "My dear brother-in-law, we are both getting old, so feel free to let it go. We'll make good arrangements for the younger ones so that we'll be seen as responsible people when we're gone."

Only now did Fang Buting realise there was someone in the world in whom he could confide. "Do you remember I disapproved of Buqiong marrying you?"

"Of course, I was a poor student then," said Xie Peidong, smiling bitterly. "The Fang family was rich and politically influential, and the governor had only one sister. Of course, you wanted her to marry your classmate."

"Nevertheless, my sister had the vision to find her own Mr Right. You were the best choice. It's such a pity the way events turned out, when calamity fell fast and furious... But no more, I'll stop there. Has Mulan gone to bed?"

"She left with Xiaoyu in the evening," said Xie Peidong. "She called at eight o'clock and said she would spend the night at Xiaoyu's house."

"Mulan resembles her mother in character," said Fang Buting. "She is twenty already. You can't afford to allow her to have her way, especially at the moment. We'll have to think about her future on her behalf."

Xie Peidong nodded his head in sadness.

"What do you think of Xiaoyu?" asked Fang Buting.

"She's a girl in a million. What's more, she's the daughter of a family friend."

"Peidong, it's you who knows me best." Fang Buting leaned forward and continued: "I'm going to make my proposition to Brother Qicang, asking him to marry his daughter to Meng'ao. What are my chances of success?"

"Your chances may be good. But considering the tension between you and Meng'ao, what would they do if they did get married?"

"They'd go to America!" said Fang Buting. "And Mulan, she'd go with them."

Xie Peidong's eyes were wide open. "You've already made arrangements for this, haven't you?"

"I've had countless challenges to overcome all my life, and this is the most difficult, so I must try the best I can. Cui Zhongshi must have been involved with the Communist Party, while Meng'ao appears to have been connected to him. To make things worse, he is being watched by the Iron and Blood Congress. Peidong, I've come to realise that the princeling's saying expresses it best: 'One revolution, fighting on two fronts.' Meng'ao shall not be used as a stooge either by the Communist Party or the Iron and Blood Congress. It's fine if he doesn't recognise me, but I won't disavow him. He will always be my son and a son of the Fang family."

"Don't worry." Seeing Fang Buting unusually excited, Xie Peidong handed the cup of boiled water to him. Fang Buting held the cup, but continued looking at Xie Peidong.

Xie walked to the door, opened it, checked both sides, closed the door again and returned. "I see eye to eye with you on this matter. We should give it further thought and discuss it later."

"There's no time to discuss it later," said Fang Buting, still very excited. "As soon as Cui Zhongshi returned to Peking, Meng'ao visited him in person. Now it's Xu Tieying who is on the doorstep. We have to make a decision now."

"Indeed, it is time to make a decision."

Fang Buting stared at Xie Peidong and sat down. He drew his chair closer to Xie's. "I want to hear your ideas."

Xie Peidong looked up at the empty sky and said: "How come Mulan's come back?"

Fang Buting heard a distant door closing in the courtyard, then the sound of someone pushing open the living room door on the ground floor and the familiar steps of Xie Mulan walking up the stairs.

"Let me find out," said Xie Peidong as he went to open the door. "It's so late, why have you come back?"

"I didn't want to stay there, I wanted to come back. Is that all right?" Xie Mulan sounded angry, obviously full of grievance. She was openly defying her father.

Fang Buting stood up with great concern when the telephone rang in the living room.

"It must be Brother Qicang," said Fang Buting. "Let me answer it downstairs."

―――――

He Qicang was very clothes conscious. In summer, he would go to bed in short silk pyjamas. Now he was on the phone in the living room of his residence in Yannan Garden: "It's good to know she's arrived home. Of course I should have arranged for a car to take her back. By the way, her teacher, Professor Liang, gave her some advice that is entirely for her own good. In the current environment, she should not get herself involved with the protests by the students from the Northeast. I'd also keep Xiaoyu at home. Please try to comfort her a bit. Well, I must go to bed now."

Beside him, Liang Jinglun and He Xiaoyu were standing respectfully. He Qicang hung up.

Liang Jinglun went over and said: "Sorry for disturbing your sleep. I'll help you go up."

"I'm not that old. Jinglun, you two can talk some more, but don't be too late." Then he went upstairs using his stick.

Liang Jinglun and He Xiaoyu followed him, helping He Qicang ascend the stairs slowly, with one positioned either side.

In the ground floor living room of his mansion, Fang Buting put down the phone. He was about to go upstairs with Xie Peidong when he saw Xu Tieying and Cui Zhongshi emerge from his office and come down the stairs.

"Thanks very much for your hospitality, Governor Fang." Xu Tieying's steps were brisk and the look on his face was relaxed. It appeared as though he was either happy that Cui Zhongshi had given him a satisfactory answer or he intended to repair the unhappiness he had caused just a few moments before.

Fang Buting had no alternative but to go up to Xu Tieying, but before doing so he looked over his shoulder at Cui Zhongshi. "Have you talked about everything you planned, Commissioner Xu?"

Xu Tieying listened attentively to Cui Zhongshi's response: "Please rest assured, governor. Regarding what to do, what not to do and how to do it, I'll give you a responsible answer."

Fang Buting looked at Xu Tieying, managing only a weak smile. "I'd be happy if you're able to give Commissioner Xu a responsible answer."

"Brother Buting," said Xu Tieying, "we both understand the purpose of the morning meeting. I will certainly put myself in your shoes. Trust me, will you? I'll take care of both Meng'ao and Mengwei."

"Sure. Let's show Commissioner Xu out together."

Fang Buting extended his hand which Xu Tieying immediately clutched, with some force. "Just walk me to the gate, please." He took the hand of Fang Buting and almost frogmarched him out.

Xie Peidong followed the pair and glanced at Cui Zhongshi. Cui returned the look. The two men went out following the two seniors.

―――

Liang Jinglun and He Xiaoyu returned to He Qicang's living room. Liang glanced back only to find He looking at him from behind.

"Sit down," Liang Jinglun said softly and sat down on the chair first. He Xiaoyu took another chair about a metre away and sat down with her knees pressed together. Their relationship was a model of propriety. Although Liang Jinglun had his own room in the house, He Xiaoyu never went there alone. Everything was discussed in the living room. He was therefore reassured.

"You really shouldn't have gone to Princess Hejing's mansion today." Liang Jinglun's voice was so low that He Qicang upstairs could not hear him. "The situation is very complicated, and your responsibility is so heavy that, from tomorrow on, you must not participate in any activities organised by the Student Government Association, including the rehearsals of the student drama club."

"What will the students think of me?" He Xiaoyu asked softly.

"Why are you still so sensitive to what others think of you?" Liang Jinglun was still gentle in his seriousness: "The Kuomintang will widen the scope of the civil war, and prices will soar. There will be corruption at all levels of government. No one can eliminate it. As for the five-member investigation group, it is little more than window dressing meant to deceive the people. Fang Meng'ao's brigade is the only one we can try to win over. We will make use of the slogan they adopted: 'To fight against the scum of the country and to save suffering compatriots!' Xiaoyu, you've been progressive, haven't you? I can't say any more now. I can only tell you that it's not my idea to assign you to work on Fang Meng'ao. Do you understand what I said?"

"A New China is arriving! We can't wait passively, nor just welcome its coming. The arrival of a New China requires many people to make selfless contributions and sacrifices. When it approaches, there shall be me and you!" Liang's voice was deep and magnetic, and his eyes were shining.

"May I join you?" As if hypnotised, He Xiaoyu felt that Liang Jinglun was shrouded in a glorious halo.

"You're already one of us!" Liang Jinglun replied encouragingly. "This is all I can tell you now. Prove your commitment with action!"

"How long will it take?" He Xiaoyu asked persistently.

"As long as the people need you," said Liang Jinglun without crossing the line. "On that day, I will show you the ideals to pursue. Is it all right?"

He Xiaoyu looked away and pondered briefly. Liang Jinglun was watching her closely.

He Xiaoyu suddenly raised her head and uttered the following words: "What if Fang Meng'ao falls in love with me?"

Liang Jinglun was stunned.

CHAPTER 9

It was morning and the clock on the wall of the meeting room in Gu Weijun's residence showed seven o'clock.

Du Wancheng, a bookish man, was panic-stricken. He was standing in front of his chair and speaking on the phone to an army officer. "Got it. Please inform General Fu Zuoyi that we will hold a meeting immediately and order the Citizens' Food-Distribution Committee to work with the Ministry of Education so that the students leave the Kuomintang's North China Headquarters for the Suppression of Communist Insurgency, and to bring the incident to an end."

"General Fu said that if you, the five-member group, can't solve the problem, it will affect the war situation in northern China and you personally will fight in this war!" said the officer on the other end of the line. Obviously, he was a prominent figure. He had a booming voice typical of an important person or a professional soldier. The caller hung up the phone with a loud bang.

Du Wancheng looked at Zeng Keda standing beside him and said: "It was agreed yesterday that we will deliver food to the students and discuss the issue of enrolment with them. What's going on today? How come it's deteriorated into such a major problem? What's the matter with the Citizens' Food-Distribution Committee? Where are the committee members now, including Mr Ma and Mr Wang? And Director Xu? Why haven't they shown up?"

Standing beside him, Zeng Keda tried to be reassuring: "Mr Du, it has indeed become a matter of urgency, but don't worry, don't rush them. We'll wait here. If they haven't shown up in ten minutes, I'll report directly to Comrade Jianfeng."

"What a mess! What an outrage!" Wang Benquan's voice came from outside the conference room.

"Clearly, they're pressuring the government," said Ma Linshen. "We must not give in any more. We must suppress it!"

Wang Benquan and Ma Linshen entered in a flurry, but they did not dare catch the eye of Du Wancheng or Zeng Keda. They went to their seats and waited for them to speak.

Neither Du Wancheng nor Zeng Keda looked at them. They were still waiting there, yet neither knew for what purpose. Ma Linshen and Wang Benquan could not sit down again, so they remained standing. The telephone on the table rang, startling Ma Linshen and Wang Benquan.

Du Wancheng was equally nervous. The phone rang three times, but he did not dare pick it up. He looked to Zeng Keda for help: "It's from Nanking..."

Zeng Keda picked up the receiver and listened. He covered the mouthpiece and told Du Wancheng: "It's Xu Tieying." Then he answered: "Chief Inspector Du is here, we are all here. Talk to Mr Du please." He handed the phone to Du Wancheng. "It's for you."

Du Wancheng took the phone: "What's the situation like... Tens of thousands! How can there be so many protestors... the professors also joined them... OK, stay where you are, maintain order. Do your best to stop the students and professors from attacking the general headquarters... Try to dissuade, try not to make any arrests... We'll hold a meeting right now and come up with solutions..."

After putting down the phone, Du Wancheng looked at Ma Linshen and said: "Did you all hear that? What about Ma Hanshan? What did the Peking Municipal Committee do yesterday?"

"Let him ask," said Zeng Keda as he picked up the phone and passed it to Ma Linshen.

Leaning on the table, Ma Linshen took the phone with both hands, put it down and turned the crank. He then picked up the receiver and said: "This is the special line for the five-member group. Connect me with Director Ma Hanshan of the Civil Affairs Bureau immediately!"

Ma Linshen was waiting to be connected. Everyone else was also waiting. Yet the words that followed still came from the female operator: "I'm sorry, Director Ma's line is busy."

"Don't give up, keep on trying to put me through," said Ma Linshen.

In the office of the director of the Peking Citizens' Food-Distribution Committee, Ma Hanshan had become so desperate that he was standing on the table, clutching the phone tightly in both hands. He turned left and right as if trying to balance on a hot wok.

"Mr Kung, my young master, my lord, permit me to say a few words, will you?" Ma Hanshan's throat was dry and his voice was hoarse. "I know you can double your profits by reselling the ten thousand tonnes of rice, but the consequence will be that people here will die... Tens of thousands of students and professors are all protesting at the doorstep of the general headquarters. The five-member investigation group from Nanking is looking for me everywhere. How do I dare see them?... I didn't say that the brothers are not entitled to a fair share in these profits. The problem is that these profits have now become poison. If you take them, you will die. I deserve it, I deserve it, I deserve the scolding. When you're done, I'll confess to the investigation group. Let them shoot me! If they shoot me, they'll come to you directly. OK?"

At last, the person at the other end was silent.

Ma Hanshan squatted down on the table and picked up a cup of tea. He drank the few remaining drops, hardly enough to moisten his lips. That cup of tea had been drunk long ago. He looked for someone to refill it with water, but the door was closed; he wanted to do it himself, yet he couldn't put down the phone. He had no choice but to put down the cup. He then used three fingers to extract some tea leaves from the cup and put them into his mouth to chew, so that he would at least be able to utter some sound.

When the person at the other end spoke again, Ma Hanshan

almost collapsed, his voice hoarse from shouting: "One thousand tonnes, that's OK... You have to call Tianjin in person, arrange for the train carriages, you must have the rice shipped to Peking today... As for the rest of the nine thousand tonnes, ship it as soon as you see fit, but I'll have to shoulder the responsibility... Or you can consult with Nanking... Don't hang up!"

Listening to further remarks made by the person at the other end of the line, Ma Hanshan soon became angry again. "The Central Bureau of Investigation is pressing me, too. Xu Tieying has turned against me. Now, if the Central Bureau of Investigation joins hands with Comrade Jianfeng, along with the Ministry of Finance, you will not be able to resist. This issue of Hou Juntang's twenty per cent shareholding must be explained to them... OK, OK! Then *you* can explain it..." Ma Hanshan went to hang up, but the other person had already done so.

Ma Hanshan was about to put the receiver back on the hook, when he stopped suddenly and thought about things. He put the phone aside and walked to the door. Without warning, he opened the door, only to find the section chiefs Li and Wang standing there.

"You bastards! Eavesdropping on my conversation?" said Ma Hanshan, his hoarse voice now seemingly recovered.

"Don't take it out on us, chief," said Mr Li. "We're here to report to you because things have become rather urgent, but we dare not knock on the door. How does that make it eavesdropping?"

Mr Wang chipped in: "We were absolutely not eavesdropping. If you don't believe us, let's swap positions and find out if you can hear what we're saying."

"You!" Ma Hanshan suddenly pointed to the phone on the table. "Put the phone back on the hook." Mr Wang had not got his breath back.

"I'm asking *you* to answer the phone!" said Ma Hanshan. "Whoever calls, tell him I'm going to transfer the food! Understand?"

"Yes," Mr Wang replied knowingly. He turned around and ran to pick up the phone on the table. Instead of leaving, Ma Hanshan stayed in the room, staring at him. Sure enough, as soon as Mr Wang put the phone back, the bell rang.

"Just do as I said!" Ma Hanshan shouted before going away in a rush. Mr Li also left.

Mr Wang picked up the burning phone, his two eyebrows being squeezed into one. The caller at the other end was swearing.

Mr Wang glanced at the door. He was determined not to be made a scapegoat: "He was here just a moment ago. He is working on food transportation, I believe... I'll try. If I find him, I'll ask him to meet with the five-member group."

In the Youth Aviation Brigade barracks, all the guards had been replaced by the young troopers selected from the Fourth Corps of the National Army. The platoon was put on three shifts a day. Each shift involved a squad standing guard at the gate of the barracks. The barracks were heavily guarded.

Xie Mulan, along with a dozen students from Yenching University Student Administration and others from the Northeast, were blocked outside the gate.

All the students were looking at her. "Tell your captain to come out and see if he will let me in!" Xie Mulan shouted to the stern-looking squad leader.

Inside the barracks not far away, the noise was heard by Guo Jinyang who was walking to the gate with two other brigade members.

"Hello," said Xie Mulan, jumping up and waving. "They won't let us in!"

Guo Jinyang came over and said warmly: "Hello, Miss Xie."

Guo turned to the guard and instructed him to let them in.

"That's not allowed," said the squad leader. "I have orders. Without General Zeng's instruction, no one can enter the barracks. Especially students."

Guo Jinyang glanced sideways at the sergeant and asked: "What's your rank?"

"Sergeant first class, sir."

"And I'm captain!" replied Guo Jinyang, putting on the airs of an officer. "Listen up! Attention!"

The squad leader had to stand to attention. The guards stood to attention.

Guo Jinyang said to Xie Mulan: "As guests of Captain Fang, please come in."

"Hurry up!" Xie Mulan was excited and proud, and rushed through the gate. The students followed quickly behind.

Guo Jinyang and the two pilots walked them to the barracks. The squad leader let them in. He rushed to the duty room and called to report the incident.

A triumphant Xie Mulan took the students into the barracks. However, on entering Fang Meng'ao's room, they were quickly silenced and stood there quietly. Fang Meng'ao was on the phone, waving to make them quiet.

"General Zeng, we have not been assigned to find Ma Hanshan," he said. "Can't *you* find Ma Hanshan with so many on the staff of the Peking Garrison headquarters and Peking Police Bureau?"

Zeng Keda was saying something patiently on the other end of the line when, to everyone's surprise, Xie Mulan ran to Fang Meng'ao and whispered into his ear in the presence of her fellow students: "Say 'yes' to him. We are here to ask you to catch that Ma Hanshan!"

Fang Meng'ao had covered the phone before she came up to him so that Xie Mulan's voice would not be heard down the line. All the students were wondering if Fang Meng'ao would believe Xie Mulan's story and help the students.

Fang Meng'ao put his arm around Xie Mulan's shoulder, but at the same time managed to cover her mouth with his hand. He spoke back into the receiver: "OK, I'll lead my brigade to find Ma Hanshan." Then he put down the phone.

Fang Meng'ao released his hand and said: "Remember, your elder brother won't listen to the Ministry of Defence, but only to you."

Xie Mulan jumped to her feet with joy. "Thank you, Brother!"

"But you're not allowed to come with us." With that, Fang Meng'ao walked out of the room and shouted to the brigade members: "Assemble, now!"

Xie Mulan looked at her fellow students whose eyes were all filled with admiration for her.

It was the summer holidays, and in the woods by Weiming Lake in the campus of Yenching University, not many students were around. Today, there were even fewer students than normal as almost all of them were on the streets in support of their compatriots from the Northeast. Everything was quiet.

Yan Chunming was standing under a tree reading a book. He looked around occasionally to see if anyone was approaching. Finally, a man appeared. Yan Chunming looked at him attentively, then he lowered his head and pretended to read.

The man was carrying a broom and dustpan. He was obviously a janitor. As he walked along, he occasionally stopped to pick up litter.

"Is that Mr Yan Chunming?" the janitor asked from a distance of no more than a metre behind him.

Yan Chunming slowly put down his book and looked at him.

The man took out a note from the top of the bamboo broomstick and handed it to him. Yan Chunming hurriedly took the note on which there was a sentence written in familiar handwriting.

The recollection of that voice in the library's rare books collection room rang out: "Something is going on at home. Please talk to the person who contacts you!" Yan Chunming tore up the note and put it into the dustpan: "Did Comrade Liu Yun send you?"

"Yes," said the janitor. "I'll be your contact person from now on."

Yan Chunming looked around and pretended to read again. He whispered: "What do I call you?"

"My surname is also Liu."

"Are you new here, or are you from Yenching?"

"Really, there is something wrong with your style of work," the janitor said in a low but stern voice. "Is that the sort of thing you should ask? Comrade Yan Chunming, when a superior makes contact with a subordinate, the subordinate is not allowed to ask questions of the superior. Have you forgotten basic discipline?"

Yan Chunming was momentarily startled, before realising that he was dealing with no ordinary man. He whispered back: "I will pay attention from now on."

"There's no such a thing as 'from now on'. You're so opinionated that it will bring about irreparable loss to the work of the party. After Comrade Liu Yun talked with you, how did you communicate his message to Comrade Liang Jinglun? Why did Liang Jinglun instigate the student demonstration at Princess Hejing's mansion yesterday? The message of the 'Sixth of July Instructions' by the superiors has been clearly stated: to protect the students and accumulate strength. Why do you always disobey the instructions of your superiors? How many members of the party are involved in today's march to the North China Headquarters for the Suppression of Communist Insurgency?"

Yan Chunming understood this was a very harsh criticism. He bowed his head and pondered for a moment before responding: "Comrade Liu, today's student protest at the Kuomintang's North China headquarters is purely an act of resistance by the people. We will not allow students to make unnecessary sacrifice, but neither will we suppress the people's voice of justice against the reactionary Kuomintang authorities."

"I was asking you how many party members were involved," said Liu, his tone hardening.

Yan Chunming was baffled, and after a short moment, he replied: "I don't quite know..."

"Once again, on behalf of my superiors, I'd like to reaffirm to you the current situation. The Kuomintang government goes against current trends, which has led to the resistance of the whole nation. Today, it is the conscious action of the students from Northeast China and students from major universities in Peking to protest against the reactionary authorities. It was a rational and legitimate protest organised by the Peking Students' Union in compliance with the so-called 'constitution' of the Kuomintang authorities. If our party comes forward to organise the protest, it will be used as an excuse by the Kuomintang authorities. First, it will seriously affect the work of the united front of our party. Second, it will result in unnecessary sacrifice on the part of the progressive students. This evening, you will hold a secret meeting on behalf of the party regarding the current student movement. The participants will be limited to those in charge of the movement. We should learn the 'Seventh of July Instructions' again so that we can reach a consensus. I'll contact you either tomorrow or the day after."

"Very well," Yan Chunming replied heavily.

As Liu walked away, he said: "You and I are to contact each other on a one-to-one basis. Don't tell anyone, especially Comrade Liang Jinglun."

Yan Chunming was seized with a sense of astonishment.

Liu stopped again and swept a fallen leaf into his dustpan. "This is the last time I'll reiterate the importance of discipline to you on behalf of the party."

It was ten in the morning, and it was starting to get warm. However, the door of the office of the director of the Peking Citizens' Food-Distribution Committee was locked from the inside. The phone was on the table, emitting an engaged tone.

Section Chief Wang was feeling drowsy having been woken up early in the morning. After working hard for several hours, he had fallen asleep on a cane chair, drooling and snoring without noticing the world outside being turned upside down.

Suddenly, there was a knock on the door. Wang sat up abruptly. "Who is it?"

"Open the door, Mr Wang. It's Captain Fang and his pilots here."

"Stop them! Just tell them I'm not here!" said a half-awake Chief Wang. "There's no one in here!"

"Who is speaking, then, if you're not there?" It was a familiar voice that brought Wang to his senses.

Fang Meng'ao was standing outside the door, and Wang had no choice but to open it. Fang Meng'ao was half a head taller than Wang, and behind him were his brigade members.

"Where is Ma Hanshan, your director?" asked Fang.

"How... how should I know?" Wang stuttered. "Captain Fang, are you looking for him?"

"Take us to look for him."

"Captain Fang," said a now desperate Wang, "I've no idea where he is. How can I help you find him?"

"Take him to the truck! Take all the section chiefs of the Citizens' Food-Distribution Committee. We won't stop until they help us find Ma Hanshan."

Shao Yuangang, who himself was a tall man, stood beside Fang Meng'ao. He grabbed hold of Wang's fat hand and dragged him to the door. "Move!" he barked.

"Stop dragging me! Let go," cried Section Chief Wang.

Fang Meng'ao saw the phone on the desk. He strode over and dialled a number. He was put through successfully.

"Is that the Peking Municipal Police Bureau?" he asked. "I'd like to speak to Deputy Commissioner Fang Mengwei."

The person at the other end said he was not available.

"Put me through to him wherever he is immediately. Tell him to take a team of policemen to the archway at Dongsi. Tell him it's Captain Fang Meng'ao of the Peking Youth Aviation Brigade who is looking for him."

Fang Meng'ao put down the phone and strode to the door.

The Tianyi Calligraphy and Painting Shop in Liulichang was well-known, but few people were aware of the collection room on the floor above the shop. It was about eighty square metres in area, with many large wooden cabinets, made of gold nanmu phoebe, huanghuali rosewood or red sandalwood. They were all arranged neatly along the wall. The wooden cabinets themselves were precious, but the items inside were considerably more so.

On the opposite side of the wall were safes used by the government to keep confidential files. They also contained rare cultural relics and antiques.

In the middle of the room was a large wooden table that was two metres long and one metre wide. It was made of Indian red sandalwood. It was said to be a royal table formerly used by Emperor Daoguang, and passed on to his favourite son, Prince Gong.

This was the secret storage place where Ma Hanshan hid the cultural relics and antiques that he seized in the name of confiscating "enemy and puppet regime assets" when he served as director of the Peking Committee for Combating Japanese Collaborators in 1945.

Ma Hanshan seldom came here, and would only do so for one of two reasons. First, when he was in serious trouble, he would raid these rare treasures to offer as bribes. A trip to this secret storage place was full of sorrow, fear and ridicule. Second, when he was in a bad mood, he would come here to take a look at these antiques, scripts and paintings. A visit to this secret storage place would enable him to forget all the humiliations and remember the finer things of life.

All hell was breaking loose around him in Peking. Both the Communist Party and the Kuomintang had it in for him. The families for whom he had worked so hard were also on his tail. Since he couldn't disappear from those whom he didn't want to see, the only place of sanctuary was here, looking at his treasures.

He opened a large wooden box and looked inside. To his surprise, it was empty. He investigated more closely and found a note in the box that read: "Given to Yunong, Director Dai, the first month of the thirty-fifth year of the Republic of China."

He opened another wooden box, and it too was empty. The note inside read: "The fourth month of the thirty-eighth year of the Republic of China. Given to Director Zheng Jiemin." Ma Hanshan noisily opened one empty wooden case after another. They contained notes appearing to state that his treasured scripts and paintings no longer belonged to him.

Ma Hanshan turned around and went to the safe. He took out a bunch of keys from his belt and sorted them out before choosing one. It opened the safe.

This safe contained a paper scroll. Ma Hanshan looked at the scroll for a long time and finally took it out. He unfolded the scroll on the red sandalwood table. It was a painting of a beautiful woman by the Ming Dynasty artist Tang Bohu. It was about two feet wide and five feet long.

Ma Hanshan climbed onto the table. Instead of admiring this work of art, he decided to lie down next to it on a narrow strip of the table about one foot wide. The scroll was on the left of the table, and Ma Hanshan was on the right. Caressing the hand of the beautiful woman depicted in the scroll with his right hand, Ma Hanshan felt it was like lying beside his beloved woman.

"I'm going to give you to a vulgar person. Please don't blame me, will you?" Looking at the ceiling, Ma Hanshan felt profoundly sad, as if he were talking to a living person.

———

A jeep came to a halt at the entrance of Liulichang Street. Two military trucks stopped behind it. Fang Meng'ao and Fang Mengwei alighted from the two rear doors of the jeep. Chief Wang struggled to emerge from the front passenger seat. The Youth Aviation Brigade members disgorged from the first military truck, while officers from the Peking Police Bureau came out of the one behind.

Section Chief Wang looked at Fang Meng'ao and Fang Mengwei, his face anguished. "Captain Fang, Deputy Commissioner Fang, do me this honour, let me find Director Ma myself. Please wait here for a moment."

"You don't deserve such face," said Fang Mengwei. "You piece of dogshit! You drive us half way round the city only to play this trick on us? Move! If you can't find Ma this time, you need to come back to the bureau with me. Go!"

He pushed Wang and ordered him to show the way. Fang Meng'ao gently buttonholed Fang Mengwei: "It will be for real this time. Let him go. We'll wait here."

Fang Mengwei still kept a close eye on Wang. "What if you can't find Ma Hanshan this time?"

"You... you can charge me and take me back to the police station," Wang replied, before holding out his hands to Fang Mengwei.

By now, Fang Mengwei was sick and tired of Wang, and he ordered him to leave. Wang went to the Tianyi Calligraphy and Painting shop alone.

As Fang Meng'ao took out a cigar, he saw the eyes of many people in the distance looking timidly in his direction. He put the cigar back in his pocket and said to Fang Mengwei: "Take your team back. With you in charge, the police department and garrison headquarters won't be hurting any students today."

"OK."

"Also," Fang Meng'ao continued, "try to reassure the students about the provision of their everyday food supply of fifteen *jin* per person per month. Promise them that they will receive it from tomorrow."

"Elder Brother," said Fang Mengwei, "I wonder if it's too early to give such a promise. The committee may not yet be in a position to supply so much rice."

"Just do as I tell you. How can we do otherwise when people are starving to death?"

"I'll go and tell them myself." Feeling that he had to comply with his brother's request, Fang Mengwei turned around and ordered the police officers: "Get back into the truck! Return to the North China Headquarters for the Suppression of Communist Insurgency!"

The military truck behind that carried Fang Mengwei and his team reversed, then drove towards the North China Headquarters for the Suppression of Communist Insurgency.

As he expected, Fang Meng'ao saw Ma Hanshan coming from afar. He was walking fast, so fast that he left Section Chief Wang far behind.

"Captain Fang! Captain Fang!" Ma Hanshan was now running to Fang Meng'ao. "Why the need for you to find me in person?"

Fang Meng'ao had seen plenty of rogues before but he had never seen anyone become rogue in broad daylight. Fang Meng'ao narrowed his eyes under the glare of the sun and looked at Ma Hanshan: "Aren't we pilots so well fed that we have nothing better to do than drive around town searching for you, a deputy director of the Citizens' Food-Distribution Committee? Director Ma, you tell me?"

Ma Hanshan was made speechless.

"Isn't it rather hot here?" said Fang Meng'ao. "It'll be nice and cool in Ambassador Gu Weijun's courtyard."

"The group of five is looking for me?" Ma Hanshan asked knowingly.

Fang Meng'ao couldn't help smiling. "Director Ma, aren't you bored of being an official? Get in the jeep."

Sitting in the back of the jeep, Ma Hanshan said to Fang Meng'ao: "Captain Fang, I have a life-long friendship with Deputy Director Cui Zhongshi..."

Fang Meng'ao didn't laugh this time. Instead, he stared at him and instructed the driver, Shao Yuangang, to drive.

―――

In the vault of the Central Bank's Peking branch, a second heavy iron door closed behind Cui Zhongshi who was following Fang Buting towards the third door.

Fang Buting opened the first lock with a key and turned the dial according to the secret combination. Cui Zhongshi promptly went over and opened the second lock with a key. There was no combination for this lock. He pushed hard and the heavy safety door opened.

Cui Zhongshi stood by the door, waiting for Fang Buting to go in first. When Fang Buting entered, Cui Zhongshi followed him. Rows and rows of wide steel cabinets lay empty. Further inside, in the rear section, two rows of steel-frame cabinets lined the walls, on which gold bars weighing fifty kilograms were neatly stacked, glowing in the light.

"When we arrived in the 1946, all these shelves were full of gold ingots," Fang Buting said with emotion.

"Yes governor," Cui Zhongshi replied.

"Where has all the money gone?"

"Yes governor," Cui Zhongshi repeated.

"If I can't explain, how can you?" Fang Buting sighed. "Zhongshi, no one in the national government knows better than you and me about the property accumulated here over this long period of time. How long do you predict it will take for the Communist Party to assume power?"

Cui Zhongshi just looked at Fang Buting.

"Walls have no ears. Tell me what you think."

"I have no opinion, governor," Cui Zhongshi replied.

"Don't you care about the current situation given that you have a family and career? Haven't you thought about a way out?" Fang Buting asked.

"It's no use me thinking about the current political situation. I'll follow the governor, either advance or retreat."

Fang Buting looked Cui Zhongshi in the eye. "You've been most faithfully true to your mission to save Meng'ao, for the sake of following me?"

Cui Zhongshi lowered his head and thought for a short while. "Yes, but also no."

"Please indulge me," said Fang Buting.

"I was promoted by the governor. The governor's business is my business. It was my original intention to make friends with Meng'ao. As time passed, I came to realise that Meng'ao is a rare national talent as well as being an excellent young man whom I admire so much. I say this from the bottom of my heart. Of course, I'm not in a position to say such things."

"Who says you're not?" said Fang Buting. "The Central Bank, the Ministry of Finance and the Kuomintang central party headquarters, you can handle them all. Cui, you're more capable than I expected."

"Governor," said Cui Zhongshi, raising his head and looking at Fang Buting, "if you're not satisfied with what I've done, or even if you don't trust me, you can tell me directly. Further, you can investigate me and discipline me if I am wrong. But one thing I must make clear is that I had no ulterior motive in going to Nanking to save Meng'ao. You can't suspect your son."

"Did I say I doubted my son? Neither the Central Bureau nor the Military Council suspect him. Why should I be suspicious? I asked you here to tell you that, no matter what you did without my knowledge, such as what you've promised to Xu Tieying, I don't care. Next, the five-member investigation group will directly check on you. In fact, it is Meng'ao who will be assigned to do that. I hope you'll speak to them as you have spoken to me today."

"I know what to say and how to do it. It will not involve the governor, let alone make things difficult for Meng'ao."

"Then you can go now." Fang Buting walked to the door. "The five-member group and Meng'ao are waiting for you in Ambassador Gu's residence. You know what to say, I am sure."

As soon as Fang Meng'ao entered the meeting room in Gu Weijun's residence, he found Cui Zhongshi sitting with his back to him. The first man to look at him was Zeng Keda.

Sitting across the table, Zeng Keda could see Cui Zhongshi sitting in front of him and Fang Meng'ao standing behind him. It was such a fleeting look.

Zeng Keda stood up and asked with great concern: "Hello, good to see you back. Did you find Ma Hanshan?"

"He's outside," said Fang Meng'ao.

Du Wancheng stood up and said: "Captain Fang, thank you for taking the trouble. Please sit down and have some tea."

Fang Meng'ao sat down under Dr Sun Yat-sen's portrait.

"Why doesn't he come in?" Ma Linshen shouted before slapping the table.

Expressionless, Ma Hanshan walked in and stopped at Cui Zhongshi's side.

"Where have you been?" Ma Linshen demanded.

"I was trying to secure the rice supply," said Ma Hanshan.

"Did you have any luck?" Ma Linshen continued.

"Only partly."

"Sit down." Ma Linshen's question seemed to help Ma Hanshan handle the ordeal. His manner of speaking became more relaxed.

Ma Hanshan wanted to sit, but found there was only one chair in this row, and that had already been taken by Cui Zhongshi. He looked at Ma Linshen, who turned to Zeng Keda's adjutant who was busy writing the minutes. Several chairs were positioned along the wall behind the adjutant.

The adjutant stood up slowly and prepared to fetch the chair. Zeng Keda stared at the adjutant who understood his meaning, and he sat down again.

Ma Hanshan was left there, standing alone. Ma Linshen was embarrassed and became angry. But what could he say about the matter since his subordinate was held responsible for the mess?

"The Peking Citizens' Food-Distribution Committee has been in operation for three months, and all the money from the Central Bank under the Ministry of Finance has been allocated to you," stated Zeng Keda. "Now, where are you supposed to secure the food supply? Where is the food?"

Ma Hanshan felt he had never been so humiliated, provoking in him a sudden burst of anger that was rooted in desperation. He simply refused to answer Zeng Keda's question. Instead, he rolled his eyes and looked up at the ceiling.

"Answer me!" roared Zeng Keda.

"Were you asking me about the food supply?" said Ma Hanshan. "Here, take it all!" He stretched out his two empty hands toward Zeng Keda.

Zeng Keda did not expect that Ma Hanshan would have the audacity to reply like this. He was simply dumbfounded. Others in the room were left equally stunned.

Normally, the next step would be to make an arrest. But in what name? Who would make the arrest? And once the arrest was made, who was supposed to try him? Du Wancheng was the first to react, his lips trembling with anger: "Look at the document! All of you, read the document! How should he be dealt with if he works against the central government like this?"

"There's no need to read it," said Zeng Keda in a calmer tone. "I can't punish him for refusing to answer my questions. However, we are here to investigate the Seventh of July Incident that has shocked both the people of China and our foreign allies. Whether or not the Communist Party is behind the incident, it is certainly true that the Peking Citizens' Food-Distribution Committee failed to distribute food to the students from the Northeast. You failed then, and you failed yesterday after we arrived the previous day. The result is that we are now witnessing an even larger student demonstration. Ma Hanshan!"

To emphasise his points, he slapped the table and stood up swiftly. "Regarding the two empty hands you showed me, there are no stipulations in the law of the party-state that allow me to cut them off. But let me remind you, the Special Criminal Court can sever your head! I had Hou Juntang's head cut off on the sixth of July shortly before coming up to Peking! Now, I propose…"

Du Wancheng, Wang Benquan and Ma Linshen all looked at him.

"…I propose that we immediately report to the central government in the name of the five-member investigation group, to remove Ma Hanshan from all posts, and escort him to Nanking where he should be tried by the Special Criminal Court!"

"Calm down! Calm down!" Ma Linshen said. "Inspector Zeng, I'm in charge of this sector. I have a better understanding of the situation. Since the establishment of the Citizens' Food-Distribution Committee in April, we have encountered many difficulties. While serving as deputy director of the Peking Citizens' Food-Distribution Committee, Ma Hanshan has done his best. General Inspector Du, we are here to investigate and solve the problem. We'll have to rely on them to do the job in Peking. I don't agree with Inspector Zeng's proposal. It won't help."

Zeng Keda turned to Ma Linshen and said: "Please go to Ma Hanshan's committee and get the food you need."

Ma Linshen was stunned, and turned to look at Ma Hanshan: "Why don't you take back your chicken feet hands? Do you have a death wish or something?"

Ma Hanshan retracted his hands, while still wearing the same fearless look.

Zeng Keda assessed Cui Zhongshi. While he was attacking Ma Hanshan, his eyes never strayed from Cui Zhongshi.

Ma Hanshan was so desperate because of a very complex reason that involved the economic interests of the top financial groups. Why did he appear so very honest and cooperative when Fang Buting was around yesterday, while today, with Cui Zhongshi present, he was so agitated?

Zeng Keda was ready to attack Cui Zhongshi. But he held back for a moment and looked towards Fang Meng'ao: "Captain Fang, where did you find Director Ma just now?"

"I'm not familiar with Peking. What's the name of that street?"

He turned to Ma Hanshan, who said: "Qianmenwai. That's where the committee transports grain by train."

Still looking at Fang Meng'ao, Zeng Keda said: "Captain Fang, did you find him in the place where the grain was transported?"

"If that's what he said," said Fang Meng'ao.

Realising that Captain Fang was now being more sensible, Ma Hanshan went on: "I can cooperate with people like Captain Fang and his team who are so conscientious and reasonable."

Ma Hanshan seemed to confront toughness with toughness. Zeng Keda did not look at him any more, and instead he turned to Fang Meng'ao with a very serious expression on his face. "Comrade Fang Meng'ao, we've a daunting task ahead of us. More than a million people in Peking are suffering, and they depend on us to provide them with the means to survive. The five-person team will launch an investigation. Next, our team of five will launch an official investigation. I hope you will understand which individuals and which departments we are to investigate."

Fang Meng'ao immediately understood what he meant. He looked at Cui Zhongshi subconsciously, then turned to Zeng Keda: "I'm clear about my task. I also know what's excluded. There's no need for General Zeng to remind me."

"That sounds good," said a reassured Zeng Keda, who now began a full-frontal attack on Cui Zhongshi. "Since the establishment of the Peking Citizens' Food-Distribution Committee in April, Ma Hanshan, executive deputy director, has personally managed the purchase, management, distribution and allocation of materials. Yesterday, we consulted Governor Fang Buting and understood that the fund appropriated by the Central Bank to purchase the materials was processed by Cui Zhongshi, deputy treasury director of the Peking branch of the Central Bank. Now that these two people have presented themselves here, I'd like to ask Deputy Director Cui if you can make a detailed report on your accounts to the five-member investigation group."

As the discussion unfolded, Wang Benquan became nervous, and he looked at Cui Zhongshi, eyes wide open. Ma Linshen was also nervous, but with Wang Benquan present, he could afford to bide his time.

Cui Zhongshi stood up slowly and looked at the adjutant. "Please," he said, "take away my chair. I can't let Director Ma stand alone."

There was a popular rule in Kuomintang officialdom, which was similar to one that prevailed in the underworld and was known as *jianghu*, literally meaning "rivers and lakes". The gangster boss Du Yuesheng once characterised it as "eating two bowls of noodles". One part involved respecting those in officialdom, the other was saving face for those in trouble. By respecting officialdom and taking personal feelings into account, one would be held in high esteem and often pardoned and released if caught.

Although Cui Zhongshi was a banker, most people he dealt with were politicians. In the circumstances in which he currently found himself, he utilised the common practice known as "two bowls of noodles". Although he was standing there in humiliation, he had taken a position that was likely to win the respect of those in the group.

Ma Hanshan was the first one to be grateful. Looking at Cui, he openly thanked him. Ma Linshen and Wang Benquan were equally appreciative. Du Wancheng nodded with admiration.

The adjutant felt confused. He looked at Zeng Keda again. To remove Cui's chair or not was the question.

Zeng Keda looked at Fang Meng'ao again, and he found his expression now somewhat unusually indifferent. He said to his adjutant: "Give Director Ma a chair." The adjutant grabbed a chair for him. "Deputy Director Cui, can you begin now?"

Cui Zhongshi remained standing and said: "I don't know how to begin. Now we're engaged in a civil war, the Central Bank has to carry out additional tasks assigned by the national government. General Inspector Du is an expert in economics and Secretary Wang is our financial person. For your information, banks are responsible for financial flows in the market. Neither the ratio of money to commodities in circulation nor the gold reserves to support the banks' issuance of money are sufficient, so it's impossible for money to circulate. Whether it's the Central Commission on Citizens' Food Distribution or the Material Management Commission, it's all about controlling the economy. As long as the economy is controlled, no one single department can form a clear picture of the accounts. Since April this year, we have been entrusted to manage the accounts of the Central Commission on Citizens' Food Distribution and the Material Management Commission. Please listen clearly, each and every one of this five-member group, we are only in charge of the accounts. We can't even see the specific materials."

Zeng Keda frowned on hearing this, because Cui's presentation was full of professional jargon and highlighted the most important corruption practices. He didn't know how to respond, so he looked at Du Wancheng.

"What he said was quite convincing," said Du Wancheng. "However, Deputy Director Cui, it doesn't prevent you from filling us in on the accounts, does it?"

"Although they only cover three months, the accounts of the two committees have been piled up in one room," Cui Zhongshi replied. "There are also dozens of departments involved, and many of them are directly related to the expenditure of the Military Commission. The headquarters of the Central Bank has clear disciplines which stipulate that some accounts should not be disclosed to any departments, unless ordered by the Central Military Commission and signed by President Chiang."

"Are you using President Chiang's name to stop us?" Zeng Keda stood up angrily. "We have been sent by President Chiang! Cui Zhongshi, I think you are more a politician than a banker. Director Ma has a background in the Military Council. Do you have any other experience? If so, just tell us. If it's the Central Bureau of Investigation, we'll go to Minister Chen. If it's the Military Council, we'll go to Director Mao. Don't hide it from those who have no inside information!"

Everyone present was aware of Zeng Keda's background, so they were shocked at what he had just said. All eyes were on Cui Zhongshi, whose own expression had also changed a little. He knew that Zeng Keda suspected his political affiliations. But it never occurred to him that instead of being charged with being a member of the Communist Party, he would be accused of being associated with the Central Bureau of Investigation or the Military Council. Would this affect Fang Meng'ao, who had been in single line contact with him?

Fang Meng'ao felt strongly affected by Zeng Keda's rebuttal. He looked at Cui Zhongshi intensely. Some images of their meetings over the past three years appeared before his eyes at the speed of a hurtling train:

> Cui Zhongshi meeting him in his Jianqiao airbase dormitory: "Comrade Meng'ao, you are an alternate member of the Communist Party of China from this day forwards..."

Cui Zhongshi meeting him on a patch of grass near Jianqiao: "Comrade Meng'ao, although you are officially a party member, due to the special nature of your job, I can't take you to any activities organised by the party..."

Cui Zhongshi meeting him outside the gates of Jianqiao: "Comrade Meng'ao, you can't read any party documents for the time being. The less you know, the safer you will be..."

Cui Zhongshi talking to him in his room: "You must be aware that you, Fang Meng'ao, have never been a member of the Communist Party of China..."

An element of doubt that he had never experienced before now appeared in Fang Meng'ao's eyes. He suddenly felt a sense of estrangement when looking at Cui Zhongshi again.

Cui Zhongshi was thinking intensely, using the silence to bide for time.

Zeng Keda had felt the effect of his "one stone, two birds" tactics. He enjoyed the silence. The longer it went on, the better the effect.

Ma Hanshan came to Cui Zhongshi's rescue and pronounced: "Deputy Director Cui, feel free to inform him of any relevant background details. We're working for the party-state anyway. No individual person can claim credit for the success of the Nationalist Revolution, nor does any one person have the final say."

Cui Zhongshi sat down and looked at Wang Benquan. "Director Wang," he said, "you're from the headquarters of the Central Bank, directly in charge of the Peking branch. I solemnly ask the Central Bank authorities to investigate my identity right away. I myself, Cui Zhongshi, am no more than a staff member of the Central Bank. If I have any other political affiliation, please dismiss me immediately."

Wang Benquan looked at Du Wancheng and said: "General Inspector Du, you are the coordinator of this group. What are we doing here in Peking? What is the reason for the investigation? Since we're supposed to be here to check the accounts, why then are we being diverted to find out about the Central Bureau of

Investigation and the Bureau of Investigation of the Military Council?"

The subject Du Wancheng feared most was politics. Background checks were a huge headache for him. "Deputy Director Cui, will you please fill us in on the accounts?" he asked.

Cui Zhongshi stood up again, and picked up his briefcase from the table. "I shouldn't say anything until the Central Bank headquarters reach a conclusion about my political background. May I ask to be excused?" With that, he bowed slightly to the group of five sitting on the other side of the table and turned around to walk towards the door.

Cui Zhongshi was not Fang Buting. The young military police guards standing at the door moved together and blocked his exit.

"Who told you to leave?" one of them barked. "Go back in!"

Cui Zhongshi stood still. Fang Meng'ao got up and looked at the door.

"Don't be rude!" said Zeng Keda as he stood up and appraised the two guards from the Youth Army. The guards moved out of the way a little, but they remained vigilant at the door.

"Captain Fang," Zeng Keda continued, "you've been assigned to check the materials and accounts specifically. Do you want Deputy Director Cui to leave now?"

Fang Meng'ao looked at Zeng Keda and read his eyes carefully, as Cui Zhongshi walked briskly between the two guards and out of the meeting room. On his way out, he said loudly: "My office is on the first floor of the Peking branch, and my home is Number Two Dongzhong Hutong. You can visit me any time."

Everyone looked at Cui Zhongshi as he walked through the door.

"Deputy Director Cui, why have you left?" The voice came from outside the door, and it belonged to Xu Tieying.

No response. Xu Tieying's sweaty face appeared at the doorway. It was as if he deliberately wanted to be seen this way, indicating to the five-member group that he had been toiling away for the party-state. "At long last! We managed to put an end to the protest, at least for the time being."

"The students have all dispersed?" asked Du Wancheng, who was the most concerned.

"Not all of them, of course," replied Xu Tieying as he went to his seat and took a sip of tea. "For the time being, we managed to persuade the students from the Northeast to go back. Food must be delivered to them tomorrow."

On sitting down, he looked at Du Wancheng and asked tentatively: "Why has Deputy Director Cui left? Shouldn't we be checking the accounts of the Peking branch?"

Du Wancheng felt intense pressure as all around him were discussing an issue to which no one could offer a solution. The most pressing thing was to distribute food to the students. No one could afford to have another demonstration. "Let's put everything else on hold for the time being," said Du Wancheng. "Can you distribute food to the students from the Northeast, first thing tomorrow? Director Ma, did you hear what Commissioner Xu just said?"

"To distribute food among fifteen thousand people, that needs time," said Ma Hanshan. "Am I allowed to do it? Do you want to continue to investigate me or let me organise the distribution of food for tomorrow?"

"To allocate food, of course," said Xu Tieying, who had now become the most authoritative person in the room. "Commander-in-Chief Fu said some harsh words. If another round of student protests take place on his doorstep tomorrow, he will resign immediately and ask President Chiang to command the troops to fight the war in person."

"Can I go now?" Ma Hanshan looked at Zeng Keda and then at Du Wancheng. Du looked at Zeng Keda.

Zeng Keda turned to Fang Meng'ao and said: "Captain Fang, you don't have to check the accounts of the Peking branch for the time being. Tomorrow, we will start to check the warehouse of the Peking Citizens' Food-Distribution Committee. First, we will check the grain against their accounts, and examine one warehouse after another under the categories of purchase and allocation."

Fang Meng'ao stood there and then gave his assent.

Zeng Keda looked at Ma Hanshan and said: "Get out and allocate the food."

On his way out, Ma Hanshan was feeling a little unsure about the whole business.

Du Wancheng felt so confused that he looked to Zeng Keda and Xu Tieying for help: "Shall we continue?"

"No, there's no need," said Zeng Keda. "Check the supplies, check the accounts! By the time the results are known, someone is going to be carried out in a coffin!"

———

Zeng Keda rushed home from the conference room and dialled the number of the Foreign Languages Bookstore where he had met Liang Jinglun.

"Now's the best time to arrange it. Captain Fang suspects Deputy Director Cui. Arrange for Miss He to contact him straight away... Well done! It's good to know that. Listen to what he said, remember the exact words and then relay them to me verbatim. Professor, pay attention to your own safety."

———

On a street to the west of Gu Weijun's residence, the Central Army had sent out two motorcycles to clear a path for Fang Meng'ao's brigade. Fang drove the jeep himself, and let Shao Yuangang sit in the front passenger seat. His foot jammed against the accelerator. It was most unlike him to drive fast.

The motorcycles in front were left behind by his jeep, and they rushed to catch up.

"Captain, you're going too fast! Please slow down," Shao Yuangang protested.

"Shut up!" Fang Meng'ao's face had rarely taken on such a ghastly expression.

"Look ahead, captain!" Shao Yuangang shouted.

Fang Meng'ao saw two girls standing in the middle of the road less than twenty metres away. To his surprise, they were Xie Mulan and He Xiaoyu!

He took his foot off the accelerator and jammed the brake, yet the momentum of the jeep still carried it forward, closer and closer to the girls. The jeep careered forward and was now less than ten metres away, when Fang Meng'ao forcefully turned the steering wheel to the left.

The jeep swerved abruptly as the rear wheels screeched across the road surface. It continued in the same direction for a short distance, as the rear wheels followed the direction of the front wheels. The jeep spun a full circle before coming to a stop.

Xie Mulan and He Xiaoyu, who were standing a few metres away, were white with fear, looking confused and terrified.

It was the two motorcyclists who came off worst, however, one crashing into a tree on the pavement and the other careering into a wall for a short distance before coming to a halt.

The jeep's door was violently pushed open. Fang Meng'ao jumped out and reprimanded the two girls: "Are you trying to get yourselves killed?"

The girls were still frightened and it took a while for them to recover. They stood in the road in a daze. Fang Meng'ao sighed, calmed down a little and went over to them: "You must be scared. My apologies."

"Captain Fang!" He Xiaoyu said with emotion. "Do you know where you are?"

Fang Meng'ao looked at her.

"This is Peking, a city with a population of two million. We're not some place in the sky, you're not flying. Are you intent on killing its citizens by driving so fast?"

Fang Meng'ao narrowed his eyes again and looked at the little sister in front of him who used to be so quiet and polite. He felt she was acting rather like Captain Chennault, whom he had once admired so much. Thinking of this, he smiled and turned to Shao Yuangang: "Was I driving too fast?"

"Yes, captain, you were." Shao Yuangang was also somewhat angry.

"He did it because he is so skilful!" exclaimed Xie Mulan, who had just recovered her poise. "My big brother, that was an almost perfect 360 degree turn you just accomplished! Bravo! How did you do it? You must teach me next time!"

"What can I do for you?" Fang Meng'ao asked.

"We're here for you, actually," said Xie Mulan. "In fact, we want to thank you. The news that you caught Ma Hanshan has been circulating among my fellow students. They praised me as well. Big Brother, I want to thank you by inviting you to dinner this evening. So don't go anywhere. Come home with us. Xiaoyu and I will each cook two dishes by way of thanks."

Fang Meng'ao was silent and after a short while he asked: "Is your younger brother at home?"

"We're inviting you, not him," Xie Mulan said.

"Is he at home?"

"Yes he is. He has dinner with Uncle Fang whenever he's not on duty."

"That's good. They can eat theirs, while we eat ours. I'd also like Miss He to teach me how to drive in Peking. Get in the car."

In the governor's office on the first floor of his mansion, Fang Buting was listening on the phone very attentively. Xie Peidong was standing beside him, equally alert.

"...Zeng Keda suspected that Cui is either a member of the Central Bureau of Investigation or the Bureau of Investigation under the Military Council," said Fang. "Director Wang, this person works for me, he is not affiliated with them. If the headquarters of the Central Bank believe he does, then feel free to transfer me and reshuffle the Peking branch... Uh huh. If the sky doesn't fall, the Peking branch won't fall. Of course, Cui is a responsible and capable person. I hope Director Wang and the headquarters of the Central Bank trust him... I know. I will visit you in person at Ambassador Gu's residence, or you can come directly to my office. There is nothing to fear... OK, goodbye."

After putting down the phone, Fang Buting's high spirits morphed into worry. He sat there, deep in thought.

"To my great surprise, Zeng Keda even suspected that Cui Zhongshi belonged to either the Central Bureau of Investigation or the Bureau of Investigation under the Military Council... What do you think?" Fang Buting looked at Xie Peidong.

"At least it shows that no one organisation suspects Cui Zhongshi is a member of the Communist Party, whether it's the Central Bureau of Investigation or the Bureau of Investigation under the Military Council, or the Iron and Blood Congress. Governor, I wonder if we are being oversensitive."

Xie Peidong did not suggest that Fang Buting alone might be being oversensitive, preferring to use the word "we" instead.

"Are we being too suspicious?" asked Fang Buting, looking even more grave. "Zeng Keda will leave no stone unturned. I just learned at the meeting that he accused Cui Zhongshi of being associated with either the Central Bureau of Investigation or the Bureau of Investigation under the Military Council. Meng'ao was there. He said this to Meng'ao!"

"Does Meng'ao believe it?"

"He has been a trusting person since childhood, like his mother, Peidong."

"I see, governor."

"Go talk to Cui Zhongshi as soon as possible. Tell him to sort out the accounts in quick time and give all the books to you. Tell him not to meet Meng'ao again."

"I'll visit him tonight," said Xie Peidong.

"Uncle! Dad! Mum!" cried Xie Mulan from the living room downstairs. "I've brought my elder brother home for dinner!"

Fang Buting and Xie Peidong were stunned.

―――

When Fang Meng'ao entered the ground floor living room of Fang Buting's mansion, he politely greeted Cheng Xiaoyun: "Mother."

Xie Mulan was not very surprised, but He Xiaoyu who was standing behind him was full of emotion, her eyes sparkling. She looked at the man who just a moment ago had stood out most prominently for his fearlessness, drive and even ruthlessness.

Cheng Xiaoyun blushed and whispered: "Meng'ao, I know you respect me and indeed all women. But after all, I'm only three years older than you. You can call me 'Auntie' in the future."

"Fine," Fang Meng'ao replied, "Auntie."

"We all call you Stepmother. Why are you allowed to call her Auntie? No way!" said Xie Mulan, who was often a source of embarrassment on such occasions. Addressing He Xiaoyu, she said: "*You* wouldn't, would you?"

"No. I think it's very appropriate for Brother Meng'ao to call her Aunt Cheng."

"I see," said Xie Mulan. "He's just copying you, isn't he?"

Fang Meng'ao turned his back on them and said: "That might be the reason. I'll do as Miss He does." With that, he turned to look at He Xiaoyu.

He Xiaoyu blushed again, and she hurriedly asked: "You people are really pedantic. Whatever you say or do, why get me involved?"

"Get you involved? That's because we've never treated you as an outsider," said Xie Mulan, deliberately adding fuel to the fire. "Whenever you're in our house, you're automatically one of us. Am I not right, Stepmother?"

Fang Meng'ao felt that his little cousin was misbehaving, and he said to He Xiaoyu: "You've been family since our childhood. Xiaoyu, come here. I'll teach you how to deal with a cheeky girl."

Fang Meng'ao was being so generous that He Xiaoyu's shyness dissolved. As might be predicted, she stepped closer to him.

Fang Meng'ao looked at Xie Mulan and said: "Could you come here, too?"

But Xie Mulan didn't want to, and she cried out: "Xiaoyu, don't be tricked. My big brother, he can be very naughty!"

Fang Meng'ao took a step forward and gently put his arm around Xie Mulan. Then, to her surprise, he did the same with Xiaoyu.

The two girls were in his embrace simultaneously. Xie Mulan seemed to enjoy the experience. By contrast, He Xiaoyu was embarrassed and refused to let him cuddle her in this fashion, but she was unable to free herself.

He Xiaoyu's voice was tense, and it revealed her childlike nature. She called out to Cheng Xiaoyun for help: "Auntie! Do please tell him to let us down!"

Cheng Xiaoyun smiled. "What a silly girl! Let me teach you how to show him up. Just stay in his arms."

As soon as he heard Fang Meng'ao enter the house, Xie Peidong cracked open the door of the first floor office and peeked downstairs.

On witnessing the scene that greeted him, he quickly made way for Fang Buting so he too could peer through the crack in the door.

Fang Buting's face brightened, and he broke into a rare smile. Xie Peidong nodded his head, grinned and closed the door gently. "I think it's high time for the governor to talk to Chancellor He."

Fang Buting bowed his head in consent.

In the living room on the ground floor, Fang Meng'ao still had his arms around the two girls as he said to He Xiaoyu: "How about it? Now, she can't... can she?"

With their faces so near, He Xiaoyu closed her eyes and neither looked at him nor replied. Fang Meng'ao discovered that He Xiaoyu's long eyelashes were wet with tears and he became flustered. He instantly let go of the girls and said softly: "Sorry for going too far. Please forgive me, Miss He."

Xie Mulan and Cheng Xiaoyun both looked nervously at He Xiaoyu.

When she opened her eyes, He Xiaoyu gave him a forgiving smile. "OK, but no more jokes like this in future."

Fang Meng'ao looked at Cheng Xiaoyun and said: "Auntie, punish me. Let me cook for them. I can cook Western food at home."

"That's not necessary," Cheng Xiaoyun said with a smile. "No one is a match for me when it comes to cooking Chinese or Western food. Mulan, you and Xiaoyu accompany your elder brother to your room. When I call you, just come down to eat." With that, she hurried into the kitchen.

"Don't be angry," Xie Mulan said to He Xiaoyu. "Please, go and show him my room."

Fang Meng'ao looked at He Xiaoyu with tenderness. He Xiaoyu smiled.

"Come on!" said Xie Mulan, dragging Fang Meng'ao to the stairway as she turned around and called to He Xiaoyu. "Come on up!"

"Get my car ready," instructed Fang Buting as he removed his hat from the peg. "Let them eat at home tonight. I'll visit Vice-Chancellor He."

Xie Peidong handed him his briefcase and opened the office door.

Fang Meng'ao was taken by his cousin Xie Mulan to her room on the first floor. The ace pilot who was famous for flying his plane like a heavenly steed across the sky, appeared quite at a loss upon entering his cousin's boudoir.

He Xiaoyu sensed it and so did Xie Mulan. "Elder Brother," said Xie Mulan, "you seem a little afraid?"

"Nonsense. What am I to be afraid of?"

"Afraid of a girl's room!" Xie Mulan said bluntly. "Am I right?"

"You're talking rubbish." Fang Meng'ao went to the table in front of the window. He was just about to sit down, when he saw on the chair an embroidered handkerchief. He picked it up with two fingers and put it gently on the bed, before he went to sit down on the chair.

Xie Mulan glanced at He Xiaoyu, and said: "What a refined man!"

He Xiaoyu had also started to relax, and she looked at Fang Meng'ao innocently like a pure-hearted girl: "It's called acting like a gentleman. Do you understand?"

"A gentleman and a knight!" Xie Mulan answered loudly in English.

He Xiaoyu looked at Fang Meng'ao and asked: "Don't you agree?"

Fang Meng'ao stood up and said something in English that made the two girls raise their eyebrows: "Where is the bathroom?"

"What a killjoy!" cried Xie Mulan in Chinese. He Xiaoyu tried to suppress a smile, then laughed out loud in a clear and pleasant manner.

CHAPTER 10

Anyone visiting the Fangs' kitchen would instantly know that they were truly upper class. It covered more than twenty square metres, an area that would represent the entire living space of a typical small family in one of China's leading cities. It contained integrated, stainless steel ovens imported from Germany, with several ventilation fans built into the walls. However, the most surprising thing was the presence of two sofas, and various paraphernalia for drinking tea and coffee on the long table. There was also a gramophone and numerous vinyl records.

None of these items were meant for the servants. They were a demonstration of a Western philosophy of life. When the housewife was cooking in the kitchen, her family members were expected to keep her company there by engaging in conversation.

While Cheng Xiaoyun lived in a separate apartment, Mrs Cai and Mrs Wang cooked for the family. But it was Xie Peidong's job to cook the favourite dishes for Fang Buting, Fang Mengwei and Xie Mulan. Fang Buting would often accompany him, while Fang Mengwei would occasionally do so. Only Xie Mulan didn't want to accompany her father to whom she didn't feel close. It was as if she feared him.

Today's arrangements were deliberate. While Cheng Xiaoyun was cooking Western food, Fang Buting made an unannounced visit to He Qicang.

Now it was Xie Peidong's turn to accompany her in the kitchen where he was about to demonstrate the Western philosophy of life. He picked one of Cheng Yanqiu's records, *The Lucky Purse – The Spring and Autumn Pavilion*, and put it on the gramophone.

"Sister-in-law," he said to Cheng Xiaoyun, "you can always ask Mulan to come down and help in the kitchen."

"What kind of help can Mulan offer?" It had been a long time since Cheng Xiaoyun had been in such a good mood. She smiled at Xie Peidong and continued: "I know what you mean and what the governor means. Normally, you do most of the cooking, but leave it to me today and let them enjoy themselves."

"Sure, I'll leave it to you. The kitchen is all yours today." Xie Peidong had always been polite and rather taciturn in Cheng Xiaoyun's company, but today he was talkative. "I'll call Mulan when I get back to my room. She must stay here and be at your disposal."

When Cheng Xiaoyun heard these admonitions, she smiled and nodded understandingly. Xie Peidong walked out of the kitchen quietly.

As Cheng Xiaoyun busied herself with the cooking, she hummed along to Cheng Yanqiu on the gramophone. She reckoned that Xie Peidong would have returned to his room by now. Then she went to the kitchen door and shouted upstairs: "Mulan, come down and help me in the kitchen!"

There was no response.

Cheng Xiaoyun raised her voice: "Come down quickly, I need help!"

"I'm coming," was Xie Mulan's reluctant reply from upstairs.

Xie Peidong did not return to his room; instead, he went into Fang Buting's office. He made sure that all the doors were locked before walking over to Fang Buting's chair in front of the desk and sitting down.

He dialled a number on the phone and soon started speaking: "Mengwei... you're done talking with the student representatives... yes, they're homeless students, you should show understanding and be more considerate of their position. Don't rush back. It's important to deal with the aftermath... Upset?... want to visit Deputy Director Cui? Have you told the governor yet? It's better not to go at this time. If you insist, then go... just say what's required, don't get emotional..."

Fang Mengwei apparently hung up, as Xie Peidong stood there looking worried. He put down the phone with a silent sigh. He then went to the door of the office, made sure it was latched and went back to the desk. He sat down in Fang Buting's chair, opened the middle table drawer and pulled out an American radio. He turned it on and tried to find the right channel.

Yang Baosen's voice sounded from the speaker. It was *Wen Zhaoguan*, a bleak and gloomy aria about how Wu Zixu, the famous military strategist during the Spring and Autumn period, had his hair turned white overnight.

This radio was a new model, equipped with a pair of headphones. Xie Peidong plugged in the headphones, and the voice sounded even more real and clear. He adjusted the FM dial and the aria disappeared.

An unexpected voice came from the headset. It belonged to Fang Meng'ao: "Can I sit down?"

Xie Peidong closed his eyes and listened calmly.

The next voice belonged to He Xiaoyu: "Of course."

By eavesdropping in this manner, Xie Peidong's actions typified the fear and suspicion that were prevalent at that time. As a high-ranking official of the Central Bank in Peking, Fang Buting helped control the financial purse strings of the Nationalist government. In that capacity, he also assisted in the money-making and money-laundering activities on behalf of those in the Kuomintang's senior leadership. The reason Fang Buting had established its office in his mansion was because many secret talks involving hidden dangers could not be conducted in the bank. Three years after victory in the War of Resistance, all eyes had been on the Central Bank. Fang Buting could make money for them, but he would not die for them. Therefore, a recording and eavesdropping device had been secretly installed in the office. Whoever came here to conduct secret talks, or speak on the special telephone line, Fang Buting would have them all recorded secretly. Self-protection was his priority.

Fang Meng'ao had unexpectedunexpectedlyly returned to the family home in Peking. Yet he had returned with the Communist Party and the Iron and Blood Congress. This had huge implications for him and his family. Therefore, this eavesdropping connection was secretly installed in every room that Fang Meng'ao might enter. Fang Buting needed to know all this son's secrets and be ready to take countermeasures to save both him and the family. The device could only be installed here. Only Fang Buting and Xie Peidong could access it.

Nobody knew how long Xie Mulan's door had been closed, yet unlocked. In the room, He Xiaoyu felt the change in Fang Meng'ao's mood. He had recently been jovial downstairs, but now he was very serious. He had been given permission to sit down, but Fang Meng'ao was still standing. He was very tall, and appeared particularly so as he loomed over He Xiaoyu. He Xiaoyu felt nervous and wanted to stand up, but she still pretended to be calm and remained seated.

Knowing she was trying to cover up her anxiety, Fang Meng'ao smiled unnaturally and took out a cigar. "May I smoke here?" he asked.

"Of course."

Fang Meng'ao sat down, lit the cigar, took a puff and exhaled. Silence followed; he was obviously thinking about how to frame his question.

He Xiaoyu had been assigned to approach him, but she did not expect their first meeting would be like this. It was Fang Meng'ao who had chosen to be with her alone. She had no alternative but to remain silent, waiting for him to start the conversation.

"When we last saw each other in 1937, you were only eleven years old, weren't you?" said Fang Meng'ao somewhat surprisingly.

He Xiaoyu nodded. "You are twenty-two this year," Fang Meng'ao continued. "For ten years, I've tried hard to disassociate myself from my family. Over the years you have grown up and changed, but I don't know your current situation at all. All the questions I will ask are just trivial things. If you know how to answer, just tell me. If you don't want to respond, please feel free not to say anything. All right?"

He Xiaoyu became even more nervous, and she nodded again.

Fang Meng'ao glanced at the door as if he were trying to establish whether there was anyone outside. His pilot's ears and eyes told him he was safe for the time being. He looked out of the window and asked: "Have you ever been in contact with a member of the Communist Party of China?"

In the governor's office on the first floor, Xie Peidong was stunned at what he was hearing through the headphones. His eyebrows quivered, and his eyes closed even tighter. How would He Xiaoyu answer? He waited anxiously.

He Xiaoyu was startled. She had never expected Fang Meng'ao to ask such a question. She believed he bore her no malice, but it was a heavy question all the same. How to answer him?

Fang Meng'ao continued to look out of the window. "Sorry for making things difficult for you. It's not obvious from the outside who is a member of the Communist Party. Most of the students in Peking tend to think that the Communists are progressive. You yourself are a progressive student and may have encountered a Communist. That's what I have on my mind. You can answer me or keep silent."

"Can I also ask you a question?" He Xiaoyu asked gently.

"Of course you can, as long as I am able to answer it."

Xie Peidong sat up straight, his eyes still closed and his attention more focused. Through the headphones he heard the voice of He Xiaoyu: "Have *you* ever encountered a Communist Party member?"

"Yes," Fang Meng'ao replied immediately.

Xie Peidong suddenly opened his eyes and picked up the radio on his desk.

He Xiaoyu was more surprised than Xie Peidong. She froze, remaining like that for a long moment. Then she asked: "How can you be so sure that you have seen a Communist?"

Xie Peidong picked up a pencil. Even though he could hear no answer from Fang Meng'ao in the headphones, he had already written the following words on the blank letter-headed paper: "Cui Zhongshi?"

He waited and waited for Fang Meng'ao to say the name!

"Of course I'm sure." Fang Meng'ao's voice came though the headphones.

Xie Peidong used a pencil to cross out the characters for "Cui Zhongshi". It was logical that he didn't want Fang Meng'ao to say the name he had written.

At this point, He Xiaoyu also opened her eyes and was anxiously expecting Fang Meng'ao to say the name.

Fang Meng'ao, however, appeared calm: "I have met many people, yet admired only a few of them. For example, I admired General Chennault when I served in the Air Force during the War of Resistance. An old man, retired from service, he managed to recruit and command a world-class squadron that was able to defeat the Japanese forces. He was respected by both the Chinese and US governments. I have admired no one since then... until three days ago, when I met this prisoner under death sentence at the Nanking Special Criminal Court."

"Is he a member of the Communist Party of China?" He Xiaoyu asked.

Xie Peidong put down his pencil – or to be exact, it slipped from his hand. Hearing this, he seemed to breathe a long sigh.

"How do you know?" asked Fang Meng'ao.

He Xiaoyu looked back at him and found his eyes shining with wonder, obviously observing her real reaction.

"You said it yourself," she said.

"I didn't say that the guy on death row was a member of the Communist Party."

"Then tell me which person you have seen who is a Communist."

Xie Peidong concentrated on the conversation again. Every second seemed to last an eternity. Finally, Fang Meng'ao's voice could be heard in the headphones: "You're right," he sighed. "The Communist I encountered was the one sentenced to death by the Nanking Special Criminal Court three days ago. He was an operational staff officer who had been hiding in the Air Force Operation Department of the National Army for many years. He had passed on lots of secret military information to his superiors. In fact, he'd been working undercover for ten years. If he hadn't intentionally exposed himself, no one would have been able to find him out. I admire him."

Xie Peidong's face took on a strange appearance, before it quickly disappeared. He once more focused his attention on the conversation. There was silence again in the headphones.

He Xiaoyu was looking at Fang Meng'ao with deep feelings. She didn't reply or ask any questions.

Fang Meng'ao was obviously not happy with He Xiaoyu's silence: "You don't want to know why I admire him?"

"You have said that you admire his ability to hide so well..."

"Wrong!" Fang Meng'ao said with a wave of his hand. "I admire him for being a real man. Besides, he's not selfish." Silence followed once more as Fang Meng'ao looked out of the window.

Xie Peidong calmly listened through his headphones, the way he had done at the beginning of the conversation. He quietly awaited the exchange that would follow.

He Xiaoyu was embarrassed by the silence, so she asked softly: "How do you know that he is honest and not selfish?"

"Isn't it your turn to answer my question?" Fang Meng'ao turned his head and looked at her. "You haven't answered me yet. Have you ever encountered a Communist?"

Xie Peidong was listening attentively when He Xiaoyu's voice was heard: "I must have met a Communist."

When was the last time Xie Peidong had experienced such a moment of surprise? Eyes wide open, he picked up the pencil again.

Fang Meng'ao's eyes shone with anticipation, waiting for her to go on.

"Just like you said, these three characters are not written on their faces, so I'm not sure which one of those I've met is actually a Communist."

The light in Fang Meng'ao's eyes faded, and his eyes narrowed into a line. Usually, this was the way he looked at those whom he hated or despised. This was the first time he had taken on this appearance when looking affectionately at a young woman. What's more, this woman happened to be He Xiaoyu!

He Xiaoyu felt that this man, who had made no secret of his affection for her when he arrived in Peking, was now showing such hostility that she became a little flustered. She tried to calm herself down.

"You don't believe me, do you?"

"It doesn't matter whether I believe you or not," said Fang Meng'ao, returning to his normal habit of observing the world while trying to appear indifferent. "Like I said in the beginning, this is just a chat. I don't mean to find out who is a Communist." With that, he rose to his feet.

He Xiaoyu quickly followed and stood up.

This eavesdropping device was very advanced, and Xie Peidong heard two people standing up and sensed that their conversation might be ending.

"Sorry for having kept you. But let me ask you again," said Fang Meng'ao. "On the fifth of July, students joined the protest at the Peking Senate. Today, many went to demonstrate at the North China Headquarters for the Suppression of Communist Insurgency. Did you go with your classmates?"

"The whole nation is expressing its support for the students from the Northeast. Of course, students affiliated with the Peking Student Federation should go in solidarity."

"You and Mulan stopped my jeep and forced me back home. What do you want me to do?"

"Of course, we hope you can expose corruption and help the students."

"Then of course I should go," Fang Meng'ao said with an absence of affection in his eyes. He was so hostile that he emphasised the words "of course". "So many students, professors and ordinary people in Peking are starving. Tonight, I need to take my team to examine whether the Citizens' Food-Distribution Committee is ready to distribute food. Sorry to have kept you so long today." With that, he made to leave.

"Big Brother!" He Xiaoyu called out from behind him. "But they're cooking dinner for you downstairs."

Fang Meng'ao stopped at the door. "Don't you find it conflicting to be eating so well while knowing that others are starving? And you claim you want to save them?" Without turning around, Fang Meng'ao opened the door and left.

He Xiaoyu stood in a daze, looking at the door close behind him. Her eyes were full of confusion.

Xie Peidong, who was sitting in the office, had resumed his normal appearance. Showing no expression, he took off his headphones and turned the dial. The "radio" resumed broadcasting Peking Opera arias. This time, it was playing Ma Lianliang's *Ma Su*

Beheaded by Zhuge Liang, featuring Zhuge Liang reading the very painful confession:

> *I say, Ma Su, how bold you are! The hermit admonishes you for camping by the mountains and rivers. But don't heed the hermit's words of wisdom. Do you have any reason for...*

Listening to Ma Lianliang, Xie Peidong picked up the phone and dialled a number. The operator quickly put him through.

Xie Peidong's tone was very modest and gentle: "Excuse me, may I speak to Chancellor He? This is Xie Peidong. Might I ask if Governor Fang is with you at your house?... Thank you. Could you please put him on?"

A short while later, Fang Buting's voice came down the other end of the line.

"Governor, if you please," said Xie Peidong, "just listen to me. They didn't seem to have an agreeable chat, and the two ended up on bad terms. It's probably not a good time to talk to him about what you had originally planned."

In the sitting room on the ground floor of He Qicang's residence, Fang Buting was on the phone. "How can there be so many instructions from the headquarters of the Central Bank?" he asked. "Well, I'll be right back." He put the phone down.

He Qicang was sitting at the dinner table. On the table was a plate of sliced, dried bamboo shoots, a dish that was particularly popular in southern China, and a bowl of shelled peanuts. The two men had clearly been eating as their chopsticks were also on the table.

Fang Buting came back to the table. "I'd really like to continue this chat, but I've got to go."

"Officials aren't always free." He Qicang stood up with the help of his walking stick. "Come back again."

Fang Buting picked up his hat and briefcase. "The Ministry of Finance and the Central Bank are pressing for the currency reform plan once more. I told them that you're helping me improve it.

They also attach great importance to the plan. If we don't reform the currency system, the people will barely survive. To save those living in dire poverty, we must rely on those in authority such as you, Brother Qicang."

"Thanks for saying so. I am in the position of being able to consult a few American friends, including Ambassador John Leighton Stuart." He Qicang's face paled with grave concern. "Monetary reform? Do the banks have reserves? Will those financial groups that have monopolised the market be willing to provide materials to support the market? Without those two conditions, it will be impossible to draft the monetary reform plan."

Fang Buting was silent for a while, before he nodded his head. "Your comment is trenchant and perceptive. Brother Qicang, just help me to improve the plan from these two perspectives."

"The plan that the currency system cannot be reformed?"

"To tell the truth, we have to rely on Brother Qicang, you're the most respected expert."

"Since you can't implement the reform alone," said He Qicang, "your plan will be just a sham. Clearly, you're falsifying data. Sorry, I can't help you."

"Let's talk about it another day," said Fang Buting. "I'll go now. Perhaps I can come and visit you tomorrow or the day after."

"Mrs Li!" He Qicang called out to the kitchen.

Mrs Li hurried out of the kitchen. "Yes, chancellor."

"Please show Governor Fang out. And you can also go home." He Qicang turned to Fang Buting. "Buting, I can't walk you out because my legs aren't so good."

"Can't you spare some time for treatment abroad?" Fang Buting said with concern. "OK, I'm leaving."

He Xiaoyu was in the living room on the ground floor of the Fang mansion. "Aunt Cheng, Mulan, I'm going home," she called out to the kitchen.

Xie Mulan came out at once. "Why do you want to go home? Dinner is ready. Where's my elder brother?"

"He's gone."

"Gone?" exclaimed Xie Mulan. "When did he leave? How come we weren't told? He promised to stay for dinner. How can he leave?"

At this moment, Cheng Xiaoyun came out and found that He Xiaoyu was a little upset. She asked her politely: "Is it because he had some urgent business to do?"

Xie Mulan's joy was suddenly swept away as if by a gust of wind. She looked straight at He Xiaoyu: "The phone didn't ring. What was it that is so urgent? Why did he leave without even saying goodbye to us? Who made him so displeased?"

Cheng Xiaoyun, who was quite a sophisticated person, noticed He Xiaoyu's sad expression. "Nonsense," she said. "Who can displease your elder brother?"

"I was the only person with him, of course," said He Xiaoyu. "It was me who made him unhappy. Aunt Cheng, I'm leaving." Paying no more attention to Xie Mulan, she hastened to the door.

"What about those students from the Northeast?" Xie Mulan called out from behind her. He Xiaoyu didn't stop, and nor did she make a reply. She was almost at the gate.

"Be quiet!" said Cheng Xiaoyun. "Her house is so far away. I'll arrange for a car to take her home." She followed He Xiaoyu to the gate.

Xie Mulan stood there deeply confused, until a little while later, she stamped her foot, before becoming stunned again. On the first floor on the east staircase, she saw her father.

"Dad," she called gently and turned to the stairs.

"Stop," said Xie Peidong. "You won't leave this place if you continue getting involved in your elder brother's business."

Xie Mulan made no reply, yet she felt profoundly aggrieved. Tearful, she scampered upstairs.

Nobody felt like eating dinner that evening in Fang Buting's mansion.

The sun was setting behind the Western Hills in Peking. Fang Mengwei, another member of the Fang family, did not want to go home to eat. Something else was weighing on his mind.

He drove the Peking Police Bureau patrol jeep and stopped at the entrance to Dongzhong Hutong. He spotted two bureau officers standing guard there. They were walking back and forth.

In the hutong, there were another two police officers, one to the east side of Cui Zhongshi's front gate, and the other to the west.

Fang Mengwei knew that Xu Tieying had sent them personally. He had informed him they were deployed to deal with the five-member investigation group in the name of cooperating with the inspection team to check the accounts. But actually, they were sent to protect Cui Zhongshi so as not to embarrass his elder brother, Fang Meng'ao. Fang Mengwei knew the reason: money!

The two policemen at the hutong entrance noticed Fang Mengwei's jeep and walked over to it and saluted him.

"Hello, Deputy Commissioner Fang."

Fang Mengwei got out of the jeep and asked: "Did Commissioner Xu send you?"

"Yes sir," the two policemen replied in unison.

Fang Mengwei's face was expressionless. "Do the job well."

"Yes sir."

Fang Mengwei went down the hutong. Now, the two policemen had some extra work to do: keeping an eye on his jeep. One of them stood guard by the jeep, while the other was positioned at the street corner.

"Which police department are you from? If you've got the guts, just go to the Peking branch of the Central Bank. Your deputy commissioner's father is there!" Ye Biyu was speaking in a high-pitched tone behind the closed gate. A sense of nervousness and impatience could be heard in her voice.

"Mrs Cui, it's me." Fang Mengwei knew that her complaint was directed at the policemen outside, and hurriedly informed her of his identity.

The courtyard gate opened immediately.

When Ye Biyu saw Fang Mengwei, the tone in her voice warmed: "Good evening, Deputy Commissioner Fang. Thanks for coming on time. What exactly did Cui do? Why is a policeman watching us on our doorstep? I'm sure you know why. Cui is Governor Fang's employee and has been working his socks off for the Central Bank. And what have we got in return? Is he under house arrest? Isn't it absurd? Why do they make our life here in Peking so difficult? You've got to help us out. Ask the governor to do us a favour by getting Cui transferred to Shanghai tomorrow..."

"Aren't you tired of all this complaining?" said Cui Zhongshi, appearing from behind her. "Why not invite Deputy Commissioner Fang in?"

"I'm tired of myself already!" When Ye Biyu heard Cui Zhongshi's voice, she moved away from the entrance.

Turning to Cui Zhongshi, she yelled: "Please ask him to speak to Governor Fang for help. If you don't leave this miserable place, I'll take Boqin and Pingyang back to Shanghai!" With that, she stomped off into the house, leaving behind Cui Zhongshi and Fang Mengwei at the doorway.

Cui Zhongshi remained the same "Uncle Cui". He still had a kind expression in his eyes. "Thanks for coming to see me. I know you're busy."

"Let's speak inside, Cui," said Fang Mengwei as he walked into the courtyard.

Cui Zhongshi's eyes flashed as he closed the gate. He had noticed Fang Mengwei's uneasiness.

"Have you got anything to eat, Cui? I haven't had dinner yet." As soon as he entered the north room and sat down, Fang Mengwei noticed a large bowl on the table and a plate covered with a cloth.

Cui Zhongshi quickly removed the cover, looking a little bit embarrassed. "Half a bowl of porridge and several pieces of cornbread. That's all we have left..."

"That's good enough. I'll eat this."

"Go ahead. Let me get you a pair of chopsticks."

"Don't bother." Fang Mengwei picked up the half bowl and took a big mouthful of porridge, after which he picked up a piece of cornbread and chewed it.

Cui Zhongshi sat down beside him.

While eating, Fang Mengwei asked: "Uncle Cui, how can you live on this stuff? Boqin and Pingyang are growing up."

Of course, Cui Zhongshi understood the implication of his

remark and looked at him sincerely: "I'm very well remunerated by the Peking branch, but no matter how much *fabi* I am paid, it can't keep up with the skyrocketing prices."

After Fang Mengwei had finished the porridge, he put down the bowl and picked up the remaining two pieces of cornbread. "But you're the deputy treasury director of the Peking branch of the Central Bank. Nobody would believe you if you said you didn't have any US dollars or foreign exchange."

"Of course I have US dollars, but they're not mine. They belong to the bank."

Fang Mengwei looked at Cui as if to scrutinise him. "Few Central Bank staff members at your level are free from corruption. I believe you, but others may not. Uncle Cui, sometimes good people do not necessarily end up well."

"You're right." Cui Zhongshi sighed with emotion. "Before you entered this room, Mrs Cui was quarrelling with me. She accused me of spending all the dollars I embezzled on mistresses. How can I prove I didn't? Well, she can do as she wishes."

Fang Mengwei finished the last piece of cornbread. Cui Zhongshi was so meticulous that he quickly went to a nearby bucket and scooped up a ladle of clean water and waited beside the washbasin shelf.

Fang Mengwei hurried over, stretched his hands over the empty basin, and the water in Cui Zhongshi's ladle was poured down like a thin thread. Fang Mengwei promptly scrubbed his hands. It took almost a ladle of water for Fang to complete the task. Cui Zhongshi handed him a clean towel.

As Fang Mengwei was drying his hands, a feeling of melancholy overcame him. He felt this way because only at this moment did he begin to connect with Cui's utter consideration and self-restraint.

"What's the matter? Has the food disagreed with you?" Cui Zhongshi asked with concern.

Fang Mengwei forced a smile as he moved back to his seat: "Not at all. I enjoy Mrs Cui's food very much. I am upset because I was thinking about what a member of the National Assembly recently said about some of the Kuomintang's generals. They could never match your honesty and integrity."

"What did they say exactly? I cannot compare myself to them." Cui Zhongshi also sat down.

"Indeed they cannot be compared to you, Uncle Cui. Do you want to hear what they said?"

"Is this some kind of joke?"

"No, it's the truth. A senior assemblyman told Chiang." Fang Mengwei sounded very serious. "The assemblyman is kind of old school. At one point, he and several others were invited for a consultation with the president. The assemblyman took it seriously. Right before the president, he cursed his generals and called them good-for-nothings. The president asked him why. He explained that they squander public money and kill people like flies. So they're good-for-nothings. The president was so angry that he left immediately."

After relating this story, Fang Mengwei lapsed into silence.

Cui Zhongshi looked at him. "It's the truth, but sometimes that's the last thing people want to hear."

"I want to hear the truth." Fang Mengwei jumped at the topic and looked at Cui Zhongshi with interest. "Uncle Cui, you have been working hard for my father for so many years. You've been very careful in managing the expenditure of the bank as well as your family finances. Now, some people in the bank have been complaining about you. Even Mrs Cui is complaining about you. Why do you put up with it?"

Cui Zhongshi was a little surprised. "I manage the money because the governor trusts me. Of course, it's only natural I should do so. What else can I do?"

"But you were throwing the bank's money about while you were in Nanking. Don't you feel guilty about it?"

Cui Zhongshi seemed to understand the reason why Fang Mengwei had visited him today. He looked back at him, yet he took a long while to respond: "Of course I do. The money of the Central Bank belongs to the national treasury. Every single penny is the hard-won property of the people. But you will get in trouble if you don't give it to them. Even if you're the governor, you still have to. If you don't give it today, or tomorrow, you will be removed the day after tomorrow and replaced by someone who is more compliant."

"I know my father," said Fang Mengwei, coming straight to the point. "But I still don't understand you, Uncle Cui. Why do you want to be deputy treasury director with all that responsibility when your family is in want?"

Cui Zhongshi sat in silence, and a short while later he replied: "Mengwei, you know something about my history. Neither my father nor my grandparents left me any money. Their last throw of the dice was for me to finish accounting school. When I met your father, it was as if he had been sent by God to help me. He hired me as a bank clerk in Shanghai. After I was transferred to Peking with him, he appointed me as deputy treasury director. Now you ask me why I'm willing to work for him. How can I answer you? If I wasn't willing to accept this position, what else could I do?"

Fang Mengwei was silent, but he was clearly experiencing mixed feelings. What Cui Zhongshi had said sounded very reasonable, and he was willing to believe him. But why had Dad been so sure about his Communist background?

Fang Mengwei raised his head. "Uncle Cui, do you understand your current situation?"

"Of course I do."

"Can you share it with me?"

"Some things I can, others I can't."

"Tell me what you can say."

"Because of my loyalty to the governor, and my friendship with you and Meng'ao, I became a suspect during my trip to Nanking. In addition, I am in charge of the accounts of the Peking Citizens' Food-Distribution Committee and those of the Military Material Management Committee. Since these books have been cooked, I'm sure to be investigated. Those from the central government were so powerful that they summoned Meng'ao to investigate me. Although the future holds many uncertainties, I am not afraid. The bank is not guilty of any embezzlement, nor did I personally embezzle any public money. They won't be able to find anything even if they initiate the investigation. There are only two major obstacles that I am unable to overcome, neither of which you can help me with."

"If I can't help you, who else can?"

"There's no one. I'm at the mercy of God."

"Uncle Cui, let me be straight with you. Listen carefully. No matter what kind of trouble you're in, I'll do the best I can to help you out. You've been kind to my elder brother for all these years, especially during this trip to Nanking, when you fought with your life to save him. Also, to ensure Mrs Cui and the two kids, Boqin and Pingyang, enjoy a happy future, I promise to help you. Just tell me what these two major obstacles are."

Cui Zhongshi looked at him intensely. "Even if you want to help me, please bury that urge in your heart. Otherwise, you will put me and my entire family in harm's way."

Fang Mengwei became emotional. "Your biggest crime is being a member of the Communist Party! To repay your kindness, I'll help you out in return."

Cui Zhongshi was startled and hurriedly went to the door and looked outside. Following her quarrel with Cui Zhongshi, Ye Biyu was still mad with him. Since she was some distance away with her son and daughter, she didn't hear what Fang Mengwei had just said.

Cui Zhongshi turned to Fang Mengwei and said: "I can't say anything. Mengwei, what you've just told me will frighten Mrs Cui to death." He sat down and said nothing more.

Fang Mengwei lowered his voice: "Uncle Cui, since I've just opened up to you, why not tell me what's on your mind?"

Cui Zhongshi thought again and looked at him. "OK, I'll tell you what. The first hurdle is the governor."

"Go on," said Fang Mengwei.

"The governor's attitude towards me changed dramatically when I came back yesterday. I had a hard time trying to figure it out the whole night. Before attending the meeting convened by the five-member investigation group this morning, the governor said something I didn't understand, but I realise now that he was highly suspicious of me. Mengwei, I can manage to live without a lot of things, but I must retain the governor's trust. Can you help me with that?"

"Well, if it has to do with my father, I promise I can. Now, what about the second hurdle?"

"As for the second hurdle, I'm afraid you can't help me with that because it involves Xu Tieying. You've seen the police officers deployed at my doorstep by your bureau. You were also there when you saw Xu Tieying's secretary, Mr Sun, who met me at the station yesterday.

"A short while ago, you were quoting the assemblyman's remarks about those corrupt generals, weren't you? I'll tell you now that your new boss is as corrupt as those generals! He's not like the others in throwing money about. But his appetite for wealth is even more insatiable. Not for the present, but in order to feather his retirement nest. When he was a member of the Central Bureau of Investigation, he never baulked at killing people. Now that he is commissioner of the Police Bureau of Peking Municipality and detective chief superintendent with the General Command of the Peking Police Force, it's easier for him to have people killed. Without doubt he won't hesitate to kill the Communists, yet he may spare those who have nothing to do with him. But there is a certain category of people he'll definitely kill – those who block his way to wealth. Mengwei, I manage the financial fortunes of many people. Yet someday in the future if I fail to do as I'm told, I might be their roadblock to wealth. Back in the past, I was fortunate to have the governor covering my back, meaning no one could touch me. Now even the governor suspects me, it's only a matter of time before someone kills me. When that day comes, I hope you'll take care of Mrs Cui, Boqin and Pingyang."

The conversation ceased abruptly. Cui Zhongshi closed his eyes and sat there, looking as if he was not expecting Fang Mengwei to make a response.

Fang Mengwei stood up and lowered his voice: "Uncle Cui, I will fight with my life to save yours, but on one condition only."

Cui Zhongshi slowly opened his eyes.

"My elder brother is a person of character, and a truly good man," Fang Mengwei continued. "My only condition is that you don't get him involved in anything you do in the future. If he is safe, I will guarantee your safety. Uncle Cui, let's say no more today. Let's keep this conversation between ourselves. It's better not to let anyone else know." With that, he strode briskly to the door.

Fang Buting was sitting where Xie Peidong himself had been sitting recently. Wearing headphones, he listened attentively with his eyes closed.

Xie Peidong stood by the door to keep watch.

Fang Buting was done with listening to all the recordings of He Xiaoyu and Fang Meng'ao. He opened his eyes, removed the headphones and thought about things carefully.

Xie Peidong walked to the built-in closet that was directly behind Fang Buting's chair. It contained the recording device, and two tapes were still turning. Xie Peidong pressed the button and the tapes came to a stop.

"Don't rush to close the machine," said Fang Buting.

Xie Peidong stopped. The closet door was still open and the device could clearly be seen. Xie went over to the opposite chair and sat down before Fang Buting's desk.

"What do you make of the conversation between Meng'ao and Xiaoyu?" asked Fang Buting.

"Let's begin with what I am sure of," replied Xie Peidong. "Xiaoyu is definitely not a member of the Communist Party."

Fang Buting nodded, with a rare look of relief on his face.

"The following is just my personal opinion, and it may differ from the judgment of the governor."

"That's why I particularly value it," said Fang Buting.

"Then I'll be honest with you, governor. Meng'ao cannot possibly be a member of the Communist Party."

"Why do you think so?"

"If he is already a Communist," Xie Peidong explained, "why the rush to find another Communist? You've heard on the tape that Meng'ao is an honest young man."

Fang Buting leaned back and shook his head.

"Then I feel confused."

"Then you're too naive," said Fang Buting. "Didn't it occur to you why Meng'ao asked about the Communists at this critical moment?"

"Why?"

"What Zeng Keda has said is true. Meng'ao began to distrust Cui Zhongshi and suspects that he is a Communist."

Xie Peidong looked down and became silent.

"What should we do next?" asked Fang Buting.

Xie raised his head again and replied: "Stop Meng'ao from visiting Cui Zhongshi again."

"Though Cui Zhongshi will not visit Meng'ao again, nothing will stop Meng'ao from approaching him. Fortunately, Xu Tieying has effectively put Cui Zhongshi under house arrest in the name of the Peking Police Bureau. Of course, he does this not because he suspects Cui Zhongshi is a Communist Party member, but because he wants his twenty per cent shareholding! Before the real fight begins on the front, the fight in the rear has already been lost. Alas, the party-state…"

After a short period of silence, he put on the headphones again and said to Xie Peidong: "Let me listen to the conversation between Cui Zhongshi and Xu Tieying last night."

Xie Peidong went to the closet and rewound the tape.

He Qicang had been suffering from chronic rheumatism throughout the year. Even in summer, he had to cover his knees with a thin blanket. Sitting on the sofa in his ground floor living room, he looked at the busy figure in front of him, eyes shining with affection.

Liang Jinglun was pouring hot water for him to wash his feet. He put his hand into the bucket to test the temperature and found it was just right.

Liang Jinglun carried the bucket and placed it before his teacher. He squatted down to lift the blanket and fold it over the older man's thighs. He slowly rolled up his trouser legs, gently helped him take off his shoes and socks, and put one foot and then the other into the bucket.

"Is it warm enough?" Liang asked.

"Surely, why ask?" said He Qicang in a manner as if he were speaking to his own son.

Smiling, Liang Jinglun massaged his legs gently like a filial son.

During this process, neither He Qicang nor Liang Jinglun would normally speak. He Qicang's eyes shone with affection, while Liang's massaging hands felt like a spring breeze.

"Have they arrested any students today?" He Qicang asked.

"All major national newspapers are reporting on the protest, so they've had to restrain themselves a bit."

"The nation is in peril. You didn't go, did you?"

"No, I didn't," replied Liang Jinglun. "In fact, very few university professors participated in the protest. I heard they are discussing the possibility of submitting a jointly written statement. Not only the students from the Northeast, but also the teachers and students in Peking have been unable to buy rations for many days. It's been eight years since the end of the War of Resistance, but the people are still suffering after that hard-earned victory. Sir, I heard that the Ministry of Finance is planning a currency reform. You and Minister Wang Yunwu are former classmates. I wonder if you can help them come up with a feasible plan."

He Qicang surveyed him, his expression hardening. "Under the current circumstances, do you think there is any possibility of currency reform? As an economics scholar, don't you think it difficult to reform the current system?"

"Indeed, it is difficult," said Liang Jinglun. "But we can't afford to wait and see the *fabi* becoming more like wastepaper every day. Today's rate has risen to twenty-three million *fabi* for one hundred *jin* of grain. It's hard for the common folk to survive, and to make things worse, many employees of public institutions are also having a hard time."

"Before you came back, Governor Fang visited me," said He Qicang. "He also mentioned the issue."

"Did he talk about currency reform?"

He Qicang forced a smile. "He is a member of the Central Bank, specialising in the national government's financial resources, so what power does he have to reform the currency system?"

"What's his opinion, then?" asked Liang Jinglun.

"He hoped I could help him draft a plan for the currency reform."

Liang Jinglun raised his head. "Sir, I don't wish to be rude, but can I say something? But then again, perhaps I shouldn't say it."

"No, go ahead."

"Don't you think it's bad for someone like you, with a clean reputation, to make friends with people like Fang Buting?"

He Qicang was a little put out and replied: "I know who I should associate with and who I should not. It's not up to you to tell me."

"Sorry. Forgive my impetuosity."

Both were silent.

He Qicang would never blame this favourite student of his, and he looked at him emotionally. He felt it was high time to share with him what had been hidden in his heart for a long time: "I have something to ask you, too. You must tell me the truth."

Liang Jinglun seemed to have a premonition of what He Qicang would say. He was silent for a short while and then said: "Sir, please go ahead."

"You have watched Xiaoyu grow up. But do you think she has actually grown up?"

Liang Jinglun lowered his head and continued to gently rub He Qicang's feet. "In your eyes and mine, Xiaoyu will always be a child."

"Is she still a child?"

Liang Jinglun didn't answer.

"Yes, you two are so close... But she is a big girl in other people's eyes. Do you know what Fang Buting intended to tell me during his visit here today?"

"Didn't he ask you to assist with the currency reform plan?"

"Not just that," said He Qicang. "He also came to talk about Xiaoyu."

Liang Jinglun's hand stopped for a moment, but he still didn't look up. "I don't quite understand you, sir."

"Don't talk to me like that!" said He Qicang, becoming quite cross.

Liang Jinglun raised his head. "Like what, sir? Nowadays, young people like Xiaoyu are pursuing freedom. I've got no right to interfere in her life."

"You know it in your heart," said He Qicang, his tone softening a little. "You're still a young man, so how come you don't pursue your own freedom?"

Liang Jinglun found it hard to answer.

"Xiaoyu has paid many visits to the Fangs these days, don't you know? In fact, Fang Buting wasn't here today to discuss his currency reform plan. Instead, he came to talk about marrying my daughter into his family."

"Really?"

"He should be fully aware of who we both are. Even if he conceived the idea, he has to seek my approval first. After all, his elder son Fang Meng'ao was quick to hold sway over many students since his arrival in Peking. You should know quite a bit about him, I guess. Now it involves Xiaoyu, but actually, it also involves you. I want to hear what you really think."

For the first time, he heard his mentor associate his name with He Xiaoyu's. Liang Jinglun took it with a heavy heart. Faced with this gentleman, who had always been a loving and caring father, he began to struggle intensely within himself. When Professor He sponsored him to study in the United States, he knew that it was actually the Kuomintang that arranged it behind his back. For years, he had kept it a secret and he believed that it must remain that way, which meant he could only keep on deceiving his mentor.

"I haven't had the chance to meet Fang Meng'ao, but I've heard a lot about him. An ace pilot in the National Air Force, a decorated hero during the War of Resistance. Not long ago, he was tried by the Special Criminal Court on the charge that he ordered his brigade not to bomb the city of Kaifeng. Later, he was acquitted. For some unknown reason, he was assigned by the Ministry of Defence and sent to Peking to investigate corruption in high places. It involves people in the ruling elite of the Kuomintang and members of the Fang family. His background is very complex. I don't want Xiaoyu to visit him and his family too often at this time..."

"Indeed, he has a very complicated background," He Qicang said, sighing. "But there's something you don't know about him. My family and the Fangs are close friends. We visited each other a lot before the War of Resistance. The mothers of Xiaoyu and Fang Meng'ao were especially close, so the children of the two families often played together. Fang Meng'ao was the eldest. He was very good to his younger brother, Mulan and Xiaoyu. Xiaoyu's mother often praised him as a sensible and promising child. But that was ten years ago. Throughout the past decade, he hasn't communicated with his father or sought to reunite with the family since his mother and sister were killed in the bombing by the Japanese. He effectively didn't have a family while living in a world of life and death, all alone. Considering the current situation, I'm quite concerned about the young man."

Liang Jinglun stood up to get a towel and came back to wipe He Qicang's feet. "Sir, what do you want me to say to Xiaoyu?"

"She also lost her mother when she was a child. As her father, I find it difficult to communicate with her. So, do me a favour by asking her what she thinks of Meng'ao. I trust that only you can talk some sense into her at this stage of her life. You can certainly do a better job than me."

"OK, I'll try to talk to her."

"Don't *try* to talk, but talk to her wholeheartedly!" He Qicang's expression became stern, but behind the obvious sternness was a degree of encouragement. "I've already called Xiaoyu. She'll come back tonight. I'm going to bed now. You wait for her here. Better talk to her tonight."

Having dried He Qicang's feet, Liang Jinglun put on his slippers and helped him up. "Don't worry, sir. I'll wait for Xiaoyu here."

With that, he walked He Qicang up to the first floor.

Jingchun Garden is located to the north of Yenching University's Weiming Lake, also known as The Lake with No Name. Although it was a time of turmoil and during the summer holidays, many students and professors still came to the lake. Some had gathered to discuss state affairs, while others tried to distract their minds from worldly worries.

He Xiaoyu was dropped off at the university gate by Fang Buting's driver. She didn't go home, but instead headed north along the banks of the lake.

At this time, the Peking authorities controlled the use of electricity with regular blackouts in certain parts of the city. The streetlights by Weiming Lake offered little visibility because four lights out of five had to be switched off. So it was very dark along the path, and He Xiaoyu felt a little afraid. She quickened her pace and came to a small gate at Jingchun Garden to the north of the lake, a place where teachers and students of Yenching rarely visited.

Jingchun Garden was a royal residence given by Emperor Jiaqing of the Qing Dynasty to Princess Zhuang Jing. It was owned by Xu Shichang during the Republican era. When John Leighton Stuart founded Yenching University, he sought to purchase the property on multiple occasions, but was rejected by the Xu family. Therefore, Jingchun Garden had become something of a sore point among students because they had to make a detour east in order to reach Langrun Garden, the faculty residential quarter, from the campus of Yenching.

There was a quick exchange of questions and answers and the door opened. No light shone in the courtyard. It was the fourth day of June in the lunar calendar, and He Xiaoyu entered the door by the dim light of the crescent moon.

The man who opened the door closed it again.

In a small room in Jingchun Garden, a weak light came through the window. The man who opened the gate showed her to the room: "He's waiting for you inside. You can go in now." With that, he walked off.

He Xiaoyu knocked on the door.

"Miss He?"

"That's me."

"Come in, please."

He Xiaoyu gently pushed the door open, but she didn't go in, because she had never met the person she was about to meet today.

The man came over. "Comrade Liu Yun has left Peking. I will be your contact from now on. Please come in."

He Xiaoyu nodded and went into the room.

When the door closed, the man turned around. It so happened that he was the same Mr Liu who had met with Yan Chunming in the morning near Weiming Lake, the undercover Communist who had been in charge of the party-led student movement.

"My surname is also Liu, Comrade Xiaoyu. You can call me Old Liu from now on," he said in a kindly manner.

"I'll call you Uncle Liu. It's what I used to call Comrade Liu Yun." He Xiaoyu felt shy in the company of this stranger before her.

Old Liu resembled a university janitor, in contrast to the more scholarly Liu Yun.

Old Liu smiled. "I'm from the liberated area, with a worker-farmer background. We don't look alike, do we?"

"Comrade Liu Yun said that intellectuals should learn from the workers and peasants. I'm expecting to learn more from you."

Old Liu smiled cordially. "I must learn from the workers and peasants, too. Let me introduce myself. I graduated from the Anti-Japanese Military and Political College in Yan'an where I earned my college degree even though the Kuomintang will never recognise it. Technically, like you, I'm also an intellectual."

He Xiaoyu felt appreciative of the effort made by Old Liu to eliminate the sense of strangeness and distance during their first meeting. She smiled. "You're already a college graduate, I'm still one year away from graduation. I should learn from you then."

"Let's agree to learn from each other," said Liu. "Please have a seat. There's not much time. We need to talk quickly."

Both sat down.

Old Liu grew quite serious as they began to talk about their work: "Did you just meet Fang Meng'ao?"

"Yes, I did," said He Xiaoyu.

"What's your impression?"

"It's hard to tell. I find it difficult to communicate with him."

"You didn't talk to him directly about your job, did you?"

"Comrade Liu Yun told me not to broach the subject."

"Then you should have enjoyed the conversation. How can it be difficult to communicate with each other?"

"He started by abruptly asking me if I had met a member of the Communist Party," said He Xiaoyu. "I was so nervous that I didn't know how to respond."

"What did you end up saying?" asked Old Liu, also becoming nervous.

"I asked him back if he himself had met a member of the Communist Party."

Old Liu immediately relaxed. "He was angry with you then, wasn't he?"

"How do you know that?" He Xiaoyu suddenly realised that Old

Liu and Comrade Liu Yun were equally wise and farsighted. She felt close to him at once.

Old Liu looked at her kindly, but his tone was very solemn: "I'll tell you everything. Comrade Fang Meng'ao is a special member of our party recruited through one-way contact. The comrade who had been in contact with him can no longer do so. Of course, he felt extremely anxious. He asked you if you have met a member of the Communist Party, which is an expression of this sentiment."

He Xiaoyu realised that Fang Meng'ao must have been deeply troubled when he asked her about that. The scene immediately appeared before her eyes: Fang Meng'ao's manner of speaking at that time, his appearance, his abrupt departure.

Liu regarded He Xiaoyu, who was busy recollecting what had happened.

"Uncle Liu," said He Xiaoyu, "I don't know how to engage him next time. Permit me to ask the organisation to send someone else to engage with him."

Old Liu, who had appeared very amicable, gradually became more solemn: "Don't think that way. This task was assigned to you based on a deliberate decision made by Comrade Liu Yun. I've no authority to change it. We have also exchanged our views. We agreed that it is quite a challenging task. But no one else is able to accomplish it except you. What's more, Comrade Liang Jinglun of the Student Movement Department has also assigned you the same task."

Old Liu paused and was silent momentarily.

He Xiaoyu felt highly agitated. She had been participating in activities organised by the Students' Union secretly led by the Communist Party's Student Movement Department as a progressive student, whereas within the larger student movement she was only accepted as a progressive youth. Even Liang Jinglun, whom she deeply respected and depended on, had been kept in the dark about the fact that he had been recruited officially as a member of the Communist Party by the top leaders of the Peking Urban Works Department. In her early twenties, she was filled with idealism. But when she returned to the real world, facing her comrades from the Students' Union, especially Liang Jinglun, she felt devoid of any such feelings; on the contrary, she felt like a fraud.

Liu had a sharp eye for detail and immediately changed his tone by resuming his amicable party elder demeanour: "Don't get stressed. The party won't press you. Continue to meet with Comrade Fang Meng'ao according to Comrade Liu Yun's instructions as a progressive youth within the Students' Union. Keep him on your radar. Your task is very simple – stay in touch with him and report to me in a timely manner if he gets into a dangerous situation. Call me before you physically report to me. But don't come here often. The most important thing for you to remember is that you approach Comrade Fang Meng'ao with the task assigned by the CPC's Urban Works Department, and don't tell anyone it was Comrade Liu Yun and me who gave you the assignment. If the Student Movement Department tells you to approach Fang Meng'ao, feel free to do so. If they tell you to recruit Fang Meng'ao to join the party, you can simply decline."

"I don't know what to say to Professor Liang when I get home today," said He Xiaoyu.

"Tell him it's hard to approach and communicate with Fang Meng'ao, just the way you told me."

He Xiaoyu nodded and stood up slowly. Old Liu also stood up, looking at her in a caring manner in order to give her encouragement and courage.

He Xiaoyu turned and was about to leave when she stopped and said: "Uncle Liu, I've got a feeling that Comrade Fang Meng'ao will be in danger if he goes on like this."

Old Liu smiled again. "Don't worry. Like you, we've been taking care of him all the time."

He Xiaoyu felt upset. It was very personal, something she could feel herself. She quickly concealed the emotion and said: "Uncle Liu, I must be going."

"Comrade Xiaoyu. There're two things we haven't done yet since we first met."

He Xiaoyu appeared confused.

Old Liu reached out his large, rough hand, and He Xiaoyu quickly held out her own. Old Liu gently held her hand and asked with a smile: "How about the second thing?"

He Xiaoyu understood what he meant, and then Old Liu uttered the first code words: *"Flowers always blooming."*

He Xiaoyu immediately joined in, and the two continued: *"The moon is always full and longevity for all!"*

The pendulum of the table clock in the sitting room in He Qicang's residence was swinging back and forth, but the sound was more muffled than was usual for this model. This particular feature was designed by the clockmaker for a special purpose. Since He Qicang had the habit of going to bed early, the house must be quiet after nine in the evening.

Liang Jinglun looked at the table clock. It was ten o'clock already! His eyes showed some suspicion. He turned to the telephone on the coffee table.

He Xiaoyu should have been home long ago. His hands reached out for the phone, but stopped midway and finally he drew his hands back. Just then the phone rang.

It rang only once before Liang Jinglun picked up the phone: "Hello."

The voice at the other end surprised him: "Mr Yan..."

It was quiet all around, so the voice of the caller was clear. There was an element of excitement in it: "We've found the materials needed for your plan. Come pick them up at the library, right away!"

Listening to the tone of the caller, Liang Jinglun realised that it must be something urgent, possibly good news, but he wanted to check with the caller first: "Isn't it too late today? I need to wait for Miss He..."

Mr Yan's excited voice was full of urgency: "Come at once. There's a response to your plan and it's a positive one!" With that, the caller hung up.

Liang Jinglun stood up. His intuition told him that behind Yan Chunming's excitement was a hidden plan. Yan Chunming might not see it clearly, but he could.

CHAPTER 11

The freight train carrying grain from Tianjin had left for Peking two hours previously. Because it was a special train dispatched by the government, the signal box staff insisted that it must arrive at the station on time at 11pm sharp.

Ma Hanshan and his entourage arrived at the freight platform of Peking railway station an hour ago. It was a hot day, and he was becoming impatient because he had arrived so early. He walked back and forth along the yellow line that separated him from the railway track about a metre away. Meanwhile, as he watched the clock above the platform, he cursed again: "Bastards, didn't they promise to arrive on time at eleven o'clock? Isn't it already eleven!"

Keeping a distance from him on the same platform, Section Chiefs Li and Wang and other members of the department were also looking at the clock that showed it had just turned eleven.

Li was more agitated than Wang. He told him: "Go to the dispatcher's office and ask them why the government train is late. It's outrageous!"

"I'll go and find out now," said Wang as he walked off, knowing too well that Ma Hanshan might implode at any time.

Ma Hanshan paced along the yellow line. He looked at the clock again and then towards Li. "How the hell did you coordinate with the station's signal box?" he asked. "How did Tianjin respond? If the grain doesn't arrive tonight, you'll report to the police headquarters yourselves! You sons of bitches! You never do your job properly. You wouldn't be able to anticipate your own death even with a scythe at your neck!"

Knowing that the business tonight was so important, Li held his tongue and turned to look in the direction where the train was due to pull in. Like a flock of geese, the staff behind him all stretched their necks and waited for the train to arrive. No one wanted to meet Ma Hanshan's eyes.

"Plainclothes team!" Ma Hanshan called out. Eleven men in Zhongshan suits, who were standing in the dark, gathered around him. Li and other members of the group were surprised, and they all looked in Ma Hanshan's direction.

Ma Hanshan trusted them, and he said to the group leader: "Brothers of the Military Bureau, thanks for joining me at this late hour." It turned out that the eleven Zhongshan suits were from the Peking station of the Military Bureau, otherwise known as the Juntong.

Ma Hanshan had formerly served as head of the Peking Committee for Combating Japanese Collaborators. Finding himself in great trouble, he had to seek help from these ghost-like lackeys from the secret police, even though it might cost him a fortune.

The head of the group in Zhongshan suits replied: "We've been instructed by our superiors that we'll listen to you tonight, our former director."

"Send two of your men to get the chief controller of the station," said Ma Hanshan. "The rest of you, get ready. Arrest anyone I point my finger at!"

"Understood," bellowed the head of the Juntong.

But before he could send someone to catch the chief controller, a breathless Wang had brought the chief controller to him.

"Director, please meet the chief controller," he said. "You can ask him yourself."

The head of the Military Bureau ordered: "Take him!"

Two of the Zhongshan suits grabbed the controller by the wrists and twisted his hands behind his back.

The chief controller's body bent from the pressure and the pain. "Director Ma! Director Ma! There is a new order... Ouch... Listen to me..."

"Fine, let him speak," said Ma Hanshan.

The two Zhongshan suits relaxed their grip on him and the chief controller said with a gasp: "I just received their call, saying that the grain train is delayed and will now arrive at midnight. They also told me that most of the freight is army provisions. So we'll have to wait until the convoy of the Fourth Corps of the National Army arrives..."

"What the fuck are you talking about?" Ma Hanshan barked. "What army food? What do you mean by the convoy of Fourth Corps? You son of a bitch! Explain yourself!"

"I received two telephone calls, one from Tianjin saying that the grain train will arrive at midnight, the other from the military supplies office of the headquarters of the Fourth Corps of the National Army claiming that eight hundred tonnes of the grain will be delivered to the National Army tonight. They demanded that we wait for their convoy..."

"One thousand tonnes of grain is all we have, but the Fourth Corps will take away eight hundred tonnes?" Ma Hanshan was so desperate he felt like his head was buzzing. "OK, it serves me right. Yangtze Construction Company, you motherfucker! Kick me when I'm down, even at this critical moment!"

Ma's entourage, including the two section chiefs and their subordinates and the Juntong, were all looking at Ma Hanshan, dumbfounded.

Ever resourceful, Ma was thinking how to deal with the situation. Suddenly, he said to Wang: "Is Captain Fang's brigade waiting for the grain in the warehouse?"

"Yes sir. They've been waiting there for quite a while to make an inventory of the grain to be delivered tonight. I've arranged everything, including tea, cigarettes, wine and some refreshments..."

"You stupid bastard! Who told you to report that?" said Ma Hanshan. "Call Captain Fang, and ask him to bring his Inspection Brigade here immediately! Tell him the Fourth Corps is going to rob the rations meant for the students and citizens of Peking!"

Wang was confused at Ma's instruction. It would lead to open conflict between Fang's brigade and the Fourth Corps of the National Army. In case it turned bloody, Wang would have to make the call and he would be held responsible for it. So he decided to act dumb and asked: "Director, director... can I not say that it is the Fourth Corps that's coming to rob the grain..."

Ma Hanshan became so furious that he instructed a member of the Juntong beside him to give him a gun. Ma loaded the weapon and handed it to Wang. "Take it!"

Wang would not take the gun. "Director..."

Ma Hanshan put the muzzle against his chin. "Take it..."

Sensing that Ma meant business, Wang took the gun with shaking hands.

"It's loaded," said Ma Hanshan. "Take your own life with it if Captain Fang and his brigade fail to reach the station by midnight."

"I'll go!" Wang said, holding the pistol with both hands as if it were a piece of red-hot iron, and handing it back to Ma Hanshan.

"Director, director, I promise to bring Captain Fang here before midnight," said Wang. "I can't use this thing anyway..."

Ma Hanshan grabbed the gun back and shouted: "Why haven't you gone yet?"

"Yes sir!" Wang answered, before turning to his two subordinates. "Come with me, come on! Let's make that call." They dashed to the control room.

Without returning the pistol to the Juntong agent, Ma Hanshan paced back and forth with the pistol in his hand. He spotted Li again. "Block the main entrance with all your trucks. If a single military truck of the Fourth Corps manages to squeeze into the station, just kill yourself!"

Looking at his subordinates, Li demanded: "Did you hear him? Follow me!"

The group dashed off.

Ma Hanshan was left alone on the platform with the eleven plainclothes Juntong agents and the chief controller of the station. He instructed the release of the chief controller and then turned to the agents.

"Brothers, it looks like there's going to be internecine strife tonight. I've made a deal with the head of your station. If anything happens, he'll cover our backs. If things get worse, I'll call Vice-Minister Zheng Jiemin of the Ministry of Defence in person. Feel free to cooperate with the MOD's Inspection Brigade. As you know, I've never failed my Juntong brothers."

"Director Ma, rest assured, we'll listen to you," said the head of the Juntong team.

"Good, good!" Ma Hanshan thought hard again. Seeing the little stool brought out by his subordinate, he turned to the chief controller. "Hey, you, put that on the railway track for me!"

The dispatcher hurriedly picked up the stool, but spun around having taken only a single step. "Excuse me, Director Ma, do you really want me to put it on the track?"

For some reason, Ma Hanshan didn't curse or shout at him this time. Instead, he made a heroic gesture by nodding in agreement. The chief controller jumped off the platform with the stool in his hands and put it on a sleeper between the tracks.

Ma Hanshan strode over and jumped off the platform and sat on the stool. "God damn it! Those sons of bitches at Yangtze Construction Company! If I can't stop you today and end up losing my life, they'll send my memorials directly to the president. When he reads them, he will curse you. You bastards!"

Seeing him like this, even the agents from the Juntong looked at each other in confusion.

After the five-member investigation group decided that Fang Meng'ao's brigade would conduct a thorough inspection of the materials at the Peking Citizens' Food-Distribution Committee, Ma Hanshan responded by vacating his own office and turning it into the temporary office of the Inspection Brigade. Almost all the furniture was moved out, leaving the director's desk for Fang Meng'ao's sole use. In addition, a large conference table was placed in the centre of the spacious office, with one chair at the head of it and ten on each side, perfect for accommodating the twenty-one members of Fang Meng'ao's brigade.

It was the brigade's first night at the warehouse. The purpose was very clear: to wait for the one thousand tonnes of grain scheduled to arrive from Tianjin at 11pm and distribute it the next morning among the students from Northeast China and the teachers and students of several universities.

As Section Chief Wang had said, sumptuous food was served on the large table, along with sweets and cakes in the middle and a pack of Hatamen cigarettes, a cup of tea and a bottle of foreign wine in front of each seat on both sides. The only exception was a pack of cigars at the head of the table for Fang Meng'ao.

The pilots were quiet and none of them touched anything on the table. It was not because of the importance of tonight's task, but because everyone could see that their captain had taken on a different appearance today.

Fang Meng'ao sat there without speaking, looking neither serious nor angry. He remained silent.

The telephone rang and he answered it. Everyone looked at him, yet they could only hear him grunt occasionally. No one else could hear what the caller was saying. He remained silent until he uttered the following words: "I've got it." Then he put the telephone to one side, walked back to the table and sat down, still expressionless, silent and contemplative.

Two staff members who had stayed to wait on the men came in, each holding a thermos bottle. They carefully lifted the teacup covers in front of each seat. A lid was removed but the cup was already full. Another one was removed, and it was full, too.

One of the staff members summoned up his courage, stood beside Fang Meng'ao with his back bent and said with a smile: "Captain Fang, it's quite hot today, could you please give the order for the men to have some tea?"

Fang Meng'ao looked at him and knew that he was only a staff member. His tone was soft: "Answer me honestly when I ask you a question, will you?"

"Yes captain. As your subordinate, I must tell the truth."

"You are not my subordinate, are you?" Fang Meng'ao waved his hand and pointed to the confectionery on the table. "Normally, who do you serve this stuff to?"

"It's all for the officials above director general level in party institutions and ministries."

"I see. You can go now."

"Yes sir." Both staff members walked off.

Fang Meng'ao looked at his team, and his face, which had been expressionless up to that point, slowly revealed the smile that everyone had been expecting. The smile, however, was different this time. It was a forced smile as if something was weighing heavily on his mind.

The men seemed to have been infected by his silence. They all looked at him in confusion, waiting for him to speak.

"Really, why have you been so oddly uncommunicative since your arrival in Peking?" he asked.

In fact, it was he himself who had been silent, troubled by his thoughts. It was therefore surprising that he asked them why they did not speak. The pilots knew they could say whatever they wanted, but they all looked at Chen Changwu.

Chen had worked for him longer than anyone else, and he was also the oldest of all the pilots. So he took the lead by asking: "Captain, are you facing any difficulties? If so, you should share them with us. You can't burden yourself alone while we stand idle. Nor will we allow you to constantly protect the twenty brothers."

How could Fang Meng'ao tell them about his worries? He squinted at Chen Changwu, before his eyes swept across the other members of the brigade. "What do you mean by 'difficulties'? We can manage the special criminal court. What else is beyond us? Remember this – don't ever try to guess what I'm thinking! You're totally hopeless. Let me ask you, all of you, a question. What's the date today?"

Everyone knew the answer, but they all looked at Chen Changwu once more.

Fang Meng'ao asked Chen Changwu directly: "Say it yourself."

"Captain, today is my wedding day!" Chen replied, before adding earnestly: "Captain, it was delayed because we were unexpectedly assigned this new mission in Peking. Our families have agreed that she and I will get married one day when we're done with the corruption investigation in Peking."

"I delayed your wedding." Fang Meng'ao sighed with sorrow and stood up. "You heard the man just now. Normally, these items are exclusively reserved for those above director general level in Peking. If we don't consume them, they will still be out of reach of the common people. We should consume them on their behalf. Though Changwu's wedding has been delayed, we must drink the wine to celebrate the occasion. Open the wine, let's have a toast to Changwu and his bride. After that, I will lead you into battle!"

Everyone got excited. They stood up one after another, countless hands reaching out for the wine bottles. Fang Meng'ao took the lead in raising his bottle. The rest of the brigade followed suit.

Fang Meng'ao glanced at Chen Changwu and then looked at his team. It was time for him to offer a toast. "Blooming flowers! Full moon! Longevity for all!" With that, he drank the entire bottle.

They followed him and drank from their bottles, all the while thinking that the captain's toast was a little odd. It differed from his usual style of address, and no one knew the real meaning of the words.

Fang Meng'ao put down his bottle, and so did everyone else. They were expecting to hear from their captain what kind of battle they would fight.

"I have received news that about a thousand tonnes of rice has been shipped from Tianjin tonight," he said. "It should be rationed to students from the Northeast and to all students and professors in Peking. But the Fourth Corps of the National Army will take away eight hundred tonnes in their own lorries. That is an act of brazen robbery of the citizens' food! Now, we shall go to the railway station and make sure that not a single grain of rice will be taken away by Fourth Corps troops. That's a direct order!"

With a swish, all twenty members stood up.

"Changwu, Yuangang," Fang Meng'ao called out.

"Yes sir!"

"Both of you, stay here in the barracks. Everyone else, follow me!" Then he strode to the door.

While Chen Changwu and Shao Yuangang were seized with confusion, the other pilots followed Fang Meng'ao out. Chen Changwu recovered his senses and shouted from behind: "Captain!"

Fang Meng'ao stopped. Everyone stopped.

"Captain, I know you want to do us a favour. But when it comes to fighting the Fourth Corps, I don't need any favours."

Shao Yuangang realised Fang's intention and came over. "When you're in danger, I am in danger, too. I have to support my mother, but all my fellow soldiers also have families to provide for. Captain, I beg you to retire me and send me home if you want me to stay put."

Fang Meng'ao watched the two men and felt that not only did they look resolute, but so did all the other pilots.

"Fine! As the adage goes, 'How can one evade one's responsibility in a time of crisis because of personal gain and loss, life and death?'" Recalling these heroic words, Fang Meng'ao called out: "Let's go."

After speaking with Comrade Liu of Peking's CPC Urban Works Department, He Xiaoyu rushed home, only to find that Liang Jinglun was absent. A note from him was left on the tea table:

Dear Xiaoyu,

I had to leave because of an emergency. I'll be back in an hour or two. When you get home, please wait up for me. I'd like to talk to you about matters related to the Fangs. If you feel tired, take a nap on the couch. Rest well.

LIANG JINGLUN

He Xiaoyu sat in a daze. She stared at the table clock beside the wall. The hands of the clock pointed to half past eleven.

Covert operations by the Communist Party against the Kuomintang had been going on for several decades. Some of those involved were regarded as outstanding, and they were known as special party members. They were special in the sense that their backgrounds were complex and the reasons for their existence were complicated. Therefore, it was hard to evaluate their deeds.

Fang Meng'ao belonged to this outstanding group of special party members. So did He Xiaoyu. Now that the long-term struggle between the CPC and the Kuomintang regime had reached a decisive stage, these two special party members were united by a common destiny.

He Xiaoyu folded Liang Jinglun's note, placed it in a book and carefully put it into her school bag. She walked out of the house and stood by the doorway.

A chirp of insects sounded from the courtyard lawn. The

flowers her father had planted were not visible in the darkness, but she could smell their fragrance. A crescent moon was only dimly visible in the western sky.

She closed her eyes and heard a mysterious, but excited voice: Blooming flowers! Full moon! Longevity for all!

She silently prayed in a voice that only she could hear: when the flowers bloom, when the moon becomes full, the married couple will live happily ever after...

The intense feelings brought about by her pious, silent prayer seemed to enable her to hear footsteps of a great phalanx of people coming from the heavy darkness of the night. They were the footsteps of the New China that she had imagined in her mind! She could feel the footsteps getting closer and louder.

She opened her eyes, only to find the courtyard quiet and peaceful and the stars seeming to cover the entire sky. It was a loneliness she thought she did not deserve. The indescribable nature of it overwhelmed her. And it wasn't just her own loneliness. She seemed able to feel the loneliness of two other people.

Liang Jinglun's loneliness was subtle and too profound to be understood. By contrast, Fang Meng'ao always stood alone and was completely independent and with no restrictions.

The clock hanging down from the ceiling of the freight platform of Peking railway station showed 11:50pm.

Though they could not hear it, the two phalanxes of people waiting for the train to arrive at midnight imagined they could sense the distant rumble of a train rolling over the tracks.

By now, an extra squadron of soldiers had arrived on the platform. The Fourth Corps had not only sent its quartermaster, but also a special battalion commander heading a company of commandos, armed with submachine guns to escort the transport of rice, all lined up in rows on the other side of the platform.

On this side of the platform, the two section chiefs and a group of staff members from the Peking Citizens' Food-Distribution Committee were very nervous. They were all hiding behind the eleven plainclothes Juntong, but they had no idea that the eleven were also very nervous.

They all knew there would be a fight, but they ignored each other, waiting for the grain train to arrive and showing that they meant business. The commandos sent by the Fourth Corps thought rather highly of themselves, acting as if Ma Hanshan and the Citizens' Food-Distribution Committee staff did not exist.

Ma Hanshan remained resolute. He was still sitting on the railway track, holding the twenty-shot Mauser pistol in his right hand and a folding fan in his left.

The most nervous person present was the chief controller, who was five hundred metres down the track, holding a red light high for fear that the incoming train might run over Director Ma who simply refused to move his position.

"Wang Yixing!" Ma Hanshan burst out in anger.

Wang, who was hiding behind the crowd, had to walk over: "Here I am, director."

Ma Hanshan pointed the Mauser at him and said: "Where is the Economic Inspection Brigade of the Ministry of Defence?"

Panic-stricken, Wang looked at the clock: "Director, director, it's not quite twelve yet... Captain Fang said it will be here on time..."

Their conversation was heard by the quartermaster and the Special Operations Battalion commander of the Fourth Corps.

The quartermaster winked at the battalion commander, who came up to Wang and asked: "What did you mean by the Economic Inspection Brigade of the Ministry of Defence?"

Wang dared not answer him, so he looked to Ma Hanshan for help.

Ma glanced at the battalion commander. "It's not too late to go now if you're sensible. If you don't, see what will happen next."

The battalion commander immediately returned the charge: "In times of counter-insurgency and nation-saving, I want to see who has the fucking balls to rob us of army provisions. He is dicing with death by acting in this way!"

"You bastard! Who did you just scold?" said Ma Hanshan, standing up from his stool. "Even you, Deputy Commander General Chen, wouldn't dare scold me. A lieutenant colonel like you, what right have you to say those words, you son of a bitch?"

"Director Ma, you seem to take pleasure in swearing. That's something we never enjoy," the colonel answered sarcastically.

The Fourth Corps were Chiang Kai-shek's own troops. Stationed in Peking, they were meant to keep General Fu Zuoyi's Northwest Army in check. As Chiang's own force, they were much favoured by the Kuomintang government. Nanking had repeatedly come to their rescue whenever they caused trouble. Naturally, they would hold Ma Hanshan in contempt.

The colonel continued: "A decisive battle with the Communist forces is imminent. Our task is to capture and kill those who rob military provisions."

"Good! Arrest me now if you have the balls!" Ma Hanshan had been pressured by the five-member investigation group over the past two days, and now he was again forced into a corner by Yangtze Construction Company. He was prepared to do something desperate tonight. As long as Fang Meng'ao's brigade showed up, he would be happy to leave the five-member group and Yangtze Construction to clear up the mess tomorrow. With this in mind, he showed his true colours as a former agent of the Central Bureau of Investigation and Statistics. He jumped onto the platform with his pistol and rushed to confront the battalion commander. Removing the safety catch, Ma took the gun and was ready to hold it against the colonel's head.

The colonel was quite a master of combat skills. In the blink of an eye, the gun in Ma Hanshan's hand was taken from him, and the black muzzle was pressed against his jaw. Ma Hanshan's head was propped up by the colonel's pistol. Knowing it was loaded, he didn't dare move because with one jerk, it could go off.

"What do you want?" The head of the Juntong group came forward and pulled out his gun with his right hand, while holding his ID card in his left. He strode across to the pair. "We belong to the State Secrecy Bureau," he said. "Don't move, neither of you!"

The ten Juntong agents pulled out their guns and followed him with their ID cards held high.

Stationed in Peking, the Army's Fourth Corps found that their grain supply line in Hebei and Shanxi was cut off by the People's Liberation Army (PLA). Now, their military provisions depended on US aid shipped from Tianjin port. The Peking-Tianjin Office of

Yangtze Construction Company called to say that 800 tonnes of grain shipped from Tianjin tonight was allocated to them. If they failed to get the grain back, they would be court-martialled, but now someone was blocking their way.

Seeing the eleven Juntong agents approaching, the colonel's eyes became red with anger and he shouted: "Captain of the special operations company!"

"Yes sir!" roared the commander of the company.

"Take their guns!"

"Sir! First platoon!" said the company commander waving his gun. It turned out that he was the company commander of the Fourth Corps who had previously cooperated with Fang Mengwei in arresting students at the hospital affiliated to Yenching University.

More than thirty American submachine guns surrounded the eleven Juntong agents in a tight ring. "Hand in your guns!"

Eleven pistols were pointed at by the muzzles of more than thirty submachine guns and the Juntong knew they would not get the upper hand. The ten agents were at a loss and looked to the head of the group.

The head of the Juntong warned: "I told you, we are from the State Secrecy Bureau of the Ministry of Defence! Do you know what will happen if you continue to attack us? You'll be shot!"

The battalion commander was even more arrogant: "Seizing military supplies of the National Army and sabotaging war efforts at the front! Which State Secrecy Bureau do you belong to anyway? Arrest them all!"

The special forces company was well-trained. But they did not rush in like a swarm of hornets. Instead, more than twenty of them closed in on the Juntong agents in a circle. About ten of them charged in, stabbing at the arms of the Juntong agents with the muzzles of their guns. All eleven guns fell to the ground.

"Move!" they roared in one voice. The ten guns held the eleven Juntong agents at gunpoint to the wall. Immediately, several more soldiers came up and collected all the pistols on the ground.

Only then did the battalion commander put down his gun against Ma's jaw and say: "Please take Director Ma and his men to the wall."

More than a dozen men ran over and pointed their guns at Wang and Li and all staff members of the Citizens' Food-Distribution Committee. "There, off you go!"

The company commander came in person to "invite" Ma Hanshan. Ma would not let him do it. No longer with the pistol pressed against his jaw, he took a breath and then jumped up and grabbed the battalion commander by the collar. "You bastard! Totally disregarding the party and the government! I dare you to arrest me. Shoot me if you've got the guts!" He then yelled back at Section Chiefs Li and Wang: "Don't go, stand your ground! Let's see if these sons of bitches dare lay a finger on us!"

Ma Hanshan was still grabbing the colonel by the collar. The colonel knew Ma's government background and didn't use force against him: "Director Ma, you'd better let go."

"Let go?" Ma Hanshan roared. "Call Commander Li Wen. Only when he comes, will I let go..."

"We're here at Commander Li's order," said the colonel. "Director Ma, are you going to let go?"

"You son of a bitch, the only way I'll let go is if you shoot me."

The colonel didn't need to strike back. Instead, he exerted all his strength by thrusting his upper body and shaking off Ma Hanshan's hands. Ma lost his balance and staggered backwards.

Suddenly, there was a long whistle, a flash of bright lights and the train that was carrying a thousand tonnes of grain puffed into the station from a few hundred metres away.

Standing still, Ma Hanshan saw the train was approaching. He tried to put up a desperate fight, but was stopped by several guns.

"Stop it!" said the quartermaster walking over to Ma Hanshan and the colonel. "Director Ma, we are acting on military orders. You're an important person. Why bother? If you end up being injured by my brothers, we can't even hold them responsible."

The grain train rumbled on.

"Our lorries, as well as those of the Citizens' Food-Distribution Committee, move in! Prepare to load up!" shouted the quartermaster.

Comrade Jianfeng appreciated the many merits of Zeng Keda. One of them was his ability to endure hardship and another was his capacity for hard work. Every night, he stayed up late to handle official business until about three in the morning. Yet he never missed the dawn and was still full of energy.

Around midnight was Zeng Keda's busiest time of the day to review official documents. At this moment, he was standing at the desk in his room in Gu's residence and was looking at a situation map recently sent by the Fourth and Ninth Corps of the National Army. He appeared grim-faced.

There was a core area in the middle of the map that was marked with the two Chinese characters for "Peking", and southwest of Peking there were huge red arrows in front of the names of the following places: Dingxing, Fangshan, Liangxiang and Changxindian.

Zeng Keda picked up a confidential telegram sent by the Ministry of Defence. It was so quiet at this time of night that people like him who were deep in concentration were prone to develop auditory hallucinations.

The first sound to ring in his ears was a secret radio message being transmitted, followed by someone deciphering the contents of a secret telegram, and then it was the voice of a person reading a confidential telegram. "According to secret reports submitted by the Fourth Corps of the National Army and the North China Headquarters for the Suppression of Communist Insurgency, more than two hundred thousand troops of the PLA's North China Field Army have advanced from the Shijiazhuang and Baoding strongholds to Dingxing, Fangshan, Liangxiang and Changxindian under the jurisdiction of Peking. Within three to five days, there will be fierce fighting with Communist troops around the above four areas. The Peking chapter of the CPC will secretly cooperate with the Communist troops' military operations in stirring up students and city residents in agitation against the government. Chief Inspector Zeng must pay close attention to it and guide the five-member investigation group to stop the spread of the Fifth of July and Ninth of July student unrests, to ensure that the military campaigns in the front conducted by the North China Headquarters for the Suppression of Communist Insurgency are not disturbed by the turmoil in Peking."

Zeng Keda closed his eyes for a moment, opened them again and looked at the military situation map and the huge red arrows. Suddenly, a burst of fierce gunfire seemed to come from the red arrows! At first Zeng Keda was alarmed, then he instinctively stepped back. When he had collected his thoughts, he discovered that the phone on the desk was ringing.

He knew that the caller must be aware of his schedule and be vetted for this line. He calmed down a little, then went over and picked up the receiver: "This is Zeng Keda. Who is speaking?"

It was quiet all around, and the voice of the caller was very clear: "Comrade Keda, we have a situation here." The caller was the young agent who had followed Cui Zhongshi from Nanking to Peking.

Zeng Keda remained calm: "Easy, speak slowly."

"Yes sir. Fang Meng'ao's brigade suddenly decided to go to Peking railway station. I also learnt that the Fourth Corps of the National Army sent their troops to the station to transport the grain from Tianjin to their base."

Zeng Keda was stunned for a moment, then asked: "Did Ma Hanshan and his Citizens' Food-Distribution Committee people go to the station?"

"They were already there," said the voice. "After learning that the Fourth Corps also wanted to have their share of the grain, they informed Captain Fang who then rushed over with his Inspection Brigade."

"I see. Continue to observe over there and report to me at any time."

Zeng Keda hadn't expected such a situation to arise. After hanging up, he thought hard for a moment before picking up the phone again and looking at the clock on the wall. It was past midnight. He hesitated for a moment and then dialled a number.

As it was a special line, they quickly put him through. "Is that Nanking special line two, please? Yes, this is Zeng Keda. Hello, you're on duty today? Yes, I have an important situation to report to Comrade Jianfeng... I hate to call at this hour of the day, but it is quite a complicated situation... Thank you."

Knowing that Comrade Jianfeng was about to take the call in person, Zeng Keda got up and stood rather straight.

"Is that Comrade Keda speaking?" A friendly voice with a strong Ningbo accent came from the other end of the phone.

"Yes, this is Zeng Keda. Permit me to report to you, Comrade Jianfeng." Zeng Keda's feeling of awe was apparent in his voice. "My apologies to disturb you at this very late hour. I'm sure you're still working, aren't you?"

Jianfeng's voice down the line was firm: "It doesn't matter. Have you received the latest confidential reports from the Ministry of Defence?"

"Yes, Comrade Jianfeng, the Communist troops' attack has worsened the situation, and in a ferocious way."

"Regarding the military deployment, it's not our responsibility. How to suppress the Communist insurgent troops will only depend on the wise strategy of the president. At present, we need to act in accordance with the president's military deployment to stabilise the economy and win the hearts and minds of the people in the interior, especially in the five major cities. Let's talk about the situation in Peking."

"Yes," Zeng Keda replied. "During the day, the Peking Citizens' Food-Distribution Committee reported to the five-member group that the Peking-Tianjin Office of Yangtze Construction Company would ship a thousand tonnes of grain to Peking tonight, which has been agreed to be allocated to local residents. Just now, I got a report that the Fourth Corps in Peking stepped in and claimed that eight hundred tonnes of this total was allocated to them. This indicates that Yangtze Construction not only controls the allocation of food to citizens, but also interferes with the distribution of military food that is the responsibility of the Resource Supply Committee. The tiger has a growing appetite."

There was silence at the other end of the line. Zeng Keda had no alternative but to wait.

In fact, the silence lasted only a few seconds before Jianfeng's voice resumed: "Today, Peking students demonstrated before the North China Headquarters for the Suppression of Communist Insurgency, which is most unfortunate. There has been negative press across the country, and the impact will only increase tomorrow. Tonight's one thousand tonnes of grain is being provided for the sole purpose of calming down the unrest among citizens in Peking. Have you investigated the cause of the issue? Why did the Fourth Corps decide to make trouble at this moment?"

"It happened so suddenly that we haven't had time to investigate, Comrade Jianfeng. My thinking is that Yangtze Construction borrowed from the Central Bank but didn't supply the citizens' food that should be rationed to Peking. Now, as we've intensified our efforts in checking the accounts, they've become so desperate that they use troops to cover up their corruption in the distribution of citizens' food under the pretext of supplying military food. Their intentions are nefarious."

"How do you manage a situation they've engineered?" asked Jianfeng.

"First, since tonight's grain has been clearly earmarked for citizens, it can't be taken away by the Fourth Corps. However, since a large-scale battle is imminent, food deprivation may affect the morale of the Fourth Corps. To address the immediate consequences, Comrade Jianfeng, permission to invite you to explain the reasons to the Fourth Corps in person. Second, take tonight's event as an opportunity to immediately launch an investigation. Yangtze Construction took a loan from the Central Bank to manage the distribution of citizens' food. How did it spend the money? Third, review the procedures surrounding the transport of grain by the Fourth Corps. How can Yangtze Construction intervene in the decision-making process of the Material Supply Committee on the National Army's Military Needs? Comrade Jianfeng, the financial markets have been completely out of control. If the Kung and Soong groups continue to manage the process of economic rebuilding, the president's military deployment in the front as well as the planned currency system reform will be adversely affected. You have to make up your mind, and let the president make up his mind, that we shall no longer allow the interests of the Kung and Soong groups to control the economic lifeline of the party-state..."

"Stay focused on current affairs," said Comrade Jianfeng in an impassioned tone.

Zeng Keda was shocked by the interruption.

After a moment of silence, Comrade Jianfeng's voice came

again: "The Republic of China is one country, one government and one leader. What do you mean by this and that group? You've even named names!"

Zeng Keda felt wronged, but he could now better understand Comrade Jianfeng's position. He quickly appreciated the sensitivity surrounding the Kung and Soong groups and replied: "Yes, Comrade Jianfeng, I accept your criticism. I will pay attention to it in the future. I feel humbly cautious and fearful."

"Caution is necessary, but there's no need for fear," replied Jianfeng, in a calmer, more encouraging tone. "We will never waver in our belief in fighting against the Communists and corruption. I agree with all three of your suggestions. Who are you going to arrange tonight to stop the Fourth Corps from misappropriating the grain?"

"This is exactly what I was going to report to you, Comrade Jianfeng. Fang Meng'ao's Economic Inspection Brigade has gone to the railway station."

"It wasn't you who told them to go there, was it?"

"No. I understand that the Peking Citizens' Food-Distribution Committee contacted Fang Meng'ao directly. They went there by themselves without requesting my approval."

This was an indirect complaint. It was meant to inform Jianfeng that Fang Meng'ao's brigade was not taking orders from him. Zeng Keda was listening attentively as Comrade Jianfeng continued: "There are only twenty people in Fang Meng'ao's brigade. Don't you worry about their safety?"

Zeng Keda felt disappointed. Instead of criticising Fang Meng'ao's behaviour as being maverick, Comrade Jianfeng was only concerned about the man's safety!

Zeng Keda intentionally made no reply, deciding instead to express his dissatisfaction with silence.

Since ancient times, many people have been following and depending on their masters; some were even ready to die the cruellest death for them. There is only one psychological barrier that can't be surmounted, and that is when his master puts others above himself. If this barrier can't be surmounted, he will be a jealous or angry type. Zeng Keda had always questioned Comrade Jianfeng's estimation of Fang Meng'ao as an important person. But he also worried that Comrade Jianfeng suspected he was jealous of others; therefore he felt reluctant to speak his mind or to control Fang Meng'ao to the best of his ability. Tonight, following the accidental clash, he felt even more conflicted about the fact that Comrade Jianfeng was allowing Fang Meng'ao to act with impunity. With this in mind, he decided to continue to let Fang Meng'ao act at his own discretion. He could use the opportunity to assess his performance and observe his relationship with Cui Zhongshi.

"Do you have any concerns?" Comrade Jianfeng asked.

Zeng Keda knew that by remaining silent he would breach etiquette and pay the cost later. So he quickly decided to respond with an element of fear in his voice: "My apologies for being disrespectful, Comrade Jianfeng. I was thinking about the question you just raised. I don't have any concerns. I believe that Fang Meng'ao and his brigade will face the Central Bank, his father and a greater force of corruption in the future. Furthermore, they will need to perform many more arduous tasks ahead. A chance presents itself tonight for them to practise dealing with such events. Only when they are capable of dealing with all forces and circumstances can they carry out the arduous task given to them by the president and Comrade Jianfeng. Of course, I will try my best to balance the attitude of the five-member group towards the Fourth Corps of the National Army. As for the safety of Fang Meng'ao and his brigade in Peking, I can assure you of that, Comrade Jianfeng."

"It's good that you understand these points." Zeng Keda was gratified to hear Jianfeng's voice at the other end. "Always remember, there must be different approaches according to who you are dealing with. Those inside our camp must be dealt with differently from those outside."

These words cheered Zeng Keda as he waited excitedly for Comrade Jianfeng to further explain that "inside" referred to himself, while "outside" referred to Fang Meng'ao.

However, Zeng Keda was disappointed by what Comrade Jianfeng said next: "The conflict that occurred tonight between the Citizens' Food-Distribution Committee and the Fourth Corps can only be handled internally. It should not be allowed to shake the morale of the army or the public. The information must not be leaked to the Communist Party, which might take advantage of it to cause adverse effects."

"I understand, Comrade Jianfeng," he replied softly.

The other party hung up, but Zeng Keda was still thinking with the receiver in his hand.

"Guard!" Zeng Keda called out.

An officer from the Youth Army entered the room.

"I'm going to meet Comrade Liang Jinglun tonight," Zeng Keda said in a stern, yet low voice. "Please make the necessary arrangements."

———

There were fifteen wagons on the extended grain train. When it stopped at the platform, the rear carriage was still not visible.

The Fourth Corps' ten-wheel trucks for grain transportation arrived at the platform. They had even temporarily requisitioned trucks from the Peking Citizens' Food-Distribution Committee. One by one, numerous lorries stopped on the platform, stretching into the distance.

Every wagon door of the train had been opened. The company of soldiers from the Fourth Corps' Special Operations Battalion were on guard, while the engineers they brought with them were busy loading the bags of grain onto the lorries.

Ma Hanshan, his section chiefs and officers, along with the eleven Juntong agents were allowed to sit on the ground with their backs against the wall, but they were still being held at gunpoint by a squad of soldiers.

By sitting down for a while, Ma Hanshan's energy reserves had just begun to recover when he suddenly rose to his feet again.

"Please sit down!" Two guns pointed at him at once.

Ma Hanshan smiled strangely and stepped forward with his chest thrust towards the guns. "I'll count to three, and if you don't shoot me, I'll say Commander-in-Chief Lee is a son of a bitch."

The two soldiers were stunned and turned to the colonel for permission to shoot. The colonel shook his head and then looked at the quartermaster next to him. The two soldiers secretly looked towards the other side of the platform, and they were confronted with a most troubling sight.

Two rows of formidable Air Force pilots were standing on the platform! They were members of the Economic Inspection Brigade of the Ministry of Defence stationed in Peking.

The colonel was very professional. He was secretly observing the leader of the brigade. Of course, that man was Fang Meng'ao. He exuded an aggressive readiness for combat. He was more arrogant than his army counterparts. He stood there smoking a cigar in an absent-minded manner. He did not even look across the platform. He appeared not to notice the many lorries and people milling about.

Professional experience informed the colonel that he was confronting a more powerful rival. At this time, Ma Hanshan issued a hysterical cry as he stared at the two soldiers who were pointing their guns at him. "One, two, three! Shoot!"

Except for Fang Meng'ao's brigade, all eyes were on the two guns. Yet the two guns did not fire.

"I dare you to shoot me," taunted Ma Hanshan. "Get out of my way if you're not going to shoot! You motherfucking Fourth Corps!" He broke through the gap between the two guns and came over to Fang Meng'ao.

Fang Meng'ao turned slowly and looked at Ma Hanshan who was walking towards him.

"Captain Fang," said Ma Hanshan, "you must have seen all that's been going on. Would you care to stop them unloading the grain?"

Fang Meng'ao smiled and replied: "Why?"

"Because this grain is to be rationed tomorrow to the students. If these supplies are taken away tonight, the students will protest once more outside the North China Headquarters for the Suppression of Communist Insurgency. As a result, Commander-in-Chief Fu will report it to Nanking, and you, the five-member group, will be sure to find fault with us at the Peking Citizens' Food-Distribution Committee again!"

Ma Hanshan was speaking loudly so the quartermaster and the colonel could hear. The two decided to ignore him.

Instead, the quartermaster called out to the troops: "Speed up! Unload the grain within the hour and ship it away immediately!"

"Did you hear that, Captain Fang?" said Ma Hanshan, pointing to the quartermaster and the colonel. "If you don't act, those motherfuckers from the Fourth Corps will have all the grain shipped away."

Fang Meng'ao did not answer; instead he was busy evaluating the situation. Ma Hanshan knew that Fang Meng'ao would not necessarily listen to him, but he kept on swearing. As long as he could provoke the quartermaster and the colonel of the Fourth Corps, Fang Meng'ao might not necessarily continue to hold back.

Holding a civilian post, the quartermaster was inured to being scolded. It was common for him to be cursed in normal times. Thus, Ma Hanshan's swearing tactics had no impact on him.

The colonel, however, was having a hard time putting up with Ma Hanshan's language. His patience snapped as Ma Hanshan continued to shout curses in the presence of so many of his subordinates. He snarled in response: "Damn you son of a motherfucking bitch! I'll see who dares to do anything!"

The colonel hardly imagined that his strong words would infuriate Fang Meng'ao since he had so cherished his mother's memory all his life. Hearing him swear, Fang Meng'ao quickly lost his air of detachment. His eyes flashed with rage and he looked at the colonel in fury.

Ma Hanshan was so cunning that he said provocatively: "Captain Fang, did you hear..."

"Go over to him," said Fang Meng'ao. "Ask him for his official designation, his rank and whose mother he cursed."

"I'm going to ask him right now!" Ma Hanshan knew that by doing so he was going to be adding fuel to the fire on both sides. He walked briskly to the colonel of the Special Operations Battalion.

Fang Meng'ao had planned to seize the lorries as soon as all the grain was loaded. Now that the colonel had pricked his sore spot, he found his sober calmness replaced by the pugnacity of youth. His looked straight at Ma Hanshan who marched over to the colonel.

The twenty pilots understood their captain so well that their eyes were blazing like torches, looking intensely at the army soldiers. They were waiting for his order on which they would act immediately.

Fang Meng'ao watched Ma Hanshan approach the battalion commander. He saw Ma Hanshan speaking with his hands waving in the air, but his voice was kept so low that Fang Meng'ao could not hear what he was saying to the colonel.

The colonel appeared scornful, and he said something in reply.

Ma Hanshan turned around and called out loudly: "Captain Fang! He said that he is colonel of the Special Operations Battalion of the Fourth Corps! During the period of counter-insurgency and national salvation, it was apparently not a problem to arrest and kill people. Calling us sons of bitches is actually quite polite! They see nothing untoward in cursing us like that."

Fang Meng'ao looked ghastly pale. "Turn left!" he instructed.

In two rows, the twenty pilots turned left.

"March!" said Fang Meng'ao as he led the brigade towards the colonel. The two rows of pilots followed him with precise steps. The battalion commander instinctively put his hand on the holster at his waist.

The platoon standing guard spread out around him. The muzzles of their submachine guns were pointing at Fang Meng'ao's brigade who were fast approaching them.

The quartermaster, who knew the scheme of things, hurriedly whispered to the colonel: "They've been sent by the Bureau of Reserve Cadres. Don't ever start a fight with them."

"Too late!" Ma Hanshan responded after hearing these words. He was so eager for the fray, he immediately shouted at the two men.

Fang Meng'ao had reached the colonel and the quartermaster. "Halt!" he shouted.

The twenty members of the brigade stood in formation behind him. Fang Meng'ao looked at the two bars and three stars on the shoulder of the quartermaster and then at the two bars and two stars of the colonel. "Officer first," he said. "Tell me your unit designation, rank and name."

The quartermaster smiled reluctantly. "Excuse me, are you Captain Fang sent by the Ministry of Defence stationed in Peking?"

An expressionless Fang Meng'ao responded: "Please report your unit number, position and name!"

The quartermaster had no choice but to comply: "Qian

Yousheng, chief of the military supplies department, colonel of the Fourth Corps of the National Army."

Fang Meng'ao smiled and held out his hand. "Chief Qian, it's a pleasure to meet you."

The quartermaster reached out and the two shook hands. Ma Hanshan looked on, unsure what might happen next.

Seeing that Fang Meng'ao was being polite to Qian, the colonel saluted Fang and reported: "Hu Anqiang, lieutenant colonel of the Special Operations Battalion of the Fourth Corps of the National Army. It's a pleasure to meet Captain Fang." He put down his hand and reached out to Fang Meng'ao.

Fang Meng'ao did not even bother to offer his hand. He stared into the eyes of the lieutenant colonel. "Were you the one who led the troops to shoot and kill the students at Peking Municipal Assembly on the fifth of July?" he asked.

The lieutenant colonel changed colour. He withdrew his hand and hardened his tone: "My current post is lieutenant colonel of the Fourth Corps of the National Army. I only receive orders from our Corps and only report to the commander of the Corps."

"Then tell me, who gave you the order to shoot the students on the fifth of July?" Fang Meng'ao persisted.

"I've said that I report my actions only to the commander of the Corps."

"Well, then. I will take you to see your commander and listen in person to your report."

The lieutenant colonel had been vigilant all the while and was ready to draw his gun, but when he reached for it, his hand felt powerless. Fang Meng'ao had moved with great speed to clip an ice-cold handcuff firmly on his wrist. Then, with a click, the lieutenant colonel felt a sharp pain. Fang Meng'ao had quickly secured the handcuffs. The steel teeth bit into the colonel's flesh and the gun fell from his hand.

Next, an Air Force boot stretched out and kicked the falling gun. Fang Meng'ao grabbed the gun before it landed and quickly held it against Hu's head. This series of moves was completed within just a second or two. Fang Meng'ao twisted Hu's handcuffed hand behind his back with his right hand while his left held the gun against his head – Colonel Hu was completely under his control.

Events happened so fast and so suddenly that everyone was still trying to react before Fang Meng'ao roared: "Shao Yuangang!"

"Yes sir!" Shao Yuangang responded.

"Take the captain's gun."

"Yes sir." Shao Yuangang was the largest of all the pilots and the most skilled in kungfu. He leapt forward and with great dexterity handcuffed the captain's right wrist and swiftly pulled out his gun and held it against his head.

"Over there!"

Holding the captain of the Special Operations Battalion, Shao Yuangang twisted his handcuffed hand against his back and pushed him to Fang Meng'ao's side. Fang handed the lieutenant colonel over to Shao Yuangang, who now had two handcuffed men to look after.

With the battalion commander and company captain arrested, the whole company of the Special Operations Battalion were dumbfounded.

"Take their guns!" Fang Meng'ao ordered.

The entire brigade, which had been in perfect formation, suddenly moved at the command. The battle formation at Fang Meng'ao's order succeeded in compelling obedience from the company of the Fourth Corps.

"Drop the guns!"

"Put down your guns!" One by one, they laid their guns on the ground.

"You scoundrels! Now you know the power of the brigade, don't you?"

No one felt more excited than Ma Hanshan, who spat on the floor and taunted the captain: "Weren't you bragging about arresting and killing people? Now you've seen what the officers from the Ministry of Defence are capable of, haven't you?"

With Fang Meng'ao's brigade avenging him, Ma Hanshan thought he should offer some advice in return. "These guys, we must take them to be investigated by the five-member group. Captain Fang, with your support, I promise to distribute this grain tomorrow. Come here, all of you. Load the lorries with grain!"

The first to recover from the scene were the eleven Juntong

agents. They immediately rose to retrieve their handguns taken by the soldiers of the Special Operations Battalion.

"Don't move!" Fang Meng'ao shouted at them.

"Don't move! All of you, get back!" Chen Changwu and Guo Jinyang blocked the Juntong agents.

Section Chiefs Li and Wang and the staff members were unable to move.

"Captain Fang," said Ma Hanshan, "these are my staff on the Citizens' Food-Distribution Committee."

Fang Meng'ao glanced at him, and then looked at the quartermaster who was frozen in confusion. "You two, come here," he instructed.

The quartermaster came over nervously. Ma Hanshan also moved closer, feeling somewhat confused. He looked at Fang Meng'ao, his expression one of puzzlement.

"Where did the grain come from?" asked Fang Meng'ao. "How come both of you received authorisation to transport it? Show me the paperwork."

"Captain Fang, is it necessary to see documents?" Ma Hanshan complained. "I promised the five-member group that this grain was purchased from Tianjin by the Peking Citizens' Food-Distribution Committee. Here's the bill of lading."

He took out the document and handed it to Fang Meng'ao, who gave it a quick look over. The bill of lading clearly stated the name of the buyer to be the Peking Citizens' Food-Distribution Committee, which was authorised by the Peking-Tianjin Office of Yangtze Construction Company to transport the one thousand tonnes of imported American rice from Tianjin to Peking.

Fang Meng'ao turned to the quartermaster and asked: "What about yours?"

The quartermaster fetched out his bill of lading and handed it over. Fang Meng'ao scrutinised the bill of lading and found that it clearly stated the buyer as the Fourth Corps of the National Army. With this paperwork, the Fourth Corps was authorised by the Peking-Tianjin Office of Yangtze Construction to transport the eight hundred tonnes of imported American rice from Tianjin to Peking.

Ma Hanshan saw it clearly and swore: "That goddamned bastard with a black heart, the same goods sold to two buyers! Captain Fang, the person who escorts the wagons is in the back of the train. We've got to catch him before it's too late!"

Fang Meng'ao turned to Guo Jinyang and said: "Take two brigade members to arrest the escort."

"Yes sir." Guo Jinyang and another member of the brigade went off to the rear wagon with their guns.

Zeng Keda was in no mood to read the documents. He was resting in a chair in order to gain some peace and quiet.

This was something that Comrade Jianfeng would do every day in order to set an example for all – to meditate quietly for an hour and reflect on what he'd been thinking and doing earlier in the day. The practice originated with General Zeng Guofan of the Qing Dynasty who meditated for an hour every day even when his troops were engaged in fierce battle. By doing this, he improved his concentration along with his capacity for thinking.

"Permission to enter," said a young army officer from outside the room.

Zeng Keda opened his eyes and said: "Please come in."

The young army officer came in and whispered in his ear: "Comrade Liang Jinglun was having a meeting with members of the Communist Party's Student Movement Committee. We had a hard time getting in touch with him. He's going to meet us somewhere in the suburbs near the campus of Yenching University. But it's so late and you'll have to change, besides which it will require a long bicycle ride. Would that be too much trouble?"

On the freight platform of Peking railway station, the young man taken back by Guo Jinyang decided to take the initiative by asking Ma Hanshan and the quartermaster: "Director Ma and Section Chief Qian, what's the matter? What's the problem?"

Ma Hanshan and the quartermaster were obviously familiar

with him, but neither of them answered. They just looked at Fang Meng'ao. Fang Meng'ao felt disgusted at the sight of him.

The young man was wearing a Hawaiian short-sleeved shirt, light silk trousers and a pair of pointed brown leather shoes. A look of displeasure was written all over his face. Beside him stood a woman wearing heavy makeup.

The man probably knew that this Air Force officer beside him was in charge, but he didn't seem to care. He only looked at Ma Hanshan and the quartermaster. "Whatever is the problem, you two can solve it through consultation. I've got to get back to Tianjin tonight."

"It's filthy here," the woman next to him complained. "I'm going back to the coach." With that, she spun around and was about to leave.

Guo Jinyang immediately blocked her way. "Stay where you are! Stay back!"

"Who do you think you are? Why are you so rude?" Without understanding the consequences of her resistance, the woman said to the young man: "Find a phone, we'll call President Kung now!"

The young man became angry: "Who's in charge at Peking railway station? Where's the telephone?"

"Just forget it, Deputy Director Kung!" Ma Hanshan looked at the young man with disapproval, and continued: "During the day, President Kung of your company promised that a thousand tonnes of rice would be delivered to us tonight. How come that grain is now destined for the Fourth Corps? You can't make a fool of us like that."

"Who's making a fool of you?" asked Deputy Director Kung in a voice much higher than Ma Hanshan's. "The market is shrinking, the roads are awful, the National Army needs food and the Citizens' Food-Distribution Committee also needs supplies. Where can we get so much grain for both of you! Director Ma, let me remind you that our business has been directly negotiated with Nanking. It's not your job to be blaming President Kung."

"But tell us whether this train-load of grain is for us or for the Fourth Corps." Ma Hanshan continued to press him to tell the truth in front of Fang Meng'ao.

"That's quite true," said the quartermaster. "You called our

Corps headquarters to inform us that eight hundred tonnes of grain would be delivered tonight. However, our men have been detained by the Ministry of Defence. How do you explain that?"

Deputy Director Kung had been giving Fang Meng'ao a severe look, thinking of himself as a tough person to deal with. He still maintained his hardline approach: "Are you from the Ministry of Defence? Which ministerial department do you work for?"

"Answer their questions," Fang Meng'ao demanded, while staring at him with eyes narrowed.

Deputy Director Kung was stunned, but he quickly regained his composure and revealed his toughness once more: "I will not answer. You have no right to ask me such questions no matter which department you're from. Anything you are unclear about, you can always ask your boss and the authorities in Nanking." And to everyone's surprise, he turned to Ma Hanshan and the quartermaster and asked: "Do you want to unload the grain or not? If not, I'll take the remaining amount back to Tianjin. What a nuisance! Let's go."

"Capture him!" Fang Meng'ao ordered in a deep voice.

Guo Jinyang had been ready and waiting for some time, and at Fang's order he handcuffed Deputy Director Kung with one cuff and the woman beside him with the other.

"What are you up to? What the fuck are you..." Kung felt a sharp pain in his wrist. It was so sore that he couldn't utter a word. Guo Jinyang exerted some strength on the handcuffs, and the steel teeth of the ratchets were clamped tight.

"These two, as well as those two men from the Fourth Corps, take them all back!" said Fang Meng'ao. "The grain will be transported to the barracks tonight. We'll deliver the people and the grain to the five-member investigation group tomorrow."

CHAPTER 12

It was two o'clock in the morning. The telephone rang loudly on the bedside table of Du Wancheng, leader of the five-member group and general auditor of the Ministry of Finance.

Du woke up, and he groped around in the darkness for his glasses, only to lay his hands on the telephone. As soon he put it to his ear, he found himself bombarded by loud voices coming down the line.

The voices seemed to be yelling alternately: "This is the North China Headquarters for the Suppression of Communist Insurgency..."

"This is the Fourth Corps of the National Army..."

"Is that General Auditor Du of the Ministry of Finance?"

"Is that Chief Coordinator Du of the five-member group?"

"Commander-in-Chief Fu asked me to pass on a message to you that if the Ministry of Finance is not up to the task of managing the money, you really shouldn't come to Peking to interfere in our war efforts at the front! If you continue to mess around in military affairs in northern China, he'll give up his command position and make way for Minister Wang Yunwu..."

"The Fourth Corps strongly protests. Who is behind tonight's incident? Why did they send people to rob our military rations? Who authorised you? What the hell is your five-member group getting up to?"

Du Wancheng was perplexed. He put on his glasses and looked at the phone. It came into focus, but he remained unclear about the two voices he was hearing. He spoke loudly into the microphone: "Are you from the North China Headquarters for the Suppression of Communist Insurgency or the Fourth Corps? What's the matter with your telephone office? What are you talking about? State your issue clearly... I'll convene a meeting. My five-member group will hold a meeting immediately to investigate..."

Unable to stand the alternating bellow of the two voices, Du Wancheng put the phone down. He sat up in bed staring blankly into the darkness.

A few seconds later, he collected his thoughts and called the operator with shaking hands: "Internal line? Put me through to the room of Director Ma Linshen."

"I'm sorry, Director Ma's line is busy," the internal line operator replied.

Ma Linshen was also awakened by the sharp sound of the telephone ringing. On waking, he was halfway through a long snore, and he couldn't catch his breath. Still startled, he picked up the phone and found himself being yelled at by two voices simultaneously down the line.

The voices were still roaring at the same time: "What the hell are you people at the Citizens' Food-Distribution Committee up to? Communist troops are going to attack us in the outskirts of Peking. You sent someone to rob us of grain. Aren't you and your committee people acting out of greed? While our troops are preparing to fight a bloody battle with the Communist Army, you've taken the money from the Central Bank but you haven't bought the grain. Instead, you have someone rob us of our grain..."

Du Wancheng held the phone as sweat streamed down his face. "Operator, internal line, operator! Put me through to Director Wang Benquan's secretary."

"I'm sorry, his secretary's line is also busy."

Du Wancheng slammed down the phone, in the process knocking over the teacup on his bedside table.

Wang Benquan, secretary general of the Central Bank, leaned on the bed headboard and held the telephone in his hands.

Two voices were bellowing on the phone: "Did you loan the money from the Central Bank to the Citizens' Food-Distribution Committee? Why the hell did you instigate the students to surround us at the North China Headquarters for the Suppression of Communist Insurgency during the day and then rob the grain meant for the Fourth Corps at night?"

"Has the money from the Central Bank been allocated to the Material Supply Committee? The military provisions of the Fourth Corps are purchased by a fund specially approved by the president. How can the Citizens' Food-Distribution Committee take our military grain..."

With no time to clean up the mess on the bedside table, and without allowing the operator to speak, Du Wancheng shouted into the phone: "Connect me with the chief inspector's room! Connect me immediately! Put me through. I don't care if he's busy or not!"

The voice of the operator made him feel hopeful: "Mr Du, Mr Du, I'm putting you through to Mr Zeng..."

"Is that Chief Inspector Zeng? Chief Inspector Zeng..." Du Wancheng called out repeatedly.

Instead of a voice, though, all that could be heard down the line was the long tone of the line being disconnected. Du Wancheng was in such a state that he banged the phone hard: "Is that the internal line? Why does no one answer the phone in Chief Inspector Zeng's room?"

"I'm sorry, no one in the room is answering," said the operator.

Du Wancheng threw the phone aside.

A crescent moon shone down on a wood beside the road that led to Yenching University in the northwestern suburbs of Peking. A few lights from the Yenching campus shone out here and there.

On the side of a road, six bicycles were parked. The adjutant and four plainclothes soldiers from the Youth Army were on guard.

The wood by the road was made up of saplings that had grown

to the height of a man. With Zeng Keda walking in front and Liang Jinglun following him, the two went deep into the trees.

"When did He Xiaoyu meet Fang Meng'ao today?" Zeng Keda asked eagerly. "What did they share with each other? I must know the details now."

Liang Jinglun was taken aback and he stopped. Zeng Keda also stopped and turned around.

Standing close to one another in the dim light, the two could vaguely make out the other's features. Liang Jinglun saw the stern look on Zeng Keda's face, but he was unable to answer his question, so he asked back: "Is Fang Meng'ao acting abnormally, Comrade Keda?"

Zeng Keda's stern look turned into one of displeasure. He would not have Liang Jinglun answer his question with a question: "It is both abnormal and normal. Comrade Liang Jinglun, please answer my questions first."

Liang Jinglun was silent for a short while. Then he replied: "I haven't seen He Xiaoyu yet. I don't know anything about her visit to Fang Meng'ao. I can ask her when I get back."

"Your most important task is to keep a close watch on Fang Meng'ao's movements," said a serious-sounding Zeng Keda. "It's two-thirty in the morning. Didn't you arrange for Xie Mulan to take He Xiaoyu to meet Fang Meng'ao during the day? Why did you fail to locate He Xiaoyu in order for you to better understand Fang Meng'ao's situation as early as possible?"

Liang Jinglun's heart sank, yet he managed to explain the situation calmly: "Actually, I was waiting for her this evening at He Qicang's house. At eleven o'clock, I suddenly got a call from Yan Chunming from the Student Movement Committee of the Communist Party in Peking, saying he had to meet me to communicate some important instructions. Therefore, I didn't have the chance to ask He Xiaoyu for more information. Besides, I didn't know that Comrade Keda needs to know more about the meeting between He Xiaoyu and Fang Meng'ao."

Hearing these words, Zeng Keda relaxed a little. With a quick wave of the hand, he said: "Let's discuss the important instructions of the Communist Party."

The meeting room of the five-member group in Gu Weijun's residence in Peking was ablaze with light. Du Wancheng was in rather a spin about what to do without Zeng Keda. He raised his voice by an octave and shouted to the Youth Army officer in charge of security outside the door: "Keep looking! Get me Chief Inspector Zeng right away, and tell him we're waiting for him to attend the emergency meeting of the five-member group."

Four of the group had showed up. Ma Linshen and Wang Benquan were seated in their original chairs facing the door. They had turned as pale as death and were mute as fish. Xu Tieying had arrived from the Peking Police Bureau headquarters after receiving the phone call. He was still sitting to the right of Du Wancheng, but he appeared like an outsider and didn't say a word.

The seat that Zeng Keda had previously taken to the left of Du Wancheng was empty. In the absence of the person at the helm, Du Wancheng was worried.

The two parties involved in the conflict had also come, sitting opposite the group of five: Ma Hanshan on the left and Chief Qian of the Fourth Corps on the right.

Ma Hanshan put the bill of lading issued to the Peking Citizens' Food-Distribution Committee on the table in front of Du Wancheng. He did the same with Chief Qian's bill of lading issued to the Fourth Corps. Written in black and white with a red seal; clearly worded with accurate numbers and official seals!

Du Wancheng hated doing this kind of work, but he had no option but to compare the two bills for grain delivery. "Damn it! What on earth is the problem? The Central Commission on the Distribution of Citizens' Food and the Central Bank should know about these two bills, shouldn't they? Here are the bills of lading for grain delivery. You can see them for yourselves!"

Ma Linshen sat there unmoved with his eyes closed, as if he hadn't heard Du Wancheng's words.

Wang Benquan seemed ready to cooperate, if a little reluctantly. He sat back in his chair and spoke coldly: "The document for buying the grain was from the Peking Citizens' Food-Distribution Committee, while the document for retrieving the grain was from the Fourth Corps, and the grain was seized by the Economic Inspection Brigade of the Ministry of Defence. None of these three documents seem to have anything to do with us at the Central Bank. Mr Du simply assumed that the Central Bank was better informed about the matter. With that in mind, I don't think I need to read these two documents, otherwise people will jump to the conclusion that the Central Bank is cognisant of the internal arrangements. If we really need to see them, we will wait for Chief Inspector Zeng to come back and review them together."

Du Wancheng almost choked with anger, and the colour rushed to his cheeks. He could only look at Xu Tieying.

Xu Tieying, however, showed some respect. He smiled, picked up the bills of lading, one in each hand and compared them. Having done so, he put them back in front of Du Wancheng.

Du Wancheng glowered at Ma Linshen and Wang Benquan: "Commissioner Xu, you have seen the bills. Both the military provisions purchased by the Commission on Material Supplies and the rations bought for the Citizens' Food-Distribution Committee have actually been purchased from the same company! What's more, with the Central Bank's appropriations and borrowings, they refused to deliver the grain. This is an outrage! We need to investigate the matter thoroughly. What's your opinion, Director Xu?"

Xu Tieying replied in a cooperative manner: "Of course, such corruption will not be tolerated by party discipline or state laws. Mr Du, while the Ministry of Finance should check the loans and their accounts, we, at the Central Bureau of Investigation and Statistics and law enforcement, are ready to make arrests. After you're done with the investigation, I'll arrest whoever you charge." With these words, he cast a glance at Ma Hanshan.

After that murderous declaration and the threatening glance directed at him, Ma Hanshan understood what Xu Tieying was implying. He was dropping a hint he would be business-like if he refused to give out the twenty per cent of shares Hou Juntang formerly possessed.

Ma Hanshan did not dare show dissatisfaction, so he quickly returned a look of indifference to Xu Tieying. By now Xu Tieying had lowered his head and was studying the two bills.

Du Wancheng stared at Ma Hanshan and said: "Director Ma, the money loaned to you by the Peking branch of the Central Bank is to buy ten thousand tonnes of grain. How much have you bought and how much have you rationed? Where did you buy the nine thousand tonnes quite apart from the one thousand tonnes you have purchased already?"

Ma Hanshan's intention to orchestrate the confrontation tonight was to signal to Yangtze Construction Company and the powerful people behind him that he was not willing to be blamed solely if no more grain was delivered. Now, in terms of Du Wancheng's questions, he could answer them accurately, yet neither could he refuse to answer them. Therefore, he replied: "I'm not the only one in charge of the Peking Citizens' Food-Distribution Committee. To answer Mr Du's question, I'll need to check our accounts as well as the grain in stock."

"The Communists are going to attack us in Fangshan and Liangxiang!" barked Qian of the Fourth Corps, while slapping the table with the palm of his hand. "Will our brothers in the Fourth Corps only fight once you're done checking your damned accounts and stocks?"

"It's none of my business if you fight or not," retorted Ma Hanshan, also banging the table. "It was you who came to rob the rations purchased by the Citizens' Food-Distribution Committee tonight! If you've got the nerve, why not check with the Economic Inspection Brigade of the Ministry of Defence!"

"You want me to go? Are you kidding!" Qian stood up. "It was you who instigated the Economic Inspection Brigade to confront us at the railway station. It is you who sabotaged our war efforts at the front. Commander-in-Chief Fu and my superiors at the Fourth Corps will make a report to Nanking in due course. Ma Hanshan, you can't get away with this!" As he was speaking, Qian slapped the table again.

Ma Hanshan stood up quickly and said: "If the one thousand tonnes of grain we unloaded tonight are not distributed to the students tomorrow, they will surround the North China Headquarters for the Suppression of Communist Insurgency in protest. In that case, Commander-in-Chief Fu and the Fourth Corps, do not come to us for an explanation! Qian Yousheng, it's down to you to explain to them."

Du Wancheng was angry at the fact that the two had disrespectfully quarrelled before the five-member investigation group established by the central government. He also slapped the table: "This is ridiculous! This is absurd! Commissioner Xu, you are also acting as commander of the Garrison headquarters. I now authorise you in your capacity as head of the five-member group to make the arrest!"

Ma Hanshan and Qian stopped quarrelling, but they were not cowed. They both looked to Xu Tieying.

Ma Linshen, who had been silent all the while, then interjected: "Mr Du, I understand you've got a reason to say these angry words, but you'll come around when the problem is solved. Just now, you were shifting your responsibility to the Central Commission on the Distribution of Citizens' Food and the Central Bank. Now you call on Mr Xu to arrest people from the Peking Citizens' Food-Distribution Committee and the Fourth Corps. It's not that easy to arrest people these days."

Du Wancheng was so angry that he seemed at his wits' end. Unconsciously, he looked to his left and found that the chair was still empty, so he turned around and looked at Xu Tieying.

"Not necessarily." Xu Tieying's words were directed at Ma Linshen. He stood up and went on: "Hasn't Captain Fang made some arrests already? Those who should be arrested, must be arrested. Of course, just make sure we don't arrest innocent people. I think we must make more arrests as a result of these two bills of lading issued by Yangtze Construction. It was agreed that day by the five-member group to deliver a thousand tonnes of grain to the Citizens' Food-Distribution Committee. How come the seller company resold it to the Fourth Corps? Now the Fourth Corps puts the blame on us, and strangely, none of the five-member group dared to speak. It's not hard to deal with the matter, Mr Du. Tell Captain Fang to bring in the two detainees from that certain company. I'm sure they'll talk and implicate a few more people!"

Du Wancheng's eyes were glittering. Looking at Xu Tieying, he said: "Commissioner Xu, please ask Captain Fang to bring them here at once!"

"Captain Fang belongs to the Ministry of Defence," Xu Tieying replied. "Chief Inspector Zeng is supposed to give the order. But as a member of the group of five, I can do it on his behalf, except that when the two arrive, they have to be interrogated together with Chief Inspector Zeng."

He left his seat as he spoke and went to the special telephone next to the wall.

Ma Linshen and Wang Benquan looked at Xu Tieying as he walked past them from behind their chairs. Their eyes met as they were both acutely aware that they owned shares in the company. They had also understood by then that this person was determined to acquire Hou Juntang's shares. For that money, he was prepared to work against them both.

Ma Hanshan understood this better than the others. But at this time, he did not know whether it was something to worry about or to cheer. Perhaps the shares should have been given up long ago. Otherwise, it would be collective suicide.

Xu Tieying picked up the phone and said: "Please put me through to Deputy Commissioner Fang Mengwei."

All eyes were on him, and at the phone he was holding to his ear.

"Deputy Commissioner Fang?" said Xu Tieying in a loud voice. "Get a team of officers to find Captain Fang of the Economic Inspection Brigade. Bring in the two people he arrested who were escorting the grain train tonight. Hand them in to the five-member group meeting. Right away!"

Du Wancheng's spirits rose and he shouted to the door: "Any luck with Chief Inspector Zeng of the Ministry of Defence? How long will you keep us waiting?"

Liang Jinglun and Zeng Keda were in the woods beside the road that led to Yenching University.

"There are things that neither you nor I can understand. It is fine if you don't understand something, the thing is you must speak up."

After hearing Liang Jinglun's report, Zeng Keda keenly felt he was not in the right state of mind. Liang expressed a willingness to cooperate fully with his in-depth investigation of Fang Meng'ao when they last met, but now he wavered. This was absolutely not allowed.

"The situation is changing faster and in a more complicated manner than you or I could have anticipated. However, you must send He Xiaoyu to approach Fang Meng'ao about whether the instructions of the Urban Works Department of the CPC Peking chapter are real or not, or even if they are merely testing you."

Liang Jinglun realised that Zeng Keda was not satisfied, or to be more precise, he anticipated that he might invite trouble on himself if he were to express his own ideas tonight. But he believed he should speak up: "Comrade Keda, I fully understand that you shoulder great responsibility, in particular to Comrade Jianfeng, so you must verify Fang Meng'ao's true identity. However, I'm afraid I can't help you with it."

"Do you mean we don't need to verify Fang Meng'ao's identity?" Zeng Keda watched him closely, his eyes glittering with disbelief, and his tone became sterner. "Tell me why. Give me your reasons."

After a brief silence, Liang Jinglun answered: "Based on my analysis of what I reported to you just a moment ago, the Urban Works Department of the CPC Peking chapter has been way ahead of us in their work on Fang Meng'ao."

Zeng Keda was startled at first, followed by an even greater sense of dissatisfaction.

"Is that based on your analysis or your personal observation?"

"My observation is based on my analysis," Liang Jinglun answered. "Yan Chunming, head of the CPC's Student Movement Committee, proposed to the Urban Works Department how to recruit Fang Meng'ao the day before yesterday. Surprisingly, he was criticised for the proposal. However, he told me that the Urban Works Department changed its mind and gave him the green light. Furthermore, it cited our proposal as proactive and significant. It's weird to see the abrupt change."

"Anyone can change an existing decision," said Zeng Keda. "The CPC is no exception. How come you know that it wasn't someone at a higher level who agreed to the proposal after the CPC's Urban Works Department in Peking had requested instructions from their superiors?"

"No," said Liang Jinglun, "they have just communicated to us the

Communist Party's Sixth of July Instruction, which clearly stipulates that no special party members shall be recruited. One day later, however, they agreed to our proposal for the recruitment of special party members. This is a clear violation of the Sixth of July Instruction. No one at the top dares to change this decision, unless it's Zhou Enlai or Peng Zhen! But within just one day, it was impossible for anyone in Peking's Urban Works Department to ask Zhou Enlai or Peng Zhen for instructions face to face."

Zeng Keda had no reason to reject Liang Jinglun's analysis, but he pressed hard with the following: "In your judgment, why did the CPC's Peking Urban Works Department reach a different decision within such a short time?"

"Two reasons," Liang Jinglun replied heavily. "First, the Communists' Urban Works Department in Peking suspected me."

Liang Jinglun looked at Zeng Keda, hoping he would show concern and care on behalf of the Iron and Blood Congress, because the issue was related to his own safety.

Yet Zeng Keda showed little concern. He asked: "What about the second reason?" Liang Jinglun was so bitterly disappointed that he felt as if a cold wind had pierced his chest and risen to his forehead.

He looked up at the crescent moon and controlled himself so he could continue in a flat voice: "The second reason is that Fang Meng'ao has long been a special member of the CPC. Just because they suspected me, they had to agree with my proposal and let me carry out the so-called task of recruiting Fang Meng'ao. The idea is to use my investigation to prove to you that Fang Meng'ao is not a member of the Communist Party."

"What do you mean by 'you'?" Zeng Keda turned more severe. "Does this 'you' not include you? Comrade Liang Jinglun, your explanation betrays your thoughts. The Communist Party wants to use your investigation to prove that Fang Meng'ao is not one of them. Why can't you prove otherwise?"

"No, I can't," replied Liang Jinglun. "As long as the Communist Party suspects me, a series of measures will be put in place to protect Fang Meng'ao. As a result, it will be difficult for me to gather any evidence to prove to Comrade Jianfeng that Fang Meng'ao is a member of the Communist Party. If, on the other hand, the Urban Works Department of the Communist Party's Peking chapter finds out that I am not a member of the Communist Party, it will be difficult for me to accomplish the task set me by Comrade Jianfeng, that is to use He Qicang to carry out the currency system reform, and that of fighting corruption within the party-state."

"Don't you believe that we will also take measures to protect you? And ultimately Fang Meng'ao is the one to be exposed, not you!"

Zeng Keda was incensed by Liang Jinglun for the way he continued to look at the moon, and for the fact that he was using Comrade Jianfeng against himself. "Comrade Liang Jinglun, please look at me when you speak!"

Liang Jinglun was forced to turn his head but his voice was still calm: "It's not a question of whether I believe or not. Comrade Keda, you can't protect me. No one can protect me. I don't need any protection."

Liang Jinglun's response was so beyond Zeng Keda's expectation it was almost intolerable. No one should be possessed by such pessimism and loneliness having been chosen by the Iron and Blood Congress and Comrade Jianfeng. This is equivocation, fear and selfishness! But he failed to examine his own errors. The fact that he forced Liang Jinglun to prove that Fang Meng'ao was a member of the Communist Party would prove to be his greatest folly.

Zeng Keda realised that he had to solve Liang Jinglun's problems tonight. After all, he needed to convince himself and find out that Fang Meng'ao was a member of the Communist Party. He had to rely on Liang to carry it out. Besides, it was Comrade Jianfeng's idea to use Liang's CPC identity to recruit economists to contribute to the currency system reform, and Liang's role in that regard should not be affected.

With that in mind, he quickly changed subject and appealed directly to his heart: "You've been working for the Communists for several years. Have you ever admired any one of them?"

Liang Jinglun understood that this line of questioning was less a reflection of Zeng Keda's strong dissatisfaction, but more an ongoing political assessment of a member of the Iron and Blood Congress.

But Liang Jinglun refused to be forced to carry out a task unwillingly because of his superior's attitude. He responded: "I don't know why Comrade Keda asks a question like this. My ideals and the principles I choose to pursue will not allow me to admire any Communists."

"It's an ideal state of mind to admire the enemy!" Zeng Keda said sternly. "Comrade Liang Jinglun, both Comrade Jianfeng and our organisation agree that you are a talented and capable comrade. But you also have fatal weaknesses."

"Comrade Keda, can you please give me some examples..."

"For example, you've just said you do not admire any Communists!" Zeng Keda said forcefully.

"It is my belief..."

"It's nothing to do with your belief!" said Zeng Keda, gruffly interrupting him once more. "Comrade Jianfeng said on multiple occasions that he admired some people in the Communist Party for their benevolence and ability. More than once, he has argued that we need to learn from the Communist Party in terms of work methodology. Does that have anything to do with faith?"

Liang Jinglun was amazed.

Seeing him silenced, Zeng Keda quickly went on: "Let me share with you something about a Communist Party member whom I do admire. His job is a bit similar to yours. Do you want to hear?"

In the name of the Ministry of Defence, Fang Meng'ao had instructed the twenty members of the Economic Inspection Brigade to each command a group of stevedores. The engineers of the Fourth Corps and the stevedores from the Peking Citizens' Food-Distribution Committee had already dispatched more than half of the one thousand tonnes of grain with great efficiency. There were a few trucks left on the Peking railway station platform, and the stevedores were busy loading the remaining grain onto the lorries.

As soon as Fang Mengwei led a team of police officers onto the platform, he saw two familiar faces shouting in his direction. "Deputy Commissioner Fang!" they called out. Fang Mengwei was startled.

The first face belonged to the Special Operations Battalion commander of the Fourth Corps of the National Army, with one hand cuffed to his captain and the other attached to an iron fence. The other person who had called out his name was the head of the Peking station of the Juntong, who was handcuffed to the same iron fence.

Fang Mengwei sized up the situation and went up to them: "Don't say anything. I'll talk to Captain Fang. You should be released soon."

"Is that all you're going to do?" cried out the woman locked to a fence not far away. "Take him to Nanking. We will only allow our handcuffs to be unlocked if the guy who had us cuffed in the first place is executed."

Fang Mengwei's face sank, and he turned to look at the woman and the man who were handcuffed there.

"Shut up!" said the deputy director called Kung, who appeared more sensible. Turning to Fang Mengwei, he asked: "Are you from the Peking Police Bureau? Can I trouble you to unlock us first so we don't need to petition the higher-ups?"

"Who are they?" Fang Mengwei asked the head of the Juntong operation group.

"They're from Yangtze Construction Company," he replied. "Goddam it! They make all the money and they also make us wear handcuffs. This is ridiculous!"

Fang Mengwei tried to comfort him. "OK, I understand your grievances," he said, not looking at the man or woman again. Then he asked: "Where is Captain Fang?"

The head of the Juntong's operation team pointed to where Fang Meng'ao was standing. Fang Mengwei looked in that direction and saw Fang Meng'ao standing on top of some grain piled up on a truck. He was receiving a bag of grain the stevedore had thrown to him. He laid the bag on top of the pile.

Fang Mengwei sighed and walked over to his big brother's lorry.

In the woods beside the road that led to Yenching University, Zeng Keda continued to grill Liang Jinglun.

"Comrade Liang Jinglun, the Communist Party member I'm referring to is called Lin Dawei. I wonder if you admire him."

Liang Jinglun kept his head down and listened in silence. Then he raised his head and looked at Zeng Keda. "I still don't understand why Comrade Keda wants me to admire him."

"Loyalty! Absolute loyalty to his own organisation!" said an enraged Zeng Keda. "A Communist agent, who has done such an important job for the Communist Party, didn't want to get paid a penny by the party in ten years, and has never proposed any protection from his organisation! He risked his life sending secret military information to his party. At one point, he had to expose himself at the cost of his own life and he went to his death unflinchingly. Apart from his beliefs, isn't this man's loyalty to his organisation worthy of your admiration?"

How could he use the loyalty of a Communist Party member to accuse me of disloyalty! Zeng Keda's comparison sent a chill to Liang Jinglun's heart. He knew that he could no longer refuse the task assigned to him on behalf of his superior in the organisation, but he would never accept the evaluation of Zeng Keda against his will.

"Comrade Keda, I accept the task assigned to me by the organisation. I will resolutely implement it and carry it out according to the letter. As for the issues we just discussed, I'd like to explain my views at another time. Since I've decided to throw in my lot with the Kuomintang, I will not admire any member of the Communist Party."

It was Zeng Keda's turn to be stunned.

"Do you have any other instructions, Comrade Keda?" Liang Jinglun continued. "If not, I'll go to see He Xiaoyu immediately to implement your decision, and tell her to further engage Fang Meng'ao and recruit him."

Having said these words, he didn't wait for Zeng Keda's reply. Instead, wearing a traditional Chinese long gown, Liang Jinglun raised his hand and gave Zeng Keda a military salute.

Zeng Keda was stunned once more. While he was still deciding whether to return the salute or not, Liang Jinglun had turned around and walked out of the trees in the direction of the weak lights of Yenching University.

Zeng Keda walked to the bicycles parked beside the road. The cloth shoes he was wearing had collected mud on the soles, so his footsteps echoed on the ground, reflecting a feeling of intolerance down deep in his heart. He tried to imitate Comrade Jianfeng in every aspect, but he never succeeded.

On the freight platform of Peking railway station, Fang Mengwei had been standing beside a truck for the past ten minutes.

His big brother had seen him from on top of the grain sacks, but he was still there piling them up. It wasn't until the last sack was put in place that he jumped down. Fang Mengwei reached out his hand to help cushion Fang Meng'ao as he leapt down from the truck.

"What are you doing here?" Fang Meng'ao asked. "I was expecting Chief Inspector Zeng and Commissioner Xu. Take your team back!"

"The five-member group told me to come," Fang Mengwei replied. "Brother, you have done everything right, but you've never worked in the police force so you've got no idea how to handle this sort of thing."

Fang Meng'ao's eyes narrowed and a smile appeared at the corner of his mouth. "Teach me."

"That's not what I mean," said Fang Mengwei. "First, you must release the people of the Fourth Corps as well as those of the Juntong. In fact, the group of five are now waiting for me to take back the pair from Yangtze Construction for interrogation. Let's deal with things on a case-by-case basis. Don't involve too many people."

"Did they ask you to bring back the two from Yangtze Construction?"

"The order I received was to take them to the five-member group at once."

Fang Meng'ao looked at his younger brother and said: "Come here."

Although they were already close, Fang Mengwei moved closer.

Fang Meng'ao whispered in his ear: "Do those company employees have any working relationship with the Peking branch of the Central Bank?"

Fang Mengwei was startled and understood the implication of the question.

"It can't possibly be so," Fang Meng'ao continued. "Do they have any relationship with the governor of the Peking branch?"

Fang Mengwei suddenly felt an inexplicable agony. Who was the governor of the Peking branch? Was he not their own father? He knew that his big brother did not recognise his father, but he could not understand why he would refer to him like this.

Fang Meng'ao didn't care what he felt at that moment. "There are so many deputy commissioners in the Peking Police Bureau headquarters. Why doesn't Xu Tieying order them to bring the pair back? Mengwei, you're a police officer. You should know how to deal with the situation. But you didn't because if you did, you wouldn't have accepted the task. I'm free to dissociate myself from the father figure who is governor of Peking branch, while you can't. If you can't, don't come to the railway station. Understand?"

Fang Mengwei now realised that his big brother was still the kind-hearted and benevolent person he had always known. He was just like he had been ten years before, standing firm and tall like a large tree protecting him. He had the vision to accomplish things. He was always humbled by the fact that he himself fell short in terms of these virtues. He stood there, stunned.

"Now that you are here, you shall listen to me," said Fang Meng'ao. "I'll leave behind those Fourth Corps and Juntong people who have been captured. I'll leave them with you. In addition, make sure to ship the grain back to my barracks, every bag. You can't afford to miss a single one!"

"Yes, Big Brother," Fang Mengwei replied.

Fang Meng'ao announced in a loud voice: "Now, all of you with the Inspection Brigade, follow Deputy Commissioner Fang Mengwei's command. Ship all the grain to my barracks. Shao Yuangang and Guo Jinyang, come with me. Escort the two from Yangtze Construction to where the five-member group are waiting."

Throughout the night, Fang Buting remained motionless, sitting in front of the balcony of his office, looking out of the window. Meanwhile, Xie Peidong was sitting at the large desk answering calls from different organisations and individuals. Fang Buting did not take any calls or make any comment. Xie was left to handle all inquiries, and he bore the brunt of the accusations. To every call, he responded by saying: "The governor is out on business."

"General Manager Kung, we are equally concerned." It was the third time Xie Peidong had received a call from him. "I am telling you for the third time, our governor has been out since midnight. Of course, our governor has to act given that it's such a major incident... There should be results when he comes back."

The tone of voice at the other end was becoming increasingly strained. It was already the small hours of the morning, and even Fang Buting, who was sitting some distance away near the window, could hear the young man's voice at the other end.

"What do you mean by waiting for him to come back? It's his scoundrel of a son who created such a fucking mess! Ten minutes, I'll give you ten minutes to get hold of Fang Buting and call me back. It's up to him to sort out this mess created by his bastard son. If not, he won't be governor tomorrow!"

Fang Buting rose to his feet and moved quickly to the phone.

Xie Peidong covered the speaker and said: "Governor, please, you don't want to bother yourself arguing with the likes of him..."

"Give it to me!" Fang Buting had never been so severe in front of Xie Peidong. "Give me the phone!"

Xie Peidong handed the phone over.

"Did you hear what I said?" Mr Kung at the other end was still roaring.

"I heard it!" Fang Buting shouted back. "I don't want to hear any more of your impudent remarks!"

Kung was silent for several seconds.

"Did you hear what I said?" Fang Buting's voice was stern. "Answer me!"

"Is that Governor Fang?" The caller sounded more polite than he was with Xie Peidong. "Aren't you away on business?"

"Where would I go?" Fang Buting retorted. "This is the Peking branch of the Central Bank, it is where my office is located. If I'm not here, where else would I be?"

"Then why didn't you answer my previous calls?" General Manager Kung said down the line. "Governor Fang, your son arrested my man and withheld our company's grain, and you didn't take my call. What the hell are you doing anyway?"

"Do you really want to know?" Fang Buting replied. "Well, let me tell you. It was Fang Meng'ao, captain of the Economic Inspection Brigade of the Ministry of Defence, not Fang Buting's bastard son! If you want him to release your people and return the grain, you can always go to your father or your uncle for help and tell them to talk to the director-general of the Bureau of Reserve Cadres and the president of the Iron and Blood Congress, personally approved by the president! I dare you to go to them for help! This is my answer to your first question. Second, I'm governor of the Peking branch officially appointed by the Central Bank. I'm not some departmental account manager of Yangtze Construction Company. I can answer if I choose, but I don't have to. Third, you just told me that I would be dismissed from my office as governor tomorrow. I will tell you that you have taken so much in the way of loans and appropriations from the Central Bank and tens of millions of dollars from its Peking branch. Now, I don't want to continue to see my bank mired in debt. Tomorrow, I'll share information with Central Bank Governor Liu Gongyun in Nanking. I'll resign so that he can wipe your arse!"

Kung was silenced. Xie Peidong looked admiringly at Fang Buting who had vented his spite on Kung.

"Now, are there any other questions?" Fang Buting asked. In the absence of a reply, he continued: "If not, Fang Buting, governor of the Peking branch of the Central Bank, will hang up."

"Governor Fang!" It was impossible to tell whether the voice at the other end was angry or deflated. "You'll be held accountable for what you've just said."

"Who am I supposed to be responsible to?" Fang Buting snapped. "I'm not obligated to be responsible for the actions of someone's bastard son!"

With a loud click, Fang Buting ended the call. After standing by the telephone for a while, he turned around and looked at Xie Peidong, his eyes full of sadness.

"Peidong, do you think the Republic of China can be saved?"

"Governor, the Republic of China is not something you can save. Think about our family. According to Mengwei, Meng'ao has escorted two people from Yangtze Construction to the five-member group. I expect Nanking will start to interfere in the morning. If the Soong and Kung families really get involved, the group of five won't be able to stand up to it any longer. Besides, they won't choose to resist. In the end, Meng'ao will be held responsible for the mess. Of course, the Bureau of Reserve Cadres will support him. But really, he'll end up being just a tool in this internal strife."

"He'll be cannon fodder in the fight." Fang Buting's worries were surging out like a tidal wave. "What I worry about most is the other person..."

Xie Peidong just looked at him and waited for him to continue.

"Did Cui Zhongshi meet Meng'ao today?"

Fang Buting stared at Xie Peidong.

"I couldn't very well raise the issue if the governor didn't ask me," said Xie Peidong.

"Did they meet with each other anyway?"

"No, they didn't. But Mengwei went to see Cui Zhongshi today. He had a showdown with him and told him not to meet Meng'ao again."

"Why did you get Mengwei involved in this?" Fang Buting's face took on a ghastly expression. "If Cui Zhongshi really is a member of the Communist Party, Mengwei is going to let him go, isn't he? I've already got one son involved in this mess, I can't risk the life of the other! Why are you hiding such an important matter from me?"

Xie Peidong bowed his head and kept silent for a while, before looking up at Fang Buting. "I'd love Mengwei to tell you in person when he comes back tomorrow. My brother-in-law, I am not a good uncle, am I?"

Unexpectedly, Fang Buting reached out and took Xie Peidong's hands. "Both my two sons are your sons. You are not just their uncle. For my part, I've always treated Mulan as a daughter, not a niece. Peidong, the current situation won't last for ever. I've spent half my lifetime working for the government of the Republic of China and I'm worthy of them. You must help me at this critical moment. Only you can help me."

"Don't say 'help'," said Xie Peidong. "My dear brother-in-law, our two families are already united as one. Regarding the children, just tell me what to do."

"Let's keep things separate. It's not just issues concerning the children, but also those of the bank. You concentrate on Cui Zhongshi. The most important thing is to take over all the accounts he is in charge of and conduct a thorough check of everything. I'm concerned that if he really is a member of the Communist Party, he will expose the corruption cases within the Kuomintang to the general public. What I fear most is the fact that he's also in charge of bank incomes and loans. He's capable of getting the money into the hands of the Communist Party. If that happens, he will certainly choose to escape, and Meng'ao may become a scapegoat."

Xie Peidong was shocked. "If that happens, I will go to check out Cui Zhongshi at his house now. I can certainly bring him back to the bank and ask him to hand over all the accounts."

"No need to rush at this hour of the day," said Fang Buting. "It's gone three o'clock. Let's see what the results will be at the five-member group meeting later in the morning. Then you can go to Cui Zhongshi's house, and I'll visit He Qicang. In any case, no matter how much it costs, I'll ask him to introduce me to Ambassador John Leighton Stuart and by working the oracle I'll be able to make friends with him. Meanwhile, I'll also talk to Ambassador Gu Weijun, in the hope that he'll give Meng'ao the position of military attaché at the Chinese Embassy in Washington, which may allow him to go to America as soon as possible."

"Will Vice-Chancellor He help you?" asked Xie Peidong.

"Ten years ago, there was an agreement between our two families. Meng'ao's mother and Xiaoyu's mother agreed that they would arrange for Meng'ao to marry Xiaoyu when the two children grew up. These days, I think they have demonstrated quite a lot of affection for each other. Vice-Chancellor He will surely work on Ambassador Stuart, for his daughter's benefit."

Xie Peidong looked relieved and said: "I've also checked with Mulan who told me that Xiaoyu was very pleasantly impressed with Meng'ao. Governor, it's going to be a workable plan."

Liang Jinglun quietly opened the gate and entered He Qicang's courtyard residence in Yannan Garden. As he was about to enter the living room, he stopped. He was poised to knock on the door when his hand froze. A thin ray of light was seeping through a crack in the door. He Xiaoyu had left the door open for him! Liang Jinglun, who told her to wait for him, was now scared at the idea that she would actually be waiting for him.

With Zeng Keda pressing him to verify that Fang Meng'ao was a member of the Communist Party, he also found that Yan Chunming had unexpectedly agreed on behalf of the Urban Works Department of the Peking chapter of the CPC that he would recruit Fang Meng'ao. His experience told him he was caught in the middle of a most complicated game between the Kuomintang and the Communists. Unfortunately, He Xiaoyu had to navigate her way through this dangerous situation. He had this vague feeling that if he pushed open the door, he was likely to lose He Xiaoyu and would prove unworthy of his mentor.

Liang Jinglun reached out and grasped the handle of the door. He did his best to open the door slowly and lightly so as not to awaken anyone in the house. It opened without any noise, just wide enough to let himself in.

He Xiaoyu was asleep in the living room, lying on an arm of the sofa with her head resting on her arms. She was sound asleep, unobserved by anyone.

Liang Jinglun stood quietly, not daring to take another step forward. The world would be a wonderful place to live in if only he could keep her sleeping like that, or without letting her accept the mission he himself was unwilling to accept.

He wanted to slip out slowly. With an eye on the still sleeping

He Xiaoyu, he tiptoed to the door. But when he realised he might wake her up, he stopped at once.

He Xiaoyu was still sleeping soundly. Liang Jinglun saw a plate containing two pieces of bread that had been fried and steamed on the tea table in front of the sofa and a cup of milk that was supplied each day for He Qicang. This was obviously what He Xiaoyu had made for herself. Two stern faces appeared in Liang Jinglun's mind, one belonging to Zeng Keda, the other to Yan Chunming.

He inched towards the tea table opposite He Xiaoyu, and sat down on the chair that she normally used. He reached out and picked up one of the golden steamed breads. It smelt delicious and he was starving. Like most residents of Peking, he had been hungry for quite a while. He stopped to look at He Xiaoyu who was still sound asleep when he was about to put the steamed bread into his mouth.

He reckoned that eating the crispy steamed bread might wake her up, so he dunked the bread into the cup of milk. Once it had become soft, he took a bite. Then he closed his eyes and let it dissolve in his mouth. He swallowed it contentedly, making no sound.

He Xiaoyu's eyes opened slowly, but her body did not move. Though her head was still half buried in her arm, she saw Liang Jinglun sitting there with the small piece of moist bread in his hand.

When Liang Jinglun finally finished the bread, he was startled to see another piece being offered to him! He Xiaoyu was looking at him, smiling.

"Did I wake you up?" Liang Jinglun asked with a shy look that was quite rare for him. "How long have you been watching me?"

"What kind of talk is that? You were peeping at me, weren't you?" He Xiaoyu still held out the piece of steamed bread. "Dad has a monthly allocation of just half a *jin* of oil. You're too wasteful. It's already been fried, there's no need to dip it in milk."

"That's enough. Let's keep it for Professor He's breakfast." Liang Jinglun felt sorry for not having asked He Xiaoyu if she wanted some. "It's midnight, you must be hungry..."

He Xiaoyu stood there and asked softly: "Professor Liang, is there such a notion in philosophy as the three difficult choices?"

"No," said Liang Jinglun. "There are only two difficult choices."

He Xiaoyu smiled. "A starving father, plus a starving professor. I'm already in a dilemma. You can't give me a trilemma, can you?" As she spoke, she picked up the leftovers and put them in the cupboard.

"Yes, for thousands of years, Chinese women never said they were hungry," sighed Liang Jinglun with emotion.

Sometimes a single, sincere sigh is enough to break the heart and depress the mind. Fortunately, He Xiaoyu swallowed the profound anguish that was welling up in her heart as she stood with her back to Liang Jinglun. As a child, she was precocious and sensible because she wanted to become something of a mother figure for her father, which deprived her of the right to cry as a girl. Since the age of thirteen, she never cried in front of her father, and over time, she never cried in front of anyone.

Liang Jinglun felt a peculiar sensation of alienation in her company, but he did not dare ask her. He could only look at her back in silence.

He Xiaoyu calmed down and turned around. "Are you done with your lament, sir?" she asked with a forced smile that no one could see. "I'll make a wild guess regarding where the great lament comes from, sir. Would that be OK?"

He Xiaoyu deliberately touched upon the subject that Liang Jinglun was most afraid of. He wanted to avoid the subject because he was still immersed in his own feelings. He said with a forced smile: "It's just a lament. It's not important, forget it."

"I didn't say that you're great. I wanted to guess who the great person was and which great work inspired you to sigh such a great sigh today."

"Well, do as you wish."

He Xiaoyu pretended to think, and then asked: "Have you been learning the script of *New Year's Sacrifice* for the student drama club? Were you moved again by the Lu Xun story?"

Liang Jinglun clammed up, staring at He Xiaoyu and waiting for her to answer. The He Xiaoyu before him now was transformed into the He Xiaoyu of that night when he assigned her to contact Fang Meng'ao: "If Fang Meng'ao has fallen in love with me, what am I to do?" Then she turned around and went upstairs.

As if he was hallucinating, Liang Jinglun visualised He Xiaoyu, who was standing in front of him, turn around and walk upstairs without looking back, the way she did that very night.

Liang Jinglun's eyes suddenly turned to the stairs! He Xiaoyu followed by turning to look in the same direction.

The stairs leading to the first floor were empty, and there was no sound. He Xiaoyu had never seen Liang Jinglun's eyes so empty. "Hey!" she called gently.

Liang Jinglun turned around, and his vacant eyes shone with light again.

He Xiaoyu, who was still standing before him, had seen the complicated change in Liang Jinglun's appearance and manner, and she asked: "What did you just see?"

In those few seconds, Liang Jinglun had decided to keep He Xiaoyu! While assigning her the task of engaging and recruiting Fang Meng'ao, he should keep her heart!

He approached He Xiaoyu and whispered: "Didn't you see someone walking upstairs just now?"

"Who was it? What did he look like?"

Liang Jinglun put his other arm around her and whispered: "No, it was a woman, wearing a cardigan with a bun at the back of her head, carrying a basket and a walking stick..."

"Have you been hallucinating?" asked He Xiaoyu, instinctively grasping his hand.

"It was no illusion, it was a real person."

"Was it Mrs Li?" He Xiaoyu said softly. "She went back home earlier. She is not like the one you described..."

"It wasn't Mrs Li, it was someone else," Liang Jinglun whispered. "I know, and you do, too."

"Who was it?"

"Sister Xianglin!"

He Xiaoyu released her grip and made to break loose from Liang Jinglun's embracing hand, but she held back and remained silent.

A profound sense of loneliness became apparent in Liang Jinglun's eyes. He said softly: "I'm answering the question you were trying to answer. You were right. I was moved by Mr Lu Xun and his sister Xianglin, the character he portrayed. Sorry to have scared you."

"I'm not afraid at all," said He Xiaoyu. "It's just a little odd. How could you be so moved by Sister Xianglin today?"

Liang Jinglun sighed deeply. "She's such a good woman, who unfortunately falls in love with two good men and is unfortunately loved back by two good men. In the end, the people she loves and the people who love her, the two good men in her heart, turn into the people who saw her in half..."

"What do you want to say?" asked He Xiaoyu, finally wrenching herself from Liang Jinglun's grasp. "Didn't you tell me to wait for you? Are we going to talk about engaging Fang Meng'ao?"

Liang Jinglun became silent again, intentionally so. Clearly, he wanted to give He Xiaoyu the impression he was unwilling to talk about the subject.

He Xiaoyu didn't like the silence: "I went to see Fang Meng'ao at the family mansion today."

"Will it be easy to engage and recruit him?"

"I don't know," said He Xiaoyu, looking into his eyes. "He's hard to engage, and even harder to communicate with."

"I'm asking if he's recruitable?"

"Yes, he is."

"But didn't you say it's hard to engage and communicate with him?"

"Well, that's because I didn't try hard enough previously."

Liang Jinglun tried to remain calm. "How are you going to engage and communicate with him to achieve your goal?"

He Xiaoyu turned around and looked up at her father's room on the first floor and then at Liang Jinglun, her eyes glittering. "I want to know who you represent in assigning me to engage Fang Meng'ao... You don't have to tell me."

Liang Jinglun just looked at her.

He Xiaoyu lowered her voice: "I'll help you out. You don't have to nod or shake your head. Just silence."

Having regarded her for a long while, Liang Jinglun nodded in approval.

"Besides being with the Students' Union, have you been sent by the Communist Party?"

Liang Jinglun did not nod or shake his head, but slowly

extended his hands to He Xiaoyu. He Xiaoyu gave her hands to Liang Jinglun.

"For those who have long suffered cold and hunger." Liang Jinglun's voice contained a touch of sorrow. "I'll answer you like this, if that's OK with you?"

He Xiaoyu's eyes sparkled with tears. "For those who have long suffered cold and hunger, I'm going to work on Fang Meng'ao."

CHAPTER 13

Seeing Fang Meng'ao enter the conference room, Du Wancheng took the lead in standing up, his eyes full of concern. Xu Tieying stood up next out of good manners. Ma Linshen and Wang Benquan also rose but they were more concerned about the two people about to enter the room. The other two individuals who seemed to have no alternative but to rise to their feet were Ma Hanshan, who was sitting to the left of the entrance, and Qian Yousheng on the other side.

"Thanks, you've had a long night. Where are the two people you arrested?" Du Wancheng asked politely, looking at Fang Meng'ao who was standing in the doorway opposite the long conference table.

Fang Meng'ao obviously had a favourable impression of Du Wancheng. He saluted him and said: "I brought them with me." He ordered the two pilots outside the door to escort them in. Then he walked to his seat under the portrait of Dr Sun Yat-sen at the head of the conference table and remained standing.

All eyes were on the door. Shao Yuangang and Guo Jinyang walked Kung and the woman to the meeting table opposite Du Wancheng, and then they withdrew.

Kung and the woman were handcuffed together. With a clang, the key to unlock the handcuffs was thrown on the table right before the deputy director and the woman. After throwing the key on the table, Fang Meng'ao remained standing in front of the chair under Dr Sun Yat-sen's portrait.

"I'm going to die!" said the woman, who had been grumbling all the way to the conference room, and was now alarmed to see Fang Meng'ao toss the key at them in front of so many people. Her complaining intensified as she was taken inside the conference room.

"Shut up!" said Deputy Director Kung as his eyes swept across the four people sitting across the table. Kung knew two of them: Wang Benquan standing on the left, and Ma Linshen to the right. The two exchanged ambiguous glances.

Obviously, he had never met Xu Tieying and Kung could only guess from his police uniform that he was the new commissioner of the Peking Police Bureau transferred from the Central Bureau of Investigation and Statistics, known as the Zhongtong.

Kung's eyes finally fixed on Du Wancheng, who was sitting opposite him. He had heard that he was the chief auditor of the Ministry of Finance and head of the five-member group.

"Captain Fang, please take a seat. Everyone, please be seated," said Du Wancheng.

Fang Meng'ao sat down and said to Kung: "Unlock the handcuffs and sit down to answer our questions."

Kung dragged the woman with him to their seats, but he didn't look at the key in front of him. Suddenly he asked Du Wancheng: "Which of you is from the Ministry of Defence? Who's in charge of the Economic Inspection Brigade?"

Seeing that Kung didn't want to unlock the handcuffs, Du Wancheng was surprised, especially when Kung enquired about the ministry and the brigade. So he asked him: "What do you mean?"

"Whichever department handcuffed us must unlock us," said Kung, closing his eyes. "Furthermore, I will only talk when all of the five members are present."

"This is outrageous!" roared Du Wancheng as he stood up again.

However, none of the other three members of the five-member group responded. Ma Linshen and Wang Benquan were still looking out of the door. Even Xu Tieying was no longer cooperating. He sat there, eyes dim with sleep.

Du Wancheng had to turn to Fang Meng'ao for help. Fang stood up and walked to Kung, as the others began to get nervous. They all looked at him.

Fang Meng'ao picked up the key from the conference table and called out: "Guo Jinyang!"

"Yes sir!" Guo Jinyang entered the room quickly and caught the key thrown to him by Fang Meng'ao.

"Take this and throw it in the garden," said Fang Meng'ao. "The farther, the better."

"Yes sir!" Guo Jinyang took the key and walked out.

The woman opened her eyes, as did Kung. But Fang Meng'ao ignored them. Smiling, he went back to his seat and said to Du Wancheng still standing there: "Please take a seat, Mr Du. It was I who handcuffed them. Now, without a key, no one can unlock them. Let them remain handcuffed forever. What do you think?"

Although he despised ruffians such as Kung, Du Wancheng was not used to Fang Meng'ao's straightforward and unvarnished way of doing things. He smiled bitterly and had to sit down.

"You stupid idiot!" the enraged woman said in Shanghai dialect, referring to Fang Meng'ao.

"Guards!" Fang Meng'ao called out to the door as he sat down, having fully understood what the woman had just said.

Guo Jinyang and Shao Yuangang came in.

"Listen," said Fang Meng'ao, "whoever curses next, carry them out immediately and throw them into the garden pond!"

"Yes sir, yes!" Guo Jinyang and Shao Yuangang replied, clearly prepared to carry out the instruction.

The woman was now afraid to utter a word, but Kung's face paled with rage and he was blinking rapidly. Both Wang Benquan and Ma Linshen shook their heads. A hidden smile trembled on Xu Tieying's lips, but he looked away at Ma Hanshan rather than at the raving woman.

Ma Hanshan seemed to know that the problem might escalate today and that Kung was likely to petition higher authorities. If that happened, it would be hard to conclude matters. Besides, he found that Xu Tieying was smiling at him discreetly. He moved his body uneasily and found himself deprived of the pleasure of being an interested spectator.

Du Wancheng appeared desperate and called out to the guards

in the doorway: "Does anyone have any news of Inspector-General Zeng?"

Zeng Keda had just entered the residence from the rear entrance. It was four in the morning and half an hour later dawn would break in Peking. It was still very dark in the garden.

Zeng Keda was seen walking circumspectly into the courtyard in the dim yellow light coming from near the back door where the Youth Army officer in charge of security was meeting him.

"Is the meeting still in session?" he asked the officer as he walked on the unlit path after entering through the mansion's back door.

"Yes, it began at half past twelve and is still in session," the young army officer behind him replied.

"Has there been any outcome?" asked Zeng Keda as he walked down the dark pathway.

"No, they couldn't agree on anything, which is why General Inspector Du has been so anxious to find you."

Zeng Keda was just turning a corner as the flickering light from the meeting room faintly illuminated the sneer on his face. "Is Captain Fang present?"

"Yes, he's just showed up. He escorted two people with him. Special line number two from Nanking has been trying to reach you in your room since three o'clock..."

Zeng Keda stopped at once.

The Youth Army officer continued: "It's four o'clock now, another call came in five minutes ago and asked you to call special line two as soon as you returned."

Zeng Keda turned around and went back to the corner where he headed to the left, saying: "Go back to the meeting room. If they ask about my whereabouts, tell them I'm still away on business."

"Permission to report to Comrade Jianfeng," Zeng Keda said in a low, nervous voice, standing in front of the special line phone. "I went to meet with Comrade Liang Jinglun. I have to find out whether Fang Meng'ao's actions tonight had anything to do with the Communist Party."

"Is it so important?" came the voice of Comrade Jianfeng down the line. "The Economic Inspection Brigade is assigned to carry out the anti-corruption investigation in Peking, which I clearly explained to you in Nanking. What Fang Meng'ao did tonight is completely correct. Why make the association with the Communist Party?"

The question was so challenging that sweat started to appear on Zeng Keda's forehead.

Jianfeng's voice was deep and serious: "I've had numerous phone calls tonight. Some accused Fang Meng'ao's brigade of disrupting the war situation in Peking and sabotaging the counter-insurgency efforts. Some begged me to immediately release the people from Yangtze Construction to avoid negative consequences. These people didn't put the blame on the Communist Party. Instead they put it on the Iron and Blood Congress. What does this tell us? It means that our resolute anti-corruption campaign was internally resisted from the very beginning. You didn't attend the meeting convened by the five-member group to support Fang Meng'ao tonight, but you went to investigate whether Fang Meng'ao's actions had anything to do with the Communist Party. Isn't the truth that only the Communist Party is doing everything to comply with the aspirations of the people?"

"Yes... no..." Zeng Keda was almost incoherent with fear. "I completely accept your criticism, Comrade Jianfeng. Could you give me a few minutes? I'd like to give you a brief report on the purpose of my meeting with Liang Jinglun."

"Very well. Go ahead."

"Thank you, Comrade Jianfeng." As he said this, Zeng Keda found that his throat was dry. Hurriedly, with one hand covering the phone, he picked up the teacup from the table and drank a mouthful of water.

While he was drinking, he sensed the seriousness of the problem and felt the need to report his action plan to Comrade Jianfeng. But before outlining the plan, he had to clarify his thinking. Only when he understood that his action plan involved the implementation of his own ideas could Jianfeng recognise and support him.

"I fully support and understand Comrade Jianfeng's determination to resolutely crack down on corruption within the party, and also fully support and understand his efforts to put Fang Meng'ao in such an important position. As Comrade Jianfeng instructs us, since this is a life-and-death situation for the party-state, we should fight the Communist forces on the frontline. Even more important, we should also commit ourselves to eliminating corruption in the rear, to winning over the hearts and minds of the public and to developing the economy. After arriving in Peking, Fang Meng'ao's brigade received the warmest welcome and enthusiastic support of the people, especially from university students in Peking and those refugee students from the Northeast. They showed unprecedented enthusiasm and optimism. This is enough to demonstrate that Comrade Jianfeng's decision is wise and correct. Because of this, I feel that I have a great responsibility regarding how to carry out the arduous mission assigned to me by Comrade Jianfeng to make good use of Fang Meng'ao's brigade... I'm sorry, Comrade Jianfeng, is my report insufficiently brief?"

"Say everything that's on your mind, and say it without reserve." The tone of Comrade Jianfeng's voice on the phone had softened considerably. Zeng Keda's clear and comprehensive report would have been well received by anyone's superior. "Go on, just finish what you have to say."

"Yes, Comrade Jianfeng." Zeng Keda was encouraged and knew that the moment had come for him to elaborate on how to combine Comrade Jianfeng's great knowledge and bold vision with his own action plan.

"I have been trying very hard to recall the famous adage since I accepted your task that day, which is: 'A person who is suspected can still be used. The key is how to use him well.' Why should we doubt the one we use and why should we use the one we doubt? This is because the party-state has reached a critical point where there are too few talents and too many parasites. How can we fight to defeat the Communist Party in the larger nationwide battlefield? The key lies in whether we can compete with them in the battlefield in the rear in terms of recruitment, economic competence and popular support. I understand that the rationale behind Comrade Jianfeng fast-tracking Fang Meng'ao into the line-up has to do with the Chinese character, to compete. What we value is the virtue of this man who recognises only reason, honours only principle and takes pride in being the loyal dissident. Because of these virtues, he was brave enough to violate military orders by not bombing the city of Kaifeng. It is because of this he chooses to become the prodigal son, and turns himself into a wedge that inserts itself into the monolithic structure of the Central Bank's Peking branch. He is committed to tackling corruption and private interest groups, and helps us fight for improving the economy and win over the hearts and minds of the Peking public. Therefore, we should use Fang Meng'ao even if he has nothing to do with the Communist Party. If Fang Meng'ao has nothing to do with the Communist Party, we should firmly prevent them from recruiting him. If Fang Meng'ao does have some kind of connection to them, we should sever those connections. We should use him to our own advantage, not to the Communist Party's advantage. Only in this way can we implement Comrade Jianfeng's instruction, namely 'the key is to make good use of him'. I don't know if I understand Comrade Jianfeng's thoughts..."

At one breath, Zeng Keda surprised himself in being able to sum up his thoughts so succinctly. He stopped there and waited for Comrade Jianfeng's response nervously and excitedly.

"With this understanding, I can assure you that you've made progress, Comrade Zeng Keda." The tone of Comrade Jianfeng's voice over the phone showed great appreciation. "Now, how are you going to implement this understanding?"

Zeng Keda was greatly encouraged. In replying, he could not conceal his excitement: "Yes, Comrade Jianfeng, I made an analysis of Cui Zhongshi based on a further investigation after I arrived in Peking. If Fang Meng'ao is a member of the Communist Party recruited by Cui Zhongshi, he is only a member through one-way contact, which means that he is a special member who has not been given any particular assignments. As long as the connection between these two men is cut off, every connection between Fang Meng'ao and the Communist Party will be severed, meaning he will no longer be a member of the party. Again, my idea is to make Fang Meng'ao suspect that Cui Zhongshi is not a Communist Party member by taking advantage of Cui's hesitation to reveal his true identity and the organisational weakness of the Communist Party.

Once Fang concludes that Cui is not a member of the Communist Party, we can completely ignore the history of when Fang Meng'ao was recruited, and give him a free hand to investigate the corruption cases of the Peking branch and the Peking Citizens' Food-Distribution Committee. All Fang Meng'ao's actions should be channelled into implementing Comrade Jianfeng's instructions, not the instructions of the Communist Party. Of course, there is a key issue here, that is, let Fang Meng'ao understand that we are also doing what the Communist Party wants to do. In this way, Comrade Jianfeng, you'll really achieve your goal of fighting the Communist Party for talent, for the economy and for the hearts and minds of the people."

In all the excitement, Zeng Keda found that his mouth had become dry, so he covered the mouthpiece again, picked up the cup and took another gulp of water, only to choke and cough violently.

"Comrade Keda, are you all right?" asked Jianfeng with great consideration.

"It's nothing, nothing at all... Comrade Jianfeng." Zeng Keda was so touched by his concern that he knew that his response tonight, including his accidental choking and coughing, had achieved the desired results. He was managing to restrain the sense of excitement he was feeling but couldn't hide the fatigue that resulted from his toiling for the party-state. He purposefully said in a hoarse voice: "Perhaps I haven't had enough sleep these past few days... Comrade Jianfeng, I don't know whether my assumptions just now are right or wrong. Please give me your clear instructions."

"I don't have any specific instructions for you since your ideas are based on such a thorough understanding and thoughtful application of my instructions." Jianfeng clearly had plenty of thoughts and feelings. "I will share with you a poem by Gong Zizhen by way of an answer."

"Comrade Jianfeng," Zeng Keda replied. "I'll grab my pen and pad so I can take notes..."

"There's no need. You can recite this poem just as well as me." Jianfeng then read:

In order to awaken, China needs a thunderstorm –
It's awful that myriad steeds are mute with blood warm.

Heaven, I pray thee to give a great shake again,
To send forth men of many talents.

"With heaven remembering my painstaking efforts, I will surely be blessed with more talents like you, including those like Fang Meng'ao!"

Zeng Keda was moved. He felt something like a stream of sour liquid rushing up from his chest. He was almost unable to utter a single word, and his eyes were wet with tears. "Comrade Jianfeng, thank you for your trust. I, Zeng Keda, am ready to die the cruellest death for our noble cause. The five-member group is expecting me, and the Yangtze Construction Company people who were detained by Fang Meng'ao are still waiting to be interrogated. How do I handle the..."

"It will be five o'clock in about half an hour. The president and Madam Chiang will soon rise. I guess they will get the news about Peking to Madam Chiang. I won't go to sleep. I'll wait here for the phone call from the president's residence. If Madam Chiang fails to see the larger issues and speaks in their favour, I will immediately dismiss the five-member group and let them return to Nanking. On behalf of the Ministry of Defence, you will continue to stay in Peking and support Fang Meng'ao, make good use of him, investigate Cui Zhongshi and the organisation behind him, as well as the Peking Citizens' Food-Distribution Committee and go all the way down to check the Peking branch of the Central Bank and the Peking-Tianjin office of Yangtze Construction. You will faithfully carry out our tenet of 'one hand resolutely fighting the Communist Party, and the other resolutely fighting corruption – one revolution, fighting on both fronts!'"

Zeng Keda replied firmly: "I understand completely and will resolutely implement your instructions, Comrade Jianfeng."

The large clock in the living room on the ground floor of the Fang mansion struck again. It was five in the morning.

Fang Buting was sitting at the breakfast table and listening to the clock in silence, his eyes turning to the open door of the living room. Having not slept a wink the previous night, he was waiting for the moment to come. He was well aware of the fact that many major events and changes in the party-state took place soon after five in the morning. Last night, his son arrested the man from Yangtze Construction. Later, he himself fell out with General Manager Kung of that same company. For all these developments, he made himself ready, and ready also for the cough from Nanking at five o'clock that might develop into a heavy cold in Peking.

Cheng Xiaoyun came in from the kitchen with a tray and gently placed it on the breakfast table. Seeing Fang Buting looking out of the open door, she whispered: "Please eat your breakfast."

Fang Buting turned his head slowly and looked at the six steamed buns on the tray. A wave of tender feelings that had been absent for a long while surged in his heart.

The delicate steamed meat buns were a favourite of people living south of the Yangtze River. The most difficult thing in preparing the buns is to carefully pinch out a petal-shaped ring at the top with a tiny hole in the middle. When steamed, they should be cooked over a moderate flame.

It was now five o'clock. In order to make the steamed bread for this hour, Cheng Xiaoyun had to prepare the ingredients in the kitchen by three o'clock in the morning. In addition, she had also made a plate of turnip cake fried on both sides, a plate of steamed Wuxi-style diamond cakes, a dish of dried tofu fried in oil and a bowl of steaming glutinous rice balls fermented in rice wine. These were all snack foods popular in the Wuxi area, and particularly liked by Fang Buting.

"This is way too much! Everyone else in the city is starving," protested Fang Buting. However, he still looked with longing at the food on the table.

"I learnt from Cai Ma that you haven't eaten these things for months," Cheng Xiaoyun replied softly. "And it's just after dawn, Mulan isn't up yet and Mengwei isn't likely to come back so early. So come on, treat yourself just this once."

Fang Buting's eyes slowly turned to her. "I thought I could live a better life for at least a short while after victory in the War of Resistance. I didn't expect we would end up in such a situation."

It was as if he had become a changed person. To be exact, Fang

Buting was more like the debonair gentleman of the past, who even recited with a heavy Wuxi accent a Peking Opera line that Cheng Xiaoyun had not expected: "My beloved concubine, what shall I do about her?"

Cheng Xiaoyun graduated from St. John's University in Shanghai. With a natural gift for the young female character role in Peking opera, she was very familiar with *Farewell My Concubine*. Hearing Fang Buting's rather amateurish rendition of Xiang Yu's line, Cheng Xiaoyun became sentimental. With tears in her eyes, she turned and went back into the kitchen.

"Peidong was up all night, too," Fang Buting called out. "Call him in, and let's eat together."

"I'll go and get him." With her back still to Fang, Cheng Xiaoyun went straight up to the first floor.

"He's not in his room, he's in my office," Fang Buting called out.

By now, Cheng Xiaoyun was already upstairs. Hearing these words, she looked worried. She was aware of the tense situation, and she also knew that neither of them had slept all night. Xie Peidong must be wrestling with a very thorny problem for him to be in the governor's office at this hour. According to the rules established many years ago, she could not interfere in the bank's business, so she had to hide her concerns and walked to the governor's office anxiously.

Cheng Xiaoyun was about to knock on the door when she heard the telephone ring inside the office. She was startled, and spun around to look towards the breakfast table down on the ground floor.

As soon as he saw Cheng Xiaoyun looking down, Fang Buting got up and moved quickly to the stairs. Cheng did not want to be suspected of eavesdropping on the phone conversation, so she scurried along the corridor on the first floor.

Pushing open the door of the office, Fang Buting discovered Xie Peidong looking very concerned, with the phone in his hand. When he saw Fang Buting come in, Xie immediately covered the phone so he could speak with Fang Buting.

"Who's calling?" Fang Buting asked, starting to lose his usually calm demeanour.

"The five-member group," Xie Peidong replied, still with his hand over the mouthpiece.

"Let me talk to them." Fang Buting moved over quickly.

"They've just hung up," said Xie Peidong as he put the phone down.

"What did they say exactly?"

"Please sit first, governor," said Xie Peidong, trying to engender a more relaxed atmosphere.

"Tell me," said Fang Buting, still standing in front of him.

"The group of five has been dissolved."

"What do you mean?"

"They didn't explain the reasons in detail. They only told me that the group had been dissolved."

"Just like that?"

"Zeng Keda of the Ministry of Defence made the call, saying that from today on the ministry and the Peking Police Bureau will jointly investigate the corruption cases involving the Peking branch and the Peking Citizens' Food-Distribution Committee. He demanded that we send Cui Zhongshi to Ambassador Gu's mansion immediately for questioning."

"Who's being questioned? Did they release the pair from Yangtze Construction Company?"

Xie Peidong stopped and looked at Fang Buting in silence.

"Say it!" Fang Buting seldom lost his temper, but to Xie Peidong's surprise, he even stomped his feet.

"The Yangtze Construction folk are still being detained there. But they demanded that Cui Zhongshi be summoned for cross examination. Zeng Keda, Xu Tieying and Meng'ao will conduct the questioning..."

Fang Buting was shocked, and he turned his gaze to the ceiling fan that had been revolving throughout the night. Suddenly, the fan appeared both larger and closer.

"Governor!" Fang's body started shaking, and Xie Peidong held out his hands to support him.

"The sky can't fall..." Fang Buting closed his eyes and tried to calm himself down. "Peidong?"

"My dear brother-in-law." Xie Peidong continued to hold his arm.

Fang Buting slowly opened his eyes and looked at him affectionately. "'When fighting a tiger, a man has to rely on his blood brothers. When fighting a battle, one has to rely on one's father and sons.' Now that they are calling on their sons to fight their fathers, we two old brothers have to fight the tigers ourselves."

Xie Peidong had also become emotional: "Meng'ao won't be so confused. He won't go so far as to fight his own father. Just tell me what you want me to do, and I'll do it."

"I never intended to get you involved in these disputes. But this time, I've got to let you in. Please go to see Cui Zhongshi now, accompany him to Ambassador Gu's mansion and keep an eye on him during the questioning on behalf of me and the Central Bank's Peking branch.

"With you present at the questioning session, we can deal with Zeng Keda and watch Cui Zhongshi. These two men are going to be at close combat with each other. One is a member of the Iron and Blood Congress, the other is a member of the Communist Party. They all took Meng'ao as a knife in their hands to cut and kill, and in the end it was all about cutting me. Do you understand what I mean?"

"I'll go right away." As he spoke, he released the hands supporting Fang Buting.

Fang Buting pulled back his arm. "Xiaoyun's made us some breakfast downstairs. Have something to eat before you leave."

"I'll take some and eat on the way." Xie Peidong moved towards the door, opened it and called out: "Sister-in-law!"

"Yes, Peidong," Cheng Xiaoyun answered quickly.

Xie Peidong was still standing in the doorway. "Please go upstairs and keep the governor company."

It happened that this was Xie Peidong's first visit to Cui Zhongshi's house after arriving in Peking more than two years ago.

Ye Biyu opened the gate of the courtyard and looked at Xie Peidong warily. "It's so early. Who are you looking for?"

Since Xie Peidong was Fang Buting's personal assistant, he seldom got involved in the bank's affairs. Therefore, he never visited the bank staff at their homes or even called in at the branch building. Indeed, few bank employees, let alone their family members, knew him personally.

"My name is Xie Peidong, a colleague of Deputy Director Cui," Xie Peidong replied calmly. "Governor Fang sent me here."

Ye Biyu appeared both apologetic and surprised: "It's Assistant Manager Xie. I'm so sorry. Come on in." The gate of the courtyard was opened, and Xie Peidong went in. Cui Zhongshi showed up at the door of the north room. Even the normally composed Cui Zhongshi was surprised. Xie Peidong winked as Cui came up to greet him, now all smiles.

"It's an honour to welcome you to my humble home. Why have you come so early?"

"A development at the branch. Shall we talk about it inside?"

Cui Zhongshi accompanied him into the house. As they walked, he turned his head to see Ye Biyu busy closing the gate. He called out to her: "We need to talk shop. Go look after the children."

Ye Biyu knew when to be excused, but before doing so she said: "Remember to make some tea for Assistant Manager Xie. I can fix some breakfast for you if you like."

"Thank you. I've already eaten," Xie Peidong replied as he followed Cui Zhongshi into the north room. Once there, they sat down and looked at each other but did not speak for several seconds.

Cui Zhongshi was facing the door, which he surveyed with vigilance. He wanted to make sure they were alone. No one, be they an outsider or close family member, should hear the conversation that was about to take place.

Xie Peidong looked around the living room and said: "Why is it that the furnishings are so simple and shabby? It's not like the home of a deputy treasury director of the Peking branch."

Cui Zhongshi smiled bitterly. "My monthly salary is twenty million *fabi*. It's not enough to buy food for a family of four. And yet I am resolved not to be as corrupt as other officials."

Xie Peidong sighed and said: "Well, there's no time for idle chat. Ten minutes at most. We'll have to go to Gu Weijun's residence to face Zeng Keda's questioning."

"Are you going there, too?" asked Cui Zhongshi in surprise.

"You can't attend such a session! Unless it is the decision of the organisation, Comrade Peidong..."

What a turn-up for Cui Zhongshi to call him "Comrade"! In fact, Xie Peidong turned out to be in charge of covert operations on the economy under the leadership of the CPC's Peking branch.

"Call me Assistant Manager Xie," Xie Peidong corrected him. "Nanking has dissolved the five-member group. Now it is the Iron and Blood Congress and the Peking Police Bureau that will investigate the Peking branch and the Peking Citizens' Food-Distribution Committee. Zeng Keda means business, unlike Xu Tieying. The thing is that since the Iron and Blood Congress has long suspected your real identity, it must have suspected Meng'ao's as well. Why did they decide to reuse Meng'ao? Because they are trying to incite defection, using Meng'ao to help them fight against corruption and private property for the purpose of deceiving public opinion and gaining the upper hand in their internal strife. To this end, they will make full use of Meng'ao, but you must be removed. Therefore, you are currently in danger. Meng'ao is safe for the time being. The party organisation has decided that you must leave as soon as possible."

"Where to?" Cui Zhongshi asked.

"The liberated area. I need to wait for my superior's notice regarding when and where."

There was a flash of yearning in Cui Zhongshi's eyes, but it was gone soon and there was silence for a moment. "I can't leave now," he said finally.

Xie Peidong seemed to be expecting such a reply, but all he did was look at him.

"Meng'ao and I are in single-line contact," Cui Zhongshi continued. "I'm the only one he trusts. If I went now, no one could gain his trust, and he will lose contact with the organisation. A full-scale war of liberation is about to begin. We need Meng'ao and his Air Force pilots. If I left, we would fall into the trap set by the Iron and Blood Congress. All our previous efforts would be wasted. Comrade Peidong... please let me finish. I know what you mean. But I can't let you take over my work. Our party needs you to stay on around Fang Buting as his trusted assistant, which would allow you to get closer to the Kuomintang's economic lynchpin. So there should be no room for risk on your side. As your subordinate, I urge you and the organisation to accept my suggestions and let me stay on. I know what I should do."

Xie Peidong glanced at the clock on the table and looked back at Cui Zhongshi. "Let's not talk about this for the moment. Let's tackle Zeng Keda's interrogation session first. Xu Tieying and Meng'ao are present. The Iron and Blood Congress somehow contrived to set this trap. They suspect you are a member of the Communist Party, and they want Meng'ao to suspect that you are not a Communist. Their purpose is clear, either to force you to expose your real identity or let you deny your real identity so that Meng'ao will cut his ties with the party. I'm here to tell you that we should believe in the party and Meng'ao's political consciousness. He chose the Communist Party, he believes in you, Cui Zhongshi. Therefore, when you are interrogated today, you must forget your true identity. You're deputy treasury director of the Peking branch of the Central Bank of the National Government, not a Communist Party spy! You must stand on the side of the Peking branch and defend it. You must take advantage of the fact that both the Citizens' Food-Distribution Committee and Yangtze Construction Company want to cover up their corruption, and that Xu Tieying wants to have a fair proportion of its shares. The idea is to let them work against Zeng Keda."

"I know how to deal with them." Cui Zhongshi smiled and stood up. "Thank you, Assistant Manager Xie, you don't have to go with me."

Xie Peidong took Cui Zhongshi's arm in a firm, warm grasp and said: "Governor Fang asked me to accompany you. Let's go together."

The meeting was convened in the same conference room in Gu Weijun's residence, but three chairs were empty, the ones formerly occupied by Du Wancheng, Wang Benquan and Ma Linshen.

Xu Tieying was still sitting in his chair on the left and Zeng Keda, who had showed up early in the morning had taken his seat on the right. Du Wancheng's chair, which was positioned between the two, was unoccupied. Fang Meng'ao was sitting in his original place under the portrait of Dr Sun Yat-sen at the head of the conference table.

As Comrade Jianfeng had predicted in his phone call, Nanking intervened in Peking's case by dissolving the five-member investigation group soon after five in the morning. Du Wancheng, Wang Benquan and Ma Linshen were instructed to return to Nanking immediately. The Bureau of Reserve Cadres should continue to deal with the aftermath of the economic corruption case triggered by the "Fifth of July Incident" in Peking, while the Peking Police Bureau should assist and cooperate with the bureau. The order also emphasised that those within the party should be dealt with differently from those outside. Cracking down on corruption should not affect the image of the party-state or jeopardise the overall situation of counter-insurgency and nation-saving efforts.

Still sitting near the door were the four people waiting to be dealt with as a result of last night's conflict, so no one could afford to relax.

Kung, deputy director of the Peking-Tianjin office of Yangtze Construction Company, was still handcuffed to the woman. She was so exhausted that she was leaning forward on the meeting room table and had fallen asleep. Kung was forced to put his cuffed left hand on the table, which he found very uncomfortable.

Ma Hanshan was still sitting to the right of Kung. He felt very weak, while the quartermaster of the Fourth Corps, who was sitting to the left of the woman, appeared equally weary.

Zeng Keda refused to release them. Without telling them how they would be handled, he just sat with a sneer on his face. Xu Tieying was also silent and appeared very "cooperative" with Zeng Keda. He sat there patiently awaiting his next move.

Fang Meng'ao was watching quietly in his own way. He had long since believed that the Kuomintang would not take any substantial action against internal corruption. He, too, sat in silence and watched how events would unfold.

Kung was becoming irritable. He pulled the handcuffs with some force and disturbed the woman who had dozed off.

The woman woke up from her dream, and with her mouth still drooling, she shouted: "God damn it!" On opening her eyes, she found that the handcuffs were still on. She said desperately: "Why don't you unlock these handcuffs?"

"Be quiet!" Kung bellowed, before looking at Fang Meng'ao and then at Zeng Keda. "Which one of you two is calling the shots here on behalf of the Ministry of Defence? You've heard Nanking's instructions. Who gives you the power to keep us here even when the five-member investigation group has been disbanded?"

Zeng Keda refused to look at him. Instead, he turned his gaze on Fang Meng'ao and said with a smile: "He's chastising us. Captain Fang, do you think we should let them go?"

For the first time, Fang Meng'ao found that Zeng Keda had created such a strong bond between the two of them, as if they were of one camp. He smiled and replied: "Even if I wanted to let them go, I couldn't."

"Why's that?"

"I don't have the keys."

Zeng Keda could not tolerate Fang Meng'ao's open defiance. His face darkened, but with so many present, he kept his temper under control. He turned to Kung and said: "Then you'll have to wait and see if the people of the Peking branch can unlock your handcuffs when they arrive."

By the time Fang Mengwei got home, it was already broad daylight. Apart from the janitor near the gate, the courtyard was unusually quiet. Those who normally came to clean the courtyard in the morning could not be seen. Someone had probably instructed them not to show up.

Fang Mengwei was right in his premonition. The janitor, who opened the door for him, lowered his head slightly. Fang Mengwei seemed to understand what was going on, and he stepped lightly towards the parlour on the ground floor of the mansion. Suddenly, he stopped and froze in amazement. From the living room came the voice of a woman singing in a soft voice:

The floating, scattered clouds,
The bright moon shines on the reunited people,

Today is the happiest reunion,

Clean and shallow ponds,
Mandarin ducks playing on the water

It was Cheng Xiaoyun who was singing! Fang Mengwei's face was transformed. Then he coughed and stood there waiting for the music to fade.

Hearing the coughing, Cheng Xiaoyun's whole expression changed. Halfway through the song, she had to stop by swallowing the next line. She glanced at the doorway in panic, and then looked at Fang Buting who was sitting by the dining table, still with his eyes closed.

"Sing, go on," Fang Buting said.

"Mengwei is back," Cheng Xiaoyun whispered.

"I know. Come on."

"I'd better be excused."

"Sit," said Fang Buting, finally opening his eyes. "No, I'll sing, you listen." Cheng Xiaoyun had never heard Fang Buting insist on her staying like this. She thought for a moment, and sat down.

Now that the singing had finished, Fang Mengwei continued his walk to the living room. However, before getting there, he had to stop again.

In the living room on the ground floor came his father's voice:

Red skirts and emerald caps,
Devoted married couples like two lotus flowers opening.
In pairs, the spouses share a mutual love.
This soft wind blows upon the beautiful flowers,
Blowing on the good flowers
Full of warmth and affection between the people.

Fang Mengwei detected a sense of loneliness and desolation in his father's voice. But he hesitated no more and proceeded to the living room.

———

"Permission to report!" said Zeng Keda's adjutant at the door of the conference room in Gu Weijun's mansion. "The staff of the Peking branch of the Central Bank are here."

Zeng Keda looked towards the doorway, while at the same time glancing out of the corner of his eye to witness Fang Meng'ao's reaction.

Fang Meng'ao responded as expected. He had been smoking and didn't look at the doorway or at Zeng Keda. However, as an ace pilot, he was very alert. Then his eyes glimpsed a man... who turned out to be Xie Peidong.

He thought Cui Zhongshi would be appearing before the panel. Or perhaps his father who had showed up the day before. However, it was Xie Peidong whom he had always loved dearly. It was so unexpected that he stood up unconsciously.

Xu Tieying saw Cui Zhongshi first, then Xie Peidong who was standing beside him. He obviously knew this man was more important to Fang Buting than Cui Zhongshi. A smile lit up his face and he stood up after the others.

Zeng Keda followed and slowly stood up. He noticed that the man standing beside Cui Zhongshi was quite special, particularly given the way Fang Meng'ao and Xu Tieying responded. He guessed that this man was Xie Peidong, Fang Meng'ao's uncle on his mother's side and Fang Buting's right-hand man at the branch.

Now knowing the identity of the man, Zeng Keda's murderous look softened. He ordered his adjutant outside the doorway in a relatively polite tone: "Please come in and add a chair where the secretary normally sits." At the same time, he purposefully cast a look at Fang Meng'ao.

Fang Mengwei stood at the living room table of the Fang mansion without looking at his father, nor at Cheng Xiaoyun. He stood there in silence. Once more, Cheng Xiaoyun wanted to stand up and leave.

"Sit down," said Fang Buting. "I'm glad to know you helped your elder brother obtain a thousand tonnes of grain for the students and teachers as well as the residents of Peking. But you should eat your breakfast properly. Look, here're some snacks from our hometown of Wuxi."

"Who made them? Uncle Xie?" Fang Mengwei asked in a low, muffled voice.

"Do you only eat food cooked by your uncle?" Fang Buting's sharp response was rather out of character.

Fang Mengwei was embarrassed, and he chose to be silent.

Fang Buting softened his tone: "Uncle Xie accompanied Cui Zhongshi to attend the interrogation by Zeng Keda and your elder brother."

"What?" said a shocked Fang Mengwei, his eyes wide open.

Back in the conference room in Gu Weijun's residence, Zeng Keda's adjutant showed Cui Zhongshi and Xie Peidong to the place normally reserved for the secretary. Then the adjutant placed a second chair there and put them both in proper order.

"Please be seated," Zeng Keda said, holding out his hand in a gesture of welcome. He turned around and looked at Xu Tieying and Fang Meng'ao. "Commissioner Xu, Captain Fang, please sit down."

Zeng Keda himself sat down, followed by Xu Tieying. Fang Meng'ao remained standing.

"Why don't you sit, Captain Fang?" Zeng Keda looked at Fang Meng'ao again, and found that his bright eyes sparkled. Fang Meng'ao seemed to be looking at something on the opposite side as if he were saluting it with his eyes. Then he looked back.

Xie Peidong and Cui Zhongshi were still standing in front of the chairs, neither sitting down.

"Please be seated," Zeng Keda persisted. "If you don't, Captain Fang can't very well sit either."

Xie Peidong gestured to Cui Zhongshi and said: "Sit." They both sat down.

Fang Meng'ao remained standing.

"What's the matter, Captain Fang?" asked Zeng Keda.

"Would it be all right for me to stand for a while?"

Zeng Keda could see Fang Meng'ao's mouth curling into a smile, and his eyes shone. Astonished, Zeng Keda had no alternative but to force a smile of his own. "Of course you can," he said.

In the living room on the ground floor of his mansion, Fang Buting told Cheng Xiaoyun: "Please go back to your room. I have something to say to Mengwei."

Cheng Xiaoyun stood up slowly.

"Hold on, Stepmother..." said Fang Mengwei.

Fang Buting and Cheng Xiaoyun were taken aback by what they had heard. They first looked at each other, and then at Mengwei.

"Could you take a seat, please?" Fang Mengwei asked Cheng Xiaoyun.

Cheng looked at Fang Buting again, who motioned with his eyes for her to sit down. She sat down slowly.

"Sooner or later, the party-state will be destroyed by its own people," said Fang Mengwei. "Stepmother, my father will depend on you to take care of him in his old age."

"Nonsense!" Only then did Fang Buting realise this younger son of his was so temperamental that he might not know what he was saying.

"What nonsense?" said Fang Mengwei. "Look what you've got in return. Dad, you have been working yourself to the bone for the party-state for twenty years. You've raised money for them and made money for them. Now, in order to fight the civil war, Chiang Kai-shek and Chiang Ching-kuo wouldn't punish their own relatives. Instead, their knives are out for you. The most hateful thing is that they're using my big brother to punish you! Whatever the concepts of allegiance, filial piety, benevolence, courtesy, righteousness and shame, they're all rules for others to observe. For sure, every single member of the Kuomintang would respond by quitting the party, not to say my elder brother. If pressed, I would switch allegiance to the Communist Party, too!"

"Shut up! Shut up! Shut up!" said Fang Buting, slapping the table. He was already out of breath.

"Calm down, you must not worry," said Cheng Xiaoyun,

stroking his back. "Mengwei was just talking in anger. He'll be cautious when speaking in public..."

"Cautious?" said Fang Mengwei. "My father was cautious all his life. In the twenty-sixth year of the Republic of China, in order to transport their property to Chongqing, his family was ruined. Will they remember these things now? What's the difference between state property, party property and private property? They have never made any distinction among themselves. Now that they are losing to the Communist Party, they'll use him as a scapegoat!"

With that parting shot, he turned around and made to storm out of the house.

"Where are you going?" Fang Buting shouted.

"Ambassador Gu's residence!" Fang Mengwei replied and walked out of the living room. "I'm going to take on Zeng Keda myself!"

In the conference room of Gu Weijun's residence, Zeng Keda started the questioning in a friendly manner.

"The day before yesterday," he said, "this was the place where Deputy Director Cui told the five-member group that the Central Bank's appropriations to the military and the loans to the Central Commission on Citizens' Food Distribution were top secret, and couldn't be disclosed without the say-so of the Central Military Commission. As a result of this statement, the group of five simply couldn't go on. But just last night, there was a problem with the Central Bank's appropriations and borrowings. The supplies for the military and the supplies for Peking were found to be operated by a single company. Furthermore, the company took funds from the Material Management Committee and loans from the Central Commission on Citizens' Food Distribution, but failed to supply the materials to the military or Peking City. As a result, the Fourth Corps of the National Army and the Peking Citizens' Food-Distribution Committee were fighting for a single train-load of grain! Now, the company's escorts have arrived. The deputy director in charge of the Peking Citizens' Food-Distribution Committee is here. The director in charge of military supplies of the Fourth

Corps is also here. Is it true that the Central Bank's Peking branch didn't appropriate the funds to the military or did it fail to give the loan to the Peking Citizens' Food-Distribution Committee? Or did the Central Bank's Peking branch allocate funds and loans to the relevant departments, but the relevant departments did not use the money to purchase materials? Or did the relevant departments pay the money to the company, but the company totally ignored the overall situation of the party-state, took the money and failed to supply the materials?

"Deputy Director Cui, the day before yesterday when you were interviewed by the five-member group, you said that you are in charge of these funds and loans and handle all these accounts. I want you to answer all the above questions today. By the way, none of them can now be regarded as what you call 'top secret'. In addition, although the five-member group was disbanded, the Economic Inspection Brigade representing the Ministry of Defence in Peking was not. Captain Fang and I, on instructions from Nanking, have the right to continue to investigate these issues, and we must carry on the investigation to the end. I apologise for not mentioning this before, but let me emphasise that Peking's economic corruption case is not only being investigated by the Ministry of Defence, but also by Commissioner Xu on behalf of the National Communications Bureau of the Kuomintang. He is under orders to cooperate with the investigation and is authorised and obligated to assist in the interrogation and apprehension of the alleged criminals involved in the case. Commissioner Xu, would you like to say a few words?"

Xu Tieying nodded in agreement. "Inspector-General Zeng has said all I wanted to say. We are here to assist in the investigation. So let them answer the questions."

With Xu Tieying's role clarified, Zeng Keda turned to Fang Meng'ao and said: "Captain Fang, I received a call from Nanking over an hour ago. My superior officer thinks highly of you and your team's actions last night. You and your brigade will be specifically assigned to investigate this case. In response to the three questions I just asked, do you have anything more to ask Deputy Director Cui?"

This was what Xie Peidong had analysed for Cui Zhongshi. The

Iron and Blood Congress would force Fang Meng'ao to choose sides and Cui Zhongshi to make a statement. Of course, only four people knew about this – Zeng Keda, Fang Meng'ao, Cui Zhongshi and Xie Peidong. Two camps, involving the single member of the Kuomintang's Iron and Blood Congress and the three Communist Party spies, were engaged in the cut and thrust of spontaneous debate. However, no one, including Xu Tieying, the two people from Yangtze Construction Company, Ma Hanshan and Director Qian, knew this was the most secret battle fought between the Iron and Blood Congress represented by Zeng Keda and these three brave souls. But the five people were well aware of the fact that the Iron and Blood Congress was making use of the son against his own father.

Different thoughts, but a familiar silence. Most of the people at the session chose to look at the table, instead of at Fang Meng'ao or Zeng Keda.

There was only one pair of eyes that were looking intensely at Fang Meng'ao. The eyes were full of understanding for Meng'ao, and of course, they were also full of a desire for Fang Meng'ao to understand others. This man was Xie Peidong.

Fang Meng'ao saw the fatherly love in Xie's eyes that he had lost ten years previously and remembered the gifts he had received from Cui Zhongshi in the name of Xie Peidong over the past decade. At this moment, he realised that during this period he had transferred all his love for his father to this uncle figure. The stronger this feeling grew, the stronger his aversion to Zeng Keda became.

"Inspector-General Zeng, can I ask you a question?" he said.

"We've all been sent by the Ministry of Defence," Zeng Keda replied. "Of course you can."

Fang Meng'ao stood there, raised his foot, stubbed out his cigar on the sole of his pilot's boot and said: "It has nothing to do with anyone being sent by the Ministry of Defence. Inspector-General Zeng, you often served as prosecutor of the special criminal court on behalf of the Ministry of Defence. You tried me before coming to Peking. So you should understand legal procedures."

As he said this, he stared at Zeng Keda with contempt. Zeng had plenty of anger inside him and wanted to get even. But he remembered Jianfeng's instructions, so he kept calm. Instead of looking at Fang Meng'ao, he just gazed down at the table.

"Which legal procedure in particular are you talking about, Captain Fang?"

"The challenge system. Inspector-General Zeng knows better than anyone else that during my detention in Nanking's special criminal court, it was Deputy Director Cui who acted on behalf of my family in Nanking and tried to rescue me. Now you want me to question Deputy Director Cui, aren't you afraid I will cover up for him? Besides, the gentleman sitting opposite me is my maternal uncle. Since he is a relative, might I not consider taking care of him during the process? Aren't you concerned that I might feel constrained from asking any substantial questions?"

Fang Meng'ao's words shocked not only Zeng Keda, but also just about everyone else in the conference room. Some of them stood gazing at each other, while others looked at Fang Meng'ao in astonishment.

Cui Zhongshi and Xie Peidong were most concerned. "There's no need for Captain Fang to question me," Cui Zhongshi said as he stood up. "Inspector-General Zeng, I can answer your questions."

Zeng Keda leaned back in his chair and said: "That's good. If you answer truthfully, Captain Fang need not be involved, and nor will I. All of us will be satisfied."

"Inspector-General," said Fang Meng'ao, pressing on, "you haven't answered my question. Do I need to be excused when they are being interrogated?"

Zeng Keda was shocked at Fang Meng'ao's honesty and directness. He had no alternative but to avoid full frontal confrontation. He turned to Cui Zhongshi and asked: "Deputy Director Cui, do you think Captain Fang needs to be excused?"

"No need at all," said Cui Zhongshi. "I'm deputy treasury director of the Peking branch of the Central Bank of the National Government. I'm now answering questions about the bank's business that doesn't involve any personal feelings. Everyone should be allowed to listen."

"That's good," said Zeng Keda. "Please go ahead."

However, the two people sitting in the interrogation seats were starting to become concerned. One was Ma Hanshan, and the other was Deputy Director Kung. As for Director Qian and the woman, they were just tired and impatient.

There was also another person who was very concerned about developments: Xu Tieying. He had been sitting there without saying a word until he chipped in: "Well said, Deputy Director Cui. We are here today to talk about real business, not to establish who is related to who. Go ahead, we're all ears." With that, he looked at Ma Hanshan and Deputy Director Kung of Yangtze Construction.

"Thank you," Cui Zhongshi replied. "The government of the Republic of China has only one Central Bank, which of course is responsible for the allocation of military supplies to millions of troops. In addition, the Central Bank is responsible for the allocation of citizens' food supplies to five major cities. In Peking, we are the branch responsible for issuing grants and loans.

"However, the Central Bank and its Peking branch are only responsible for appropriation and borrowing. The appropriations to the army are directly allocated to the Material Management Committee in accordance with the requirements of the Nanking authorities, while the loans to purchase food for urban citizens go directly to the Citizens' Food-Distribution Committee in accordance with the requirements of Nanking again. As for the channels from which the Material Management Committee purchases military supplies and the Citizens' Food-Distribution Committee purchases daily necessities for the public, these are the business of the two committees. The Central Bank is not responsible for purchasing, nor is the Peking branch. So I can only answer one of the three questions raised by Inspector-General Zeng. Have I explained things clearly?"

Zeng Keda seemed to have expected that he would answer this way, and he emitted a long drawl; "Understood. That's to say the Peking branch has already put in place the appropriated funds and loans. Therefore, it has nothing to do with the Central Bank or the Peking branch whether the military supplies or daily necessities for the public have been embezzled or allocated or not allocated at all. Is that what Deputy Director Cui means?"

"That's what I mean."

"Then I must ask you another question. The money to be allocated has been allocated, the loans to be loaned have been loaned, so why is the book-keeping being conducted by the Peking branch?" Zeng Keda stared at Cui Zhongshi to see if he was looking at Fang Meng'ao.

Cui Zhongshi's eyes were fixed on Zeng Keda. "The Central Bank has clear stipulations that all the funds appropriated and loans issued must be accounted for by the bank to ensure that the special funds are used exclusively for their intended purposes."

"Did they spend the money you set aside and the money you lent out to purchase either military supplies or daily necessities for the public?" asked Zeng Keda. "Is the destination and use of each sum of money reflected in the accounts you keep?"

"We have the responsibility and try the best we can to supervise the money appropriated and ensure that the loans issued are earmarked for their specified purpose only."

"That I can't understand. Do you mean it's for its intended purpose or not?"

"We allocate funds and issue loans on a monthly basis," said Cui Zhongshi. "When the situation becomes urgent, we do it on a daily basis. But when they make the purchase, we need to solve various difficulties, such as transportation and finding out the source price, so some accounts can only be disclosed at a future time."

Cui Zhongshi's reply provoked a reaction among the panellists.

The first to respond were Kung, deputy director of Yangtze Construction Company, and Ma Hanshan. Both were sitting at the interrogation table, and both were relieved at Cui's reply. They appeared appreciative and grateful, though in a discreet manner. Cui Zhongshi had been so loyal and so professional in answering Zeng Keda's questions. They didn't have to worry about who would bear responsibility on their behalf.

Xu Tieying also expressed his appreciation and gratitude to Cui Zhongshi, while ignoring Zeng Keda's presence. This was someone who could be extremely responsible and loyal. Once he had secured his own shares, he would be happy for them to be managed by Cui.

Xie Peidong was the only one who understood why Cui Zhongshi had responded in this manner. He knew that Cui was protecting Fang Meng'ao. There was also a hidden motive, which was to further strengthen his relationship with various departments of the Kuomintang government, including making the senior management of the Central Bank feel that the Peking branch could not function without him. Obviously, he was unwilling to accept the organisation's arrangement that involved him withdrawing from Peking and going to the Communist-controlled area.

"It seems that there is no way to check the accounts of the Peking branch," concluded Zeng Keda. "More than 1.7 million teachers, students and residents in Peking are starving every day. It seems that very few in the party-state care about the fate of these people, so let's wait for the Communist Party to enter the city to open the granaries to provide relief! But it will take a while for the Communist troops to fight their way into Peking."

He turned to Fang Meng'ao and continued: "Captain Fang, you just mentioned the challenge system. Now you can see their action was conducted with a complete disregard for the life and wellbeing of the people. As head of the Economic Inspection Brigade dispatched to Peking by the Ministry of Defence, do you still have the heart to use your privilege?"

A loud voice came from outside the meeting room: "No, no, a challenge is required."

Everyone looked towards the doorway, including the four people with their backs to the door. Fang Meng'ao was shocked to see Fang Mengwei entering the room.

CHAPTER 14

Fang Mengwei was responding to Zeng Keda from outside the conference room. He marched into the room and took the seat that was formerly occupied by Wang Benquan, the one next to Zeng Keda.

Everyone was shocked, including Fang Meng'ao. Zeng Keda glanced at Xu Tieying: "Commissioner Xu, what's the problem here?"

"Permission to report to Commissioner Xu," said Fang Mengwei without waiting for Xu Tieying. "Last night, we got orders from the five-member investigation group to arrest the people from Yangtze Construction. I took my men to the railway station where we found they had been arrested by the Economic Inspection Brigade of the Ministry of Defence. We cooperated by transporting the one thousand tonnes of grain to the barracks of the brigade. Many of the student refugees from Northeast China and those from Peking's various universities heard news of its arrival. They have now gathered at the barracks to demand the immediate distribution of their rations. Are we supposed to distribute a thousand tonnes of grain to the university students or to the Fourth Corps? Furthermore, if there is a new wave of student protests, will the police respond by making arrests as happened during the Fifth of July Incident? I'm here specifically to ask the group of five for instructions."

The row of chairs that were formerly taken by other members of the group of five were empty. Du Wancheng, Wang Benquan and Ma Linshen had all left. Where the hell was this five-member investigation group?

Every one of the assembled company knew that Fang Mengwei's forceful questioning was directed against Zeng Keda. Zeng's face darkened. Was Fang Mengwei's move instigated by Fang Buting or by someone else? Before he could make a judgment, however, the first person he looked to was Xie Peidong.

Xie Peidong regarded Fang Mengwei with surprise and concern. His eyes appeared to indicate that he should stop.

Zeng Keda could not read Xie Peidong's facial expression, so his eyes turned to Cui Zhongshi who also found himself horrified, something that Zeng Keda believed he was incapable of faking.

However, at this moment a cloud of suspicion began to hang over Zeng Keda. He knew that Fang Mengwei had been with Fang Meng'ao the previous night when they seized the grain and arrested the pair from Yangtze Construction Company. If the two brothers were conspiring against him, it would be impossible for him to complete the mission Comrade Jianfeng had assigned. Slowly, he turned his eyes towards Fang Meng'ao.

In fact, Fang Meng'ao was also surprised by Mengwei's sudden intrusion. Deep in his heart, he would never want to get his younger brother embroiled in this most difficult emotional tangle. He was the last person he wanted to involve in a matter that was likely to be so unpredictable. After hearing Fang Mengwei's straightforward statements, he immediately understood that his younger brother was resolved to rescue his father and himself from the clear and present danger. Facing Zeng Keda's scrutinising gaze, Fang Meng'ao's extraordinary wit began to show itself, and he returned the look with an equally scrutinising stare of his own.

Zeng Keda knew that he had to avoid direct conflict with Fang Mengwei, so he turned to Xu Tieying again and said: "Commissioner Xu, he's your subordinate, please explain."

Xu Tieying wanted to offer an explanation, but he would not help to solve the problem facing Zeng Keda: "Deputy Commissioner Fang, there is no longer a five-member group. You don't have to report about your mission last night. As for how to deal with the thousand tonnes of grain, I don't have an answer. The priority for our bureau is to cooperate with the investigation team of the Ministry of Defence. I'd appreciate it if you were to head back to the barracks to help the Economic Inspection Brigade guard the grain."

"Commissioner, are you saying that the five-member group has been disbanded, and now you're telling me to take my people to help the Inspection Brigade guard the thousand tonnes of grain?"

While Fang Mengwei despised Xu Tieying, his main target today was Zeng Keda. He turned from Xu Tieying to Zeng Keda, his eyes radiating menace. "With so many starving students outside the barracks, and more due to come, we're not guarding a thousand tonnes of grain, but a thousand tonnes of gunpowder! Now that the group of five has been dissolved, who the hell is in charge here? How long will we need to stay there guarding the one thousand tonnes of gunpowder? What if we lose control, and there's a repeat of the Fifth of July Incident? Can you give us a specific instruction?"

"It surely won't be that bad, will it?" said Xu Tieying, who was aware of Fang Mengwei's bad mood and had decided to steer clear of the dispute. "I tell you to guard the barracks, and not just with guns. First, make it clear to the students that the Investigation Group of the Ministry of Defence is calling a meeting to discuss the issue, and there will be a reply very soon. Inspector-General Zeng, it's really difficult for my subordinates to execute your order. Could you explain this to Deputy Commissioner Fang?"

"I can't offer an explanation. In fact, it's the Peking branch that should offer one." Zeng Keda cast his eyes like a silver dagger at Cui Zhongshi. "Deputy Director Cui, you must have heard this. You too, Assistant Manager Xie. Is the one thousand tonnes of grain to be allocated as military supplies to the army with the appropriations to Yangtze Construction Company or to the residents of Peking with the loans to the Citizens' Food-Distribution Committee? Please give us a definite answer now so that we can make an immediate decision."

When Fang Mengwei heard that Zeng Keda intended to draw the fire against the Peking branch, especially Cui Zhongshi, he decided to fight him head-on. "I don't quite understand your question, Inspector-General Zeng. Could you clarify? I overheard you say that more than 1.7 million people in Peking were starving. But Captain Fang of the Economic Inspection Brigade, that's my elder brother, is assigned to take charge. My question is why Captain Fang has been singled out to head this group of Air Force pilots to carry out the job? Isn't there another person or department in the party-state qualified to do it? I'm sure you know as well as I do who is responsible for this mess in Peking's economy. To investigate the issue, many departments in Nanking and Peking should be the proper targets. Why should the accusation now be made against the Peking branch? Obviously, these allegations are against my father! My father is just the governor of the Peking branch, a subsidiary of the Central Bank. How come he has such great power and bravery to starve more than 1.7 million people in Peking? Why did the Ministry of Defence appoint my elder brother to investigate him? Yesterday, in response to the potential big student demonstration at the North China Headquarters for the Suppression of Communist Insurgency, you promised to distribute rations to them immediately. However, the Citizens' Food-Distribution Committee had no grain to distribute. Once again, it was left to my elder brother and others to force the Distribution Committee to send a thousand tonnes of grain, which the army's Fourth Corps tried to seize for themselves. Then the five-member group appointed me to go to the railway station to cooperate with my big brother to make the arrest and seize the grain. Last night, the two of us foolishly withheld a thousand tonnes of grain, unaware that the group had been dissolved this morning. Now, as we speak, many students are waiting anxiously outside the barracks for their rations, and instead of distributing the grain, you ordered us to guard it. Furthermore, you called the meeting to check the accounts at the Peking branch. Are you sure you can thoroughly check them today?

"Inspector Zeng, I think it's wrong for you to ask the Peking branch to offer an explanation. Instead, you owe *us* an explanation. Under the guise of investigating the corruption cases and improving the livelihoods of Peking residents, you use the two of us as gunners. While watching so many people starving in the city, you're demanding my brother and I investigate our own father. What on earth is going on?"

None of the assembled company had expected Fang Mengwei to be so blunt. They experienced a mixture of shock, worry, admiration, pride and joy.

Zeng Keda sat there, his face ghastly pale. Failing to keep his anger under control, he slapped the table with his palm and shouted: "Fang Mengwei! Aren't you aware of the discipline of the party-state? You served at the Three Principles' Youth League headquarters at the age of sixteen, the headquarters of the Kuomintang Central Committee at nineteen and you became deputy chief commissioner of the Peking Police Bureau... in your early twenties! You need to understand that even though you have powerful connections, it's the party-state that cultivates you! When the party-state cultivates you, does it teach you how to handle the relationship between public and private affairs correctly?"

"Inspector-General Zeng!" said Fang Mengwei, banging the table even louder. "Why bring up my personal history? Is it because you can't answer my questions? Since you've disclosed my past, let me disclose yours! During the War of Resistance, you were an adjutant at the brigade headquarters of the Youth Army in the south of Jiangxi Province. Within three years of the war ending, you were promoted to the rank of major general at the Ministry of Defence. Were you promoted based on your meritorious services, say fighting the Japanese during the war, or for fighting the Communists after the war, or for consolidating the economy in the rear by raising money and food for the party-state? How did the party-state cultivate you? You know as well I do, indeed everyone knows exactly how things stand!"

Zeng Keda was furious, and he stood up and yelled: "Guards!"

As the argument progressed inside, the young officer and two Youth Army sergeants outside had been nervously preparing for a possible arrest. They now broke in and stood at the door, waiting for Zeng Keda to give the order.

Under the table, Fang Meng'ao stubbed out his cigar on the palm of his hand. He sized up the young soldiers at the door.

Xie Peidong suddenly looked at Fang Mengwei and shouted: "Mengwei!"

"It's none of your business, Uncle!" Undaunted, Fang Mengwei continued his face-off with Zeng Keda: "I am ready to be tried at the special criminal court today. Wasn't it you who had my brother tried at the court several days ago? You claim that I became an official of the party-state by virtue of my connections and background. Why didn't you look at my brother's personal background when he was sentenced to death in Nanking? Engaging the Japanese Air Force in countless battles, countless sorties flown over the Hump of Death. You may have passed the death sentence, but he has already faced death countless times. Did you interrogate him about his history when you tried him?"

As he was speaking, Fang Mengwei had tears in his eyes and was choking with emotion. But he quickly composed himself, and said angrily: "Now you are making my elder brother probe into the branch's activities and tell him not to worry about the judicial notion of the challenge system. Then why was it that when my elder brother was interrogated at the Nanking special criminal court a few days ago, you insisted that the person my father sent to help had violated the legal code of the judicial challenge system? Inspector-General Zeng, as someone with no citations for any military service, do you get some kind of sick pleasure from bringing down my elder brother, a decorated war hero?"

Zeng Keda's face had turned from livid to pale, and his teeth were clenched.

The young army officer whipped out a pistol from his waist and looked at Zeng Keda. The two young soldiers with carbines followed his lead. The whole conference room was dead silent.

Fang Mengwei had already taken off his police hat, pulled out his pistol and put it in the hat. He pushed it across to Xu Tieying. Then, he looked at Fang Meng'ao emotionally.

Fang Meng'ao's eyes, which were as wide as the sky, returned the look.

"Elder brother," said Fang Mengwei, "there's something I must tell you. I dreamt about Mum last night. She told you to give up your hatred of my father, and not to work for them any more. Settle down and have a family as soon as possible." Then he walked to the Youth Army soldiers at the door.

The silhouette of Fang Mengwei walked to the door.

The silhouette of Fang Meng'ao slowly stood up.

What would happen next? Everyone held their breath.

The most anxious person of all was Xie Peidong. He was thinking hard and fast how to respond to the fast-changing situation.

The person who felt most embarrassed and was busy contemplating what to do next was Zeng Keda. Fang Mengwei had by now reached the door and said to the young army officer: "Shall we head to Nanking or somewhere? Let's go."

The young officer froze in astonishment. He looked anxiously at Zeng Keda, waiting for his order. Zeng had intended to derive personal benefit from this complicated situation. But he didn't expect that Fang Mengwei, who was so very deeply bonded with his brother Fang Meng'ao, to complicate things by suddenly turning up and having a fit of rage.

It was only then that he realised that Fang Meng'ao would pose the stiffest test. He had to implement the grand strategy meticulously designed by Comrade Jianfeng.

How to resolve the dilemma? Zeng Keda found himself grilled by the countless eyes that left him suffering in agony. Cui Zhongshi and Xie Peidong were looking at him. So were Ma Hanshan and the two people from Yangtze Construction, along with Chief Qian. Fang Meng'ao, however, the key person present, did not look at him.

Xu Tieying was the person who should have caught his eye. To his dismay, Zeng Keda saw him leaning on the table, staring down, pretending to be deep in thought.

The familiar voice of Comrade Jianfeng suddenly rang in Zeng Keda's ears: A minister without support at court and a prince fallen from grace. Then came another voice, also with a Zhejiang accent:

Reinvigorating China requires a thunderstorm,
It's awful that myriad steeds are mute with blood warm.
Heaven, I pray thee to give a big shake again,
To send forth men of many talents.

Surely, heaven will reward me with more talents like you, including those like Fang Meng'ao...

There was a sudden flash of light in Zeng Keda's eyes. Then, looking at the army officer, he called out: "Get me the phone!"

"General, what did you say?" asked the dazed young army officer.

"Get me the phone!"

"Yes sir!" The officer fully understood the order and he moved to the wall on which the phone was secured. He held the phone and cord in both hands and walked up to Zeng Keda and put it on the table.

They all expected him to call Nanking, and Comrade Jianfeng, in particular. Apart from Fang Meng'ao and Fang Mengwei, everyone including Xu Tieying now looked at Zeng Keda's hand that was working the handle.

A profound silence hung over the conference room, and the voice of a female operator could be heard clearly: "This is the special line for the five-member investigation group. Sir, who would you like to speak to?"

"Connect me with the governor of the Peking branch of the Central Bank," Zeng Keda said. "Tell him it's Zeng Keda from the Ministry of Defence. Please ask Governor Fang Buting to answer the phone in person."

Zeng Keda was calling Fang Buting! This was way beyond the expectation of everyone.

The breakfast Cheng Xiaoyun had cooked was still sitting on the living room table of the Fang mansion. Fang Buting sat motionless at the table, having not eaten a thing.

Cheng Xiaoyun knew Fang Buting well, and instead of trying to persuade him to eat, she just sat beside him.

Fang Buting's eyes, which were looking out at the doorway, slowly turned to Cheng Xiaoyun. "Do you remember when we were in Chongqing, you hid the newspaper fresh off the stand one morning, and instead took *A New Account of the Tales of the World* to read me the story of the statesman Xie An?"

"Of course," Cheng Xiaoyun whispered.

"My most vivid memory is that you were able to tell that story in everyday Chinese. Darling, tell me the story again." Then he closed his eyes and waited.

The past was like yesterday, but also like another life. Where could Cheng Xiaoyun rediscover that previous mood? Looking at an anxious Fang Buting before her, she had no option but to adjust her mind and begin the story: "In AD 383, Fu Jian of the Former Qin Dynasty commanded a million troops to conquer the Eastern Jin Dynasty. Xie An sent his younger brother and nephew with eighty thousand troops to meet them head-on at Feishui. It was a battle of life and death, a battle of vital importance for the survival of the State of Jin."

The phone on the tea table behind Fang Buting rang sharply. Cheng Xiaoyun looked at Fang Buting who slowly turned around and looked at the phone, but he had no intention of picking it up.

"Maybe it's Uncle Peidong," said Cheng Xiaoyun. "Answer it."

Fang Buting reached out and picked up the phone, only to put it to one side. He then turned to Cheng Xiaoyun and said: "Carry on."

Holding the phone in the conference room, Zeng Keda continued to hear the voice of the operator: "I'm sorry, General Zeng, Governor Fang's line is busy."

"Continue trying to connect me."

With the telephone put aside on the table, Cheng Xiaoyun looked at Fang Buting waiting with his eyes closed: "Buting..."

"Go on with the story."

Cheng Xiaoyun shook her head sadly. "Where was I?"

"It's a battle of life and death."

Cheng Xiaoyun continued: "Though Xie An is playing chess with his guest at home, in actual fact, he is expecting the battlefield report from the front. Finally, the report arrived. Xie An took a look and put it aside. He kept quiet and continued to play the game until it was over. The guest couldn't help but ask him whether it was a win or loss. Xie An replied..."

Fang Buting suddenly waved to stop Cheng Xiaoyun from

continuing. He opened his eyes and said loudly: "Xie An said: 'My son has defeated the invading army!'"

He stood up and looked at Cheng Xiaoyun affectionately. "Then you spread out the newspaper in front of me, pointing to the report, and told me that Meng'ao had shot down three enemy aircraft in the air battle with the Japanese Air Force!"

Fang Buting paused for a short moment, before a wry smile appeared on his face. "By then, Meng'ao had stopped seeing me as his father. You were sensible and tried to comfort me with this story. In fact, I'm not Xie An and I never could be Xie An. But I'm still happy to have this son anyway... My son is here to conquer the enemy again! Xiaoyun, do you think I'm his enemy?" As he spoke, he extended his hand.

Cheng Xiaoyun held his hand and cried out: "It's so hot!" She checked Fang Buting's forehead with her other hand. "Buting, you're having a fever! Driver..."

"Stop it!" said Fang Buting. "Put the phone... back."

"Buting!"

"It was an important call just now... Put the phone back."

Finally, Zeng Keda was put through to Fang Buting.

"Is that Governor Fang?" he asked, very much like a pupil might speak to his teacher. "Hello, Governor Fang. This is Zeng Keda from the Ministry of Defence... I'm not his boss... I'm humbled. Captain Fang and I are colleagues."

Zeng Keda's eyes were focused on the speaker, as if no one else present existed. Other people were looking at Fang Meng'ao, while for his part Fang Meng'ao was looking at the sky outside.

Fang Buting stubbornly held the phone, while Cheng Xiaoyun could only hold Fang Buting's hand with one hand, while helping him to sit upright with the other.

Fang Buting spoke into the microphone: "Inspector-General Zeng, it's very kind of you to say so... We met at the ambassador's residence... In fact, I should have called on you long ago, but to steer clear of suspicion..."

"It's all my fault," said Zeng Keda. "Before I came to Peking, Comrade Jianfeng repeatedly instructed me to visit Governor Fang... I must call on you to show my respect. Please give me the chance to make up for the error of my ways. I'd also like to thank you for allowing your assistant manager Xie to accompany Deputy Director Cui to work with us today... Yes, Mr Cui's been working so hard to manage all those accounts that it might be quite difficult to sort out in just a day or two. Besides, the people from the Central Bank have all gone. Neither I nor Captain Fang are economists. So I'm calling for your help. If I may, I suggest that Mr Xie help Director Cui to sort out the accounts... Thank you, Governor Fang, for your understanding. It's almost seven o'clock. We shall distribute a thousand tonnes of grain to the students today. I'll visit you either in the afternoon or in the evening... I look forward to being informed."

After the call, Cheng Xiaoyun helped Fang Buting stand up. She found that his cheeks were flushed, his forehead was damp, but his eyes were still flashing. "It turns out that this prodigal son of mine is powerful... But perhaps he didn't realise that those hiding behind him are even more powerful..."

"Well, forget about it for the time being. Let's see the doctor now."

"Attention!" commanded the sergeant at the gate of Gu Weijun's residence. Several armed guards stood to attention. Fang Meng'ao exited briskly, closely followed by Fang Mengwei. Ma Hanshan, Guo Jinyang and Shao Yuangang were the next to leave.

Fang Meng'ao strode to the jeep parked on one side of the street, while Fang Mengwei looked hesitantly at his police jeep parked opposite.

Guo Jinyang and Shao Yuangang walked Ma Hanshan over to Fang Meng'ao, yet they were no longer acting like guards or escorts to Ma.

Instead of going to his own jeep, Fang Mengwei decided to join his big brother. Fang Meng'ao glanced at his younger brother and then turned to Ma Hanshan. "Director Ma, we've been cooperative since you requested our assistance in seizing the one thousand tonnes of grain last night, haven't we?"

"Indeed. I'm humbled!" It was hard for Ma Hanshan to laugh, but he had to force a smile. "Previously, I only heard about the heroism of Captain Fang, but now I can see it with my own eyes! You're the reincarnation of the valiant general Zhao Zilong in the Battle of Changbanpo!"

"Cut the crap!" Fang Meng'ao interrupted him. "So, are you going to let us distribute the grain?"

Ma Hanshan thought deeply.

Fang Meng'ao glanced at his watch and said: "It's seven o'clock. Assemble your staff from the Citizens' Food-Distribution Committee at eight o'clock. Register the students one by one and distribute the food among them."

"Captain Fang!" Ma Hanshan said nervously. "It's impossible to get people to your barracks in an hour. Besides, I need to find the register... I couldn't do it even if you threatened to shoot me, brother."

"Then I'll give you half an hour more," replied Fang Meng'ao, looking at him sharply. "If you fail to come with the register to distribute the grain, I'll ship it all to your committee compound. I trust there will be tens of thousands of students coming to you for the grain."

The sweat on Ma Hanshan's face became more evident. "I'll do it right away! Captain Fang, if I can't make it by eight-thirty, I'll be there before nine. Would that be OK?"

Fang Meng'ao no longer looked at him. "Guo Jinyang, Shao Yuangang!"

"Yes!" they replied.

"Drive the guard's motorcycle and sidecar combination, and accompany Director Ma."

Ma Hanshan didn't dare to delay and moved quickly to the military vehicle parked at the gate. He was followed by Guo Jinyang and Shao Yuangang.

Fang Meng'ao watched the motorcycle start and drive away carrying the three people. Then he looked to Fang Mengwei.

Fang Mengwei regarded him with emotion: "Elder Brother, there will be a huge number of people wanting to get their rations. It will be quite a challenge to control the situation. Let me help you distribute the grain."

"Are you sure you can control it if you're there? I can tell from that speech you delivered just now that you're quite well informed about the current situation. You'll do a better job than I can. You'll make a triumphant general, I'm sure!"

"Big Brother..."

"Believe it or not, I must confess something," said Fang Meng'ao. "I often see Mum in my dreams. She always said I was right. She understood me. She understood the reasons for all my actions. She was always troubled by your choice of career. She wanted you to strip off that uniform and quit the job." He opened the door.

Fang Mengwei stopped Fang Meng'ao at the jeep door. "Elder Brother," he said. "You've never witnessed starving students demonstrating in the streets. Let me help you."

"I think you need to understand this. That one thousand tonnes of grain is food, and food for saving lives, not gunpowder. The starving are waiting to be saved. In my heart, they are all my fellow compatriots. They should not be regarded as a powder keg and there will be no student unrest. Go back, and don't forget the person who is most concerned for you."

He hopped into the jeep and closed the door. Fang Mengwei watched it speed away into the distance.

Inside the Austin sedan, Xie Peidong and Cui Zhongshi sat silently in the back. Not far ahead was a fork in the road.

"Let's not go back straight away," Xie Peidong said to the driver. "Dongzhong Hutong. Let's drive Deputy Director Cui home."

"Yes sir," said the driver, as he turned right at the fork.

Fang Buting's Austin sedan squeezed into the hutong and parked outside Cui Zhongshi's house.

Displaying impressive deference, the driver was soon standing beside the car near the gate, holding the back door open and waiting smilingly for Cui Zhongshi's two children to hop in.

Neither Boqin nor Pingyang had seen such a luxurious vehicle before. They were so excited at the prospect of going for a ride in it. Boqin in particular could not wait, and he dragged his sister over to the car.

"This is embarrassing!" said Ye Biyu, pulling her son back, with a look of gratitude and honour on her face. She caught sight of Xie

Peidong standing at the gate and said gratefully: "Assistant Manager Xie, thank you for giving Zhongshi extra rations. We couldn't very well ride in Governor Fang's car…"

"Deputy Director Cui has been working for the bank for almost his entire career," Xie Peidong replied with a smile. "We've not taken sufficient care of him. These twenty catties of flour are the appropriate ration for someone in his position. Don't be embarrassed."

He turned to the driver and instructed him: "When you get to the community grain store, give them the grain coupon. Here's some money. Take the kids to Daoxiangcun to buy some cakes and then come back to pick me up."

"Yes sir."

"Zhongshi." Ye Biyu looked at Cui Zhongshi standing beside Xie Peidong. "On the second shelf of the kitchen cabinet there is some Longjing tea from Hangzhou. It was picked this year. It's in the little porcelain pot on the left. Remember to make some tea for Assistant Manager Xie."

"I know. Get into the car," Cui Zhongshi replied.

Boqin was beside himself with excitement. He broke free of his mother's hand and dragged his sister into the back of the car. Ye Biyu tried to be more reserved and approached the car at a slower pace.

"Madam, please take the front seat," said the driver as he closed the rear door gently and opened the front door. With his hand on the door rim to protect the passenger, he waited for Ye Biyu to get into the car. Ye Biyu could not remember when she had last been given such special treatment and she couldn't help throwing a rare, tender look at Cui Zhongshi before entering the car.

The figure of her husband standing at the door appeared much larger than usual.

―――

"Why didn't you report Mengwei's visit to you to the party organisation?" asked Xie Peidong in the north room of Cui Zhongshi's house.

"I couldn't contact you at that time," Cui Zhongshi replied.

"Are you all alone?" Xie Peidong asked sternly. "At every level of our structure we have a party organisation, and any party member must report in a timely manner, especially in situations like this. After all, Mengwei is deputy commissioner of the Kuomintang's Peking Police Bureau. What he said to you has proved to be extremely important. If you had reported in time, we could have avoided today's situation. Do you know the serious consequences of Mengwei's boldness today?"

Cui Zhongshi became silent. Xie Peidong looked at him with profound care. He sighed, his tone softening: "Please make me a cup of Longjing."

Remembering his wife's instruction, Cui Zhongshi grabbed the teacup on the table and stood up.

"Omitting any details will bring irreparable losses to the party organisation and yourself," said Xie Peidong.

Cui Zhongshi looked directly at Xie Peidong. In his mind, Xie was his superior, his sponsor when joining the party, and party elder and personal mentor in the underground battle against the Kuomintang.

"Commissioner Xu has received instructions from Nanking to release the two Kung employees," said Zeng Keda. "But I have received orders from the Ministry of Defence demanding that you hand over the rations of the Fourth Corps."

Zeng Keda looked coldly at Kung and the woman. Nobody knew when and how their handcuffs were unlocked. He then turned to Xu Tieying and said: "Commissioner Xu, you can release them as you see fit. Regarding the Fourth Corps' rations, it's up to you whether they can be delivered in three days or not. Of course, you can also watch the disintegration of the party-state from a comfortable distance."

"Don't get me wrong..." Xu Tieying knew Zeng Keda was addressing him. Zeng Keda had turned abruptly to the stone path in the yard.

Xu Tieying's face was cold and silent. He turned his attention to

Chief Qian of the army who had been such a coward the whole night: "Chief Qian, feel free to go back."

"Mr Xu, do you intend to let me go back to my commander empty handed?"

"Then you can take Kung with you, take him to see the commander of your regiment." At long last, Kung had found someone on whom he could vent his anger! "Qian Yousheng! I've never been so damned wronged as I was last night. You son of a bitch! Why didn't you put in a word for us? And now, why are you deliberately making it difficult for me? Don't you want any grain? Well, there's a thousand tonnes of it in the barracks controlled by Captain Fang. Do you, the Fourth Corps of the National Army, have the balls to go there and claim it? You horseshit-eating commander of the Fourth Corps, if you hadn't embezzled part of what should've been delivered to your troops, you would have had enough food for the whole year! To make things simple, I won't head back to Tianjin. If you have the guts, you can come down to Nanking with me!"

Qian flushed bright red and he dared not stay any longer. He turned around and walked quickly out of the back door of Gu Weijun's residence.

"It's not your responsibility to cover for Meng'ao or me. Besides, you're not capable of doing it," said Xie Peidong, putting down his teacup. "In three days, sort out the accounts and hand them over to me. Stand ready to leave at any time."

Cui Zhongshi was taken aback: "Where to?"

"The Communist-controlled liberated area."

Cui Zhongshi was shocked. "The accounts in my possession involve many departments of the Kuomintang. It's complicated. It's impossible to explain them in detail if they were handed over to anyone else. Comrade Xie, you can't possibly take over the books at this critical time."

Xie Peidong stared at him. "Are you concerned about whether I can deal with those people from the Kuomintang, or the fact that those accounts can't stand up to the examination of the party organisation?"

"Mr Xie!" Cui Zhongshi, who had always been calm and even frail in appearance, suddenly stood up and became quite emotional. "As a subordinate under your single-line leadership, please make a record of my words and report them to the party organisation."

"What are those words?" Xie Peidong looked at him for a while. "Go ahead."

"The man who transferred money that belongs to the people from the Kuomintang's Central Bank to the pockets of corrupt Kuomintang officials is Cui Zhongshi, deputy treasury director of the Peking branch of the Central Bank, but it's not Cui Zhongshi, member of the Communist Party of China. If Cui Zhongshi hadn't done such a thing, the Kuomintang would have assigned others to do it. Although I feel guilty every time I do these things since I'm also a member of the proletariat, I'm not afraid of being scrutinised by the organisation, as it should be."

Xie Peidong was greatly shaken, but he appeared very calm. "There's no need to make a report to the superiors. I'll answer you on behalf of them right now. In the past few years, all you have done with people from various departments of the Kuomintang has been necessary for your work and all stand up to the scrutiny of the party organisation and the test of history. What you just said, and your work performance in recent years, I will include them in your personal dossier in the future. Remember, when you arrive in the liberated area, no matter which new department you report to, you should continue to conceal your previous actions to your new superiors. Any other requests?"

"Yes," said Cui Zhongshi, sitting down again. "Three days isn't enough for me to sort out the accounts and leave. Please reconsider your decision to evacuate me on behalf of the party organisation."

"It's impossible for the organisation to reach a new decision. Arrange the books at once, wait for my notice and be ready to leave at any time." Without further discussion, he moved towards the door.

"Xie!" Cui Zhongshi stood up and shouted to stop him. "My last request is my responsibility and also my right. Please respect my rights."

Xie Peidong stood by the door. "Be brief and to the point."

Cui Zhongshi walked over to Xie and said: "Before my departure, allow me to see Meng'ao."

"What do you want to say to him?"

Cui Zhongshi forced a smile. "Of course, something meant to protect him. But how to put it to him, it all depends on his reaction. Please trust me."

"You can't meet with him at this critical moment."

"He will come to me."

Xie Peidong thought for a while. "In three days, if he hasn't come to you, you must leave."

"Good." Cui Zhongshi followed Xie Peidong out of the door.

Xie Peidong's car had not yet returned. He stood under the large locust tree and looked around at Cui Zhongshi's courtyard. Then he turned and appraised Cui Zhongshi up and down. For the first time, his face was lit up with a smile.

"You're going to be liberated. Be happy. Zhongshi, have you ever thought about what you might look like in a military uniform?"

Cui Zhongshi had to smile back but he didn't say anything.

"Let's make a deal. When Peking is liberated, Meng'ao and I will put on our military uniforms. The three of us will take a photo at Desheng Gate!"

"OK, agreed," said Cui Zhongshi.

At last, the faint sound of a car engine came from the hutong outside the courtyard.

"They're back." Cui Zhongshi went to the gate and opened the door.

"Dad! Dad!"

The two children had never appeared so happy.

Ye Biyu was so elated to be carrying such a large package of cakes. When she saw Xie Peidong standing under the tree, she yelled: "Zhongshi! What are you doing? Why are you letting Assistant Manager Xie stand in the yard?"

The driver came in with a bag of flour on his shoulder. Cui Zhongshi simply ignored Ye Biyu and took the bag of flour.

Xie Peidong walked over with a smile. "We came out when we heard the sound of the car. Biyu, let me give you a word of advice."

"Mr Xie, whatever you have to say, I'm all ears."

Xie Peidong was still smiling as he admonished her: "A woman isn't supposed to talk to her husband like that. The children may look down on their father."

Ye Biyu smiled awkwardly and said: "I see."

"Let's go," Xie Peidong said to the driver.

Walking out of the door, Xie Peidong did not even look back at Cui Zhongshi behind him, but said: "Don't bother to see me out."

The doctor had gone. Cheng Xiaoyun was sitting on the side of the bed in the bedroom, counting the number of drops administered from the infusion bottle.

The infusion tube was connected to the back of the hand of Fang Buting, who was resting quietly on the large bed, propped up by three pillows. He was smiling.

"This happens all the time. When I sob, you smile." Xie Mulan, who was squatting beside the bed, composed herself and let go of Fang Buting's hand that she had been holding tightly a moment ago.

Fang Mengwei was standing quietly behind Xie Mulan. He looked at his father's face, but his father didn't look back.

Fang Buting continued to regard Xie Mulan. "Do you know why I'm smiling?"

Xie Mulan took her uncle's wandering hand again and said coyly: "I'm sure you will tell me."

Fang Buting's smile faded, but he appeared more gracious and said: "In this house, I know you care about me the most." As he was speaking, Fang Buting glanced at Fang Mengwei who remained standing behind her.

Xie Mulan held her uncle's hand more tightly. "Uncle, please tell me what I should do now."

Fang Buting gave Xie Mulan an encouraging look and said: "With your auntie here, you don't have to worry about me. Since all your classmates have gone there, I won't stop you like your dad. Go, join them at your big brother's barracks and help distribute the food to the students from the Northeast."

Xie Mulan couldn't bear to see her uncle's eyes radiating a

loving and caring quality. She looked at Cheng Xiaoyun and said: "Auntie, it's nothing serious, is it?"

Cheng Xiaoyun smiled and said softly: "No, nothing serious. The doctor said it's just the heat. After taking the medicine and IV, he'll be fine."

"Then I'll go?" Xie Mulan looked at her uncle again. Fang Buting nodded his head. Xie Mulan stood up, still holding her uncle's hand.

Fang Buting glanced at Fang Mengwei, who was standing silently. "I'll tell him to drive you there." He then looked at Xie Mulan kindly. "When you see Xiaoyu, ask her to help your elder brother more. Do you understand what I mean?"

"I certainly will," Xie Mulan said, her face lit up with excitement. "Uncle, Auntie, I'm leaving. Little Brother, let's go."

She stooped down again, took her uncle's hand and kissed it, and moved to the door.

"Dad..." said Fang Mengwei, who had been silent during this entire period of time.

Fang Buting still declined to look at him. "Remember, they claim to be 'lone patriots', but you're not one of them. There's no such a thing as a lone patriot who can save the nation or the family. Send Mulan to the barracks and find yourself a place where you can contemplate. Let's talk when you come back."

Fang Mengwei walked out with his head down.

Again, melancholy returned to Fang Buting's eyes. "Why hasn't Peidong come back?"

Cheng Xiaoyun stood up and helped Fang Buting lie down. She plumped the pillow for him to lean on. "Rest assured that Peidong has everything in hand."

"Brother Mengwei, I'm going to my big brother's barracks. You took the wrong road!" cried Xie Mulan, as they drove through the northwestern suburbs of Peking. She was sitting in the front passenger seat of the jeep, looking at the ruins of the Old Summer Palace in the distance.

Fang Mengwei was driving. "I'd like to have a word with you. When I'm done, I'll drive you to the barracks."

"That'll be too late!" said an upset Xie Mulan.

Fang Mengwei gently applied the brakes to stop the jeep. He looked at Xie Mulan and said: "Then let's speak now. It will only take a minute."

Xie Mulan had never before seen such an expression of such desolation, loneliness and even desperation in her cousin's eyes. She immediately panicked: "Mengwei, what's the matter with you today? What do you mean by 'a minute'?"

Fang Mengwei realised that his appearance had frightened his little cousin, and he smiled to conceal his mood. "Nothing. I'll drive you to my big brother's barracks." Fang Mengwei changed gear and reversed the jeep.

"Brother Mengwei!" said Xie Mulan, grabbing Fang Mengwei by the hand. "It'll take all day to distribute the grain. I'll go with you."

Although there were many slabs of white marble in the abandoned site of the Old Summer Palace where they could sit down, Fang Mengwei took Xie Mulan to a more hidden meadow. The sloping fields were covered with thick grass. Fang Mengwei broke some foliage from the nearby trees and made a proper cushion for her.

"Sit down," he told her.

Xie Mulan sat down obediently, but left a sufficient part of the soft leaf cushion for her cousin to sit as well.

However, Fang Mengwei did not sit. "I'd like to say what I'm going to say while positioned behind you. If you want to answer, you can answer. If you approve, you can nod. If you don't approve, just feel free to shake your head."

Xie Mulan was a little scared. She looked up at her cousin standing there, his silhouette almost blending into the night sky.

"Do you hate me and fear me like those classmates of yours?" asked Fang Mengwei.

Still facing each other, Xie Mulan shook her head vigorously.

Fang Mengwei was relieved but smiled a little bitterly. He slowly walked behind Xie Mulan, about a metre away from her, and sat down on the grass.

Xie Mulan turned her head: "Brother Mengwei, why can't you face me? Let's talk face to face."

"Well, listen up. Turn around if you think you can tell me face to face."

Xie Mulan was even more nervous, so she straightened herself up and looked into the empty space ahead of her: "Brother Mengwei, please speak slowly..."

"Do all the students of the Students' Union in your university hate the Kuomintang?"

Xie Mulan nodded but paused once more. "Not all of them."

Fang Mengwei's eyes glittered. "What do you mean by that?"

"They hate the Kuomintang, but not everyone in the Kuomintang."

"Give me some examples. Who don't they hate?"

"My big brother!" Xie Mulan said excitedly. "Brother Meng'ao is the ace pilot in the Kuomintang's Air Force. The students admire him and some even worship him."

"Who else?"

Xie Mulan thought, and finally offered another name: "Mr He Siyuan. He used to be the mayor of Peking Municipality in the Kuomintang government, but he has the people in his heart. My classmates and teachers respect him very much."

Fang Mengwei pondered for a short while. "Who do they hate most? For example, the Central Bureau of Investigation, the Military Bureau or the police force?"

"Yes, they hate their guts."

"Including me?"

Xie Mulan was stunned. She now realised why her cousin had driven her here to ask these questions. She shook her head, even though she herself didn't know whether she was responding on behalf of herself or all the Students' Union members.

"Your cousin is deputy commissioner of the Peking Police Bureau, and also deputy director of the Investigation Department of the Peking Garrison headquarters. Don't they hate me?"

"Not really," said Xie Mulan, turning around. "On the fifth of July, you refused an order to fire on the students. You also secretly opened up a channel for them to escape. Brother Mengwei, many students told me you are a man of conscience."

Fang Mengwei looked away, apparently unwilling to let his cousin see his face – his eyes were wet with tears.

Xie Mulan turned her head back, with her back to Brother Mengwei. "I know you are a good man, Mengwei, and in the future more people will know you are a good man. The Communist Party doesn't regard all Kuomintang officials as bad people... Brother, did you bring me here today simply to ask these questions?"

Fang Mengwei's expression became more solemn: "Do you know any Communists?"

"Brother, are you asking me to name individuals?"

Fang Mengwei realised that the look on his face betrayed him, and he immediately sought to clarify: "It's not my business to find out about the Communists. I wouldn't do it even if I were asked to. Besides, you can't possibly know who really is a Communist."

Xie Mulan also softened her tone: "Then why did you ask?"

Fang Mengwei tried his best to keep his voice soft: "I have to check out the background of a particular person. You can tell me if you're willing to cooperate because it concerns my big brother and whether this person is a member of the Communist Party."

Xie Mulan understood what Mengwei had asked, and she had some idea who he was referring to: "Go ahead... though I might not know the answer."

Fang Mengwei tried his best to speak in a friendlier tone as he slowly uttered a name: "He Xiaoyu."

This was the name Xie Mulan expected to hear and she shook her head immediately: "No, she isn't."

"Like you, a progressive student?"

Xie Mulan nodded her head but then shook it again. "She's actually much more progressive than me."

"Mulan!" Fang Mengwei called her name from behind.

Xie Mulan turned her head, and saw that Fang Mengwei had stood up and was approaching her. Xie Mulan watched her cousin squat down in front of her.

"I want her to be my sister-in-law," said Fang Mengwei. "Would you like her to be your sister-in-law?"

Xie Mulan gave him a firm nod, but she appeared hesitant again.

"Tell me, what's the problem."

"No matter how popular brother Meng'ao is among the

students, none would marry him now," said Xie Mulan. "After all, he is a colonel and captain in the Kuomintang Army."

"What if he retires from the army and resigns his captaincy? If he leaves the army and goes to the United States, Xiaoyu can follow him and study there. I guess Uncle He would agree. As long as Uncle He approves, he can approach Ambassador John Leighton Stuart to assist us in the matter."

Hearing this, Xie Mulan's eyes were full of concern. She looked at her cousin and said: "And if Uncle He doesn't agree?"

"Why?"

Xie Mulan hesitated, looked at him in a daze and thought. She suddenly said: "Brother Mengwei, you'd better stand behind me."

Fang Mengwei was right in the premonition that was buried deep in his heart. He stood up and walked behind Xie Mulan. He didn't sit down. "Please carry on."

"Because of one man."

"Who is he?"

"Professor Liang," said Xie Mulan. "He's Uncle He's favourite student, and Xiaoyu has also been very close to him."

"Is he the same progressive professor worshipped by many of your female classmates?" Fang Mengwei did not try to conceal his disgust.

"Brother Mengwei!" Xie Mulan didn't look back, but she could tell his tone was full of anger. "What do you mean?"

"Nothing. I'm not speaking on behalf of the Kuomintang. Both Xiaoyu and you are free to like this person or even worship this person, but he is not suitable for either of you."

"Brother Mengwei, can you take me to the barracks now?"

"I will." Fang walked past Xie Mulan and down the slope.

Xie Mulan realised that the young cousin whom she had grown up with was utterly alone. She vaguely sensed that he had thoughts buried deep in his heart, but she dared not think more about them. An unprecedented rush of panic surged up within her. Stepping on the soft grass, she was on the verge of tears as she followed her cousin.

On the first floor of Yenching University's Foreign Languages Bookstore, the eyes of a young lady were looking affectionately at a male figure in the gloom.

Liang Jinglun was standing by the window that overlooked the army barracks where Fang Meng'ao's Youth Aviation Brigade was stationed. In the distance, he could see that a crowd had gathered outside the gates, appearing like countless black spots.

The grain was being distributed and many people were collecting their rations in an orderly fashion. It was such an amazing spectacle that a massive crowd had assembled.

"Can you hear the sound of the crowd?" Liang Jinglun asked softly, still looking out of the window.

Sitting at the desk, He Xiaoyu, who had been gazing at his silhouette, listened carefully and said: "No, it's very quiet."

"Does it remind you of a particular poem?"

"I'm not in the classroom, and I don't want to be reminded of it."

"'Amid the silence comes the crash of thunder!'" said Liang Jinglun, quoting Lu Xun's poem. "Come and see if you can make out Fang Meng'ao from among the crowd."

"I see him," He Xiaoyu replied seriously. Liang Jinglun was perplexed. He turned to look out of the window once more, then back at where He Xiaoyu was sitting. "Can you really see him from where you are?"

He Xiaoyu looked out of the window and replied: "Of course. He's already in my heart. Do I need to see him with my eyes?"

Liang Jinglun was even more surprised. He walked slowly to the stool beside He Xiaoyu.

Liang Jinglun imagined himself lifting up a corner of his thin gown and sitting next to He Xiaoyu who was in her short student summer dress. But instead, he went to He Xiaoyu's desk, raised the hem of his long gown and sat down on another stool, thereby blocking He Xiaoyu's view of the window. He looked at her and said: "You shouldn't attend such a big gathering in the future, but I don't mean to keep you from going today."

He Xiaoyu felt the breeze blowing as Liang Jinglun walked by in his gown. She felt that the breeze was gently turning the pages of the book in her heart.

Now that her view of the window was blocked, she had to look at him instead. "Didn't we agree to invite Captain Fang Meng'ao's flying brigade to attend a student party? I'm supposed to invite him, yet I can't attend myself, is that right?"

"Of course you can."

"Didn't you just say that I couldn't go to the meetings?"

"Sorry, I didn't mean that." Liang Jinglun smiled bitterly. "I was referring to the gathering of petitions and protests, including today's large gathering where food is being distributed to so many students from the Northeast."

"Then I'll pretend to be willing to marry him, visit his home, go to his barracks, or ask him out and go for a moonlit walk amid the flowers?" He Xiaoyu looked into Liang Jinglun's eyes.

"Xiaoyu..."

"I know, this is for the New China!" He Xiaoyu rushed to say the words. Liang Jinglun had to remain silent.

He Xiaoyu looked at Liang whose melancholy she had always valued, but the thought of having to hide her real feelings from him suddenly made her heart ache. She wanted to tell him they were comrades who shared a common ideal, albeit within two organisations, but she could not.

"Tell me about the New China we are looking forward to. What kind of place will it be?"

Liang Jinglun's heart seemed to plunge into a bottomless valley. He raised his head, stood up and held the falling heart in his arms. He recited the following passage with enthusiasm: "'It is like a ship far out to sea whose masthead can already be seen from shore. It is like the morning sun in the east whose shimmering rays are visible from a high mountain top. It is like a baby about to be born, moving restlessly in its mother's womb.'"

He Xiaoyu stood up in great excitement.

CHAPTER 15

"I've no idea about tonight's get-together, Comrade Liu."

Through his thick glasses, it was possible to see the consternation in Yan Chunming's eyes. He was sitting on a stone bench in the woods by Weiming Lake. He seemed to have lost his temper, and putting down his book, he was about to stand up.

"Pick up your book, Professor Yan," said Liu, continuing to sweep the leaves nearby. "Remember, you are chatting with a school janitor."

The slanting sunbeams filtered through the foliage of the trees. There was silence all around, an absence of anyone talking. Yan Chunming was well aware of the strict discipline of the party's underground organisation, but that should not mean that everyone is suspicious. Therefore, a trace of dissatisfaction welled up in his heart. He picked up his book with apparent disapproval.

Again, Liu swept a pile of leaves, straightened up and smiled. "Professor Yan, many teachers are protesting against the Nationalist government. But you seem to be in something of a relaxed mood. I'm amazed you are able to concentrate on your reading."

The sun shone on Liu through a gap in the trees. The smile on his face was honest and humble, but in Yan Chunming's eyes, Liu's figure was covered by a golden halo, and the smile on his face was not genuine, but a representation of the party's draconian disciplines.

"Hold the book in your hand, let's carry on chatting." Liu continued sweeping the leaves.

Yan Chunming had to resume what he was doing. Holding the book in one hand, he smiled a reluctant smile and continued to pretend to be a professor chatting with a school janitor. He said to Liu: "Really, I had no idea up to now that the Students' Union planned to invite Fang Meng'ao to this party at the university. Was it a spontaneous act?"

"Has the party's student movement department lost its leadership over the Students' Union," Old Liu said with a smile, "or have you given up leadership over the student movement department of Yenching University?"

Old Liu squatted down and put down his broom. He picked up some leaves from the lawn with his hands. "There's no need for an investigation. It's all the work of Comrade Liang Jinglun."

He Xiaoyu was standing in front of the Foreign Languages Bookstore window. As the setting sun shone through the window and framed her body, the view of her from behind appeared graceful.

Liang Jinglun's long gown slowly floated to where she stood. The hem fluttered slightly even after he had stopped behind her. He was taller than He Xiaoyu so he could see over her head. But he found that his eyes were stabbed by the flash of sunlight. The military barracks in the distance appeared merely as a dazzling white.

Liang Jinglun knew that He Xiaoyu was not looking for Fang Meng'ao whom she could not see anyway. He felt so relieved that he exhaled a long breath that ruffled her beautiful hair.

He Xiaoyu's desire was aroused. She slowly reached up a hand, but she didn't use it to brush her hair, it was just held in mid-air.

Liang Jinglun was momentarily stunned. He had been looking forward to this moment for many months, only to find it arrive today when they were bathed in full sunlight. Was it happiness or pain, or pain accompanied with excitement?

He bent his face slowly to He Xiaoyu's delicate fingers. Her fingertips touched his face. The gentle hand was soon all over Liang

Jinglun's cheek. Both her hand and his face were suspended in the space of a moment – the clinging hand and the face. Perhaps both hoped this moment would be fixed for an eternity.

At least on He Xiaoyu's part, she just wanted the face that she was holding to stay still. For her, it would be consoling enough to keep her hand close to his hair without actually touching it.

But there was no eternity.

Liang Jinglun's hands reached down He Xiaoyu's back, hugging her waist gently yet tightly. He buried his head in her palm and on her shoulder.

He Xiaoyu nervously closed her eyes even though she still found herself bathed in sunlight. Suddenly, she felt a little moisture on her neck and shoulders – not sweat, but tears.

She was so startled that she opened her eyes and turned around quickly. She saw tears in the eyes of this erudite and strong-willed man in front of her.

She didn't know if she should hesitate any more. Finally, she embraced him and put her face on his chest, with her tears falling on the lapels of his gown.

Comrade Liu had moved around and was sweeping the leaves behind the stone bench on which Yan Chunming was sitting. Yan was still listening to him while wearing a forced smile, his book in his hand.

Liu said: "Comrade Peng Zhen made it clear in his Sixth of July Instruction that the number of activists among the broad masses should be small, well trained and well disguised. Only within a certain organisational limit can certain events be hosted, to host the events permitted by the situation. Comrade Liang Jinglun involved so many important activists among the students for tonight's event. He went so far as to invite Fang Meng'ao's brigade to the get-together under such complicated circumstances, which clearly violates the spirit of the party's Sixth of July Instruction."

"I'll find out which student activists were involved in organising the event." Yan Chunming was motivated by a desire to evade severe reprimand by the party organisation.

"Let's just wait until your party is over!" Liu still smiled, but his deep voice sounded very stern. "Do you think the Kuomintang will be merciful enough to use the money that they appropriated to fight the civil war as well as the corrupt foreign currency held in their American accounts to save their suffering compatriots? Is that right? If not, it will lead to a new 'Seventh of July Incident', by exposing the majority of students, especially our valued activists, to possible arrest by the Kuomintang secret police. Comrade Liang Jinglun failed to form a clear assessment of the situation. Nor can you, the party chapter that controls the Student Movement Department in Peking."

Hearing these words, Yan Chunming stood up.

"Mind your step, Professor Yan," said Liu. "Find Professor Liang immediately and abort the action before it takes place."

Having given this instruction, Liu ambled to the other side of the woods with his dustpan and broom.

Liang Jinglun tried his best to find the glow in He Xiaoyu's eyes which were awash with tears. However, He Xiaoyu closed her eyes softly once more.

Liang vaguely sensed her ambiguity by shedding tears the way he did on her shoulder, much like the ancient sentiment of "returning pearls to the one she could not afford to love". Nevertheless, he hoped that it was just the shyness of a young woman.

He gently turned her around again, put his arm around her and whispered into her ear: "Fang Meng'ao defied orders to bomb Kaifeng, and had the guts to seize the grain for the people of Peking from the Fourth Corps of the Kuomintang Army. I daresay he will come to join us this evening. The purpose of the get-together is to tell the people of Peking that the Kuomintang government did not run short of food, but instead used it to fight the civil war. They embezzled the food as well. So this event is highly significant. Many Students' Union members are already at the barracks. Xie Mulan must be there already. When you get there, you can join others in inviting Fang Meng'ao and his brigade."

"What would the Kuomintang authorities think of Fang

Meng'ao, knowing that he's going to attend our event? If there's some kind of negative impact, will they disband his team? They're an important force we should endeavour to win over, aren't they?"

"The Kuomintang is divided into two factions," said Liang Jinglun. "It is the newly rising faction that has elevated Fang Meng'ao to this important position. It has powerful political backers and is more reactionary in its politics. That is, to try to save the Kuomintang government that is about to collapse. Therefore, they are also desperately striving for popular support. Of course, the nature of their actions is to deceive public opinion. Fang Meng'ao's attendance at our get-together is also in line with their intention, so it would not result in the dismissal of his brigade... It is estimated that all the food will be distributed in an hour from when you arrive at the barracks."

Liang Jinglun paused and listened. The faint sound of a telephone ringing downstairs could just be heard.

After a short while, Ms Sofia's voice came from below: "Liang, it's for you."

He Xiaoyu turned her head and looked at Liang Jinglun.

Liang Jinglun continued to hug her gently. "Thank you," he called out. "Do you know who's calling?"

Sofia's voice grew louder from downstairs: "It's the school library."

Liang Jinglun was shocked, but his face showed an earnest wish for understanding. "I really don't want to leave you now."

"Go," said He Xiaoyu, smiling with the reserve of a young woman. "I should get going myself to the Aviation Brigade barracks."

Liang Jinglun could not show his eagerness to answer the phone, but by now He Xiaoyu had gently broken loose from his embrace. "Go, take the call."

Liang Jinglun walked to the door, and then he stopped to look back at He Xiaoyu.

He Xiaoyu whispered but her voice was loud enough for Liang Jinglun to hear: "I will not fall in love with him... Nor will I fall in love with you."

Liang Jinglun trembled with a little pain. But when he saw He Xiaoyu's loving smile, he quickly returned with a confident smile of his own. As he spun to open the door, he found himself in pitch darkness.

His smile disappeared and his figure vanished against the dark of the stairwell.

———

An impromptu meeting had been convened a short while ago. Zeng Keda was standing in front of his desk in the meeting room in Gu Weijun's residence, wearing a white Hawaiian short-sleeved shirt.

The other participants were in short-sleeved military uniforms. Standing in the living room, they were all holding their military caps. This group of young soldiers included the two military agents who had followed Cui Zhongshi all the way from Nanking; two more were the student agents who had escorted Zeng Keda on bicycles to see Liang Jinglun on multiple occasions, while the final pair were Zeng Keda's adjutant and the officer of the Youth Army.

"Did you inform our reporters from the news agencies?" Zeng Keda asked the two agents from the Chiang Kai-shek Student Society.

"Yes general, they've all been informed," one of the students replied.

"Tell them that at tonight's party, they are requested not to appear as journalists, especially when they take photos. All photos must be taken in secret. Two points must be highlighted in their coverage of the event in tomorrow's newspapers. First, students from Northeast China and the staff and students from Peking universities and the Economic Inspection Brigade dispatched by the Ministry of Defence to Peking are of one family! Second, the Nationalist government regards eliminating the suffering of the people as its highest priority. The Fourth Corps of the National Army has given its own military grain to the students from the Northeast and the teachers and students of the universities in Peking. Have I made myself clear?"

"Very clear, general," the two student agents replied in unison.

"Are you certain you're clear?"

The two students looked at Zeng Keda in puzzlement.

"All of you know Comrade Liang Jinglun," Zeng Keda continued, "but you must not have any contact with him at the gathering."

"Understood," the two students replied.

"All right, act now."

"Yes sir!" Holding their military caps, the two secret service students saluted simultaneously. They turned around neatly and walked out of the door after putting on their caps.

Zeng Keda's eyes turned to the two military spies from Nanking. "Your job is still to focus on Cui Zhongshi. Since he can identify both of you, don't do it yourselves. Tell our comrades from the Military Intelligence Department of the Ministry of Defence in Peking to monitor him and report the situation to you."

"Yes sir," the two answered.

"Go."

They saluted him, turned around and walked out of the room.

Zeng Keda looked at the Youth Army officer and asked: "How many people were originally assigned to protect Fang Meng'ao's brigade?"

"One platoon, general," the young army officer replied. "Three shifts a day."

"Too few," Zeng Keda said as he looked out of the window. "Add another reinforced platoon to ensure the safety of Fang Meng'ao and his brigade. No matter who they are – the Fourth Corps, the Central Bureau of Investigation or the Military Bureau – those powerful men and scumbags who were hurt by Captain Fang may endanger his life at any time. If any signs are detected, identify yourselves as members of the Bureau of Reserve Cadres and restrain them!"

"Yes sir!" The alert young army officer saluted, and he immediately turned around and went out.

Only Zeng Keda and his adjutant were left in the room. Zeng Keda appeared extremely fatigued and sat down. The adjutant looked at him with concern.

"Sir, I'll heat some water so you can take a bath and then have a nap. I'll wake you in time for you to visit Governor Fang."

"Good. Prepare a set of plain clothes for me. Also, tell Chairman Zhang of the Chiang Kai-shek Student Society to return the Yixing purple sand tea set with Comrade Jianfeng's name engraved on it. I want to give it to Governor Fang."

Yan Chunming was sitting in the rare books section of the Yenching University library. His appreciation of and trust for Liang Jinglun sitting opposite him were gone. He just stared at him through his thick lenses and awaited his answer.

"I didn't know that until quite recently. As for tonight's gathering, it's hosted by the Students' Union at the urgent request of the students themselves."

Liang Jinglun sensed the existence of a powerful force behind Yan Chunming. Weighing his words carefully, he went on: "I called you before we met. I planned to report to you about it. No one answered the phone."

"I don't understand you." Yan Chunming's sternly scrutinising attitude reinforced Liang Jinglun's premonition. "Did the Students' Union tell you after they had reached their decision or consult you before they did?"

Liang tried to control his inner shock. Aware that any lies he told would soon be exposed, he had no alternative but to answer truthfully: "They asked me before making a decision."

Yan Chunming frowned at his reply, but the scrutinising look in his eyes was disappearing, with only sternness remaining. "That's to say, you made the decision on behalf of the Students' Union! Comrade Liang Jinglun, what you did today has seriously violated the working principle of the party's spy network. You acted in complete disregard of the organisation."

"Is it really so serious, Comrade Chunming?" Liang Jinglun had to pretend to be surprised. "Now is the time to further expose the truth about the Seventh of July Incident caused by the reactionary resolution made by the Peking Senate of the Kuomintang to disperse the Northeast students. Isn't this gathering an opportunity to further expose the corrupt and reactionary nature of the Kuomintang from within?"

"Are you advising or lecturing the party organisation?" Yan Chunming was so angry that he stabbed the table with his finger.

"If you are giving advice to the organisation, it should have happened a few hours ago. If you are lecturing, Comrade Liang Jinglun, you have no right or qualifications to do so."

Liang Jinglun responded with silence.

"You are quite a talent," Yan Chunming continued. "You can even recite many of the works of Marx, Lenin and Chairman Mao. A few days ago, you were able to reel off whole paragraphs of Comrade Peng Zhen's Sixth of July Instruction, almost word for word, weren't you? Why did you act today against the spirit of this instruction? It's time you stopped being presumptuous, Comrade Liang Jinglun. Since you're directly in contact with all the important Students' Union activists, find them immediately and cancel tonight's gathering."

"Comrade Chunming..."

"This is the decision of the party, and it is final!"

Liang Jinglun lowered his head and pondered for a short moment, then raised his head slowly. "But the students from the union have already gone to Fang Meng'ao's barracks. How can I inform them?"

"Don't you have legs? Is it not a public event? You've been working openly as a liberal professor all the time. Go to the barracks now and cancel the party!"

The last Dodge military truck, the last truckload of grain and the last batch of Northeast students sitting on grain bags loaded on the truck. Slowly, the trucks rolled through the iron gate of the Youth Aviation Brigade barracks as the sun was setting over the Western Hills.

The students who were sitting on the grain bags stood up. Some cried and waved emotionally to the student representatives of Peking Students' Union on the other side of the iron gate who were in charge of grain distribution. They returned their shouts and waves.

Xie Mulan was the first to climb onto the long table, waving desperately and with tears flashing in her eyes. Many others followed, standing on the table and waving to the receding grain trucks.

Behind the students, the staff of the Citizens' Food-Distribution Committee slouched around the warehouse. It was difficult to tell if they were exhausted, angry or just helpless. Some slumped on stools, others simply lay down on the spot, enduring the shouts of the students standing on the long table with notebooks and receipts that had piled up around their feet.

Fang Meng'ao was nowhere to be found either inside or outside the barrack gate. Section Chief Li came out of the guard room, followed by Section Chief Wang.

Seeing what was going on, Li's face appeared like an aubergine withered by the sun, while Wang's face resembled a bitter melon that had been picked several days ago. Li looked at Wang and said: "Go ahead, you tell them please."

Section Chief Wang, who was beginning to lose his stamina, shouted to the student representatives in a voice that started to quaver: "Students! Dear students..."

None of the students could hear him. "Can't you speak up?" Section Chief Li complained. "I can't hear you."

"I wasn't born with a loud voice. Would you prefer to speak to them?"

"It's up to you." Li glanced at his office workers who were slumped on chairs and on the ground. Unwilling to talk to the students again, he glanced at one of his clerks who was sitting on a chair in front of him. The man stood up lazily and gave up the chair to him.

He slumped down in the chair vacated for him. "I can tell you that I'm from the Social Welfare Bureau. Director Ma Hanshan, the King of Hell, can control my hands but not my feet. When it comes to you, however, he can control your vital organs... your intestines, liver, stomach and lungs. If you fail to sort out all these receipts, and if he can't finish what he's been assigned to do for Captain Fang, let's see whose skin he'll strip off." With that, he simply ignored Wang and closed his eyes as if he were about to fall asleep.

Wang was both miserable and angry: "Even if I speak to them, you just can't doze off here. Can't you at least advise me?"

Li, still with his eyes closed, said: "Do you see the female student who is standing tallest?"

Wang looked to where the students were standing. "Which one?"

"The one with wings like a phoenix. She is Fang Meng'ao's cousin. This is the last time I'll advise you. Hope it's useful."

Wang's eyes widened and searched for any students who might match the description. He was able to recognise the animated and beautiful Xie Mulan, who was still standing on the table. He went up to her with a forced smile.

———

The sight in the barracks of the Youth Aviation Brigade was barely believable. All day long, between ten and twenty thousand people were collecting their rations outside the barracks, but the dorms inside were closed and all members of Fang Meng'ao's brigade were ordered to take their noon naps.

It was a scorching summer day, twenty strong pilots in twenty beds were sleeping, all stripped to the waist. The whole scene resembled a Renaissance painting.

A pair of eyes secretly opened. Guo Jinyang had heard some movement outside the barracks, and he looked at other members of the brigade. Some were still asleep, while several others opened their eyes. They all heard the movement outside the dorm. They winked at each other and then looked at the open door of Fang Meng'ao's room at the far end of the dormitory.

There were two idioms used by the ancients to describe the great men and generals before major battles. The first referred to one who sleeps in his armour with his weapon under the pillow, the other was one who is as quiet as a virgin.

Around this time, Fang Meng'ao seemed to fit both descriptions, or neither. He was lying on his side on the copper bed propped up by two large pillows. A hand was positioned under his head, his face quiet and his breathing even. With his legs curled up, he looked like a sleeping child.

Almost without noise, Guo Jinyang stuck his head through the open door, looking at the captain on the bed. He was so surprised that he stood there frozen.

He saw the captain smiling, smiling like a child for a few seconds, then frowning before his face became calm again. The captain was fast asleep. Guo Jinyang's eyes flashed a trace of love and admiration. He withdrew his head slowly.

Another five pilots secretly got up, with Guo Jinyang in the front, four behind him. They walked like cats, quietly to the door.

A large lock secured the inside of the door, and there was a barred window above the door. Guo Jinyang made a gesture, and a tall pilot squatted down. Guo Jinyang stepped on his shoulders, and when his teammate stood upright, Guo Jinyang was able to look through the window at the terrace outside.

"You sons of bitches! I know you've had a long day, but you can't quit your jobs like this. Damn it! Get off your arses and sort out the accounts!" Ma Hanshan, followed by Section Chief Wang, was cursing all the way from the guard room.

Li stood up lazily, and so did the staff.

When Ma Hanshan saw the staff were still standing and had no intention of organising the accounts, blue veins stood out on his temples. Looking at the lieutenant in the guard room, he yelled: "Gun! Give me a gun!"

All the students looked at him in astonishment. However, like dead pigs, his subordinates were inactive and unresponsive.

"Director Ma, what do you need a gun for?" asked the lieutenant.

"In troubled times, the lazy must be punished with harsh measures. Pity the party-state if I don't manage to kill at least one or two people today!"

"Director," Section Chief Li said, "trust me, none of the brothers has said that they won't sort out the accounts. Captain Fang has issued specific instructions on behalf of the investigation team of the Ministry of Defence that we must work together with representatives of the Students' Union to sort out the accounts today.

But the representatives aren't cooperating. So who exactly are you going to shoot?"

Ma Hanshan was stunned and looked at the dozens of student representatives standing together out there.

Xie Mulan straightened up and went up to him. "Our Students' Union has decided to invite Captain Fang and his brigade to a party this evening. All the accounts should be sealed up for safekeeping. We'll send someone to take care of them tomorrow. Does Director Ma still want to execute anyone?"

How come there was a party? How could she speak in such a disrespectful way?

Ma Hanshan was about to rage at Xie Mulan when Wang whispered in his ear: "Director, it is her, the cousin of Captain Fang."

The students gathered behind Xie Mulan and looked at Ma Hanshan. Ma was rendered speechless, unable to show either anger or resentment. He stretched out his spindly fingers and rubbed his temple a few times before looking at Xie Mulan and saying: "I think you should call it a day. Why do you have to mess things up and complicate matters during the period of counter-Communist insurgency?" Turning to his subordinates, he said: "We must sort out the accounts today. If they don't cooperate, we won't be to blame. Let's pack the books and return them to the distribution committee."

Xie Mulan was about to speak again when a male student beside her, apparently the head of the Students' Union, stopped her and said to Ma Hanshan: "Without the approval of the Students' Union representatives, you mustn't take the books away."

"Army! Police!" shouted Ma Hanshan, looking at the officers standing inside and outside the gate. "On behalf of the Nationalist government, I order you to take these students out of the barracks!"

The students didn't speak, but the lieutenant of the guards came up to him and said: "Director Ma, that is not a good idea."

"What do you mean?"

"Captain Fang gave us an order. We must handle the books together with these student representatives. We can't get rid of them."

"Well, well! It's hard to tell the difference between the Kuomintang and Communist Party!" Ma Hanshan got so exasperated that he raved again: "Then please, ask Captain Fang immediately!"

"I'm sorry, the whole brigade is taking a nap. We can't very well disturb them before six."

Ma Hanshan jumped up and shouted: "We all worked through the night, without sleeping a wink. How come they're sleeping and preventing us from sorting out the accounts? And why this get-together anyway? My life is on the line. I'll wake them up myself."

"Do as you please."

Ma Hanshan took a few steps, looked at the closed door and stopped again, turned around and pointed to Wang and Li: "You, and you, go wake them up!"

Neither Li nor Wang dared to knock on the door. Both turned away to look at the ground.

The students laughed in delight, none more so than Xie Mulan before she felt someone tugging at her side. She looked back, only to find He Xiaoyu standing beside her.

―――

The pilots were known for their sharp eyesight and keen hearing. Guo Jinyang, who was looking out through the window above the door, had been enjoying the scene for quite a while.

"What do you see?" one pilot asked in a low voice.

"A get-together. They're going to invite us to a party tonight!" Guo whispered.

"We heard that, too. How many female students are there? Are they pretty?"

"They're pretty, all of them, prettier than pretty!" said Guo Jinyang.

"Come on, let me look, then it's your turn," the pilot below said to another, signalling he should squat down.

Guo Jinyang jumped down. "No more looking, let's try to get rid of those bastards from the Citizens' Food-Distribution Committee, or they'll end up ruining tonight's party."

"The door's locked. The captain has the key. How can we get out?"

"Just watch me," Guo Jinyang said as he tiptoed to Fang Meng'ao's room.

Fang Meng'ao was still sound asleep as Guo Jinyang slipped into his bedroom. He measured two spoons of instant coffee into his cup, added hot water from a thermos bottle, then quietly stirred it with the spoon.

When the coffee was ready, he went to Fang Meng'ao's bed and continued to stir it, as he hummed the music to *Blooming Flowers, Full Moon*.

Fang Meng'ao's eyes opened.

Guo Jinyang smiled slyly. "Good evening, captain," he said as he handed over the coffee.

Fang Meng'ao did not take the coffee, but sat up and then got out of bed. He looked at his watch and said: "Do you know what makes me so unwell?"

"I've no idea," Guo Jinyang replied seriously. "Please tell me."

"Motherless at the age of three and rising at the fifth watch before dawn. Guo Jinyang, you've just disturbed my sleep. Do you know how I'll punish you?"

"Captain, sir, it's not the fifth watch before dawn, it's half past five in the afternoon. So there's no need for any punishment." Then he handed the coffee to him with both hands.

Fang Meng'ao took the coffee with one hand and handed the key to him with the other. The key to the door!

Guo Jinyang's eyes glowed with excitement. He took the key with a military salute, his knees touching. With the key in his hand, he strode out of the room.

As soon as he stepped out of Fang Meng'ao's room, Guo Jinyang was heard shouting outside: "Get up! Put on your clothes. Let's carry out our task!"

"Resign! I'll go to Peking municipal government to resign now!" Ma Hanshan stood on the large terrace and called out to Guo Jinyang and the pilots. "We'll leave all the books to you in your barracks. Don't come to me if you want them checking."

Following the tirade, Ma Hanshan turned around and went to

his car parked at the gate. "Where is the driver?" he bellowed. "Where the fuck is the driver?"

The driver had been waiting for him at the door where he usually got into the car. But because of the throng of people who blocked his sight, Ma Hanshan went to the wrong side. He continued to yell: "Damn that stupid driver."

"Director, you are on the wrong side. Come round this way." The driver was also angry today.

"Damn it, forget about coming to work tomorrow!" said Ma Hanshan as he opened the door himself and got in.

The driver shut the door on the other side of the car and muttered to himself as he walked around the front of the car: "You're impossible to serve. But it's no big deal. The worst that can happen is that my family starves to death."

Seeing Ma Hanshan's car pass through the gate, Li and Wang looked at each other and almost simultaneously said: "Off we go."

With all the grain receipts left on the long table, the clerks from the Citizens' Food-Distribution Committee moved to the two trucks parked outside the barracks gate.

The representatives of the Students' Union clapped. The students sang happily even though nobody knew who took the lead in singing these lines:

Two tigers, two tigers, run fast, run fast!
One has no tail, one has no ears, how strange, how strange!

"My fellow students!" shouted the male student in charge of the Students' Union. "Help to seal up the grain receipts."

All the other union representatives rushed to the long table to sort out the receipts. The male student in charge of the Students' Union and He Xiaoyu discussed something in a low voice, after which He Xiaoyu whispered to Xie Mulan. Xie gathered the girls together. A group of female students stood in lines and said in unison to Guo Jinyang and his pilots: "On behalf of students from Northeast China and the universities in Peking, the Students' Union of Yenching University sincerely invites all pilots of the Youth Aviation to our party tonight. Thank you for being on the side of the people!"

Guo Jinyang and the pilots smiled and looked at each other.

"This needs to be approved by our captain," said Guo Jinyang.

"Let's prepare the invitation," said Xie Mulan, jumping with joy. "He Xiaoyu and I are going to give Captain Fang the most sincere invitation ever!"

"Please go," said Guo Jinyang, looking at the male student in charge of the Students' Union. "The captain's room is small, so no more than two of you."

"He Xiaoyu, Xie Mulan, please tell him that it is our common wish to invite him to the party," said the male student in charge of the Students' Union.

"Don't worry," said Xie Mulan. "If he doesn't accept the invitation, the two of us will kidnap him!"

Guo Jinyang beckoned the other pilots to stay, and he himself walked Xie Mulan and He Xiaoyu to the brigade dorm in the barracks.

Liang Jinglun was the only one left in He Qicang's house. He needed to use his phone in order to call the Ministry of Education in Nanking.

With the door and windows closed, Liang Jinglun quickly started winding the telephone handle. "This is Chancellor He's home at Yenching University. I've urgent business, please put me through to Inspector-General Zeng's room in Building Number Two in Ambassador Gu Weijun's residence. He is from the Ministry of Defence."

The call was actually connected, but only a dull sound could be heard. In order to let Zeng Keda sleep, his adjutant had wrapped the phone in several thick towels.

The adjutant immediately picked up the phone with the speaker still wrapped in the towels.

The caller's voice at the other end sounded faint: "Is this the room of Inspector-General Zeng of the Ministry of Defence?"

The adjutant glanced at the clock on the wall and kept his voice as low as possible: "Who is calling? Listen, Inspector-General Zeng is dealing with some urgent business. Except for calls from Nanking, all other calls will be redirected after seven o'clock."

The adjutant waited for the caller to hang up before putting the phone back on its base. Again, he wrapped up the phone with towels. Then he tiptoed to the door of the living room connecting the bedroom and listened to make sure that Zeng Keda had not been woken. Relieved, he went back to the phone and sat down.

Liang Jinglun held the phone to his ear and closed his eyes. After about ten seconds, he put down the phone in despair and walked to the door.

He Xiaoyu and Xie Mulan had obviously finished what they had to say, and they were quietly looking at Fang Meng'ao, waiting for him to give approval.

Fang Meng'ao took out two pieces of chocolate from an iron box with Chinese and English words printed on the outside. One he gave to Xie Mulan standing alone, the other to He Xiaoyu sitting on the chair. "Please, have some."

"Are you going to or not? I won't eat your chocolate if you say I can't." Xie Mulan handed back the chocolate she had been given.

Fang Meng'ao took back the chocolate she handed over. "If you don't want it, give it to her." He handed the chocolate to He Xiaoyu as he was speaking.

Xie Mulan clasped Fang Meng'ao from behind and hugged his neck. "You must go, and you should go!"

Due to his good nature, Fang Meng'ao let her ride on his back. "But my shirt is rather dirty."

"I don't care. You have to go anyway."

"Then feel free to ride on my back." He carried Xie Mulan on his back and strolled over to the washstand where he washed his face.

He Xiaoyu's vision started to become blurred. Before her eyes, two images rose up: one was the gentleman-like Fang Meng'ao in Xie Mulan's room, the other was the shy and reserved Fang Meng'ao.

The Fang Meng'ao in her eyes now appeared to be two totally

different people. In his eyes, Xie Mulan was only a child, and in her eyes, he was one too.

Then, something unexpected happened. Right in front of He Xiaoyu, Fang Meng'ao pulled up his shirt and started to unbutton it. All this took place after he had washed his face with Xie Mulan still on his back.

He put down his towel and said: "Come down, wash my shirt first, will you?"

"Does that mean you agree?" Xie Mulan cheered and jumped off his back.

Fang Meng'ao had taken off his shirt, exposing his impressive physique. "Can you wash it clean?"

"He agreed!" Xie Mulan snatched the shirt from her cousin's hand, smiled at He Xiaoyu and shouted with joy. She put his shirt in the basin of water.

Before long, Xie Mulan felt a little uncomfortable and glanced at He Xiaoyu who was looking outside of the door. There was no joy, only embarrassment.

Xie Mulan turned around to look at her cousin again. To her surprise, Fang Meng'ao had stooped down and was washing his body with another wet towel.

Xie Mulan slowly withdrew her hand from the basin, looked at He Xiaoyu, and whispered: "Xiaoyu."

At this moment, He Xiaoyu pictured the cultured and elegant Liang Jinglun with his long gown flowing and his melancholy eyes.

"Xiaoyu," Xie Mulan called again.

He Xiaoyu turned around at her call. As she turned, her eyes swept past the semi-naked Fang Meng'ao and looked directly at Xie Mulan.

"This collar's still dirty," said Xie Mulan. "I can't do it by myself... Come and give me a hand."

"No way," said Fang Meng'ao, who was still bent over and scrubbing the shirt. "You're my sister, but she's my guest."

"Then why are you so rude to your guest?" Xie Mulan blurted out.

"What? Me, rude?"

Fang Meng'ao stood up straight, turned around and looked at the two young women. He Xiaoyu now looked him in the eyes.

Xie Mulan was confused.

Fang Meng'ao threw the towel into the bucket, took another clean shirt from the hook on the wall and walked to He Xiaoyu while he put it on. "Why don't you eat my chocolate?" he asked.

"Captain Fang, we are representatives of Yenching University Students' Union," said He Xiaoyu. "We're not little children who come here for your chocolates." She put the two chocolate pieces back on the table.

Fang Meng'ao picked up one of them and put it into his mouth. "Then I guess I am a child."

He Xiaoyu was shocked again.

Fang Meng'ao chewed his chocolate and turned to Xie Mulan: "Here, let me. I've been doing my own laundry since the Thirteenth of August Incident in 1937."

"Did you change your mind again?" Xie Mulan tightly clutched his shirt in the washbasin and looked at her cousin.

He Xiaoyu's heart sank. This was the little brother who cared for her during childhood, but now he's not only an ace flyer in the Kuomintang, but also a special member of the Communist Party. A man with multiple shades of glamour and charm all wrapped into one legendary character.

She seemed to recognise that she still did not understand why she cared. The only thing she did understand was her mission tonight. She stood up, went over to Mulan and said: "Mulan, let me do it for you."

"Good!" said Xie Mulan, getting out of the way. He Xiaoyu stood by the basin, and picked up the shirt and the soap on the stand.

"Put it down," said Fang Meng'ao. "I never tell anyone to do my laundry, even my orderly."

"Can I not do it for you on behalf of my classmates from both Northeast China and Peking?"

He Xiaoyu held his wet shirt in one hand and the soap in the other.

"Bullshit, what has my laundry got to do with your classmates?"

"Elder brother!" screamed an angry Xie Mulan.

When had He Xiaoyu suffered such a grievance? Gripping his

wet shirt in her left hand, she struggled to hold onto the slippery bar of soap in her right hand.

Fang Meng'ao looked at an angry, anxious Xie Mulan and pretended to be puzzled: "I say, what's wrong with you two today?"

Xie Mulan stamped her feet and said: "You've gone too far this time!"

Fang Meng'ao glanced at He Xiaoyu beside the basin. "Please don't be offended. I didn't mean to hurt anybody. I never like being told what to do."

He Xiaoyu was determined not to show any sign of upset as a result of her treatment. She tried her best to say calmly: "Do you mean we have to force you to join us at the get-together, or do we have to force you to allow us to do your laundry?"

Fang Meng'ao was silent for a short moment. "It's about washing my shirt now."

"Can I wash it on behalf of Mrs Fang, your mother?"

He Xiaoyu's remark was devastating, and Fang Meng'ao was overwhelmed.

He Xiaoyu turned her head and looked straight at Fang Meng'ao. "Both Mrs Fang and my mother died on the same day on the thirteenth of August. If my mother were here, would you say the same thing if she wanted to wash your shirt for you?"

"I am sorry." Fang Meng'ao said these three words gently and repeated them in English. "Sorry."

He Xiaoyu paid no more attention to him. She applied the soap to the shirt collar. She could not hide her emotions any more. The twinkle in her eyes was dimmed by tears.

What had happened today? She had never shed tears for any man before, so why did tears well up for two different men on the same day?

"They are all my comrades…" He Xiaoyu did not know why she would have repeated this sentence in her heart at this moment. She tried to avoid shedding tears for this man. However, as she was scrubbing the collar, tears fell from her eyes and splashed into the water drop by drop.

A perspiring cyclist came racing from Yenching University to the barracks. He was one of the student agents who had escorted Zeng Keda that night. Liang Jinglun was perched on the back seat. When the bike came to the fork leading to the barracks, it suddenly stopped and Liang Jinglun jumped off.

"Go to Ambassador Gu's residence as fast as you can and report directly to General Zeng. Tell him tonight's party is cancelled."

"Cancelled?" the student agent said in amazement. "How can it be? How can I explain to General Zeng..."

"I'll explain everything." With that, Liang Jinglun dashed to the main road leading to the barracks on the right.

Now alone, the cyclist put his foot on the pedal and headed towards the railway.

"Assemble! Assemble!" Guo Jinyang came out of the barracks and whistled. The pilots stood in two rows. Guo Jinyang also lined up. Captain Fang was coming out. The students were so excited that they held their breath and looked at the dorm entrance.

Fang Meng'ao came out of the room having put on the shirt. He was followed by Xie Mulan who was still excited, but she tried to appear composed. She lowered her head and quickened her step to catch up with Fang Meng'ao's pace, but in vain.

"Hello, captain!" the students cried out in orchestrated fashion.

Fang Meng'ao was about to join his pilots. But, greeted by the students, he felt obliged to stop and walked over to them.

"Captain Fang! Captain Fang!"

Watching the approaching Fang Meng'ao, the students' spontaneous greetings were unrestrained. The voices of some of the female students seemed to tremble with excitement.

Fang Meng'ao, who had exuded masculine power just a moment ago, now appeared quite shy. He stood there looking to Xie Mulan for help.

Xie Mulan smiled. "They're saying hello. Answer them quickly!"

"What do I say?"

"Just say 'hello'!"

"That's bullshit, it's not a military review," Fang Meng'ao

answered, before turning to see the dozens of excited faces. "Are you hungry?"

The students were surprised. A decorated war veteran and ace pilot, the people's hero who refused to bomb the City of Kaifeng had decided to engage in casual conversation.

"Yes, we are," a male student in the crowd answered.

"We're starving," came the cry from many other students.

Fang Meng'ao turned to his line of pilots and shouted: "Chen Changwu, Shao Yuangang!"

"Yes sir," the two men answered as they stepped out of the line.

"It's time for dinner. Go to the kitchen and bring out all the steamed bread and porridge."

"Yes sir." Chen Changwu and Shao Yuangang answered loudly and trotted to the kitchen next to the barracks.

The male student in charge of the Students' Union asked: "Excuse me, Captain Fang, are you coming to join us at our get-together?"

Countless eyes looked at Fang Meng'ao.

Xie Mulan was smiling and nodding to the many female students behind Fang Meng'ao. All eyes were still on Fang Meng'ao, waiting for him to answer in person.

"Food is the most important thing," he said. "I don't necessarily have enough, but what I do have I'll pay for."

As he was speaking, a succession of large bamboo steamers could be seen coming from the barracks' kitchen. Chen Changwu walked in the front holding eight steamers in his arms. With the steamers almost obscuring his entire body, only his legs were visible. Shao Yuangang followed, carrying two buckets of congee balanced on a shoulder pole and in one hand a basket containing bowls and chopsticks.

The two heavily-laden men reached the students. The steamers were soon spread out on the long tables, revealing several dozen steamed buns made of white flour. The heat from the buns seemed to turn into countless hooks, which caught the students' attention. Fang Meng'ao's heart ached. Turning around, he asked Chen Changwu: "How many buns have we got?"

"There are eighty in total, captain," said Chen Changwu.

Fang Meng'ao turned around, took a quick glance at the

students and announced: "Sixty-seven students, plus one inside. I'm afraid I don't have a bun for everyone."

He paused for a brief moment before continuing: "What a poor host I am!"

"Report to Captain Fang," Guo Jinyang chimed in. "There are twenty of us, and if we each had half, that would leave one for you and one for each of the students. We would even have one left over!"

There was silence before head of the Students' Union called out: "Captain Fang..."

"Do you know who he is?" Fang Meng'ao anticipated what the student was going to say, and immediately interrupted him. He considered Guo Jinyang and changed the subject of conversation: "He is a famous Shanxi native! His ancestors were bankers for generations. He's very good at calculating. Let's listen to what he says. You deserve something better, but do us a favour by having a steamed bun! That's it. Go on boys, tuck in. Guo Jinyang, for the female students, you must deliver them to each and every one of them. Also, serve the porridge and divide it evenly."

"Yes sir!" said the twenty pilots, loud and clear. Fang Meng'ao spun around and walked alone to the dorm, with tears in his eyes.

Xie Mulan took two steamed buns in one hand, and a white enamel cup in the other. The cup was full of porridge. She walked into Fang Meng'ao's room and put the porridge on the table carefully: "Time for dinner!" Then she walked over to He Xiaoyu by the window.

"What's for dinner?" He Xiaoyu was hanging up the washed shirt near the window. Looking back, she saw Xie Mulan hand over a steamed bun.

"My brother shared his dinner with the students," said Xie Mulan. "Each of them has one piece, but they will only get half. Many of the students were moved to tears."

He Xiaoyu looked at the steamed bread while listening to Xie Mulan. Her eyes were full of surprise.

"Please enjoy your dinner, princess," said Xie Mulan.

"What did you call me?" The look on He Xiaoyu's face abruptly changed. "Does a princess wash clothes for soldiers?" she asked.

"Of course not," Xie Mulan replied. "Doing the laundry for your prince, Princess He?"

"What did you just say?" He Xiaoyu shook the wet shirt and looked out of the window.

Xie Mulan handed the steamed bread to her from behind. "Are you really mad at me?"

He Xiaoyu didn't respond.

"Ah, what a great job you've done! It's so clean!" said Xie Mulan, unable to figure out what was on He Xiaoyu's mind.

He Xiaoyu was still looking out of the window. After a short moment of silence, she turned around without taking the bun Xie Mulan handed over to her. She now looked at her intensely: "Promise me never to say such things again, all right?"

Xie Mulan nodded her head.

"Remember, your elder brother is also my elder brother. Always our big brother."

A feeling of disappointment overwhelmed her, but Xie Mulan managed to hide her feelings: "He's been our big brother since childhood."

He Xiaoyu took the steamed bread from her hand apologetically. "Shall we make another agreement? If the New China fails to materialise, neither of us shall get married. What do you say?"

Xie Mulan stared at He Xiaoyu. "Neither of us shall fall in love?"

He Xiaoyu tried to make sense of that look of sophistication in Xie Mulan's eyes, but she did not know how to respond.

"I'm afraid you can't do it," said Xie Mulan.

He Xiaoyu still did not know how to answer her, but Xie Mulan continued staring into her eyes.

Then came the sound of rapid footsteps, and both turned to look at the door. Guo Jinyang had showed up with the male student from the Students' Union.

"Mr Liang is here," said the student. "Please, come quickly."

At first there was a look of surprise in their eyes, then they both avoided looking at each other.

Xie Mulan was confused. "Why has Mr Liang come here?" she asked.

He Xiaoyu also looked at the male student doubtfully.

"It's likely the party will be cancelled," said the student. "Go out quickly."

He Xiaoyu and Xie Mulan stepped out of the pilots' dorm.

Liang Jinglun had just finished talking with the members of the Students' Union. He was turning around and slowly walking towards Fang Meng'ao, who was on the other side. They were about fifty metres apart.

While the members of the Students' Union were all on the side close to the entrance of the barracks, the men from the Aviation Brigade gathered near their dorm. Between the two groups was open ground.

The silhouette of Liang Jinglun was approaching the lone figure of Fang Meng'ao.

He Xiaoyu's eyes.

Xie Mulan's eyes.

They expected Fang Meng'ao would also step forward out of courtesy...

"Attention!" Fang Meng'ao's loud and clear word of command called them back to reality.

The pilots, who were still standing apart, lined up. Fang Meng'ao strode to Liang Jinglun and held out his hand. Liang Jinglun extended his hand. The two men's steps and two outstretched hands were getting closer.

CHAPTER 16

In the Youth Aviation Brigade's large, open terrace, Fang Meng'ao was holding Liang Jinglun's hand. When their eyes met, Liang Jinglun was taken aback even though he had already been fully prepared for the meeting. He found that the pupils of Fang Meng'ao's eyes were shrinking slowly, eventually forming into two bright lights.

Liang Jinglun, who felt oppressed by some external forces, sensed that it was the wrong time and the wrong place to meet the man whom he should not have met. Yet he had to face these two eyes so intensely fixed, while forgetting the presence of the Students' Union members behind him, especially He Xiaoyu's stunned and confused eyes.

Yan Chunming and the Urban Works Department behind Yan Chunming, Zeng Keda and the Iron and Blood Congress for Nation Saving behind Zeng Keda, both could be forgotten. What he had to face with all his strength was the sheer intensity of Fang Meng'ao at this moment.

Is he a member of the Communist Party?

Fang Meng'ao's intense eyes, which were capable of distinguishing between enemy and friendly aircraft from a great distance, had turned into two laser swords that penetrated into the pupils of Liang Jinglun. However, Liang Jinglun's pupils turned out to be so dark and misty that the "aircraft" Fang

Meng'ao tried to identify appeared to be partly hidden, partly visible.

Slowly, the "aircraft" became visible, even without markings. It gradually approached, flying to one side of his own aircraft, then in close formation as if it were his own wingman.

Fang Meng'ao held his hand and clenched it unconsciously.

But right at this moment, his "wingman" Liang Jinglun appeared to change position. He now flew above his own aircraft, slightly to one side. His wingman had become his "leader" in the formation.

The sudden change brought Fang Meng'ao back to reality. Then he saw the eyes of two other people he would never forget. The first belonged to Cui Zhongshi when they shook hands for the first time; it was his appreciative eyes, caring eyes and trusting eyes. The second belonged to Lin Dawei when he saluted him on his way out of court; they were the eyes of appreciation, the eyes of love and the eyes of trust.

Cui Zhongshi was gone, Lin Dawei was gone. The eyes were still the same, but the person in front of him now was Liang Jinglun.

Is he a Communist? The voice immediately sounded in Fang Meng'ao's mind! His head slowly turned to the students, his gaze fixed on He Xiaoyu and Xie Mulan. It was an inquiring look.

He Xiaoyu appeared a little nervous. She looked at no one, not even at Liang Jinglun; instead, she stood gazing at the ground.

Xie Mulan did not try to hide her excitement and joy. She looked over at the eyes of her big brother and watched Liang Jinglun intensely.

Fang Meng'ao seemed to have got the answer, but it was quite obvious that it was not an exact answer. When he turned his head again and looked at Liang Jinglun, he held Liang's hand even more tightly. Liang Jinglun also firmed his grip.

The handshake, the penetrating look, his masculinity and his eyes sharper than those of a falcon and more innocent than those of a child made Liang Jinglun search for the most accurate four characters to describe this legendary figure: "Diligence and perseverance, concentration and simplicity." These were the attributes in Fang Meng'ao that Liang Jinglun valued so highly.

He now understood the profound reason why Comrade Jianfeng had put him in such an important position. He felt that he could appreciate Comrade Jianfeng's brilliance better than Zeng Keda; he would utilise his persistence and simplicity like the Communist Party. By making him believe that everything was for the people, this person would give the last full measure of devotion.

Based on this accurate judgment, Liang Jinglun became fully aware of the fact that it was his reputation as an agent of the Communist Party of China, which had been hard earned over a long period of time, along with his natural charm, that had left a most positive impression on Fang Meng'ao.

He broke the silence discreetly and most reasonably: "I've heard so much about you. Nice to meet you."

"Mr Liang, please follow me." Without any further exchange of greetings, Fang Meng'ao released his hand and walked with him to the pilots who were standing neatly in formation.

"Salute!" Fang Meng'ao barked. The pilots saluted Liang Jinglun with both hands and eyes.

"Hands down!" Fang Meng'ao ordered again. The pilots obeyed neatly.

Fang Meng said to the pilots: "Do you know why we took a nap while they were distributing the grain? Very simple. None of us are experts in economics. Just like with flight training, you can't fly without knowing the theory. But there are experts, of course, for example the students who majored in economics and helped us supervise those working for the Food-Distribution Committee today. Now, let me introduce you to a real expert in economics."

As he spoke, he earnestly asked Liang Jinglun to step forward. "Professor Liang Jinglun, Department of Economics, Yenching University, the top student of Mr He Qicang, a famous economist in China. Professor Liang has a doctoral degree from the London School of Economics. He has several publications to his name. In fact, over the past two years, he has written many articles exposing the economic corruption of the Kung and the Soong families!"

The pilots and the students applauded.

Xie Mulan clapped her hands, but when she looked next to her, she found He Xiaoyu was not responding as enthusiastically as others. Xie Mulan subconsciously slowed down the speed and intensity of her clapping. Nor did she look as excited as before.

Fang Meng'ao waited for the applause to finish and then he announced: "I'd like to share with you two items of news. One will make you happy, the other will make you sad."

The pilots were silent, as were the students.

"The sad news is that tonight's party is cancelled. The reason is simple. Huge numbers of people in Peking are starving, including teachers and students. So there is really nothing to celebrate."

The pilots looked disappointed. Many students also felt dismayed. "The happy news," Fang Meng'ao continued, "is that the students have invited Professor Liang to address us. On behalf of the whole brigade, I'd like to welcome Professor Liang to instruct us on how to investigate the corruption cases in Peking."

After these words, he did a ninety-degree turn and gave a salute to Liang Jinglun.

Twenty pilots followed him with neat salutes.

Liang Jinglun had to bow a little to the saluting brigade, but stood there silent after the bow. Countless eyes were watching him.

"This will put the party-state in harm's way!" With a roar, Zeng Keda grabbed an item off the table and smashed it to the floor.

The object splintered into pieces. Zeng Keda was furious!

The student spy who came to report the cancellation of the party turned white with fear. Zeng's adjutant was simply confused.

Zeng Keda himself seemed to have been awoken from his violent act. He looked at the pieces on the floor. What he had broken was actually a cup in the purple clay tea set that was meant for Fang Buting!

His eyes wandered over the tea set respectfully placed on the table – originally there were three cups along with the priceless purple clay teapot with bamboo and plum drawings on it.

The teapot gradually appeared larger and larger to Zeng Keda. One by one, the words on the teapot were forcefully visible to him:

A bamboo stem is humbled by having leaves that bow their heads, a lofty and unyielding plum blossom takes pride in having no flowers, proudly rewarded by Mr Chiang Ching-kuo. Fan Dasheng, Yixing, made in the thirty-sixth year of the Republic of China."

Slowly the majestic back of Comrade Jianfeng sitting at his desk appeared on the teapot!

Zeng Keda was so astonished that he seemed to be in a trance. He crouched down, kneeling on the carpet, picking up the broken cup shards piece by piece.

The adjutant and the student spy, who were standing nervously to one side, did not dare help him pick up the fragments. However, when they saw him doing it so gently and slowly, the two men exchanged a glance.

The second hand of the clock on the wall appeared to move fast and loudly.

"Sir!" The adjutant knew that the situation was urgent and brooked no delay. He risked being scolded and tried to rouse Zeng Keda.

"Well," said Zeng Keda, slowly raising his head.

"Tonight's party is cancelled," said the adjutant. "Should I inform..."

"Go and separately inform those at the Yenching chapter of the Iron and Blood Congress."

Realising the enormity of his faux pas, Zeng Keda said in a somewhat hoarse voice: "Both of you, go! Cancel the operation immediately! No one shall go to Yenching University."

"Yes," the adjutant answered in a low voice, winking at the student who was still cowed and showing him to the door.

Zeng Keda had picked up the last piece of the broken cup, stood up and said suddenly: "How could this cup break..."

The adjutant and the student stopped at the door and turned around.

Zeng Keda looked at the fragments of the broken cup in his palm. "Haven't I told you already? Go."

The adjutant stayed where he was and continued without hesitation: "General, I accidentally broke the cup just now. I'm ready to receive punishment."

Zeng Keda's eyes slowly turned to the adjutant, then to the student.

"It's not his fault," said the student. "I dropped it when handing it over to you."

Zeng Keda shook his head lightly. "I dropped this cup on the ground and broke it. You don't need to cover up for your boss's mistakes. Remember, face the party-state and the leaders with absolute loyalty and sincerity at all times."

"Sir!" The reply of the two young men seemed neither gentle nor firm. But they turned around and walked out of the room.

Zeng Keda put the pieces into the pocket of his military uniform, then walked to the door and closed it behind him. He went to the phone, picked up the receiver and turned the handle. "Put me through to the Bureau of Reserve Cadres in Nanking straight away. Special line number two."

"I really appreciate Captain Fang's concern," Liang Jinglun said sincerely, looking at the twenty pilots assembled on the open ground outside the barracks of the Youth Aviation Brigade. "If someone really wants to put me in jail and shoot me, it has nothing to do with my party affiliation. Mr Wen Yiduo didn't belong to any political party, and nor did Mr Li Gongpu. But they still had them murdered. The public did not want them to die. No opposition party wanted them to die. Even those with a conscience in the ruling Kuomintang did not want them to die. Still, no political party could save them. Besides, I can't compare myself with Mr Wen or Mr Li. I share with you the anguish of our four hundred and fifty million compatriots who are suffering from war and corruption. I don't understand politics, much less military affairs. But one thing I do understand is why, after eight years of the War of Resistance, our nation is still caught in a civil war! Whose interest does the war, the highest form of political expression, represent? I specialise in economics, and from the perspective of economics, I can only say that this is all about economic interests. I'm impressed with your sincerity Captain Fang and what you have done for the people since arriving in Peking. I would like to gratefully make a brief report based on my limited knowledge of economics."

"Mr Liang, please hang on," said Fang Meng'ao politely and solemnly.

Liang Jinglun turned to look at Fang Meng'ao beside him.

Fang Meng'ao smiled most respectfully at him, then turned to Xie Mulan. "Mulan, there is some paper on the table. Please, would you mind taking notes for us?"

"Sure!" Xie Mulan answered in an eager voice, and she ran to the table where the bound receipts were still piled. Meanwhile, she said to the two male students in the Students' Union: "Help me get a table."

Xie Mulan picked up a stack of paper from the table, took out her pen and walked over to Liang Jinglun.

The two male students carried a table and followed her.

"You're right, Comrade Jianfeng," Zeng Keda answered in a low voice. "I underestimated the ability of the Communist Party spy network. This incident further proves the difficulty of what you call 'one revolution, fighting on two fronts'. But I must report to you that, based on my recent observations in Peking, I have discovered many dangerous tendencies in Comrade Liang Jinglun. Let me be frank, if I may... That's not likely. The dangerous tendency I'm talking about is that he is too opinionated. It is precisely because of his self-conceit that he has compromised tonight's organised operation, and it is likely to arouse suspicion of him from the spies based in the Peking chapter of the Communist Party. If this goes on, we cannot rule out the possibility that the Communist spies will have the goods on him and convert him into one of their real spies!"

Liang Jinglun was speaking enthusiastically: "At present, the so-called national financial institutions include four banks, two bureaus, one treasury and one committee. The four banks are the Central Bank, the Bank of China, the Bank of Communications and the Farmers' Bank of China, with the Central Bank being the core.

The two bureaus are the Central Trust Bureau and the Directorate-General of the Postal Remittances and Savings Bank of the Nanking National Government. The treasury refers to the Central Cooperation Treasury, and the committee refers to the National Committee for Economic Affairs. These four banks, two bureaus, one treasury and one committee have one thousand, one hundred and seventy units and more than twenty-four thousand staff. These institutions control the assets and property of the whole of China. However, there are no official records of any kind in the national government budget plan, no files for them in the competent departments of finance, no records for them in the organs in charge of auditing, and no traces of them in the organs in charge of the civil servants' examination. Why? Because the twenty people who manipulate and secretly control these eight institutions are all operating above the ministries and commissions of the national government! In other words, these twenty people control the whole fiscal and financial power of the country and the lifeblood of all the people, and determine the fate of the country and all the people!"

Liang's remark sent shivers down the spines of the students. It also made their blood boil. The most excited and anxious of all was Xie Mulan, who was taking notes, her face dripping with sweat.

Someone was watching Fang Meng'ao particularly closely. It was He Xiaoyu. She found that Fang Meng'ao's face showed a seriousness that had never been seen before and his eyes had never been so contemplative. She was observing his possible next move.

Sure enough, Fang Meng'ao looked at Xie Mulan: "Have you written all this down?"

"Yes, I've written it all down," said Xie Mulan, having finally finished the last sentence, taken a long breath and raised her sweat-drenched head. Then she looked at Liang Jinglun with her eyes fixed on him.

Fang Meng'ao also looked closely at Liang Jinglun. "Professor Liang, may I ask you a question? You don't have to answer if you don't want to."

"Please go ahead."

"Mr Liang, the twenty people you just mentioned. Do they include the governors of the Central Bank branches in major cities?"

The twenty pilots were stunned. So was He Xiaoyu. But Xie Mulan was unmoved by the question, as she was busy watching Liang Jinglun intensely.

As was known to all, Fang Meng'ao's question was referring to his father. Liang Jinglun fully knew it, so he replied clearly: "Not included. The governors of the Central Bank's branches in major cities are merely directors or supervisors of the one thousand, one hundred and seventy units of the eight institutions. They slave for these twenty men and their families, but they have no control over the lifeblood of the country and its people."

"Thank you for your answer, Professor Liang." Fang Meng'ao's face did not reveal any expression. "Please continue."

Back in his room, Zeng Keda's facial expression had transformed. He stood there stupefied, listening to Comrade Jianfeng's admonition coming from Nanking.

Jianfeng's thick Ningbo accent was clearly discernible down the line: "I must remind you, Comrade Keda, that you are far more prone to self-righteousness than Comrade Liang Jinglun."

"Yes," Zeng Keda answered.

"You misunderstand what I said about 'being suspicious of those you use'. If we have doubts about our loyal comrades, we will end up being without followers! Let me tell you this, I never doubted you when I put you in this important position."

"Yes." Zeng Keda's reply obviously choked in his throat.

"You are now representing me in Peking," Jianfeng continued down the line. "Every action, every sentence, even every idea of yours will have consequences beyond your own authority. With regard to Comrade Liang Jinglun, let me put it bluntly. The role he can play within the Communist Party's organisation, and especially the role he can play in the upcoming currency reform, cannot be replaced by any other comrade, nor by you. He is not only the best economic talent in our organisation, but also the best political talent who is able to tackle all kinds of dangerous tests. You have a lot of work to do. One of the most important tasks is to protect two people and use those people well at work. One is Fang Meng'ao, the other is Comrade Liang Jinglun."

"Yes..." Zeng Keda replied, but the person at the other end had already hung up.

Outside the barracks of the Youth Aviation Brigade, the sun was disappearing behind the top of the Western Hills. The half of the sun still visible was shining on Liang Jinglun, shrouding him in a halo.

"These are the four banks," he continued, "two bureaus, one treasury and one committee. Under the banner of business development, under the cloak of the state, these twenty individuals control the government with their right hand, kidnap the people with their left hand, with one foot in China and the other overseas. After victory in the War of Resistance, China's foreign exchange reserves were five hundred million US dollars. Do you know how much of that sum belongs to the Chinese government and how much to the Chinese people? I'll tell you – three hundred and thirty million is controlled by these twenty individuals!"

All the twenty pilots became emotional with indignation.

"Why are so many people starving in China today? The refugee students from the Northeast who are receiving food here today are representative of the nation's suffering! Of the five hundred million dollars in foreign exchange reserves, only one hundred and seventy million is in the hands of the government. The military needs money, numerous government agencies need money, to the extent that many public servants and educators can no longer support their families. My question is: what money is left for the relief of the people? Even with this little money, some insist on taking it out of the mouths of the starving and stuffing it into their own pockets! Respected Captain Fang, my dear friends of the Youth Aviation Brigade, I am here today not to stop my students from thanking you by hosting this party, but because it's no time for celebration. My students!"

Liang Jinglun glanced back at the members of the Students' Union and concluded: "Please join me in bowing to them on behalf of the two million suffering compatriots in Peking!" He gave a deep bow.

All the students bowed to Fang Meng'ao and his brigade.

"Salute!" Fang Meng'ao said with a loud command.

The pilots responded with a military salute.

Liang Jinglun stood up straight and looked at Fang Meng'ao the way he did when they first met. Then he raised the hem on one side of his long gown and went straight to the gates without saying a word.

While the students were bowing respectfully, the pilots all held their salute by touching their fingers to the rim of their visors. Like a farewell ceremony, they watched in awe Liang Jinglun walk away.

Jianfeng had hung up, but Zeng Keda was still standing by the phone. He thought long and hard before finally picking up the phone again to place another call: "Please connect me to the secretary's duty room of the Bureau of Reserve Cadres in Nanking."

The call was soon put through.

"Secretary Wang? Hello, this is Zeng Keda. I'm really sorry that I haven't finished the report for Comrade Jianfeng. Would you please make a request on my behalf... OK, please take notes..."

When the secretary at the other end was ready, Zeng Keda began to speak at a speed that allowed him to take notes. He spoke as if he was making an official report: "The cancellation of today's party by the Urban Works Department of the CPC Peking chapter is by no means a simple political operation, but they have taken cognisance of the economic action plan of the party-state to carry out the currency system reform and the great significance of Comrade Jianfeng in reusing Fang Meng'ao and his brigade, and have become suspicious of Comrade Liang Jinglun through the mole lurking inside the core of our economic organisation. It is imperative that the key figure sent by the Communist Party hiding at the heart of our economic decision-making body be eradicated immediately... Yes, it's Cui Zhongshi, Fang Buting's right-hand man... The best way to solve the problem is through Fang Buting. Therefore, I suggest I pay a visit to Fang Buting right now to straighten things out with him and try to get his cooperation. Report finished. OK, I'll be expecting Comrade Jianfeng's instructions. Thank you."

Zeng Keda held the phone to his ear and waited as the secretary at the other end placed the phone on the table.

Back at the Youth Aviation Brigade, many students realised that their professor was no longer present.

"Where is Mr Liang?" Xie Mulan cried out, looking at He Xiaoyu. He Xiaoyu studiously avoided her gaze and looked at Fang Meng'ao. The other students were all looking at each other in dismay.

Fang Meng'ao did not look at anyone, but stood there alone. The sun had now set behind the Western Hills and dusk was gathering.

"I am, I'm listening." Zeng Keda's room was still dark. His figure was shadowy and his voice down the line was a little muffled. "Please read me Comrade Jianfeng's instructions."

Secretary Wang replied: "Comrade Jianfeng's instructions are as follows: Approval for you to visit Governor Fang."

"Yes!" Zeng Keda answered loudly, before lowering his voice. "Please give me the specific instructions."

"Ten words, please learn them by heart: Touch him with true feelings, warn him of the consequences."

"I understand. Please, tell Comrade Jianfeng I will follow his ten-word guiding principle." Zeng Keda clicked his heels, even though the person at the other end was merely Secretary Wang.

It was getting dark. Fang Meng'ao surveyed the students gathered on the open ground and then back at the pilots who were still standing neatly in line.

The students over there, the pilots over here, one could tell they wanted to stay on in the barracks. Some pilots stared at the female students under the cover of twilight. The female students saw them watching. Some were so excited that they even looked back; others were nudging each other secretly in embarrassment, while a few were so nervous that they tried to avoid their gaze.

Only two people had not been watching the pilots all this while. They seemed lost in a trance. One was He Xiaoyu, the other was Xie Mulan.

The looks on the faces of the pilots and the female students, especially He Xiaoyu and Xie Mulan, were all observed by Fang Meng'ao. He changed his grave countenance, and a smile appeared on his lips. He turned to the students and said in a loud voice: "If I may, I would like to make a few requests."

All eyes were on the male student leader of the Students' Union, who replied: "Captain Fang, please feel free to speak. We will comply with any request you make."

"Well, let me first make the request before you accept anything."

"We'll accept anything!" the students responded.

"Well, boys, can you please stay and help us sort out the receipts for today's food distribution? Girls, can I trouble you to help our brigade members better understand Mr Liang's report?"

"Yes sir!" cried the pilots.

"We will!" the students responded in unison. It was their collective voice.

"Changwu." Fang Meng'ao looked at Chen Changwu, who was standing at the head of the line. He didn't call him by his surname and he waved him over to indicate that he was going to have a word in his ear.

Chen Changwu came over from the formation. "Captain."

Fang Meng'ao whispered in his ear: "Take care of these weasels. I'm going to run an errand. When I get in the jeep, turn on all the lights and let them get to work." With that, he went alone to the jeep parked at the main entrance.

As the formation was dismissed, the students were still standing in orderly fashion. Watching Fang Meng'ao stride towards the gate alone, they had no idea what was going on.

Watched by the silent crowd, Fang Meng'ao got in the jeep and ordered the lieutenant who saluted him: "Open the gate."

The lieutenant officer was surprised: "It's getting late, sir. You can't leave alone..."

"Open the gate!" Fang Meng'ao's face darkened perceptibly. He started the engine and drove towards the iron gate.

"Open the gate, quick!" The lieutenant panicked, and the two soldiers rushed to open the iron gate.

Fang Meng'ao's jeep roared out of the barracks.

Only a short while ago, it was Mr Liang who had left suddenly. Now Captain Fang also departed in abrupt fashion. However, it did not take the students long to realise what was going on. Together, they watched the jeep driving away.

He Xiaoyu extended her hand to Xie Mulan. The two hands were quietly held together. The image that flashed across their minds was the handshake between Liang Jinglun and Fang Meng'ao earlier in the day.

"Turn on the lights!" Chen Changwu shouted to the guards. He was so loud that he startled He Xiaoyu and Xie Mulan, who had to let go of their entwined hands.

The barracks lights were switched on. Two strong searchlights were mounted on twenty-metre-high concrete poles along the east and west walls of the barracks. The whole barracks were illuminated as if it were broad daylight.

Chen Changwu turned to the pilots and announced: "The captain has instructed me to take command here. Let's start work!"

Fang Meng'ao's jeep screeched to a halt at the entrance to Dongzhong Hutong. The street lights were dim. He turned on the headlights as the jeep approached the hutong entrance. The headlights illuminated the policemen standing in the open and the plainclothes officers standing in the dark.

The fact that Deputy Commissioner Shan was assigned to be in charge of the police surveillance here tonight indicated that Xu Tieying took Cui Zhongshi seriously. Although he didn't know the identity of the driver, the experienced Shan realised that he must have influential backing. With the headlights shining on his face, he came over with a smile and said: "Excuse me…"

Fang Meng'ao was still sitting in the driver's seat. He had no idea about who the man was, but his badge showed that he held the same rank as his brother. When the police officer came close and leaned over, Fang Meng'ao asked: "What's going on?"

Deputy Commissioner Shan was adjusting to the strong light, but he recognised Fang Meng'ao. At first, he was surprised, then he greeted him warmly: "Captain Fang!"

Fang Meng'ao replied with a smile: "I'm sorry, we don't seem to have met."

"Captain Fang, my surname is Shan. I work in the same bureau as your younger brother. I am deputy commissioner of the Peking Municipal Police Bureau. When I picked up Director Xu from the airport, I had the chance to meet Captain Fang."

"Oh," Fang Meng'ao answered casually, as his eyes swept across the police officers lit up by the headlights of his jeep. "Mr Shan, is there anything wrong here?"

"Nothing. Did Captain Fang find anything wrong?"

"Then why are so many people deployed here? And why have you been put personally in charge?"

Shan had long ago heard about this big shot. Today was his first opportunity to have a face-to-face encounter with Fang Meng'ao. Fully appreciating his powerful backing and his own position, he humbly answered: "It's a routine check during a period of counter-insurgency and nation saving. Just a routine check."

"All right. I'm looking for a person who has something to do with the case that the Ministry of Defence investigation group is working on. Since you're in charge here, please help me find this man."

Shan was quick to understand the idea, but he had to pretend otherwise: "Excuse me, who is it you're looking for, Captain Fang?"

"Cui Zhongshi, deputy treasury director, Peking branch of the Central Bank."

Shan, who was a cunning rascal, replied: "Deputy Director Cui? Does he live here? Let me go and find out."

"There's no need. Number Two, Dongzhong Hutong. Go

through the hutong to the second door on the left. Please find this man at once. I'll wait here."

Fang Buting had always been fond of traditional Chinese clothing, but as he stood in his living room, he decided to change into a Western suit. His face was a picture of health after Cheng Xiaoyun had put some make-up on his face. Without any visible sign of illness, he looked a little like a scholar studying in the United States.

Zeng Keda, wearing his army clothes, shook hands with Fang Buting. Their different temperaments were instantly discernible.

Fang, whose way of dressing allowed him to dispense with the usual Chinese etiquette, stretched out his hand and said: "Please sit down."

Zeng Keda was still carrying that boxed tea set. According to social etiquette, the hostess or right-hand man of the host should receive the gift on his behalf. However, as far as Zeng could see, there were only two people in this huge living room, the host and the guest.

Looking at Fang Buting, who had stretched out his hand and sat down ahead of him, Zeng Keda stood there hardly knowing what to do. But he was well prepared, so he remained standing respectfully and smiled. "This is nothing much, but it's the thought that counts. Here is my humble gift. Governor, please take a look." He put the box on the table and waited respectfully.

Fang Buting had to stand up, and he said: "Forgive me, General Zeng, but I forgot to tell you. Although I work in the financial sector for the government in Peking, I never accept gifts from others."

"The governor is incorruptible and prudent, we know that. But today's gift has nothing to do with Governor Fang's professional ethics. You must accept it."

"Must I accept it?" Fang Buting wore a smile, but his tone indicated that he would decline it anyway.

"At least, you must come and have a look," said Zeng Keda. "If you won't accept it, I'll take it back with me." Zeng was all smiles, but his eyes shone like torchlights.

Fang Buting thought for a moment. "OK, let me have a look." Slowly he moved over to where Zeng Keda was standing.

Zeng Keda opened the gift box. Being a connoisseur, Fang Buting's eyes lit up immediately. "This is the work of Master Fan?" he blurted out.

Zeng Keda looked at Fang Buting with great admiration. "Governor Fang, you have the eyes of Dharma. What is the current market value of this tea pot?"

"Five hundred pounds," replied Fang Buting. "If we're talking *fabi*, then more than a truckload's worth. General Zeng, please don't reveal the name of the gift-giver. This is something I can never accept."

"Then I won't mention any names." As he spoke, Zeng Keda took the pot out with both hands. "I'd simply like to ask Governor Fang to appreciate it." He held out the pot for Fang's inspection.

Fang Buting still refused to take it, but the side with the inscriptions that appeared before his eyes amazed him.

Nothing else mattered – his personal experience, professional background, the inscriptions on the pot, the signature of the pot maker. The only thing that mattered were the large characters inscribed on the side of the pot that read "Elegant work of art given by Mr Chiang Ching-kuo".

To take it or not to take it?

Fortunately, the telephone rang in the living room, and Fang Buting turned around. "Excuse me, let me answer that first."

Zeng Keda continued to hold the pot, but he sensed that Fang Buting was now a little more open to persuasion.

Fang Buting picked up the phone and said in a tone of surprise: "Yes, he's here." He turned to Zeng Keda. "General Zeng, you're wanted on the phone."

How did anyone know he was here? Zeng Keda carefully put the teapot on the table and made a gesture of apology to Fang Buting as he answered the call.

After listening for a few seconds, Zeng Keda's face regained its composure. All the while, he sensed that Fang Buting was behind him. So he answered in a low and stern voice: "Captain Fang is the head of the Economic Inspection Brigade of the Ministry of Defence. Who gives you the right to say that he can't see Deputy

Director Cui... It's OK for him to be taken out for a ride. No one shall interfere, not you nor the Peking Police Bureau!"

With the phone in his left hand, Zeng Keda's right hand gently pressed the switchhook to hang up the call. When he looked back, he found Fang Buting facing the door. "Governor Fang," he asked, "may I make another call?"

"Of course, General Zeng. If you need to make a business call, I can wait outside." He was about to go out when Zeng Keda stopped him.

"Governor Fang, my apologies for being so rude. Absolutely, Governor Fang, you're free to listen."

Fang Buting stopped at the door. "Are you sure you want me to listen, General Zeng?"

Zeng Keda felt he could see the reflection of the elder son from this father figure, which pained him. He added apologetically: "Once again, my apologies." Then he began to make the call.

"Is that Lieutenant Colonel Zheng? Take a squad to find Captain Fang at once. He left Dongzhong Hutong for somewhere in the northwest. Remember, keep your distance, just protect the safety of Captain Fang and Deputy Director Cui, and don't interfere in their conversation."

Zeng Keda gently put down the phone and turned around only to find that Fang Buting had been staring straight at him.

"I want to know which four banks, two bureaus, one treasury and committee."

Fang Meng'ao was driving at top speed down the road cordoned off under martial law. Cui Zhongshi sat in the passenger seat, looking ahead. The two had lost the feeling they had for each other when they first met.

"They are the Central Bank, the Bank of China, the Bank of Communications and the Farmers' Bank of China, and the core is the Central Bank. The two bureaus are the Central Trust Bureau and the Directorate-General of the Postal Remittances and Savings Bank of the Nanking National Government. The treasury refers to the Central Cooperation Treasury and the committee is the National Committee for Economic Affairs."

"How many units under them are there in total?" asked Fang Meng'ao.

"One thousand, one hundred and seventy," said Cui Zhongshi.

"How many people supervise these units?"

"One thousand, one hundred and seventy directors and supervisors."

"Can you name them?"

"Do they need the full list?"

"Who do you mean by 'they'?" Fang Meng'ao still didn't look at him. "I don't have anyone behind me. If you mean the Bureau of Reserve Cadres, I won't ask."

"Comrade Meng'ao..."

"If you can't name the one thousand, one hundred and seventy people, then you should at least be able to remember the names of the twenty. Am I right?"

Cui paused for a short moment. "Find a convenient place to stop. Let's talk."

"Tell me where we're going."

"Let's go to Desheng Gate."

"Why there?"

Cui Zhongshi looked ahead. "The peasant army commanded by Li Zicheng entered the city of Peking from there."

Fang Meng'ao's foot on the accelerator relaxed for a while and the jeep slowed down. In the space of a moment, he stepped on the accelerator again and said: "OK, let's go to Desheng Gate."

It was hard to find such a dense purple bamboo grove in a Peking courtyard house. It was even harder to find a stone path illuminated by street lamps on both sides, lighting up the bamboo leaves that were swishing in the night breeze.

Out of courtesy, Fang Buting slowed down as they entered the bamboo grove so he could walk side by side with Zeng Keda. Zeng, however, was careful to follow Fang Buting by a distance of one shoulder in order to show due respect. All of a sudden, he stopped in front of a particularly lush patch of bamboo illuminated by a street lamp and looked around at the individual stems that were six to eight metres tall. "Governor Fang, did you have this bamboo grove before you moved in, or did you landscape it later?"

Fang Buting also stopped. "It was planted after I moved here."

"Amazing! You also had bamboo groves in your old residence back in Wuxi, didn't you?"

"Yes, I left home when I was young. It's hard to go back now. It's been more than thirty years."

"I'm ashamed," said Zeng Keda. "I've been away from my hometown for only three years. As Governor Fang's second son said today at Ambassador Gu's residence, back then I was just an adjutant in the Youth Army in my hometown in southern Jiangxi."

Fang Buting answered him earnestly: "I heard about that. Forgive him, my younger son is still young, General Zeng."

Zeng Keda pretended to be sincere and said: "Manager Fang, it's very kind of you to say so. But we're all mere juniors before you. In front of my house and behind my ancestral house and in the mountains, they all are covered with bamboo. By the same token, perhaps during the Qing and Ming dynasties, Governor Fang and I, as well as your two young sons, were fellow townsmen."

Fang Buting did not respond. Instead he continued to listen.

"Both Jiangsu and Jiangxi belonged to the two-river administrative region in the Qing Dynasty, then they belonged to southern Henan Province in the Ming Dynasty, but throughout this time they were subject to the rule of one governor-general."

"Then Anhui will be added," said Fang Buting. "But it may not be a good idea to have these three provinces governed by one person."

Zeng Keda was momentarily stunned, but in order to appear ignorant he looked at Fang Buting in a childish way. He was pondering the man in front of him, the man so highly valued by the Soong and Kung families, and at the same time, he understood the rationale behind Comrade Jianfeng's decision to use Fang Meng'ao to deal with his father. This man was so tough to deal with. But he must be dealt with no matter what. Just now he had been trying to move him with sincere feelings; now was the time to warn him of the consequences: "I fully agree with Manager Fang's view. If one person in each province or several provinces has the final say, we will end up in a situation of separatism where China will totally disintegrate. As a result, the country will end up in chaos and the people will suffer. China can only be one China, that is the Republic of China. The Republic of China can only have one leader, President Chiang. In this context, and as fellow countrymen, our views should be the same whether it is Governor Fang or Captain Fang or Deputy Commissioner Fang."

"Do our opinions differ?" Fang Buting had been worried about the last card that the other side would deal. It looked as if the final showdown would occur today.

"Some people do indeed hope that our views are different," said Zeng Keda.

Fang Buting looked at him dead in the eyes and said: "The Communist Party of China!"

Zeng Keda looked up at the street lamp. "Mao Zedong publicly pronounced in Yan'an that there would be no two suns in the sky. He was intent on showing President Chiang that he was the only sun up above."

Since the other side had dealt the final card, the only thing Fang Buting could do was wear an indifferent smile. "General Zeng, what you mean is that someone on my side agrees Mao Zedong is the sun. Or is it both Meng'ao and Mengwei who recognise Mao Zedong as the sun?"

Zeng Keda suppressed a laugh, because that might have appeared insincere. "I just said, there is only one sun in the sky. Mao Zedong is not the sun, nor should he ever be considered as a second sun. But besides the sun, there is also the moon. There is only one moon in the sky, and it shines everywhere on Earth. Governor Fang, I hope you understand me."

Fang Buting stopped smiling. "I don't understand. General Zeng, are you alluding to Zhu Xi's 'the moon being reflected on a thousand rivers and lakes'?"

"Manager Fang, you're always wise and farsighted."

"Well then, I can only tell you, General Zeng, that there are moon shadows in the middle of the river."

"As for the moon of the Communist Party of China, as long as there is one basin of water, that moon can be easily reflected in the water."

"Have I got that basin of water?" asked Fang Buting.

"Yes... Cui Zhongshi!" Finally, Zeng Keda said the name aloud.

———

About fifty metres ahead was Desheng Gate where troops were deployed. Searchlights were positioned on a tall building that illuminated the night sky as if it were day.

"Who's there? Stop!" shouted troops deployed under the city gate. The officer on duty approached with two soldiers in helmets.

Fang Meng'ao didn't slow down his jeep. Instead, he continued to drive a further twenty metres before slamming on the brakes.

The driver of the truck that was following also applied the brakes, the vehicle skidding to a halt just five metres behind Fang Meng'ao's jeep.

"Out of the jeep," said Fang Meng'ao, opening the door and getting out. Cui Zhongshi did the same.

The officer on duty at the city gate approached Fang Meng'ao and Cui Zhongshi and asked: "Which army do you belong to? What's your unit number?"

The battalion commander called Zheng and a group of Youth Army soldiers jumped out of the truck. Fang Meng'ao went to Zheng and asked: "Are you here to protect me?"

"Yes," Zheng answered with embarrassment.

"Then tell them our unit number."

Zheng went up to explain it to the officer on duty.

Fang Meng'ao said to Cui Zhongshi: "How long does it take to get from here to Shichahai?"

"It'll take ten minutes to get to Houhai, which is the northernmost lake."

"Let's go to Houhai. It's closest."

Cui Zhongshi could not very well say anything. He took Fang Meng'ao towards a small alleyway.

"You don't even know the unit number zero-zero-zero-one?" Lieutenant Colonel Zheng was yelling at the garrison officer. "You've not heard of the Ministry of Defence?"

The sergeant of the Youth Army came up to report to Zheng:

"Reporting to Lieutenant Colonel, Captain Fang went to that small hutong."

Zheng quickly turned around and saw the figures of Fang Meng'ao and Cui Zhongshi disappearing into the entrance of the hutong. He shouted: "Follow them and make sure they're safe!"

On the seventh day of the seventh lunar month, the moon at the first quarter would set in about an hour. At this time, it was slanting on the surface of Houhai. Half of the moon was in the sky while the other half was in the water.

The two men stood on the lakeshore at arm's distance from each other. Fang Meng'ao looked at the half moon in the sky while Cui Zhongshi looked at its reflection.

The floating, scattered clouds,
The bright moon shines on the people as they arrive

Fang Meng'ao seemed to speak to Cui Zhongshi or perhaps to himself alone. While still watching the moon, he said: "You sang that song when you first visited me at Hangzhou Jianqiao airbase. It sounded like you had just learned it from someone."

"No," said Cui Zhongshi. "I had learnt it some time before meeting you, although I never could sing it well."

Fang Meng'ao shook his head. "I'm capable of passing my own judgment on whether you can sing it well or not, or whether you just picked it up."

"So call me a liar, you may as well be up front about it."

"Why are you lying to me?" Fang Meng'ao's question seemed to be in defence of Cui Zhongshi. "It's not necessary."

"I would if I really needed to."

"Why?" Fang Meng'ao could make out a suspicious look in Cui Zhongshi's face that he had never noticed before.

"Because I am not a Communist Party spy," said Cui Zhongshi.

Fang Meng'ao froze. He glared at Cui Zhongshi, but the glare receded. Instead, he now looked confused.

Cui Zhongshi then said softly: "Therefore, you are not a CPC spy either."

"For nearly three years, you've been telling me lies?" Again, there was a glare in Fang Meng'ao's eyes.

"Not really."

"Which were lies and which weren't?"

"I don't know myself."

Fang Meng'ao stared at him, and he was silent for a long moment. Suddenly he said: "Take off your clothes."

"What?"

"You said you couldn't swim. Take off your clothes and jump into the water."

Cui Zhongshi looked at this fellow comrade who had been closer than his own brother. A sense of desolation that overwhelmed him almost made him cry, but he would not. He gasped, but managed to keep his breathing even. He pretended to smile at Fang Meng'ao. "If I can't swim, then I won't be able to get out of the water."

"You'll come out of the water." Fang Meng'ao's eyes had never been so cold and detached.

Looking at the moonlit water, Cui Zhongshi resolutely turned his head to face Fang Meng'ao. "No matter how many lies I've told you before, I'm telling you the truth now. As you know, I have a son called Boqin and a daughter called Pingyang. I swear to you in their names that I am telling the truth."

Fang Meng'ao's heart ached and the look in his eyes softened immediately.

Cui Zhongshi continued: "I am not a CPC undercover agent, and neither are you. But it does not matter because when you volunteered to join the Communist Party, you weren't doing it for me. You were willing to follow the party not because you believed in me, but because you chose it in your heart, because you want to save China and do everything for your fellow citizens. Don't believe in me, but believe in yourself."

Again, Fang Meng'ao looked at Cui Zhongshi with a faraway look in his eyes. He waited until Cui Zhongshi finished what he was saying.

Cui Zhongshi had begun to unbutton his chiffon gown.

Fang Meng'ao looked at him closely, and he was quite startled again. It was clear that, having taken off his long gown, Cui Zhongshi was wearing a false white collar attached to his old shirt. Is he truly living in poverty, wondered Fang Meng'ao.

Cui Zhongshi took off the false collar and his glasses, put them on the long gown on the ground and clumsily jumped into the water.

The splash startled Zheng and his platoon of Youth Army soldiers standing guard about a hundred metres away. They ran over to Fang Meng'ao.

"Quick!" Lieutenant Colonel Zheng shouted as he ran. In less than twenty seconds, a dozen soldiers had arrived at where Fang Meng'ao was standing. They were relieved to see him safe on the bank.

"What's going on, sir?" Zheng gasped.

"Back to where you were," Fang Meng'ao replied, looking at the water.

"Sir..."

"Back off!" ordered Fang Meng'ao. "Don't come any closer!"

Lieutenant Colonel Zheng was forced to comply, and the crowd of soldiers returned to where they came from.

The surface of the water was so calm that Fang Meng'ao couldn't help looking at his wristwatch – thirty seconds had passed!

Fang Meng'ao removed his cap, took off his short-sleeved uniform and scanned the water. Finally, he found that there were ripples about seven or eight metres away from the shore.

Like an arrow, Fang Meng'ao jumped to his feet and plunged himself like a javelin into the lake. He entered the water about four metres away.

The lieutenant colonel, who had been watching intently, shouted again: "Quick! Prepare to jump in!"

A dozen men came running over. Suddenly, someone's head emerged from the water, then a shoulder.

Zheng looked anxious. "Anyone who can swim, take off your clothes! Get them out of the water, *now!*"

Several guards took off their clothes in a hurry.

Two guards stopped and looked at the water surface nervously while others ceased undressing themselves. They all looked at the water surface intently.

Lieutenant Colonel Zheng was about to scold them when he could vaguely make out Captain Fang supporting Cui Zhongshi with one arm, while paddling with the other. They were only about three metres from the shore.

Lieutenant Colonel Zheng stretched out his hand and several other guards followed.

"Back to where you were!" Captain Fang demanded. His voice was loud and clear, and he wasn't out of breath despite the exertion involved in holding Cui Zhongshi under his arm while swimming in the water.

"OK, OK," said Zheng, waving his men slowly back to their original position.

Upon arriving at the shore, Fang Meng'ao raised both of his hands and lifted Cui Zhongshi up onto the bank and laid him flat without knowing whether he was alive or dead. He climbed up by supporting himself on a rock beside the lake.

Then Fang Meng'ao leaned over Cui Zhongshi who was lying on his back. He squeezed and pressed his hands rhythmically down on his abdomen.

Cui Zhongshi spat out a lungful of water, then another.

Next, Fang Meng'ao stepped over to the other side of Cui Zhongshi's head, lifted his torso and supported his back with one hand. He looked closely at his face.

Fang Meng'ao's eyes glittered as Cui Zhongshi's eyes slowly opened.

ABOUT THE AUTHOR

Liu Heping was born in Hunan Province, southern China in 1953. He spent his childhood in the theatre and went on to become an acclaimed screenwriter, novelist and historian known for his deep insights into the events of Chinese history. His pioneering historical drama about the Ming Dynasty, *Da Ming Wang Chao 1566*, was first published as a novel in 2006 and sold nearly a million copies. The following year, it was broadcast as a 46-episode TV series that garnered popular and critical acclaim in China. His Chinese Civil War TV drama, *All Quiet in Peking*, gained a cumulative 400 million online views in the month following its first broadcast in October 2014. The series made waves among China's intellectual circles and was picked up for international distribution by Netflix. Liu's realist approach to the historical and contemporary transformation of China has been hugely influential and well received in the Chinese-speaking world.

ABOUT THE TRANSLATOR

Teng Jimeng lives in Beijing, China. He teaches interpreting, translation, and film studies. He also translates from Chinese into English and vice versa. Teng has translated over 10 award-winning independent Chinese films and documentaries, dozens of scripts, song lyrics, and essays by authors such as Wang Meng and filmmakers such as Chen Kaige of *Farewell My Concubine* (Palm D'Or winner, 1993), Li Yang of *Blind Shaft* (Silver Bear, Berlinale, 2003), Wang Chao of *Luxury Car* (Un Certain Regard, Cannes winner, Cannes International Film Festival, 2005), Geng Jun of *Free And Easy* (Grand Jury Award, Sundance International Film Institute, 2017), and Bob Dylan of *No Direction Home: The Life and Music of Bob Dylan* (by Robert Shelton, U.S.A.).

ABOUT THE SERIES

The *All Quiet in Peking* series follows Fang Men'gao, a Communist Party member working undercover in the Chinese Nationalist Air Force. It is 1948, and civil war is raging between the Communists and the Kuomintang, ravaging the economy of Peking. Fang is ordered to investigate a corruption case involving the Peking Citizens' Committee and the Peking branch of the Central Bank, the president of which is none other than his own father. Fang's desire for the peaceful liberation of Peking is a race against the clock. The nation doesn't know it yet, but the happiness and peace of the people depends on him. *Under Turbulent Skies* is the first of three books in the *All Quiet in Peking* series, translated into English for the first time by Teng Jimeng.

About Sinoist Books

We hope you enjoyed this exciting story of Feng Meng'ao's quest for peace.

SINOIST BOOKS brings the best of Chinese fiction to English-speaking readers. We aim to create a greater understanding of Chinese culture and society, and provide an outlet for the ideas and creativity of the country's most talented authors.

To let us know what you thought of this book, or to learn more about the diverse range of exciting Chinese fiction in translation we publish, find us online. If you're as passionate about Chinese literature as we are, then we'd love to hear your thoughts!

sinoistbooks.com
@sinoistbooks